STUDIES IN JOSEPHUS AND THE VARIETIES OF ANCIENT JUDAISM

ANCIENT JUDAISM AND EARLY CHRISTIANITY

Arbeiten zur Geschichte des Antiken
Judentums und des Urchristentums

Editors
Martin Hengel
Pieter W. van der Horst
Martin Goodman
Daniel R. Schwartz
Cilliers Breytenbach
Friedrich Avemarie
Seth Schwartz

Number 67

Louis H. Feldman

STUDIES IN JOSEPHUS AND THE VARIETIES OF ANCIENT JUDAISM

Louis H. Feldman Jubilee Volume

Edited by

Shaye J. D. Cohen and Joshua J. Schwartz

SBL PRESS

Atlanta

Copyright © 2007 by Koninklijke Brill NV, Leiden, The Netherlands

This edition is published under license from Koninklijke Brill NV, Leiden, The Netherlands, by SBL Press.

All rights reserved. No part of this work may be reproduced or transmitted in any form or by any means, electronic or mechanical, including photocopying and recording, or by means of any information storage or retrieval system, except as may be expressly permitted by the 1976 Copyright Act or in writing from the publisher. Requests for permission should be addressed in writing to the Rights and Permissions Office, SBL Press, 825 Houston Mill Road, Atlanta, GA 30329 USA.

Library of Congress Control Number: 2016932776

Printed on acid-free paper.

CONTENTS

In Appreciation of Louis H. Feldman vii

Josephus on Ancient Jewish Groups from a Social Scientific
    Perspective 1
    ALBERT I. BAUMGARTEN

Maccabees, Zealots and Josephus: The Impact of Zionism
    on Joseph Klausner's *History of the Second Temple* 15
    DAVID BERGER

'Your covenant that you have sealed in our flesh':
    Women, Covenant, and Circumcision 29
    SHAYE J.D. COHEN

Who are the Kings of East and West in Ber 7a?: Roman
    Religion, Syrian Gods and Zoroastriansim in the
    Babylonian Talmud 43
    YAAKOV ELMAN

The Meaning of 'Fisci Iudaici Calumnia Sublata' on the
    Coinage of Nerva 81
    MARTIN GOODMAN

The Abuse and Misuse of Josephus in Eusebius'
    Ecclesiastical History, Books 2 and 3 91
    GOHEI HATA

Justus of Tiberias and the Synchronistic Chronology of
    Israel 103
    CHAIM MILIKOWSKY

'Women are (Not) Trustworthy'—Toward the Resolution
    of a Talmudic Crux 127
    LEIB MOSCOVITZ

Josephus and the Books of Samuel 141
    ETIENNE NODET

Lysias—An Outstanding Seleucid Politician 169
    URIEL RAPPAPORT

Document and Rhetoric in Josephus: Revisiting the
    'Charter' for the Jews 177
    TESSA RAJAK

Adnotationes criticae ad Flavii Iosephi *Contra Apionem* 191
    HEINZ SCHRECKENBERG

Josephus on His Jewish Forerunners (*Contra Apionem*
    1.218) 195
    DANIEL R. SCHWARTZ

Are the 'Halachic Temple Mount' and the 'Outer Court'
    of Josephus One and the Same? 207
    JOSHUA SCHWARTZ AND YEHOSHUA PELEG

Conversion to Judaism in the Second Temple Period:
    A Functional Approach 223
    SETH SCHWARTZ

Jews and Gentiles from Judas Maccabaeus to John
    Hyrcanus according to Contemporary Jewish Sources 237
    ISRAEL SHATZMAN

The Ancient Lists of Contents of Josephus' *Antiquities* 271
    JOSEPH SIEVERS

Index of Sources 293
Index of Scholars Cited 308

IN APPRECIATION OF LOUIS H. FELDMAN

To know Louis Feldman is to love him. Has Louis (pronounced LOO-ey by all his admirers) ever had a student who did not subsequently become an acolyte, a devotee, a *hasid*? His affection for his students, his concern for their well-being and success, his delight in their accomplishments—all these were experienced by legions of students. Louis is devoted not only to his students but also to his subject. He has single-handedly kept alive the study of Greek and Latin at Yeshiva College for over fifty years. He routinely teaches five or six courses *a semester*, sometimes more, so that his students in Beginners' Latin, Intermediate Latin, Advanced Latin, Beginners' Greek, Intermediate Greek, and Advanced Greek would be able to take a course at the level appropriate to them. No class was too small for Louis; if even a single student showed up for a course, Louis offered it. When I was a student at Yeshiva College, I took a total of fourteen courses with Louis (eight in Latin, six in Greek). If memory serves, the enrollment in these courses ranged from two to five. And yet, everyone at Yeshiva College knew that these courses were among the best offered in the school and were second to none in seriousness and effectiveness. In 1981 Louis received an award from the American Philological Association for excellence in teaching the classics.

This heavy teaching load did not impair Louis' scholarship. On the contrary, from the 1950s to today a steady stream of articles and books has flowed from his active pen. Josephus, of course, has long remained his particular favorite; we may safely say that Louis is dean of Josephan studies in the United States. Louis has given us the immensely useful Loeb edition of books 18–20 of the Jewish Antiquities, and innumerable studies of Josephus's paraphrase of the Bible. These studies have been collected in his *Studies in Josephus' Rewritten Bible* (Leiden: Brill, 1998) and *Josephus's Interpretation of the Bible* (Berkeley: University of California Press, 1998). The capstone of his work on Josephus no doubt is his translation of, and extensive commentary on, books 1–4 of the Antiquities for the new Josephus series published by Brill (2000).

But this is not all. Louis has long been interested in the place of the Jews in Greco-Roman society, especially in questions relating to conversion to Judaism (proselytism). An early article of his, 'Jewish "Sympathizers" in Classical Literature and Inscriptions,' *Transactions of the American Philological Association* 81 (1950) 200–208, is a classic. Louis has gone on to write many other classic studies of the social and religious interactions between Jews and gentiles in antiquity, notably *Jew and Gentile in the Ancient World: Attitudes and Interactions from Alexander to Justinian* (Princeton: Princeton University Press, 1993). Even those who do not fully accept Louis' assumptions and interpretations will acknowledge that this is the work of a master scholar who knows all the relevant sources in Greek, Latin, Hebrew, and Aramaic. And who knows how many essays Louis has written on Philo and pseudo-Philo, on the Greek and Latin authors who refer to Jews, on Midrash and Septuagint, and on related topics?

Louis has spent virtually his entire career at Yeshiva University, an institution with a very modest PhD program in Jewish studies. The result is that Louis has not trained many PhD students. But nonetheless he has profoundly affected the field of Jewish studies through his numerous students who, inspired by his example and his teaching, went on to earn PhD's elsewhere and to become scholars of note in Jewish studies. A fair number of these students appear as contributors to this book.

Blessed by a deep and real piety, an unswerving dedication to what is right, and a wonderful sense of humor, Louis is a model Jew, teacher, and scholar. May he live until one hundred and twenty, full of good health, cheer, and enthusiasm.

Shaye Cohen
Joshua Schwartz

JOSEPHUS ON ANCIENT JEWISH GROUPS FROM A SOCIAL SCIENTIFIC PERSPECTIVE*

ALBERT I. BAUMGARTEN

INTRODUCTION

Josephus' comments on the 'philosophies' prevalent among ancient Jews have been subject to much criticism. Can Josephus really be believed when he claimed that he spent a year studying the doctrines and practices of Pharisees, Sadducees and Essenes, or is this one example of a *topos*, according to which an intellectual claimed to have learned from all possible sources?[1] Was Josephus a Pharisee, as he asserted, or was this a late in life commitment, undertaken when it was politically expedient, of which there are few if any indications in his earlier works (his loyalty to priestly traditions seems much more important)?[2] What were his sources for the two extensive excurses on the Jewish groups? Who was the audience for which these excurses were written and how might his sources and/or the audience have shaped the presentation of these movements?[3] Since

---

* This paper is a revised version of lectures presented to the Graduiertenkolleg 'Religion und Normativität,' Heidelberg University, Heidelberg, Germany, in February 2000, and as part of my responsibilities as Altman Visiting Professor of Jewish Studies, University College, London, London, England in March 2000. I would like to thank my host in Heidelberg, Professor Jan Assmann, and my hosts in London, Professors Mark Geller and Mary Douglas, for the opportunities to present my ideas and benefit from discussion.

I presented the theoretical analysis of sectarianism outlined below in my *The Flourishing of Jewish Sects in the Maccabean Era: An Interpretation* (Leiden: E.J. Brill & Co., 1997) 1–14. In that book, I did not show how these observations were confirmed in detail by comments of Josephus on the various groups. I am pleased to demonstrate the specific connection between my model of sectarianism and the work of Josephus in this volume, dedicated in honor of Professor Louis Feldman, whose contributions to the understanding of Josephus have taught us all.

[1] See S.J.D. Cohen, *Josephus in Galilee and Rome: His Vita and Development as a Historian* (Leiden: E.J. Brill & Co., 1979) 106–107.

[2] This is one of the consistent conclusions of S. Mason, *Flavius Josephus on the Pharisees* (Leiden: E.J. Brill & Co., 1991).

[3] R. Bergmeier, *Die Essener Berichte des Flavius Josephus* (Kampen: Kok Pharos, 1993). See also R. Bergmeier, 'Review of A.I. Baumgarten, *The Flourishing of Jewish*

the discovery of the Qumran scrolls many scholars have been tempted to identify Josephus' Essenes with the community that produced the sectarian documents found at Qumran. These scholars have wondered whether we should now correct Josephus, now identified as a less reliable external witness, in the light of the supposedly internal evidence, now newly available from the group.[4]

These are only a few of the critical questions that have been asked. This paper offers an indirect defense of the accuracy of Josephus' comments. In the process I also hope to show the keenness of Josephus' insight into the social and religious dynamics of his era. To accomplish these objectives this paper will have two parts. In the first I will offer a model of how dissident religious groups, which I choose to call sects, arise. This model will be based on examples *other than* ancient Judaism. To the extent possible, it was elaborated without any conscious reference to the groups of the Second Temple era. In the second part I will show how this model illuminates numerous comments on the Jewish groups of the Second Temple era made by Josephus. When a model helps explain instances on which it was not based, the model proves its descriptive validity. Conversely, when a set of sources is made more meaningful by analysis in the light of an independent model, I believe that to be indirect confirmation of the accuracy of the information conveyed by those sources.

The Social Dynamics of Sectarianism[5]

The dynamics by which dissident religious groups arise and flourish can be identified through the study of instances of the proliferation

---

Sects in the Maccabean Era: An Interpretation,' Theologische Literaturzeitung 124 (1992,2): 162–163. Bergmeier's evaluation of my book is a direct consequence of our disagreement about the nature of Josephus' evidence. Compare n. 10 below.

[4] For one early attempt to wrestle with this question see J. Strugnell, 'Flavius Josephus and the Essenes, Antiquities xviii 18–22,' *Journal of Biblical Literature* 77 (1958): 106–115.

[5] The definition of sect proposed below should be compared with that suggested by S.J.D. Cohen, *From the Maccabees to the Mishnah* (Philadelphia: Westminster Press, 1987) 125–127. While I stress the voluntary nature of sectarianism a bit more, as well as the role of boundary marking in separation from the new class of alien, and Cohen underscores the sectarian claim to absolute truth—the agreement between our definitions is substantial. Cohen and I also share the concern to define sect in such a way as to apply to the full range of Jewish groups known from the Second Temple period.

of such movements. Seventeenth century Britain and the Jewish world since emancipation and since the rise of Zionism and the establishment of the State of Israel are particularly fruitful examples. These cases have benefited from the insight of distinguished historians, sensitive to social and religious processes, such as Christopher Hill[6] and Jacob Katz.[7]

I choose to call these groups sects, although I am aware of the Christian origins of the term, and of the difficulties social scientists have encountered in attempting to isolate and define the meaning of the term. Nevertheless, numerous scholarly attempts to characterize sects indicate that the term resonates with meaning and should not be abandoned.[8] I would begin my definition of a sect with one of the oldest commonplaces in the academic discussion of the term, going back to Weber and Troeltsch. One is not born a sectarian. Rather, one elects to join a sect: a sect is a voluntary association. Accordingly, it requires great effort to educate succeeding generations born into a sect to adopt the way of life and ideological stance of their predecessors, who joined the sect voluntarily from the outside. Profound changes in the nature of the sect often ensue, in the process.[9]

Voluntary associations are numerous, and of many different types; not every small voluntary religious group is a sect.[10] Further precision

---

[6] From among many works see especially, C. Hill, *The English Bible and the Seventeenth-Century Revolution* (Harmondsworth: Penguin, 1993).

[7] For a convenient summary see J. Katz, *Halacha in Straits: Obstacles to Orthodoxy at its Inception* (Jerusalem: Magnes Press, 1992) 9–20 [Hebrew].

[8] See L. Dawson, 'Church/Sect Theory: Getting it Straight,' *North American Religion* 1 (1992): 5–28. As E. Gellner, *Saints of the Atlas* (Chicago: University of Chicago Press, 1969) 11 notes, the definition of a term such as sect is shaped in advance by those examples one takes as a paradigm. Had one taken the groups in North Africa Gellner studied as the paradigm, the notion of sect would be quite different.

[9] Despite criticism and refinement of the thesis by others, the classic study of this process remains H.R. Niebuhr, *The Social Sources of Denominationalism* (New York: Holt, Rinehart & Winston, 1929). For a brief summary of the criticisms see B. Wilson, 'Historical Lessons in the Study of Sects and Cults,' *Religion and the Social Order— The Handbook on Cults and Sects in America, Volume 3, Part A* (D.G. Bromley and J.K. Hadden eds,; Greenwich, CT: JAI Press, 1993) 55.

[10] Compare I. Gruenwald, 'The Problem of Jewish Sectarianism in the Second Temple Period,' *Cathedra* 92 (1999): 177–184 [Hebrew]. Gruenwald's comments on my work on sectarianism are an intellectual disgrace. Pretending to write a review that turns the author's dross into precious metal, he sets the stage for his supposed contribution by ignoring much of what I wrote. He disregards the nuanced argument I offered, in which for example I explained why I was defining 'sect' as I had (see a summary of these points, below, at nn. 16–19). He then fills the artificial

in the definition is therefore necessary. I suggest that sects are voluntary associations of protest, who object to the way others live their religious life. I would understand a sectarian in the light of a derogatory seventeenth century definition of a Puritan, as someone who 'loved God with all his soul and hated his neighbor with all his heart.'[11]

The reasons a sectarian so hates his neighbor may be numerous, but one in particular seems worthy of attention. I believe sects flourish when religious identity becomes more voluntary due to changes in the political or ideological environment. Instances of religious identity becoming more voluntary include the new freedom Jews acquired with emancipation, or the end of censorship coupled with the flourishing of printing (cheap handbills, broadsides and pamphlets, in particular) and the rise of a rootless urban class in Britain of the seventeenth century. When some take advantage of the new freedom in ways of which others disapprove, the hatred which will spawn sects emerges.

The social consequences of this hate are far reaching. Every group distinguishes between its members and those it considers outsiders by means of boundary marking. The latter includes issues such as with whom do you eat (commensality), whose prepared food do you accept, what clothes do you wear, whom do you marry, with whom do you pray and with whom do you do business? Sects revise the ordinary scheme of things, and establish a new class of alien, from among those normally considered insiders. They then proceed to boundary mark against these new aliens, in much the same ways as the old 'real' outsiders were distinguished. They do not eat with these new aliens, they dress differently, are unwilling to marry them, do not pray with them and restrict their business dealings with them. From among these boundary marking mechanisms food is of special importance, as it is the most universal. Commensality and those from whom one accepts prepared food define the limits of one's identity.

---

intellectual vacuum of his own creation with various proposals, arguing against a straw man of his own creation. In the end I agree with a number of his suggestions, as they can be found in my work. For a different assessment of my work, focusing on the same issues on which Gruenwald criticized me, but which takes full account of my argument see L. Schiffman, 'Review of A.I. Baumgarten, *The Flourishing of Jewish Sects in the Maccabean Era: An Interpretation*,' *Zion* 55 (5761): 379–381.

[11] C. Hill, *Society and Puritanism in Pre-Revolutionary England* (London: Secker & Warburg, 1964) 41.

When properly prepared food or acceptable fellowship companions are unavailable, the last resort of a sectarian is always food taken direct from nature, eaten alone raw, which has no social restrictions.[12]

Even at this stage of the discussion we should take account of one important variable that distinguishes some sects from others. The degree of boundary marking is not necessarily uniform. Some groups erect higher and thicker walls, with fewer exits and entrances against the outside world, while the walls of other groups are lower, thinner, and have many more openings.[13] In the terminology proposed by Wilson, some sects are reformist, the others introversionist.[14] Sects of the former type have not despaired of changing the larger society, hence maintain greater contact with it, and erect lower barriers against it. In contrast, groups of the latter type, who have turned inwards, and whose only concern is for themselves and their own purity, construct higher walls.

Another scale of measurement for classifying groups is suggested by the work of Coser. He investigated 'greedy institutions' that require sacrifice of sexual identity, and placed sects among these greedy institutions.[15] In fact, however, sacrifice of identity is not limited to the sexual realm. It can also be financial (property assigned to the sect) or biological (biological family replaced by sectarian family). In general, the scales of reformist/introversionist overlap with those of greediness. The more introversionist a sect the greater the sacrifice of identity it demands.

When this definition is applied to the Jewish groups of the Second Temple period, Pharisees, Sadducees, Essenes and the Dead Sea Scrolls, as well as many other groups that emerged in the first century C.E. were sects. I recognize that there are other ways of classifying

---

[12] For the conceptual background of this paragraph see M. Douglas, *Purity and Danger—An Analysis of the Concepts of Pollution and Taboo* (London/New York: Ark Paperbacks, 1984); M. Douglas, *In the Wilderness—The Doctrine of Defilement in the Book of Numbers* (Sheffield: Sheffield Academic Press, 1993) 42–62; E. Sivan, 'Enclave Culture,' *Fundamentalism Comprehended* (M. Marty ed.; Chicago: University of Chicago Press, 1995) 11–68; L. Dumont, *Homo Hierarchicus* (Chicago: University of Chicago Press, 1980³); C.L. Strauss, *The Raw and the Cooked* (Chicago: University of Chicago Press, 1969).

[13] One should note that no matter how extreme the degree of closure, no group ever shuts itself hermetically against the outside world. That would be suicidal, as if it were depriving itself of conceptual oxygen to breathe.

[14] B. Wilson, *Magic and the Millennium* (London: Heinemann, 1973) 18–26.

[15] L. Coser, *Greedy Institutions—Patterns of Undivided Commitment* (New York: Free Press, 1974).

the ancient groups. Some would restrict the term sect to extremist movements such as the Dead Sea Scrolls and call other groups parties or movements.[16] Others would argue that sectarianism is only possible when there is an established church from which sects can dissent.[17] My definition is deliberately broad, so as to include as many groups as possible. It does not require an established church in order to permit the existence of sects.[18] It takes account of the difference in degree of extremism between groups by another route, the distinction between reformist and introversionist suggested above. I believe that this more flexible definition has the distinct advantage of allowing greater comparison and contrast between the groups so that they can shed better light on each other as competing answers to the same set of problems.[19]

THE EVIDENCE OF JOSEPHUS: THE NEW CLASS OF ALIEN[20]

Philo of Alexandria, in his *Hypothetica* 11.1–2 was explicitly aware of the voluntary nature of sectarianism. He wrote about the Essenes: 'these people are called Essenes... their persuasion is not based on birth, for birth is not a descriptive mark of voluntary associations.' The voluntary nature of the Jewish groups is also reflected in the terms Josephus employed for them. While he called them 'philosophies' in *War* 2. 119 and in *Ant.* 13.289, 18.9,11,23, he also called them *haireseis* in *War* 2.137 and in *Ant.* 13.171, 293. He twice employed the term *proairesis* (*Ant.* 13.293, 15.373). The author of Acts followed

---

[16] See E.P. Sanders, *Paul and Palestinian Judaism* (London, SCM, 1977) 425–426.

[17] See e.g. S. Talmon, 'Qumran Studies: Past, Present and Future,' *Jewish Quarterly Review* 85 (1994): 6.

[18] See further Wilson, 'Historical Lessons,' 56 on the implausible results that follow from requiring a church in order to acknowledge the existence of sects in the study of American religious experience.

[19] See the full scale discussion in Baumgarten, *Flourishing*. I argue there that one of the principal reasons for the emergence of sectarianism in ancient Judaism was the fall of the boundaries which separated Jews from the surrounding world, in particular as a result of the encounter with Hellenism. I take this to be the factor which caused Jewish identity in that era to become more voluntary and to have sparked the flourishing of different groups as competing answers to how to cope with the new situation.

[20] As the reader will notice, there are fewer footnotes in this section. On the whole the passages from Josephus discussed have attracted little scholarly attention. Lacking the conceptual framework to make Josephus' remarks meaningful, scholars had little to say on these sources.

in Josephus' footsteps, calling the Pharisees a *hairesis* (Acts 15:5, 26:5). He employed the same term for the Sadducees (Acts 5:17), as well as for the Nazoreans, i.e. the early Christians (Acts 24:5). Acts also teaches us that *hairesis* might be employed in a pejorative sense. Paul, defending himself before Felix, explained that he followed the Way, which enabled him to worship the God of his fathers, believing everything laid down by the law or written in the prophets. Nevertheless, others called this way a *hairesis* (Acts 24:14). The terms *hairesis, haireseis* and *proairesis* all have a basic meaning of 'choice.' In that sense they reflect well the voluntary nature of sectarianism that was my point of departure.

Josephus also explicitly acknowledged the creation of the new class of alien by the groups he described. He writes about the Essenes (*War* 2.150):

> They are divided according to the duration of their discipline into four grades; and so far are the junior members inferior to the seniors that a senior, if but touched by a junior, must take a bath, as after contact with an alien.

This bit of data omits a crucial point, perhaps because it might reflect poorly on the Essenes whose praises were sung by Josephus in the excursus as a whole. What would an Essene do if touched by an ordinary Jew? I suggest that if an Essene purified himself, as if after contact with an alien when touched by an Essene of lower grade he would certainly have purified himself, for the same reason, if touched by an ordinary Jew.[21]

The application of old rules of treating 'real' aliens to the new class of aliens also emerges from another comment of Josephus (*War* 2.129):

> After this purification they assemble in a private apartment which none of the uninitiated is permitted to enter; pure now themselves, they repair to the refectory, as to some sacred shrine.

Non-Essene Jews were not allowed to participate in the Essene meal. The reason supplied by Josephus is most interesting: in Essene eyes, the refectory in which the meal was served had the status of a sacred shrine (*hagion ti temenos*). Access to the Temple proper was limited to

---

[21] Compare the interpretation of this passage suggested by J. Klawans, 'Notions of Gentile Impurity in Ancient Judaism,' *AJSReview* 20 (1995): 300–301.

properly purified Jews, and warning inscriptions were erected to inform non-Jews of the limits they should not cross.[22] As non-Jews were excluded from the sacred shrine of Jerusalem so were non-Essene Jews prohibited from sharing the Essene meal in their private communal sacred shrine.

Essene behavior may help explain yet another comment by Josephus (*War* 2.119): 'The Essenes have a reputation for cultivating peculiar sanctity. Of Jewish birth, they show a greater attachment to each other than do others.' Why did Josephus feel this need to stress that the Essenes were Jews by birth? I suggest that perhaps Josephus realized that his reader, familiar with Essene behavior and with their treatment of other Jews as if they were aliens, might conclude that the Essenes were not Jews. In order to counter this possible mistaken conclusion Josephus felt obligated to remind his reader that notwithstanding their way of life, the Essenes were, in fact, Jews by birth.

Creation of the new category of alien is explicitly noted by Josephus for the Sadducees. He comments in *War* 2.166: 'The Sadducees... in their intercourse with other Jews are as rude as to aliens.' While Josephus included the Sadducees among the Jewish philosophies it is not always clear that they belong among groups of protest and fit my definition of sect. Against whom or what was a small priestly group, centered in Jerusalem (*Ant.* 18.17) and often in control of the Temple, protesting? Nevertheless, the remark from *War* 2.166 cited above indicates that the Sadducees were involved in boundary marking against fellow Jews. Perhaps their boundary marking was of the reformist type, as was that of the Pharisees, but it existed nonetheless. The Sadducees were a sect.

The same pattern is true of the so-called Sicarii. They attacked other Jews without compunction. Perhaps their most famous action was the assault by the Sicarii in Masada on the Jews of Ein Gedi during Passover (*War* 4.402–405). Josephus denies the validity of the justification offered by the Sicarii for such actions. Nevertheless he performed a valuable service as he allows us to see how the Sicarii would have wanted to be understood (*War* 7.255):

---

[22] See especially the two classic studies of these texts by E.J. Bickerman, 'Une proclamation séleucide relative au temple de Jérusalem,' *Studies in Jewish and Christian History, Part Two* (Leiden: E.J. Brill & Co., 1980) 86–104 and 'The Warning Inscriptions of Herod's Temple,' *Studies, Part Two*, 210–224.

> Those who consented to submit to Rome... were no other than aliens, who so ignobly sacrificed the hard-won liberty of the Jews and admitted their preference for the Roman yoke.

The 'alien' status of collaborators justified the way Sicarii treated these Jews.[23]

The consequences for food consumption of this new categorization of fellow Jews are also explicit in our sources. Josephus writes of ex-Essenes (*War* 2.143):

> Those who are caught in the act of committing grave faults are expelled from the order. The individual thus excluded often perishes, the prey to a most miserable fate; for bound by his oaths and customs he cannot even share the food of others. Reduced to eating grass, he perishes, his body dried up by hunger.

Perhaps Josephus' former master Bannus was someone with an Essene past, as he '... dwelt in the wilderness, wearing only such clothing as trees provided, feeding on such things as grew of themselves (*Life* 11).' John the Baptist may have been yet another figure with an Essene past. His diet consisted of locusts and wild honey (Matt. 3:4), foods taken directly from nature (note: John would not fit our definition of vegetarian, as he ate locusts). John's behavior evoked a distinct hostile reaction from his contemporaries. They suggested that John was possessed by a demon, for why else did he not eat bread and drink wine like any 'normal' person (Luke 7:33).[24]

The behavior of an ex-Essene, of Bannus or of John should be contrasted with that of ordinary Jews. Josephus writes of his priestly friends, in jail in Rome (*Life 14*):

> I was anxious to discover some means to deliver these men, more especially as I learnt that even in affliction they had not forgotten the pious practices of religion, and supported themselves on figs and nuts.

At the time of the persecutions of Antiochus IV, according to 2 Macc. 5:27:

> Judah Maccabee with about nine others got away to the wilderness, and kept himself and his companions alive in the mountains as wild

---

[23] On the license people felt to seize the property of foreigners see also *Gen.R* 862 (Theodor-Albeck).
[24] Compare the heavily theologizing treatment of John by J. Taylor, 'John the Baptist and the Essenes,' *Journal of Jewish Studies* 47 (1996): 256–285.

animals do; they continued to live on what grew wild, so that they might not share in the defilement.

As the author of 2 Macc. makes clear, this was not a mere tactical necessity, but a requirement of a life of purity. The ex-Essene, Bannus and John the Baptist were not in Roman captivity. Nor were there persecutions of the sort promulgated by Antiochus IV in their time. Why were they behaving as they did? From whose impurity did they seek to protect themselves by eating food taken directly from nature? From that of the new class of aliens, composed of 'ordinary' Jews, created by their former sectarian brothers, I submit.

The Evidence of Josephus: Sacrifice of Identity

Another crucial aspect of the model of sectarianism offered above was sacrifice of identity in order to belong to the sect. Again, writing of the Essenes, Josephus acknowledged their sacrifice of biological identity (*War* 2.134):

> In all other things they do nothing without orders from their superiors; two things only are left to individual discretion, the rendering of assistance and compassion. Members may of their own notion help the deserving, when in need, and supply food to the destitute; but presents to relatives are prohibited, without leave from the managers.

Aid to strangers is a matter of individual decision. Yet an Essene who showed remnants of loyalty to biological kin must receive permission.[25]

Sacrifice of physical identity of another sort emerges from Essene requirements concerning defecation. Josephus wrote (*War* 2.147–149):

---

[25] Philo discussed Essene celibacy in similar terms (*Hyp.* *11.14–17*): 'They eschew marriage because they discern it to be the sole or the principal danger to communal life ... for he who is bound fast in the love lures of his wife or under the stress of nature makes his children his first care ceases to be the same to others and unconsciously has become a different man and has passed from freedom into slavery.'

The Qumran cemetery is another example of sacrifice of biological identity. An ordinary Jew of the Second Temple era expected to be buried with his biological kin, 'gathered into his fathers,' in the family tomb. Those Qumran members who chose to be buried with their sectarian brothers were making a powerful statement whom they regarded as their true family.

According to 4Q477, published by E. Eshel, '4Q477: The Rebukes of the Overseer,' *Journal of Jewish Studies* 45 (1994): 111–122, one reason Hananiah Notos was rebuked by the overseer was for love of near kin.

(On the Sabbath) they do not even go to stool. On other days they dig a trench a foot deep with a mattock—such is the nature of the hatchet which they present to the neophytes—and wrapping their mantle about them, that they may not offend the rays of the deity, sit above it. They then replace the excavated soil in the trench. For this purpose they select the more retired spots. And though this discharge of the excrements is a natural function, they make it a rule to wash themselves after it, as if defiled.

Belonging to a group whose manner of defecation was such that it was forbidden one day a week, on the Sabbath, was a most significant concession to a 'greedy institution.'[26]

The final sentence of the passage just quoted allows a further insight into the nature of the Jewish groups. Ordinary Jews, as Josephus noted, did not consider defecation defiling. But as we learn from other sources, priests, especially serving priests in the Temple, did. Ezekiel, a righteous priest, was commanded by God to bake his bread on human feces (4:12). He begged God for a special dispensation, in light of the holy status he had maintained throughout his life, and received permission to employ animal dung instead (4:12–13). The Mishnah informs us that the Temple had a special latrine with an adjacent pool for purification for those priests who needed to defecate while serving in the Temple (*mTam.* 1:1).

An Essene modeled his life on that of a priest and considered defecation defiling. I take this as an example of a phenomenon widely known in religious experience. Someone who wishes to raise the quotient of spirituality in his life does this by adopting some of the requirements characteristic of those higher up on the ladder of sanctity.[27] One interesting example of this pattern in the Biblical tradition

---

[26] As I have argued elsewhere (A.I. Baumgarten, 'The Temple Scroll, Toilet Practices and the Essenes,' *Jewish History* 10 [1996]: 9–20) the Temple Scroll also prescribed a manner of defecation (latrines placed 3,000 cubits from the camp) that effectively prohibited defecation on the Sabbath (when one may walk only 2,000 cubits outside the camp). Yet while the results were the same, one should distinguish between the practices that brought Essenes to that conclusion and those of the Temple Scroll. In fact, I suggest that these differences prove that the Temple Scroll was not Essene. Indeed, if a latrine is ever definitely found at Qumran I would take that as conclusive evidence that Qumran was not Essene. Compare J. Magness, 'Qumran Archeology: Past Perspectives and Future Prospects,' *The Dead Sea Scrolls After Fifty Years—A Comprehensive Assessment, Volume I* (P. Flint and J.C. Vanderkam eds. Leiden: E.J. Brill & Co., 1998) 65–70.

[27] See Dumont, *Homo Hierarchicus*, 192.

is the Nazirite.²⁸ The contrast between the Essene and a priest is noteworthy. While the priest considered defecation defiling a condition imposed on him by birth and as the embodiment of sanctity acknowledged by all, the Essene, a priest *manqué*, behaved as if he were a priest as a voluntary protest against the way other Jews were living. As other groups, such as the Pharisees, also imposed priest-like restrictions on their members,²⁹ the pattern I propose for the Essenes has its equivalents among other contemporary sects.

Conclusion

Viewed from the perspective of the theory of sectarianism I have proposed Josephus' comments take on new meaning and allow insights previously impossible. These insights suggest that for all its flaws Josephus' evidence must be taken seriously and should not be dismissed easily.

On the whole, in his two excurses, in particular, Josephus described the groups as they would have wanted to be portrayed. He never approaches an account of the Essenes which might have been written by someone whose brother or son joined the group and ultimately transferred his share of the family property to the order, thus damaging the economic interests of the remaining family members.³⁰ We hear little or nothing in Josephus of the resentment which groups aroused, of the sort concerning John the Baptist's refusal to eat bread and drink wine in Luke 7:33. The only exceptions to this pattern are the groups of the revolutionary anti-Roman camp whom Josephus

---

[28] See further A.I. Baumgarten, 'Hattat Sacrifices,' *Revue Biblique* 103 (1996): 341. The Nazirite served as a model for the sectarian who lived according to the rules of the Damascus Documents, as we now can see clearly from the opening line of that work, as known from fragments from Cave Four at Qumran. See 4Q266 1.i.1.

[29] See H. Harrington, 'Did the Pharisees Eat Ordinary Food in a State of Purity?' *Journal for the Study of Judaism in the Persian, Hellenistic and Roman Period* 26 (1995): 42–54.

[30] We have such accounts for modern groups which required their members to hand over assets to the group and they are eye-opening by contrast to pious accounts which seek to praise and justify the sectarian movement. See further S.J. Stein, *The Shaker Experience in America* (New Haven: Yale University Press, 1992) 50. In order to appease angry relatives Shakers regularly settled claims by family members for assets transferred to the order, rather than pursue a defense of these transfers in the courts, *ibid.*, 142. In general, on Shakers as viewed by outsiders, both favorably and unfavorably, see *ibid.*, 215–237.

regularly denounced and was happy to point out the gap between their professed ideals and the reality as he saw it. For other groups, however, Josephus was a friendly witness. What he wrote about them usually reflected the way they wished to be perceived.[31] We may never know fully how Josephus came to this information, but its value cannot be denied.

---

[31] This is not the place to enter into extended debate with Mason's contention that Josephus was consistently anti-Pharisaic from his earliest works to his last. For a preliminary discussion of this point see A.I. Baumgarten, 'Rivkin and Neusner on the Pharisees,' *Law in Religious Communities* (G.P. Richardson ed.; Waterloo: Wilfrid Laurier University Press, 1991) 109–126. Furthermore, even if Mason were correct the criticism of the Pharisees in Josephus would not approach the harshness of the polemic to be found in the New Testament.

MACCABEES, ZEALOTS AND JOSEPHUS: THE IMPACT OF ZIONISM ON JOSEPH KLAUSNER'S *HISTORY OF THE SECOND TEMPLE*

David Berger

It is hardly a secret that Zionist ideology had a profound impact on Joseph Klausner's historiographic enterprise. Even a superficial perusal of his works reveals a powerful Zionist commitment expressed in both rhetoric and analysis, so much so that his right to teach the period of the Second Temple in the Hebrew University was held up for years on the grounds that he was more of a publicist and ideologue—and of the Revisionist variety no less—than a historian.

Nonetheless, I believe that there is much to be said for a serious examination of the nationalist element in his multi-volume work on the Second Temple.[1] However we assess the political and scholarly arguments for and against his appointment, a man who had nothing of the historian in him would not have been appointed to Klausner's position in the world's flagship institution for Jewish Studies. With all his abundant methodological flaws, he was not a publicist pure and simple.

Since readers of this article, which will sharply underscore some of those flaws, may ultimately question this judgment, let me move immediately to a second, even more important point. The ideological use of selected episodes in a nation's history is an integral part of any nationalist movement or educational system. Zionism was no exception; indeed, its unusual, even unique, character generated a particularly acute need to establish a national history that would provide models for the struggling yishuv and the early state. The pedagogic utilization of the ancient paradigms of Jewish heroism had to draw upon academic, not merely popular, legitimation. From this perspective, the fact that Klausner stood with one foot in the world of academic research and the other in the public square, where he exercised considerable influence, lends special interest to an analysis

---

[1] *Historia shel ha-Bayit ha-Sheni*, 2nd ed., 5 vols. (Jerusalem, 1951), henceforth *Historia*.

of his scholarly-ideological approach to key developments in Second Temple history.[2] As Klausner confronted the dilemmas of military, political and religious policy in ancient Israel, his own dilemmas illuminate not only Zionist historiography but the political and moral challenges facing the nascent, beleaguered State.

It is self-evident that Klausner was sensitive to the charges leveled at him by his colleagues at the university, and so his inaugural lecture on the Second Temple, which is also the opening chapter of the book, was devoted to the question of historical objectivity. The argument in that lecture is so strange that only the extraordinary defensiveness generated by relentless criticism can serve to explain it.

The objective study of history, says Klausner, leads to 'necessary conclusions,' to 'absolute evaluations.'[3] It is true that each generation sees the past through its own experience, but as long as the historian seeks truth to the best of his ability, his conclusions are absolute for that generation. This is an idiosyncratic use of the term 'absolute,' and when Klausner proposes a concrete example, the peculiarity of the argument is thrown into even bolder relief. A Jew and a Pole, he says, *must* evaluate Chmielnicki differently, but precisely because of the ineluctable nature of this difference, 'there is no subjectivity involved at all.' Chmielnicki persecuted the Jews but strove to improve the lot of his own people. Consequently, 'the honest scholar must see both sides of the accepted historical coin.'[4] Thus, in virtually the same breath, Klausner speaks of the absolute necessity compelling a Jew to evaluate Chmielnicki in a one-sided fashion and proceeds to present him in all his mutivalent complexity. This almost incoherent argument for untrammeled, unmodulated historical objectivity was surely generated by the subjective realities of Klausner's personal situation.

When we turn to the period of the Second Temple, we confront a series of personalities and events central to the self-image of both yishuv and State: the return from the Babylonian exile, the revolt of Mattathias and his sons, the achievement of independence and

---

[2] Klausner's profound impact on certain sectors of the yishuv, an impact grounded precisely in his combined personae of scholarly researcher, Zionist thinker, and public personality, is strikingly evident in the tone of the admiring intellectual biography written by two disciples during his lifetime. See Yaakov Becker and Hayim Toren, *Yosef Klausner, ha-Ish u-Po'olo* (Tel Aviv and Jerusalem, 1947).

[3] *Historia* 1:10.

[4] *Historia* 1:11.

the pursuit of territorial expansion under the Hasmoneans, the great revolt, and the heroic stand at Masada.[5] The longest lasting of these developments was the Hasmonean dynasty, rooted in the most successful and spectacular event of the entire period, a revolt emblematic of Jewish military might and remembered not only by historians but by every Jewish child who has ever seen a Hanukkah menorah.

That revolt and that dynasty were pivotal to Zionist self-consciousness. Pinsker lamented the servile state of a people that had produced the Maccabees; Herzl declared that the Maccabees would arise once again; and in one of the most wrenching passages in all of Jewish literature, Bialik portrayed with bitter sarcasm the cellars in which 'the young lions of the prayer 'Father of Mercy' and the grandsons of the Maccabees' lay hidden in their miserable cowardice.[6] Jabotinsky sharply criticized the ghetto mentality that intentionally blotted out the memory of the Maccabees, and Gedaliah Alon's refutation of the thesis that the rabbinic Sages had done something similar was formulated in particularly sharp fashion: 'Did the Nation and Its Rabbis Cause the Hasmoneans to be Forgotten?'[7] Who then were these Maccabees, and are they really worthy of this extraordinary veneration?[8]

Klausner examined the Hasmonean period—and not that period alone—in an analytical framework reflecting categories of thought more characteristic of a twentieth-century Zionist scholar than of Judaean fighters in the second pre-Christian century. Granted, he says, Judah Maccabee fought for the religion of Israel, but he understood that his success was nourished by 'another non-material and non-measurable force—the national will to live. When a nation has

---

[5] In the last decade or so, several important works have, in whole or in part, analyzed the use of these and similar models in Zionist education, literature, and civic life. See Yael Zerubavel, *Recovered Roots: Collective Memory and the Meaning of Israeli National Tradition* (Chicago and London, 1995) and the literature noted there; Nachman Ben-Yehudah, *The Masada Myth: Collective Memory and Mythmaking in Israel* (Madison, Wisconsin, c. 1995); Mireille Hadas-Lebel, *Masada: Histoire et Symbole* (Paris, c. 1995); Anita Shapira, *Land and Power: The Zionist Resort to Force, 1881–1948* (New York, 1992). As early as 1937, Klausner himself had contributed to the popularization of the Masada story as a heroic, paradigmatic event. See *Land and Power*, p. 311.

[6] See the references in *Land and Power*, pp. 14, 37.

[7] *Mehqarim be-Toledot Yisrael* I (Tel Aviv, 1957), pp. 15–25.

[8] For a useful survey of Jewish perceptions of the Hasmoneans from antiquity through the twentieth century, see Samuel Schafler's 1973 Jewish Theological Seminary dissertation, *The Hasmoneans in Jewish Historiography*. On Klausner, see pp. 164–67, 199–204.

no choice other than to achieve victory or pass away from the world, it is impossible for it not to be victorious. So it was then and so it has been in our time and before our eyes.'[9]

And the essential element in this 'understanding'—the knowing incorporation of a nationalist consciousness into a religious ideology—characterized Judah's father as well. '[Mattathias] recognized clearly that it is appropriate to desecrate one Sabbath in order to observe many Sabbaths—in order to sustain the entire nation.'[10] The undeclared shift from the Talmudic formula—that the Sabbath may in certain circumstances be desecrated so that many Sabbaths may be observed in the future—to the nationalist formula that Klausner created as if the two were self-evidently interchangeable is a striking example of ideological sleight of hand.

It emerges, moreover, that this integration of the religious and the national characterized not only the Maccabees but the bulk of the Jewish population. 'Most of the nation' overcame 'all manner of torments' to stand against the decrees of Antiochus.

> Tens of thousands of spiritual heroes arose in Judaea who could not be coerced to betray the Torah of their God by any torment in the world or by any threat of bizarre death.... There was an intuitive feeling here that by betraying their God they would also be betraying their people, and if the Torah of Israel would be destroyed so too would the People of Israel.[11]

Finally, Klausner takes a remarkable further step by elevating land over spirit, and doing so through an original piece of speculative biblical exegesis so bereft of any evidentiary support that it is mildly unusual even by the anarchic standards of the Bible critics of his day. It is likely, he says, that the Psalm asserting that 'the heavens belong to the Lord but the earth He gave over to man' (Ps 115:16) was written during the great victory of Judah Maccabee. The warriors,

> suffused by a sense of the sanctity of the Homeland (*kedushat ha-moledet*) and the joy flowing from fulfilling the divine command, felt no need for the world to come. Through their conquest, they had acquired earthly life for themselves and for their nation and were prepared to leave the heavens to the Lord their God, provided that he would give

---

[9] *Historia* 3:19.
[10] *Historia* 3:17.
[11] *Historia* 2:199.

them the land as an inheritance—the land of their fathers and their children.[12]

Though the verse appears to speak of a contrast between the heavens and an earth given to humanity as a whole, the true, deeper meaning refers to the land of Israel granted to its chosen people.

Although Klausner asserts that even the pietists—the 'hasidim' of the sources—were nationalists, he underscores the contrast between their primarily spiritual interests and the political orientation of the Hasmoneans. In itself, such a perspective is eminently defensible.[13] Klausner, however, goes further by ascribing to his heroes from the very beginning of their appearance on the historical stage a fully formed, unambiguous ideology that is not expressed in the sources but accords perfectly with that of the historian.

'From the outset,' Judah and his brothers sought 'absolute freedom.' They understood that 'inner—religious and national-social—freedom' is impossible without 'absolute political sovereignty (*qomemiyyut*).'[14] Thus, the distinctive categories of religious freedom, national-social freedom, and political sovereignty did not merely animate Judah's policies on a subconscious level; they were a key element of his conscious ideology from the first moment of the revolt. Nor was this ideology created ex nihilo in the Hasmonean period. The spiritual creativity that Klausner ascribes to the four centuries between the Babylonian exile and the revolt would have been impossible in his view in the absence of 'a profound yearning for political freedom.'[15] Once again—an argument resting not on a documented source but on a psychohistorical generalization rooted in this instance in a sense of what the author's ideologically honed instincts have declared impossible.

When Klausner moves to the very different contrast between early Hasmoneans and Hellenizers, he describes the former, not surprisingly, as 'the national party.' In this instance, however, the interplay of ideological factors was potentially more complex. While the Zionist movement was in one sense a reaction against the classical Haskalah,

---

[12] *Historia* 3:29.
[13] See *Historia* 2:182–83, and cf. 3:38. For a discussion of the role of land and politics in this context, see Doron Mendels, *The Land of Israel as a Political Concept in Hasmonean Literature* (Tuebingen, 1987).
[14] *Historia* 3:41.
[15] *Historia* 2:273.

to a very important degree it was its offspring. Klausner, whose other, less controversial field of expertise was modern Hebrew literature, surely identified with the movement to broaden the intellectual and cultural horizons of Eastern European Jewry, and he could not dismiss the value of Greek culture even for the Jews of antiquity. Indeed, in another work, he described his central credo as follows: 'To absorb the culture of the other to the point of digesting it and transforming it into our own national-human flesh and blood—this is the ideal for which I fought during the prime of my life, and I will not stray from it till my last breath.'[16] Might it not be possible, then, even necessary, to say something positive about the Jewish arch-enemies of the Maccabees?

In order to avoid this undesirable consequence, Klausner mobilizes another presumably ineluctable law of history to help him conclude that the Hellenizers' objective was not the incorporation of Greek values into Jewish culture but the annihilation of the latter in favor of the former. Some scholars, he says, maintain that the Hellenizers were correct in their desire to open provincial Jewish society to the wide-ranging culture of the Hellenistic world. This, however, misperceives the Hellenizers' intentions. 'If they had possessed a liberating, essentially correct ideology, it would eventually have prevailed and been realized in life, even if little by little. The truth bursts forth and makes its way, sometimes immediately, sometimes after the passage of time.'[17]

Here Klausner's questionable rhetoric about the inevitable success of 'truth' conceals an even more extreme and implausible position upon which his argument really rests. In light of the progressive Hellenistic influence on the Hasmonean dynasty, what he sees as the essentially correct ideology of integrating Greek ideas and Judaism was indeed realized after the passage of time. So far so good. But how does Klausner know that this correct objective, which arguably did prevail, was not the goal of the Hellenizers? The answer cannot be the circular argument that their ideology did not prevail; rather, despite the plain meaning of his language, it must be that the group failed as a political entity, a failure that proves that it could not have had a correct worldview. In other words, his argument—if it is to be granted any coherence at all—amounts to the assertion that not

---

[16] *Bereshit Hayah ha-Ra'ayon*, p. 172, cited in Becker and Toren, p. 13.
[17] *Historia* 3:155.

only proper ideas but the political group that originates them must survive and ultimately triumph. Since this was not true of the Hellenizers, it follows that their goal was not integration but Jewish cultural suicide.[18]

The Hasmoneans ultimately attained genuine political freedom; this alone, however, did not satisfy them, and here Klausner mobilizes religion to explain and justify even more far-reaching national ambitions. Because the new rulers regularly read the Torah and the Prophets, 'it was impossible for them not to sense how unnatural their situation was—that of all the Land of Israel promised to Abraham and ruled by David and Solomon, Israel remained with only the little state of Judaea.'[19] Once again Klausner declares something impossible, and once again the assessment leads to a conclusion identical to the ideology of the historian, this time in its Revisionist form.

This orientation appears even more clearly in Klausner's lament over the civil war in the days of Alexander Jannaeus. If not for this internal war, he suggests, the king may have taken advantage of the opportunity afforded by the weakness of the Seleucid Empire to conquer the coastal cities of the Land of Israel—and even Tyre and Sidon. And this too is not the end of it. 'There are grounds to believe that Jannaeus, like his ancestors, dreamed the great dream of returning the Kingdom of David and Solomon to its original grandeur, and even more than this—of inheriting the Seleucid Empire itself.'[20] It cannot be ruled out that Jannaeus dreamed such dreams, but it is difficult to avoid the impression that the historian's vision has merged with the ambition of the Hasmonean king to the point where the two can no longer be distinguished.

Dreams, however, collide with realities, and these collisions can spawn not only practical difficulties but serious moral dilemmas. In describing the Hasmonean wars in general and the expansion of the boundaries of Israel in particular, Klausner must confront the leveling of pagan temples, expulsions, the destruction of cities, and forced conversions. The ethical problems posed by such behavior disturb him, and he is occasionally prepared to express disapproval. Thus, it is as if Judah Maccabee forgot what he himself suffered from religious persecution and ignored 'the slightly later dictum, "Do

---

[18] Cf. also *Historia* 2:145.
[19] *Historia* 3:31.
[20] *Historia* 3:151.

not do to your fellow that which is hateful to you.'"[21] Similarly, the destruction of the Samaritan temple 'can only be explained but not justified.'[22] Nonetheless, Klausner's basic inclination is to provide mitigation for such acts and sometimes even to justify them.

The most striking example of such justification appears in his reaction to Simon's expulsion of pagans as part of the policy of judaizing sections of the land of Israel. It is true that these actions involved considerable cruelty, he says, but had the Hasmoneans behaved differently, the tiny Judaean state would have ceased to exist under the pressure of its neighbors, 'and the end would have come for the People of Israel as a whole.' Under such circumstances, 'the moral criterion *cannot help* but retreat, and in its place there comes another criterion: *the possibility of survival.* . . . For our "puny intellect," this appears to constitute the very antithesis of justice; for the "larger intellect," *this is the way to justice*, the footstool of absolute justice' (emphasis in the original).[23]

Elsewhere, he returns to the 'biblical view of the Land of Israel,'[24] arguing that in light of this tradition, the newly formed Judaean state 'had [was *mukhrahat*] to expand eastward—toward Transjordan, northward—toward Shechem, and southward—toward Idumaea.'[25] The conquest of Idumaea, complete with the forcible conversion of its inhabitants, was unavoidable. Stolen land was being recovered; a Jewish majority was a necessity for the nation; Judaea could not have been left surrounded by enemies forever. What follows is very difficult to read today: If we are concerned with 'the admixture of blood, almost all the neighboring peoples were Semites, and so the race remained unaffected even after the conversion of the Idumaeans.'[26] The major themes repeat themselves in Klausner's evaluation of the policies of Alexander Jannaeus: 'Out of historical compulsion—deeply regrettable in itself—Jannaeus was forced to destroy cities . . . whose inhabitants did not agree to accept Judaism. . . . Is it plausible that in territories called by the name "Land of Israel" that were part of Israel in the days of David, Solomon, Ahab, Jeroboam II and Josiah, aliens and enemies should reside forever?'[27]

---

[21] *Historia* 3:33, 35.
[22] *Historia* 3:86.
[23] *Historia* 3:65–66.
[24] *Historia* 3:78.
[25] *Historia* 3:85.
[26] *Historia* 3:88.
[27] *Historia* 3:160.

Klausner makes a point of emphasizing that the Jewish people as a whole supported the Hasmonean rulers no less than he. First, his idyllic characterization of this people is noteworthy in and of itself. 'The true Jewish democracy [consisted of] farmers owning small homesteads, day laborers, craftsmen, and workers in fields and homes.' This was 'a large nation, assiduous and wise, religious-moral, laboring and satisfied with limited wealth.' The typical Jewish farmer was 'a religious conservative and a nationalist patriot.' And this nation 'defended the Hasmonean family and its aspirations as one man.'[28]

Klausner provides four arguments for rejecting the historicity of the story asserting that Jannaeus crucified eight hundred of his opponents in a single day. Two of these strikingly underscore his attitude to the Hasmoneans themselves as well as his emphasis on their popular support. First, a king and high priest of the Hasmonean dynasty could not have been capable of such behavior.[29] Second, if this had really happened, 'the nation would not have been devoted to the Hasmoneans with all its heart and soul and would not have spilled its blood like water for anyone in whose veins there coursed even one drop of Hasmonean blood.'[30] Elsewhere, Klausner is a bit more cautious, speaking of support from 'the decisive majority of the activist nation,'[31] but the fundamental emphasis remains unchanged. Finally, we hear of the special qualities of Hasmonean blood on more than one further occasion. Aristobulus II, for example, refused to accept one of Pompey's demands because 'the blood of the Maccabees coursing in his veins did not allow him to debase his honor excessively.'[32] One wonders what sort of blood coursed in the veins of Aristobulus's brother Hyrcanus II.

When we turn from war and politics to cultural life, the spectrum of Klausner's views becomes wider, richer, more varied, more nuanced, and more interesting. In some respects, the single-minded nationalist perspective persists. Thus, in the aftermath of political liberation following centuries of submission to foreign rule, 'it was impossible' that spiritual life would remain unchanged. 'This will become clear in the course of time in the young State of Israel as well even though

---

[28] *Historia* 3:12; 5:132; 3:43, 82.
[29] This point was noted by Schafler, p. 201.
[30] *Historia* 3:155.
[31] *Historia* 3:235–36.
[32] *Historia* 3:222.

in the early years this is not yet very evident.'³³ One of the prime characteristics of the Hasmonean period was the revival of the Hebrew language. Political independence led to 'an exaltation of the soul' that 'greatly reinforced national consciousness and prepared the ground for any powerful national-religious aspiration. And what national-religious possession could have been more precious and sacred to the nation than the language of the Torah and prophets that had been nearly suppressed by Greek on the one hand and Aramaic-Syriac on the other?'³⁴ Thus, as Klausner sees it, 'the national government' along with the Council of the Jews nurtured this development and helped determine its form almost along the lines of the twentieth-century Academy for the Hebrew Language.

At the same time, conflicting ideological commitments led Klausner to less predictable evaluations as he examined larger cultural developments. In his view, a central group among the Pharisees concentrated on religious and moral concerns at the expense of the political dimension, and we might have expected him to evaluate such a group pejoratively. He understood, however, that this group laid the foundations of Jewish culture for generations to come, and his own nationalist orientation was light years removed from that of the so-called 'Canaanites' in the early years of the State. For all of Zionism's 'negation of exile,' the stream with which Klausner identified saw itself as an organic continuation of authentic Jewish culture freed to develop in new and healthy ways in the ancient homeland. Thus, a man like Hillel could not be seen through a dark lens, and we suddenly find very different rhetoric from that to which we have become accustomed.

Hillel, we are told, had to refrain from taking a political stand during the terror regime of Herod. This was the only way that he could achieve his sublime objectives.³⁵ As to the Pharisees in general, their emphasis on religion over state 'afforded the nation eternal life" even though "it stole away its political power. The Pharisees achieved the *survival* of the nation at the expense of its *liberty*' (emphasis in the original).³⁶ In virtually every other context, Klausner, as we have seen, perceives the liberty of the nation as a condition of its sur-

---

[33] *Historia* 3:9.
[34] *Historia* 3:105.
[35] *Historia* 4:125, 129–30.
[36] *Historia* 3:228.

vival. Here, looking back at the founders of rabbinic Judaism through the prism of a millennial exile, he speaks with a very different voice.

We have already encountered Klausner's reaction to the Hellenizers' efforts to open Judaea to Greek culture. In other contexts as well, he mobilizes the imperative of national survival for an even more surprising defense of cultural perspectives narrower that his own. Philo, he tells us, was a proud Jew, but in the final analysis the great Alexandrian thinker maintained that Moses and Plato had said the same things. 'The nation's instinct, its feeling of self-preservation, whispered to it... that it may not admit this compromising ideology into its home.'[37] This instinct, he adds, also explains the attitude of the anti-philosophical party during the Maimonidean controversies many generations later. This understanding, almost supportive analysis of the anti-Maimonist position adumbrates Yitzhak Baer's critical approach to Jewish openness to general culture in the Middle Ages, an approach that impelled Charles Touati to formulate a particularly sharp critique.

> According to Baer, the Jewish religion belongs to the category of myth, a term never defined but clearly understood favorably. Judaism is placed in danger by philosophical culture. For Baer, all philosophers are suspect throughout Jewish history; their adversaries... always enjoy a favorable presumption. The position of the eminent historian, the product of a German university who was reared in rigorous scientific disciplines, seems odd (*cocasse*) to us. Is Judaism, then, to be devoted always, in its entirety, by its very essence, to lack of culture (*l'inculture*)?[38]

Klausner does not go as far as Baer, though he was motivated by similar instincts, and it is fascinating to see his willingness to empathize with Jews who banned and even burned the works of the hero of generations of maskilim who were in large measure role models for Klausner himself.

Klausner's cultural instincts lead to a particularly interesting deviation from the anticipated line with respect to an even more pivotal figure than Philo, a figure whom historians of the Second Temple period confront every hour of every day. Klausner is acutely aware

---

[37] *Historia* 5:85.
[38] Charles Touati, 'La controverse de 1303–1306 autour des etudes philosophiques et scientifiques,' *Revue des Etudes Juives* 127 (1968): 37, n. 3.

that his attitude to Josephus will surprise us, and in a passage demonstrating with painful clarity how insecure he felt in the face of criticism, he points to this explicitly as evidence that he is an objective historian.[39] He understands that we would expect him to disdain the historian-traitor; instead, he sees him as a man of initial good intentions who, even after his act of genuine treason, deserves regard as an exceptional historian. Perhaps this is indeed a sign of objectivity, but it is more likely the product of a collision of two subjective impulses. Of course Klausner was repelled by Josephus' treason, but his belief that the capacity to explain history is one of the quintessential qualities of the Jewish people[40] moved him toward an almost visceral appreciation of the talents of the major Jewish historian of antiquity.

The emotional tie that Klausner felt toward his illustrious predecessor emerges from a gripping, almost amazing passage. Josephus tells us that he chose to survive in Jodephat because had he died before transmitting the message (*diangelia*), he would have betrayed the divine charge. Klausner contends that this does not refer to the message that Vespasian would become Emperor. It refers, rather, to the destiny of Josephus himself, who somehow understood that he was fated to become the historian of the Jewish people. 'A supernal force impelled him to live in order to write books that would endure for thousands of years, to survive so that he could be revealed as one of the great Jewish historians of all generations.'[41]

The career of Josephus transports us to the final days of the Second Temple. Despite Klausner's qualified sympathy for the spiritually oriented Pharisees, his deeper identification is with the group that he calls 'activist Pharisees,' to wit, the Zealots, who enjoyed the support, as he sees it, of 'the nation in its masses.' Here too he must confront moral questions, which he resolves in part by recourse to a slightly altered version of a famous line in Judah Halevi's *Kuzari*. 'Their intentions were desirable, but their actions were not always desirable.' Nonetheless, even if they sometimes engaged in robbery, they had no alternative. 'Since they were constantly guarding the national interest, it was impossible for them to pursue remunerative work.'[42]

---

[39] *Historia* 3: introduction.
[40] *Historia* 2:270.
[41] *Historia* 5:190–91.
[42] *Historia* 5:29–30.

And so we arrive at the great revolt that these Zealots precipitated. In addition to the routine reasons that Klausner proposes to explain that revolt, he suggests that the Romans encouraged it through intentional, blatant provocations inspiring an uprising that they could then exploit to destroy the threat posed to them by the 'metropolis of world Jewry.'[43] Once again, warring tendencies in the historian's psyche produce a slightly unexpected result. Klausner is prepared to depict his heroic Jewish rebels as dupes of a successful Roman stratagem in order to magnify the importance, power, and centrality of world Jewry.

Finally, even the failure of the revolt does not demonstrate that it was mistaken. On the contrary, simple submission to Rome would have led to decline and, ultimately, to the disappearance of the nation. Instead,

> a destruction following glorious, remarkable wars of the sort fought by the 'bandits' and 'ruffians' against the dominant Roman Empire, wars that remained in the memory of all generations, was not an absolute destruction. It was not the Torah alone that sustained us in our exile. The memories of a monumental struggle with the great world power preserved in Talmud and Midrash, in Josippon and other of our narratives also led to long life, indeed, to eternal life. [Such a] nation will never be destroyed.[44]

It is difficult to agree that the actions of the 'bandits,' which were sharply criticized in most of the sources informing the consciousness of Jews in exile, played a central role in sustaining the spirit of persecuted Jews in medieval and early modern times. But in the Zionist period, refashioned in the works of Klausner and others, they surely did. Even one who reads Klausner's *History* for the purpose of analyzing its ideological *Tendenz* cannot help but feel the deep pathos that informs his work, and there can be no question that readers were inspired, educators energized, students instructed, and public opinion molded. In full awareness of Klausner's historiographic sins, some observers with Zionist sympathies may nonetheless set aside an academic lens and conclude that not only were his intentions desirable, but, under the pressing circumstances in which he wrote, even his actions may have achieved ends that partially atone for those sins.

---

[43] *Historia* 5:132, 140, 141.
[44] *Historia* 5:136–37.

'YOUR COVENANT THAT YOU HAVE SEALED IN OUR FLESH': WOMEN, COVENANT, AND CIRCUMCISION*

Shaye J.D. Cohen

There are only two passages in the rabbinic prayer book whose language prevents, or has been thought to prevent, their recitation by women. The first is the benediction 'who has not made me a woman,' which has been discussed often by historians, jurists, and apologists.[1] As is well known, this daily benediction is not recited by women. The second is the benediction in the *birkat ha-mazon* (Grace after Meals) which thanks God for 'your covenant that you have sealed in our flesh,' that is, circumcision. As we shall see, in medieval Europe some women omitted this phrase in their recitation of the *birkat ha-mazon* because the covenant of circumcision does not apply to women. This brief essay is devoted to the history of this phrase.

Pelimo and Rav

The core of the rabbinic *birkat ha-mazon* consists of three paragraphs, each of them phrased as a blessing. The first thanks God for the gift of sustenance; the second thanks God for the gift of the land of Israel; the third is a prayer for the restoration of Jerusalem. The Talmud discusses the precise wording of the second benediction:[2]

> R. Eliezer says: whoever does not (thank God for) 'a desirable, good, and spacious land' in the blessing concerning the land, and (whoever does not pray for the restoration of) 'the kingdom of the house of David' in the blessing concerning the building of Jerusalem, has not fulfilled his obligation (of reciting the *birkat ha-mazon*).

---

* This essay is an expanded version of a portion of chapter five of my *Why aren't Jewish Women Circumcised?*, (2005), a study of circumcision and gender in Judaism. I am delighted to dedicate this essay to my teacher Prof. Louis Feldman, a model Jew, teacher and scholar.

[1] Joseph Tabory, 'The Benedictions of Self-Identity and the Changing Status of Women and of Orthodoxy,' *Kenishta: Studies of the Synagogue World*, ed. Joseph Tabory (Bar-Ilan: Bar-Ilan University Press, 2001) 107–138.

[2] B. Berakhot 48b.

Nahum the Elder says: one must (also) include in it 'covenant.'
R. Yosi says: one must (also) include in it 'Torah.'
Pelimo says: 'covenant' must precede 'Torah,' because the latter ('Torah') was given in three covenants but the former ('covenant') was given in thirteen covenants.

The blessing for the land must contain appropriate praises of the land; we thank God for a 'desirable, good, and spacious land.' We must also thank God for covenant and Torah, because the gift of the land is intimately linked with these other gifts. Pelimo, an obscure figure whose name is transmitted in various forms and who is known only from several citations in the Bavli,[3] says that the mention of 'covenant' must precede the mention of 'Torah,' because the Torah was given in three covenants, but the covenant, that is, the covenant of circumcision, was given in thirteen covenants. Numerous rabbinic texts state or assume that the Torah was given to Israel in three covenantal ceremonies; the precise identification of the three was the subject of abundant discussion by the medieval commentators.[4] Numerous other passages state or assume that the covenant of circumcision has the force of thirteen covenants, since the word *berit* appears thirteen times in Genesis 17, the chapter in which God enjoins the observance of circumcision upon Abraham.[5] Pelimo has juxtaposed these discrete bits of information and drawn a novel conclusion: since thirteen is greater than three, the covenant of circumcision should precede Torah in the second paragraph of the *birkat ha-mazon*.

For our purposes, the intellectual cogency of Pelimo's exegesis is not important. What is important is Pelimo's assumption that 'covenant' in the *birkat ha-mazon* means 'the covenant of circumcision,' an interpretation that is by no means obvious or inevitable. The same assumption appears on the next page of the Talmud in an interesting story:[6]

> R. Zeira said to R. Hisda: let the master come and teach us (how to recite the *birkat ha-mazon*).

---

[3] The vocalization 'Pelimo' is just a guess.
[4] For example, see Rashi here and R. Hai Gaon in Lewin, *Otzar Hageonim: Berakhot* p. 83 no. 234. For full discussion see Lieberman, *Tosefta K'Fshutah Sotah* 707–710.
[5] M. Nedarim 3:11; Y. Nedarim 3.14 38b; B. Shabbat 132a and 133a; B. Pesahim 69b; B. Yevamot 5b.
[6] B. Berakhot 49a.

(R. Hisda) replied: the *birkat ha-mazon* I have myself not learned (correctly), and shall I teach it?

(R. Zeira) said to him: what is this? (What do you mean?)

(R. Hisda) said to him: once I was at the house of the Exilarch, and I recited the *birkat ha-mazon*. R. Sheshet (was so amazed that he) stretched out his neck at me like a serpent. Why? Because I said neither 'covenant' nor 'Torah' nor 'kingdom' (of David).'

(R. Zeira said:) and why did you not say them?

(R. Hisda said: because I followed the view) of R. Hannanel in the name of Rav.

For R. Hannanel said: Rav did not say[7] 'covenant,' 'Torah,' and 'kingdom' (when reciting the *birkat ha-mazon*). 'Covenant,' because it does not apply to women. 'Torah' and 'kingdom,' because they apply to neither women nor slaves.

(R. Zeira said:) you abandoned all of these Tannaim and Amoraim (who require the recitation of 'covenant,' 'Torah,' and 'kingdom') and you followed Rav?!

This wonderful story reveals a great deal about the history of the *birkat ha-mazon*, about the relations between the rabbis of Babylonia and the Exilarch (the leader of the Jewish community of Babylonia), about the interrelationship of various Babylonian rabbis, and about the authority of Rav versus the authority of other sages. All of this is fascinating and important, but none of this is important for our purposes. What is germane for us is R. Hannanel's report of Rav's behavior.

When reciting *birkat ha-mazon*, Rav did not thank God for covenant and Torah in the second benediction and did not pray in the third for the restoration of the Davidic kingdom. Why not? The Talmud supplies an explanation, but it is impossible to be sure whether the explanation is Rav's own, R. Hannanel's (who reported Rav's behavior), R. Hisda's (who is adducing Rav as the model of his own behavior), or the editor's (who helpfully supplied an explanation where none had existed). In any case, we are told that Rav did not say

---

[7] I follow the reading of various medieval testimonia; this reading is endorsed by Lieberman, *Tosefta K'Fshutah Berakhot* 38. The vulgate printed editions read: 'For R. Hannanel said in the name of Rav: whoever does not say covenant, Torah, and kingdom has (nevertheless) fulfilled his obligation.' As Rabbinowicz remarks in the *Diqduqei Soferim*, this reading is not as smooth as the alternative because R. Hisda needs to adduce in support of his position not permission after the fact but an injunction before the fact. This is supplied by the reading that I have followed. The reading of the printed editions was perhaps created to solve the problem raised by Rav's omission of obligatory words.

'covenant' because 'it does not apply to women,' and did not say 'Torah' and 'kingdom' because 'they apply to neither women nor slaves.' 'Covenant,' that is, the covenant of circumcision, does not apply to women.[8] 'Torah' and 'kingdom' apply neither to women nor to slaves. Torah, because women and slaves are exempt from the obligation to study Torah. Kingdom, because women and slaves will be subordinate to their husbands and masters even after the restoration of the Davidic monarchy. The lot of Jewish men will be much altered—improved—by the messianic restoration, but the lot of women and slaves will remain the same, forever servile.

The logic of Rav's argument is the following:[9] women and slaves are obligated to recite the *birkat ha-mazon*;[10] the phrases 'covenant,' 'Torah,' and 'kingdom' do not apply to women; the phrases 'Torah' and 'kingdom' do not apply to slaves; therefore, if these phrases are to be retained in the *birkat ha-mazon*, women and slaves will be required either to omit them or to recite something else in their stead; but the sages made no provision either for the omission of these phrases or their emendation by women and slaves; therefore, Rav concludes, the phrases should not be said at all by anyone in the *birkat ha-mazon*. Rav's solicitous concern for the feelings of the Other, women and slaves, is remarkable. We are curious to know what Rav thought about the recitation of the benedictions 'who has not made me a gentile, who has not made me a slave/boor, who has not made me a woman.' Too bad that his opinion is nowhere recorded.

Rav lost. In the liturgical tradition of Babylonia, shaped by the Bavli's citation of Pelimo, the word 'covenant' was retained in the second paragraph of the *birkat ha-mazon* and the allusion to circumcision was made clear and unmistakable. A medieval Babylonian version reads:[11]

> We give thanks to you, Lord our God, (for) the desirable, good, and spacious land that you willed to inherit to our forefathers, for your covenant that you have placed in our flesh, and for the Torah that you have given us, and for life and favor, grace and sustenance.

---

[8] The covenant of circumcision, however, does apply to male slaves: M. Bava Qamma 1:3; B. Gittin 23b; B. Qiddushin 41b.

[9] I follow the commentary of the Rashba.

[10] M. Berakhot 3:3.

[11] I translate the version of R. Amram; for a large collection of variants see Louis Finkelstein, 'The Birkat Ha-Mazon,' *JQR* 19 (1928-29) 211-262, at 247-249.

'The covenant that you have placed (in other versions: sealed) in our flesh' is an indubitable reference to circumcision. This Babylonian version forms the basis for the version that would become normative in the communities of Ashkenaz (including, of course, the contemporary Ashkenazi communities of the United States and Israel).[12]

THE TOSAFOT

Rav realized that if 'covenant' means 'the covenant of circumcision,' women would have difficulty in reciting the second paragraph of the *birkat ha-mazon*, and therefore omitted the phrase himself. R. Hisda followed suit. Their position is rejected by R. Sheshet, R. Zeira, and apparently by the Bavli itself. The question that Rav raised is a real one, however; can women thank God for the gift of circumcision? The question is ignored by the Talmud but reasserts itself in the middle ages.

The Mishnah states that women are obligated to recite the *birkat ha-mazon*. The Bavli asks: is this obligation a function of Torah law or rabbinic law? In other words, does the Torah itself (as construed by the rabbis) require women to recite the *birkat ha-mazon* or was this requirement instituted by the rabbis? After some give and take the Talmud concludes that the obligation derives from the Torah itself. The medieval commentators object: why was the Talmud uncertain? isn't it obvious that the verse *When you have eaten your fill, give thanks to the Lord your God* (Deuteronomy 8:10) applies to women too?[13] Rashi (1040–1105) explains that the doubt was caused by the last part of the verse, *give thanks to the Lord your God for the good land which he has given you*. Since the land was distributed only to the males and not the females,[14] perhaps the phrase *the good land which he has given you* implies that women are to be excluded from the obligation of giving thanks. This is how Rashi explains the Talmud's question.

---

[12] For example, see Shlomo Tal, *Siddur Rinat Yisrael Nusah Ashkenaz* (Jerusalem: Moreshet, 5737/1977), 120; Philip Birnbaum, *Daily Prayer Book Ha-Siddur Ha-Shalem* (New York: Hebrew Publishing, 1949) 829–830.

[13] The Yerushalmi has no doubt that the verse applies to women too: Y. Berakhot 3 6b. On the Bavli's question see Lieberman, *Tosefta K'Fshutah Berakhot 83*.

[14] As the biblical story about the daughters of Zelophehad abundantly attests, Numbers 27 and 36.

The Tosafot, glosses on the Talmud written by Rashi's school in the twelfth and thirteenth centuries, suggest a different interpretation.[15]

> The reason (for the Talmud's doubt) is that it is written (in the *birkat ha-mazon*) '(We give thanks to you, our God) for your covenant that you have sealed in our flesh, and for your Torah that you have taught us.' But neither covenant nor Torah applies to women, and the Talmud says further along[16] 'whoever does not (in the second paragraph of the *birkat ha-mazon* thank God) for the covenant and the Torah has not fulfilled his obligation.'

Since circumcision and Torah do not apply to her, a woman cannot say '(We give thanks to you, our God) for your covenant that you have sealed in our flesh, and for your Torah that you have taught us.' Her inability to recite these words led the Talmud to suggest that perhaps her level of obligation was a function only of rabbinic law, not Torah law. Thus the Tosafot.[17] Various other sources confirm that medieval Jewish women, in those areas that followed the liturgical custom of the Babylonian Talmud, either did not, or were not supposed to, include these words in their recitation of the *birkat ha-mazon*.[18]

The Tosafot's explanation eloquently attests two important but contradictory strands of medieval Jewish piety in Christian Europe: the increased participation of women in the sacred and the increased effort by rabbis to minimize or circumscribe that participation.[19] In the high Middle Ages women did recite the *birkat ha-mazon,* but by omitting (or being required to omit) 'your covenant that you have sealed in our flesh' and 'your Torah that you have taught us,' they were reminded of their womanly status. Even when observing a

---

[15] Tosafot, Berakhot 20b, s.v. *nashim*; see also Tosafot Harosh.

[16] B. Berakhot 48b–49a; see above.

[17] Perhaps in their support the Tosafot would adduce Rav who clearly felt that 'covenant' excludes women. But support such as this is a two-edged sword. First, according to the vulgate reading, perhaps the reading that the Tosafot had, Rav validated, at least after the fact, the recitation of the *birkat ha-mazon* without the mention of 'covenant.' This ruling completely undercuts the Tosafot's argument. Second, the Talmud rejects Rav, implying that Rav's concern is not valid. This too undercuts the Tosafot's argument.

[18] Lewin, *Otzar Hageonim: Berakhot* pp. 49–50 no. 123; Tosafot, Arakhin 3a, s.v. *mezamnot*; Meiri on Berakhot 48b; the gloss of R. Moses Isserles on Shulhan Arukh Orah Hayyim 187.3 (and see the Magen Avraham ad loc.).

[19] On these tendencies, see Avraham Grossman, *Pious and Rebellious: Jewish Women in Europe in the Middle Ages* (Jerusalem: Shazar Center, 2001; in Hebrew) 309–342.

commandment that is incumbent upon them, they are not equal with men.

Does 'Covenant' in the *Birkat Ha-Mazon* Mean Circumcision?

All of this is only half the story. Rav, following Pelimo, assumes that the word 'covenant' in the second paragraph of the *birkat ha-mazon* means 'the covenant of circumcision.' The liturgical traditions based on the Bavli, as we have just seen, make the reference to circumcision unmistakable. But there was and is an alternative. The Yerushalmi does not know the comment of Pelimo or the story of Rav, and contains not a hint that 'covenant' means 'circumcision.'[20] If not a reference to circumcision, then surely the word 'covenant' refers to the covenant that governs the relationship between God and Israel. That covenant was first contracted between God and the Patriarchs: the covenant between the sections (Genesis 15); the covenant of circumcision (Genesis 17); God's repeated promises to Abraham, Isaac, and Jacob to multiply their progeny and give them the land of Israel as an inheritance. This covenant, which I shall call the general covenant, was then renewed at various junctures during the exodus from Egypt and the wanderings in the desert. Under the terms of this covenant God promises *inter alia* to give the people of Israel the land of Israel, and a reference to this covenant makes perfect sense in a benediction thanking God for the gift of the land. The covenant of circumcision is part of the general covenant, to be sure, but the latter is broader and more inclusive than the former.[21]

In prayer books that follow the rite of the land of Israel, the word 'covenant' in the second paragraph of the *birkat ha-mazon* refers to the general covenant, not circumcision in particular. Thus one such text reads, 'We give thanks to you, Lord our God, that you have given to us to inherit a desirable, good, and spacious land, (that you

---

[20] Y. Berakhot 1 3d; cf. T. Berakhot 3.9 p. 14 ed. Lieberman. In fact, even in the Bavli, if we exclude the comment of Pelimo and the explanation for Rav's behavior, there is no sign that 'covenant' refers to circumcision.

[21] Rabbinic literature often uses the word *berit* to refer to this general covenant. See e.g. B Gittin 60b; Y. Peah 17a, Hagigah 76d, Megillah 74d (covenant with Israel only for sake of the Oral Torah); B. Shabbat 33a (covenant is Torah; see below note 34).

have given us) covenant and Torah, life and sustenance.'[22] This version is very close to that still used by many Sephardic and Near-Eastern communities.[23] Surely the plain meaning of the word 'covenant' here is 'the covenant between God and Israel' or 'the covenant between God and the patriarchs,' not 'the covenant of circumcision.' This interpretation of the word is the only possible one in the following version:[24]

> Hear our request, and in our land may there not be want. We thank you for the land and for sustenance when we eat our fill from your sustenance, as it is written, *When you have eaten your fill, give thanks to the Lord your God for the good land which he has given you.* Remember for us speedily the covenant of our fathers. Blessed are you, Lord, for the land and for sustenance.

'Covenant' here can only mean 'the covenant with the patriarchs.'

Elsewhere too rabbinic liturgy uses the unmodified word 'covenant' to refer to the general covenant between God and Israel. Perhaps the best example is the *zikhronot* ('memorials,' 'remembrances') section of the Rosh HaShanah liturgy, which almost certainly dates from rabbinic times.[25] This section refers several times to 'the covenant' and concludes with a benediction of God who 'remembers the covenant.' The covenant that God remembers is not (only) the covenant of circumcision but (also) the general covenant between God and the Patriarchs, between God and Israel.

---

[22] I translate the version of R. Saadyah Gaon as presented by Finkelstein, 'Birkat Ha-Mazon,' 247–249, who also assembles numerous variants. R. Saadyah is a champion of Babylonian Judaism, but his Siddur follows the rite of Eretz Israel.

[23] For example, see Shlomo Tal, with the assistance of Amram Aburabia, *Siddur Rinat Yisrael Nusah Sephardim Ve-edot Hamizrah* (Jerusalem: Moreshet, 5736/1976) 116.

[24] Simha Asaf, 'From the Prayer Book of the Land of Israel,' *Sefer Dinaburg: Studies offered to Ben Zion Dinaburg*, ed. Y. Baer et al. (Jerusalem: Qiryat Sefer, 1949) 116–131, at 129. Similarly, as far as I can see, none of the medieval poetical expansions of the *birkat ha-mazon* published by Habermann and Ratzhabi understand the word *berit* in the second paragraph to mean 'circumcision'; in all these texts it means 'covenant.' See A.M. Habermann, 'Poetical Blessings after Meals,' *Yediot ha-makhon le-heqer ha-shirah ha-ivrit* 5 (1939) 43–105, and Yehudah Ratzhabi, '*Birkot mazon mefuyatot hadashot,*' *Sinai* 54 no. 108 (5751/1991) 193–231.

[25] Ismar Elbogen, *Jewish Liturgy: A Comprehensive History*, trans. Raymond Scheindlin (Philadelphia: Jewish Publication Society, 1993) 118–121.

Does 'the Covenant' Include Women?

Does the general covenant between God and Israel include Jewish women? As far as I have been able to determine, among the relatively few rabbinic texts touching on this question, not a single one implicitly or explicitly excludes women from the covenant, and several explicitly include them. On the verse *Then will I remember my covenant with Jacob; I will remember also my covenant with Isaac, and also my covenant with Abraham* (Leviticus 26:42), the Sifra comments:[26]

> The verse mentions only the patriarchs; how do I know that the matriarchs are included too? Scripture says *et* (the Hebrew word which indicates the direct object and which is often construed in the midrash as a sign that the verse should be understood expansively.)

God remembers the covenant with the matriarchs as well as the covenant with the patriarchs. Male slaves who have been circumcised in accordance with the requirement of Genesis 17 have become *bene berit*, 'sons of the covenant' or 'people of the covenant'; according to at least one rabbinic passage female slaves too become *bene berit*, presumably through immersion.[27] If female slaves can be thought to belong to the 'people of the covenant,' we may assume that the same would be true of native women. In fact, various passages demonstrate that the phrase *bene berit* includes women.[28]

The midrash emphasizes that women were present at the revelation at Mount Sinai and are indeed partners to the covenant between God and Israel. In its paraphrase of Exodus 19, the chapter that describes the revelation at Mount Sinai, the midrash consistently finds a way to include women, who are otherwise missing from the text or excluded.[29] On the phrase *Thus shall you say to the house of Jacob and declare to the children of Israel* (Exodus 19:3), the midrash

---

[26] Sifra Behuqotai pereq 8 112c.
[27] Male slaves: see above note 8. Female slaves: Mekhilta Bahodesh 7 230 ed. Horovitz-Rabin (in the parallels the inclusion of women is ambiguous). The Covenant of Damascus 12.12 prohibits an Israelite owner from selling to gentiles 'his (male) slave or his female slave, because they entered with him into the covenant of Abraham.' For this author even the covenant of Abraham can include women.
[28] See e.g. B. Berakhot 16b bottom (a prayer that entered the siddur); B. Gittin 23b; T. Berakhot 3.7 13–14L; T. Sanhedrin 11:4 431 ed. Zuckermandel; M. Bava Qamma 1:2 is ambiguous (see 1:3).
[29] Well noted by Shmuel Safrai, 'The *Mitzva* Obligation of Women in Tannaitic Thought,' *Bar Ilan Annual* 26–27 (1995) 227–236, at 228–230.

comments '*the house of Jacob*—these are the women, *the children of Israel*—these are the men.'[30] Moses warns the Israelites *do not go near a woman* (Exodus 19:15). The midrash understands this phrase as evidence not for the exclusion of women but rather for their inclusion: Moses wanted to ensure the ritual purity of the *women*, and therefore ordered that *they* abstain from sexual intercourse.[31] At Mount Sinai the women too, no less than the men, 'came under the wings of the divine presence.'[32]

If 'covenant' in the second paragraph of the *birkat ha-mazon* means the general covenant between God and Israel, Rav's problem, the exclusion of women, was not a problem at all. Women belong to the people of Israel and are part of the covenant between God and Israel. In the *birkat ha-mazon* all Jews, men and women alike, thank God for the gift of the covenant, because the covenant embraces all Jews, men and women alike. In the Sephardic and Near Eastern communities that follow a non-Babylonian version of the second paragraph of the *birkat ha-mazon*, there was never any question or any doubt that women would thank God for the gift of *berit*, because Jewish women are part of the covenant between God and Israel no less than Jewish men.[33]

From 'Covenant' to 'Covenant of Circumcision'

If in the liturgical tradition of the land of Israel 'covenant' in the second paragraph of the *birkat ha-mazon* means the general covenant between God and Israel, why do Pelimo, Rav, and R. Hisda assume that it means the covenant of circumcision? I do not have a satisfactory answer to this question.

A partial explanation can be found in the general readiness of rabbinic exegetes to understand the word *berit* as circumcision, even in Biblical passages where the 'original' intent is clearly not circumcision, and even in rabbinic passages where, as in the second

---

[30] Mekhilta Bahodesh 2 207 ed. Horovitz-Rabin and parallels; cf. too Mekhilta Bahodesh 2 209 ed. Horovitz-Rabin.
[31] Mekhilta Bahodesh 3 214 ed. Horovitz-Rabin and parallels.
[32] B. Yevamot 46b.
[33] See, for example, *Siddur Tefilat Rahel le Vat Yisrael . . . lefi minhage ha sefaradim ve edot ha mizrah . . . lefi pisqe . . . ha rav Ovadiah Yosef* (Jerusalem: Midreshet Rahel, nd [5758/1998]) 316.

paragraph of the *birkat ha-mazon*, the meaning circumcision is not required. This tendency is not restricted to the Bavli, to be sure, but is well attested there.[34] A good illustration of this tendency is the interpretation of the phrase *lehafer berit*, 'to break the covenant,' in rabbinic texts.

The Mishnah reads:[35]

> All Israel have a portion in the world to come ... But the following have no portion in the world to come: he who maintains that there is no resurrection of the dead, (and he who maintains that) the Torah was not divinely revealed, and an Epicurean.

The Tosefta comments on this Mishnah by expanding the list of those who have no portion in the world to come:[36]

> (The sages) have added to these (the following): he who throws off the yoke, he who breaks the covenant, and he who misrepresents the Torah [alternative translation: he who shames the Torah] ...

The context indicates that the phrase 'he who breaks the covenant,' like its companion phrase 'he who throws off the yoke,' is a general description of radically 'unJewish' behavior, that is, practice or belief that the rabbis deemed to be completely outside the pale of the acceptable. There is no reason to think that circumcision is intended. True, the phrase 'to break the covenant' does appear in Genesis in connection with the violation of the commandment of circumcision (*And if any male ... fails to circumcise the flesh of his foreskin ... he has broken my covenant*, Genesis 17:14), but the phrase also appears regularly in the Tanakh to describe the Israelites' wayward relationship with God. For example, in one verse God threatens to punish the Israelites *if you reject my laws and spurn my rules ... and break my covenant* (Leviticus 26:15). In another God tells Moses that after his death the Israelites *will forsake me and break my covenant which I made with them* (Deuteronomy 31:16). In these and other such verses the covenant is the contractual bond between God and Israel, not the commandment of circumcision. We may presume that anyone who by his heinous behavior or outrageous theology violates the sacred bond between God and

---

[34] This is a tendency, not a universal rule. For example, in an interpolation in B. Shabbat 137b Jeremiah 33:25 is understood to refer to circumcision, but in B. Shabbat 33a it is understood to refer to the Torah.
[35] M. Sanhedrin 10:1.
[36] T. Sanhedrin 12:9 433 ed. Zuckermandel.

Israel could be said to 'break the covenant.' As R. Hilkiah said in the name of R. Simon, 'He who studies Torah only from time to time (and not all the time), behold he is a breaker of the covenant.'[37]

Many other passages, however, in both the Bavli and the Yerushalmi, understand 'he who breaks the covenant' to be a reference to circumcision. Breaking the covenant was taken to mean either ignoring the commandment of circumcision or hiding its physical effects.[38] In these passages we see the same pattern that is evident in the interpretation of the second paragraph of the *birkat ha-mazon*. The general covenant of God with Israel has been replaced by the specific covenant of circumcision. Why? Because the word *berit* automatically triggered association with circumcision, even where that is not the original meaning or the best meaning of the passage in which the word appears.

The tendency to understand 'covenant' as 'covenant of circumcision' seems to occur across the full range of rabbinic documents, and I have not been able to attribute it to a specific geographical, chronological, or documentary source. The rabbinic concepts of *qiddush ha-shem*, 'the sanctification of God's name,' and *tzedaqa*, 'righteousness,' seem to undergo a similar metamorphosis. Originally the 'sanctification of God's name' was any act by a Jew that enhances the prestige of Judaism in the eyes of gentiles; gradually it was restricted to the act of martyrdom. Originally *tzedaqa* was any act of righteousness, but gradually in the Talmud was restricted to refer to charity, the giving of alms. Here again we have the same tendency to constrict the reference of religious terms that originally were employed more broadly.[39] It is not so surprising, then, that the Bavli, in the persons of Pelimo and Rav, understood the term *berit* in the

---

[37] Y. Berakhot 9 end 14d.

[38] Breaking the covenant in the flesh: Sifre Numbers 112 121 ed. Horovitz; B. Keritot 7a, Shavuot 13a, Yoma 85b, Sanhedrin 99a. Breaking the covenant of Abraham our Father: M. Avot 3:11. Breaking the covenant by stretching the foreskin: Y. Peah 16b, Sanhedrin 27c; cf. B. Sanhedrin 38b. See Nisan Rubin, 'The Stretching of the Foreskin and the Enactment of *peri'ah*,' *Zion* 54 (1989) 105–117.

[39] On *qiddush ha shem* and *tzedaqa* see Shmuel Safrai, 'Martyrdom in the Teachings of the Tannaim,' *Zion* 44 (5779/1979) 28–42, at 29–32, reprinted in his *In Times of Temple and Mishnah: Studies in Jewish History* (Jerusalem: Magnes Press, 1994) 2.406–420, at 407–410. I am grateful to Prof. Zeev Safrai for pointing out to me the analogy between the rabbinic treatment of *berit* and the rabbinic treatment of *qiddush hashem* and *tzedaqa*.

birkat ha-mazon as the covenant of circumcision and not as the general covenant.[40]

Conclusion

The simple, and, it would appear, original, reference of the word *berit*, 'covenant,' in the second paragraph of the *birkat ha-mazon* is the covenant between God and Israel, what I have called the general covenant. This meaning persisted in the liturgical traditions of the land of Israel, including many Sephardic versions of the *birkat ha-mazon*. Such an understanding of *berit* did not pose any problems for women, since women certainly were—and are—part of the covenant between God and Israel.[41] The Bavli, however, understood *berit* here to mean 'the covenant of circumcision.' Rav, followed by R. Hisda, argued as a result that the word should be omitted from the *birkat ha-mazon*, since it excludes women from a prayer that women are obligated to recite. The Bavli ignores this objection, and in the later Ashkenazic versions of the *birkat ha-mazon* the interpretation of 'covenant' as circumcision becomes explicit. The Tosafot conclude from this that indeed women should not say the phrase 'your covenant that you have sealed in our flesh' and that women's obligation to recite *birkat ha-mazon* is lower than that of men.

Victor of Karben, a fifteenth-century apostate from Judaism to Christianity, argued that Jewish women were more passionately committed to Judaism and more ready to be martyred for it than were Jewish men. The explanation for this phenomenon, he said, lay in the women's sense of their own inferiority. Not circumcised, they saw themselves as excluded from the blessings of the world to come unless they could remedy their defect through supererogatory devotion such as martyrdom. Circumcised Jewish men had less soteriological need for martyrdom than uncircumcised Jewish women. Thus

---

[40] I do not know why the Yerushalmi kept *berit* as 'covenant,' and why the Bavli, in the persons of two sages from Eretz-Israel, Pelimo (if indeed he is a genuine tanna) and Rav, took *berit* to mean 'circumcision.'

[41] As a result, in the Sephardic realm women never became accustomed to omit 'covenant.' See, for example, *Siddur Tefilat Rahel le Vat Yisrael . . . lefi minhage ha sefaradim ve edot ha mizrah . . . lefi pisqe . . . ha rav Ovadiah Yosef* (Jerusalem: Midreshet Rahel, nd [5758/1998]) 316.

Victor of Karben.[42] In other words, exclusion from the covenant of circumcision is tantamount to exclusion from the covenant between God and Israel. I cannot here comment on Victor's striking claim that Jewish women were more devoted to Judaism than were Jewish men, but surely his explanation for this alleged phenomenon is a decidedly Christian reading of Judaism. Victor assumes that circumcision occupies a position in Judaism akin to that of baptism in Christianity, so that an uncircumcised Jew (a woman, for example) is as anomalous as an unbaptized Christian. But Judaism is not Christianity, and circumcision is not baptism. As we have seen, rabbinic texts assume that Jewish women are included in the general covenant between God and Israel, even if they are excluded from the covenant of circumcision.

---

[42] Grossman, *Pious and Rebellious* 356 and 507, citing a study by Hava Frankel-Goldschmidt.

WHO ARE THE KINGS OF EAST AND WEST IN BER 7A?: ROMAN RELIGION, SYRIAN GODS AND ZOROASTRIANISM IN THE BABYLONIAN TALMUD

YAAKOV ELMAN

Louis Feldman, who has been a wonderful colleague during all the years I have been privileged to share a campus with him, has devoted his scholarly career to investigating the intersection of Greco-Roman and Second Temple Jewish culture, in the main. I trust that the following discussion of a rabbinic text that dates from a somewhat later period, but which investigates the relation of that text to its surrounding cultural context will conform to the spirit, if not altogether the letter, of Prof. Feldman's work.[1]

The subject of the following remarks is a baraita, attributed to R. Meir, which has been incorporated within a large, highly structured sugya on the subject of divine anger. The sugya itself appears in various permutations in several places, Ber 7a, A.Z. 4a–b, and Sanh 65a–b, with various additions and deletions. I have analyzed this complex of sugyot elsewhere;[2] here I wish to concentrate on one element of the whole, which appears only in Berakhot. The sugya there is the most cohesive of the three, and probably the earliest, but that does not, as we shall see, aid us in dating the baraita, or even determining its provenance.

> It was taught in the name of R. Meir: At the time when the sun rises and all the kings of the East and the West put their crowns upon their heads and bow down to the sun, the Holy One, blessed be He, immediately becomes angry.

This baraita is cited as an answer to the redactor's question of the time of God's anger. We have already been informed, from a prooftext in Ps 7:3, that 'God is angry every day.' The question is when

---

[1] My sincere thanks to Vivian B. Mann, who discussed several aspects of this paper with me, and reviewed a large part of it. She is of course not responsible for any errors or opinions she does not share.

[2] '"Is there Then Anger Before the Holy One?" Aspects of the Theology of the Stam.'

exactly is he angry, and, secondarily, what triggers his anger. It is clear from the context that this question is secondary because it is not one of the questions that serve as the framework, or backbone, of this sugya. These questions are 'Is there anger before God? How long does it last? How long is the *rega‛* that it is said to last? These questions are then repeated in reverse order in order to provide the chiasmic structure that underlies the sugya. The question of what motivates that anger does not appear in either set of questions. Again, the answer to the first question, given in the name of Abaye, explains how to determine the exact moment of God's unleashed anger but does not explain the reason for God's anger. The baraita, which comes at the end of the sugya, deals with a different, though related issue: Why God becomes angry. However, it may be that the redactor saw this as another source for dealing with the question of when God becomes angry. This in turn depends on whether the opening phrase, 'at the time when the sun rises,' which is not in all manuscripts, is authentically part of the sugya. We will examine that question below.

Note that baraita is introduced by 'we learned in the name of R. Meir' (*tanna mishemeih de-R. Meir*) rather than the more usual 'we learned' or 'our rabbis taught' (*tanna, tanya,* or *teno rabbanan: R. Meir omer*). Whether this teaching then goes back to R. Meir of the mid-second century is then uncertain; the question of its historicity is then problematical—certainly for that period, as we shall see.[3]

There are a number of peculiarities regarding this baraita and its placement. It appears without a proof-text, a rare phenomenon in aggadic material. As noted above, it has been placed at the end of the sugya, and does not relate well to the foregoing material. Aside from the structural reason, however, there is another problem: there is a real disjunction between the theological assumptions made by this baraita and the foregoing sugya. R. Meir's comment is based on the general rabbinic teaching of measure for measure: God's anger is aroused as a response to idolatry. But our sugya up to now has spoken of God's anger as a recurrent, almost 'natural' phenomenon; one might nearly set one's clock by it. It does not seem to depend on human action at all, and may be directed at any convenient target despite the target's merit or lack of it. Balaam may

---

[3] See H. Albeck, *Mehqarim ba-Beraita ve-Tosefta ve-Yahasan la-Talmud*, 15–43.

direct it at the Israelites or R. Joshua b. Levi at an a Christian who annoys him, without regard to the merits of the case. The fact that both were saved by God's mercy does not change the fact that without that mercy God's anger may wreak havoc. This is part and parcel of a number of Babylonian sugyot that stress the demonic aspect of divine anger that I have examined elsewhere.[4] This sugya emphasizes the arbitrary, unfocused nature of divine anger/judgment, which, once unloosed, may be redirected even against the righteous, that is, the Israelites.

In a sense, our sugya both confirms and contradicts the baraita. God's anger is aroused at regular intervals, but not necessarily in response to any specific piece of wrongdoing at that moment. It is unfocused, and may therefore cause harm to individuals or communities. This is supported by a literal reading of Ps 7:3. R. Meir, on the other hand, stresses the connection between 'every day'— that is, the rising of the sun, and God's anger, by pointing out that sunrise was a time for idolatry. This proof-text may have originally been part of the baraita, which, as noted, now lacks a proof-text. When the sugya's redactor decided to emphasize the literal reading of Ps 7:3, and thus the non-measure-for-measure aspect of divine retribution, R. Meir's teaching was gradually pushed further back; it now comes at the very end of the sugya.[5] As noted, R. Meir's explanation reflects a more general rabbinic teaching on the causes of divine anger in the world, similar to a baraita which now appears at the end of Sanhedrin.

> Our rabbis taught: When the wicked enter the world, [divine] wrath enters [the world], for it is written, 'When the wicked comes, then comes also contempt, and with ignominy, reproach' (Prov 18:3). When the wicked perish from the world, good comes to the world, as it is written, 'And when the wicked perishes, there is exultation' (Prov 11:10).
>
> When the righteous depart from the world, evil enters [the world], as is written, 'The righteous perishes, and no one lays it to heart; merciful men are taken away, none considering that the righteous is taken away from the evil to come' (Is 57:1). When the righteous comes into

---

[4] See my 'Righteousness as Its Own Reward: An Inquiry into the Theologies of the Stam,' 35–67.

[5] Araham Weiss pointed out a similar phenomenon in the case of the opening sugya of Shab; see *Heʻarot le-Sugyot ha-Shas ha-Bavli veha-Yerushalmi*, 144–45 (= *Heʻarot ve-Haʼarot le-Shabbat ch. 1, Talpiot* 1944, not paginated).

the world, good comes into the world, as is written, 'This same shall comfort us in our work and in the toil of our hands' (Gen 5:29).[6]

The general rule is that evil enters the world with the wicked; R. Meir's teaching is a specific application of that rule. Divine anger enters the world when the kings of the world engage in idolatrous worship of the sun. The question of whether that worship takes place daily or yearly is reflected in the manuscript variants of a phrase in the sentence at the very beginning of the baraita: 'At the time when the sun rises.' This phrase, which serves to connect the baraita with the proof text of Ps 7:12, which connects God's anger with the *daily* rise of the sun, appears in about half of the manuscripts of these parallels, without regard to the tractate in which it appears.[7]

On the other hand, this lack of consistency in the manuscript evidence is hardly surprising. The redactors (in A.Z. 4b) would have had a stake in connecting the baraita of R. Meir to the statement of R. Joseph, that an indivudal reciting the Musaf prayer on Rosh Hashanah should delay his prayer until the period of divine anger that occurs during the first three hours of the day has surely passed, that is, after those three hours. This statement was annexed to the core-sugya in A.Z., though not in Berakhot. R. Joseph's advice refers to divine anger on the first day of the year, the annual day of judgment, and thus may imply that R. Meir's description of the kings of East and West was limited to an annual ceremony, analogous to Rosh Hashanah.[8] But the core sugya, beginning with the proof text of Ps 7:12, explicitly states that divine anger is a daily occurrence. No amount of literary juggling can close that gap.

Not that that redactor failed to try. This sugya is a carefully constructed unit, though its constituent elements are clearly discernible, as we have noted. The latest 'layer' is represented by the collection of statements by R. Yohanan (in Ber 6b–7b) into which the sugya

---

[6] Said of the death of Noah. The entire baraita appears in B.Sanh 113b. A somewhat more elaborate version appears in tSot 10:1; see ed. Lieberman, *Tosefta Nashim*, vol. II, 213–214.

[7] The text in Berakhot appears in MS Florence II I 7–9 and Paris 671, but not in Oxford O Add. Fol. 23 or Munich 95; that in Avodah Zarah appears in Paris 1337 but not in JTS Rab 15, nor in Munich 95; in Sanhedrin it appears in Munich 95, but not in Karlsruhe Reuchlin 2, nor in Florence II I 7–9.

[8] See H.H. Scullard, *Festivals and Ceremonies of the Roman Republic*, 51–58, for a description of festivities during the first two days of January. Of course, Sol and Apollo were hardly important yet, but the republican calendar allowed little room for a ceremony described by the baraita.

has been placed by association. The linkage is the theme of God's anger, which cannot be assuaged at the moment of its outbreak. The sugya itself is made up of at least two 'proto-sugyot,' each dealing with the question of how long God's anger lasts, and each punctuated with the questions of how long the anger lasts and the duration of a moment, a *regaʿ*. These questions and their answers are arranged chiasmically.

A.   Is there then anger before the Holy One?
B¹. How long is His anger?
B². How long is a *regaʿ*?
B¹'. How long is His anger?
B²'. How long is a *regaʿ*?
A'. How do we know that He is angry?

The last question, A', is parsed in two different ways. The first is: How do we know that He is angry?—that is, what biblical proof do we have for this. In answer the sugya supplies two proofs. The second way of interpreting this question is as follows: How may we determine when He is angry? It is to this question that the statement attributed to Abaye is appended. Its application, or rather, its lack of application, is illustrated by the story of R. Joshua b. Levi, and, finally, we have the concluding baraita in the name of R. Meir.

The relation of R. Meir's baraita to the sugya depends on the reading or interpretation we adopt. The other reading, without the phrase 'when the sun rises,' may relate to the end of the sugya as it appears in A.Z. Here R. Joseph, Abaye's teacher, offers advice on how to conduct Rosh Hashanah prayers.

> A person should not pray the Musaf prayer during the first three hours of the day on the first day of Rosh Hashanah [when praying] in private, lest when [his turn] comes up, they will investigate his deeds, and his prayers will be rejected.

Now, without the phrase 'when the sun rises,' R. Meir need not have been referring to Ps 7:3, nor to God's daily anger. 'When the kings of east and west... bow to the sun' may refer to a ceremony which takes place at fixed times during the solar year, but not necessarily daily. Indeed, it may refer to a new-year's enthronement ritual, of which we know nothing in R. Meir's time, the middle third of the second century. Indeed, solar worship in the Roman Empire did not become prominent until after R. Meir's time, although

Augustus, who apparently believed that Apollo was his personal protector, emphasized worship of the sun god in 36 B.C.E. Giving Apollo prominence in the Secular Games he promoted was also a political move, inaugurating a 'new age.'[9] In 28 B.C.E., he built a new temple dedicated to Apollo.[10] However, as John Ferguson noted a generation ago, Hadrian used the rising sun as a symbol of the dawning of a new age. At his accession there was a dramatic performance at Heptacomia in Egypt, in which the actor representing Phoebus, the sun, spoke the following lines.

> I have just risen on high with Trajan in my white-horsed chariot
> I come to you, People—you know me—Phoebus, god,
> To proclam Hadrian as the new ruler
> Whom all things serve for his ability
> And the genius of his divine father, gladly.

Ferguson continues:

> In the same way, a relief from Ephesus... shows Trajan, deified, ascending in glory in the chariot of the Sun. So when Hadrian climbed Etna to see the sunrise we must see the act as going beyond scientific curiosity and almost as a religious sacrament. So also he removed the colossal statue which Nero had made of himself as the Sun, eliminated Nero's features and had it rededicated to the Sun. Antoninus Pius pays honor on his coins to Apollo Augustus.... So we find Marcus Aurelius on his death-bed, asked for the password for the day by an officer, saying, 'Go to the rising Sun; I am setting.'[11]

The phrase, 'when the sun rises,' serves to connect R. Joseph's statement with the sugya proper in those manuscripts in which it appears. It may even be, though it is unlikely, that the R. Joseph-pericope, which may have constituted part of the original sugya was displaced when the daily *ritha* theme became dominant.

R. Joseph's remarks are restricted to the first three hours of Rosh Hashanah; in their current setting, Abaye's remark would apply to the daily time of divine anger. In both Avodah Zarah and Berkahot his comment clearly refers to the core-sugya on divine anger than to R. Joseph's 'application' of the concept to the liturgy. The first quarter of the day is a time of anger and judgment.

---

[9] See J.H.W.G. Liebeschuetz, *Continuity and Change in Roman Religion*, 82–85.
[10] See Alan Wardman, *Religion and Statecraft Among the Romans*, 68.
[11] See John Ferguson, *The Religions of the Roman Empire*, 49–50. See also Robert Turcan, *The Cults of the Roman Empire*, 176–183.

Still, even if we separate Abaye's teaching from that of his teacher R. Joseph, there is still the question of how they relate to one another. Certainly, whoever added this segment to the sugya of Divine anger saw a connection. Indeed, it may be that in its original form R. Joseph advised not to pray the Musaf service during the first quarter of the day because it was a time of anger. Be that as it may, R. Joseph's narrowly applicable teaching, as currently formulated, conflicts to some extent with Abaye's, though Abaye might agree that on Rosh Hashanah God's judgment takes precedence over God's anger. But while the sugya as it now stands deals with a contradiction between R. Joseph's teaching and a baraita on 3b, it makes no attempt to relate R. Joseph comments to Abaye's. The most likely conclusion, I submit, is that R. Joseph's advice was understood as being predicated on the concurrence of a period of Divine anger and judgement. If so, this segment is an integral part of the sugya. But even if this is not so, the sugya itself prefers the more generalized version of Abaye to the limited teaching of R. Joseph, since the sugya as a whole takes Divine anger as flashing forth every day.

As it stands, the connective phrase 'at the time when the sun rises' reinforces the theme of daily divine anger set by Ps 7:12, but serves no particular purpose in Avodah Zarah, where R. Joseph's advice changes the placement of divine anger from a daily occurrence to a *yearly* one. However, though the phrase does not appear in the Paris or Munich manuscripts, it *does* appear in the best manuscript we have of that tractate, the Seminary manuscript of Avodah Zarah. Its absence makes it easier to connect R. Joseph's statement regarding the occurrence of divine anger once a year, though, as we have noted, this change is only cosmetic, since ultimately the core-sugya and R. Joseph's statement cannot be reconciled. His advice applies only to the first day of the year; it does not even apply to the second day of Rosh Hashanah, which would have been celebrated in Babylonia in R. Joseph's time. The core sugya emphasizes from the outset that God's anger is a daily occurrence. This cosmetic tampering with the sugya is apparent in the Seminary manuscript elsewhere in this sugya, where the scribe (or his source) substituted the phrase 'the kings of the Nations of the World' for 'the kings of East and West' which occurs in all the other manuscripts of all the parallels. The scribe apparently attempted to level the terminology of the core sugya within the larger mosaic of A.Z. 2a–4b, which deals with the fate of the 'Nations of the world' on Judgment Day. However, for the reasons noted above, this change cannot really integrate the core sugya into its new context.

Thus, while the core sugya asserts the daily nature of God's anger, the baraita attributed to R. Meir refers to God becoming angry when the gentile kings worship the sun, which may—but may not—occur on a daily basis. Whether this statement is R. Meir's or not, and whether it originated in his time or later, we must still deal with the problem of the origin of this description of an idolatrous daily rite. Is this description based on a ceremony reported to R. Meir or another sage? Does this baraita really belong in a sugya devoted to the subject of divine anger as a daily phenomenon? To put it another way: is there any evidence regarding either imperial Roman or royal eastern ceremonies involving solar worship that would enable us to decide between these divergent interpretations? Did the kings of either East *or* West prostrate themselves to the sun on a daily, yearly, or occasional basis? What is the possible (or probable) historical venue of the baraita's report?

More precisely, is the original context and meaning of that baraita reflected in the chiasmic structure of the sugya, as outlined above, and in our assertion that Ps 7:12, originally served as the proof text of the baraita? If we assume at least heuristically, that the baraita does reflect a second century provenance, let us examine each element of the baraita in turn in light of what is known of sun worship around the time of R. Meir or his contemporaries or successors.

There are four elements that make up this description of solar worship. It is 1. a royal prerogative perhaps carried out 2. at sunrise (at least for those manuscripts which contain the phrase 'at the time when the sun rises'). In the course of the ceremony, 3. the king places his crown on his head, and 4. he prostrates himself to the sun. Quite apart from the difficulty of finding an exact parallel to all of these elements taking place at the same time and place, there is one major circumstance that the baraita does not describe. These kings are described as neither sacrificing nor praying. Both acts however were generally part and parcel of the religious rites of the world of Late Antiquity, with perhaps one exception: the rite of prostration to the sun takes place in a vacuum. If the baraita's point was that prostration alone arouses God's anger, even without prayer or sacrifice, the text would have been formulated in a more abstract manner: Prostration alone transgresses the prohibition of idolatry. Thus, for example, mSanh 7:6 includes 'one who accepts it [= the idol] as a god' violates the prohibition of idolatry, along with 'one who prostrates himself' and 'one who sacrifices.'

The baraita's intent is not legal but theological; its focus is not on the prohibited action, but on its consequences. At the time (*be-sha'ah*, 'at the hour') that this action is carried out, God's anger flares forth. We may well ask, however, why the baraita insists on prostration being the crucial act that arouses God's anger, rather than any other element of idol worship.

The baraita speaks not only of the emperor, but of all 'the kings of East and West.' Though state religions were powerful in Rome and Persia, the world of the second century was rife with local cults and national religions of all types, and the third century even more so. However, since we are best informed regarding religious rites in the Roman republic and empire, we shall begin with those—and here we find that matters are indeed problematical.

Sacrifice was an essential element in worship in the world of Late Antiquity. Moreover, during the Principate, the emperor assumed a larger and larger role as pontifex maximus, and thus as a sacrificant. On the other hand, this did not mean that the emperor actually performed the laborious and grisly job of sacrifice himself, and so the absence of sacrifice in the baraita may be historically accurate.[12] Still, that absence is noteworthy.

Thus, despite the lack any explicit mention of them, we will assume that the occasion was one of sacrifice; this means in turn that some sort of prayer would have accompanied the offering.[13] Prayer may have been so much a part of all religious rites—Roman[14] and non-Roman

---

[12] See the enlightening discussion in Richard Gordon, 'From Republic to Principate: priesthood, religion and ideology,' in Mary Beard and John North, eds., *Pagan Priests: Religion and Power in the Ancient World*, 199–232, esp. 202–219. The surviving evidence is somewhat paradoxical. On the one hand, the emperor was the sacrificant; on the other, as Gordon puts it, 'to be sacrificant in this type of sacrifice is not to labour. ... Sacrificing meant to introduce the ceremony by making the preliminary offerings. ... The labour involved in sacrifice is, in the visual record, vividly performed by only muscular slaves; the social status of the sacrificant is marked by his separation from that labour' (206). Thus the lack of emphasis in the baraita of royal or imperial involvement in sacrifice conforms, in a sense, to Roman practice!

This symbolic sacrificial activity on the part of the emperor was also widely represented in Roman coinage; see Gordon, 215–216.

[13] The exception is Zoroastrian daily prayer, which was not necessarily accompanied by sacrifice, at least in the world of Late Antiquity and beyond. We shall return to this possibility below.

[14] See Pliny, *Natural History*, XXCIII, 10–11, where he emphasizes that 'we see too that senior magistrates make their prayers using a precise form of words: some-

alike—that the author of the baraita would have felt no need to mention it. Thus, 'prostration' may serve as *pars par proto* for worship in general. Generally, while rabbinic sources demonstrate an awareness that pagans offer sacrifices, pagan prayers are not mentioned explicitly, though, as noted, one idolatrous act for which *a Jew* is culpable is 'one who accepts [an idol] as his god.'[15] However, the absence of sacrifice and prayer are only two of the many problems that arise in attempting to view the baraita's description of idolatry as descriptive of Roman practice.

First, although Augustus promoted the Greek Apollo, the sun-god, as his own protector,[16] after his reign Rome was not hospitable to solar worship. Indeed, in the East Augustus received cult honors as Zeus Olympios, and not as Apollo.[17] As an indication of just how insignificant the worship of Apollo or Sol became until late in the Empire, note the following list of deities honored (by a *vota pro salute imperatoris*, a vow for the imperial safety) for preserving the lives of various emperors (Nero, Domitian and Trajan). The list of gods other than any sun god is long indeed: Jupiter, Juno, Minerva, Mars, Salus, Providentia, Genius Augusti, Honos, Aeterbutas (for Nero); Jupiter, Minerva, Mars, Salus, Fortuna, Victoria Redux, Genus Populi Romani (Domitian); Jupiter Optimus Maximus, Juno Regina, Minerva, Iovis Victor, Salus Rei Publicae Populi Romani Quiritum, Mars Pater, Mars Victor, Victoria, Fortuna Redux, Vesta Mater, Neptunus Pater, Hercules Victor (for Trajan)![18]

In part, this is because Jupiter already served as a sky and fertility deity; Sol was not needed. If the baraita does date to R. Meir's time, it is difficult to fit it into the scheme of imperial worship.

---

one dictates the formula from a written text to ensure that no word is omitted or spoken in the wrong order; someone else is assigned as an overseer to check 'what is spoken'. . . . There are records of remarkable cases of both types of fault—when the actual sounds of ill omens has spoilt the prayer, or when the prayer has been spoken wrongly. Then suddenly, as the victim stood there, its head 'that is, a part of the liver' or heart has disappeared from the entrails, or alternatively, a second head or heart has been produced.' See Beard, *et al.*, vol. 2, 129.

[15] See M.Sanh 7:6.
[16] See J.H.W.G. Liebeschuetz, *Continuity and Change in Roman Religion*, 82–85.
[17] See J. Rufus Fears, 'The Cult of Jupiter and Roman Imperial Ideology,' *ANRW,*' II/17.1, 3–141 and the literature at n. 437 on 88. However, see the discussion on 97–98, and that of Daniel N. Showalter, *The Emperor and the Gods: Images from the Time of Trajan*, 22–27. The wider critique of Fears' position does not affect our use of his data, however.
[18] *Ibid.*, 98.

However, in the third century, solar worship of various types constituted one of Christianity's main competitors! But that was not yet the case in the second.

Indeed, there is an even more compelling reason not to see this baraita as intended criticism of Rome. Even in R. Meir's time, the middle third of the second century, the imperial cult was important enough for it to be the object of derision or condemnation. However, as Martin Goodman has noted,

> It is recognized by the rabbis that emperor worship, known from other sources to be enthusiastically performed in Palestine and its environs, is both prevalent and sincerely felt, though astonishing by lack of any diatribe against humans who set themselves up as gods may well reflect a rabbinic, rather than a common, provincial, inability to identify the object of worship with the emperors they otherwise discuss.[19]

The baraita clearly addresses the issue of the ruler as worshiper and priest, not as the object of worship. However, given the lack of criticism of emperor worship, it is difficult to take the baraita's reference to the 'kings of East and West' as necessarily referring to the emperor. As noted, the historical problems for doing so are formidable. Nevertheless, the following exercise is useful, if only heuristically. It also permits an entrée into the rabbis' view of other cultures, even when their knowledge of that culture was limited. More than that, the fact that this baraita singles out solar worship for condemnation,

---

[19] Martin Goodman, *State and Society in Roman Galilee, A.D. 132–212*, 153. For a different view of the rabbis' knowledge of Roman court ceremonial, see Samuel Krauss, *Paras ve-Romi ba-Talmud uve-Midrashim*, 35–36. Krauss, however, does not address the question of emperor worship; similarly, see I. Ziegler, *Königsgleichnisse des Midrasch beleuchtet durch die römische Kaiserzeit*, 1903, xxvi. However, more recently, see S.R.F. Price, *Rituals and Power: The Roman imperial cult in Asia Minor*, and in particular, 170–171, but also 220–2221. Price notes that sacrificing for the emperor rather than *to* him was not a problem (except for Gaius Caligula, who was more intent on asserting his rights, or rather, his rites, than others) until the Great Revolt. But the history of Judaism under the Empire continued for at least two-and-a-half centuries until Constantine, and the problem would have been endemic. Price's passing reference rather understates the problem, apparently in order to emphasize the greater problem that Christians had. But Jews would have had the same problem, if Jews and Judaism were treated on a par with Christians and Christianity. It is evident that, save for exceptional circumstances, they were not, and it may be for this reason that the Rabbis did not evince much interest in the problem. Still, even if we assume that the Roman demands on the Jews increased with time, as did the cult of emperor-worship itself, a second-century date for this baraita would be possible. Nevertheless, the solar worship element would then present us with the difficulties mentioned above.

when so many other cults existed, is noteworthy. It also adds to our corpus of examples of Roman-Jewish misunderstandings.[20]

The baraita's description is difficult to view in a Roman context not only for what it does *not* contain but also for the elements it *does* include. Crowning as part of a religious rite is not known from Roman sources, at least in the way described in the baraita, nor is it part of the description of Heliogabalus' rites. The intensity of religious devotion required of daily attendance at public rites could hardly be expected of Roman emperors, even those like Marcus Aurelius, whose private piety was deep and sincere. Generally speaking, the Roman Emperor, even in his role as *pontifex maximus*, was not required to attend to the daily rites. As Alan Wardman put it,

> The imperial way of life imposed some religious duties. Piety or the assertion of that virtue enabled the living ruler to associate himself dynastically with a celebrated god. He was also expected to build temples (without being extravagant) and to maintain or repair them. Augustus' own temple, we might say, to anticipate a little, outlived its own dynasty and was repaired by emperors who lived in a different world from the one he had prepared. . . . As Marcus Aurelius said of his father, the ideal was to show respect in a conventional way without being superstitious.[21]

Nevertheless, Suetonius reports that Nero would sacrifice three times a day to a small image of a girl, but this is the exception that proves the rule, since Suetonius' disapproval of Nero's behavior is all too apparent.[22]

> He utterly despised all cults, with the sole exception of that of the Syrian goddess, and even acquired such a contempt for her that he made water on her image, after he was enamoured of another superstition, which was the only one to which he constantly clung. For he had received a gift from some unknown man of the commons, as a

---

[20] See Sacha Stern, 'Dissonance and Misunderstanding in Jewish-Roman Relations,' in Martin Goodman, ed., *Jews in a Graeco-Roman World*, 241–250.

[21] Alan Wardman, *Religion and Statecraft Among the Romans*, 84–85, and see his n. 9 and the literature therein.

[22] Needless the say, the same is true of Dio Cassius' description of Heliogabalus' rites; see Fergus Millar, *A Study of Cassius Dio*, 169–170: 'To Dio the whole episode was an outrage. . . . His attitude to the introduction of the god Elagabal and the Carthaginian Urania is of a traditional Roman pattern: shock relieved by derision.' It should be noted that Dio was in Asia throughout Heliogabalus' reign, and so that all of his account is from hearsay. According to the *Historia Augusta*, his body was dragged through the streets, thrust into a sewer and hurled into the Tiber; see the Loeb edition trans. by David Magie, Cambridge: Harvard UP, 1993, II, 141.

protection against plots, a little image of a girl; and since a conspiracy at once came to light, he continued to venerate it as a powerful divinity and to offer three sacrifices to it every day, encouraging the belief that through its communications he had knowledge of the future. A few months before his death he did attend an inspection of victims, but could not get a favourable omen.[23]

Undoubtedly, part of Suetonius' disapproval was sparked by the extravagance of the practice; note that Wardman emphasized that the extravagant restoration of temples was to be avoided.

However, the baraita does not mention sacrificial rites at all, but merely prostration to the sun, perhaps modeled on the idolatrous elders of Ezekiel 9. Indeed, the *Sitz im Leben* of this royal ceremony is unclear in Roman terms. Ryberg summarizes the emperor's appearance at religious ceremonies in the second century as follows.

> While representations of religious ritual in the second century are no longer occupied primarily with ceremonies centering around the ruler cult, the emperor's role as chief priest of the state ceremonies continues undiminished in prominence. But the sacrifices are rites of the old Roman religion, the Suovetaurilia to Mars and the making or paying of vota to Jupiter. The Vota Publica cover a variety of occasions, the departure, arrival, or return of the emperor, the inauguration of the triumphal close of a military campaign, and, finally, the successful completion of the decades of the current reign. Throughout the century the mode of presentation used for sacrificial scenes remained purely descriptive. Allegorical elements were freely introduced into other phases of these same imperial events... Not until the reign of Septimus Severus does the sacrificial scene lose its hold on a sense of concrete reality to the extent of introducing into cult ritual deified abstractions along with human participants.... The concept of cult ritual as a human activity was thus maintained as long as the emperor retained his human status, and was lost only when the ruler combined in his own person the roles of priest and god.[24]

As noted above, sacrifice was the *sine qua non* of state religious observance. It accompanied advents, departures and triumphs. Unless the baraita was directed at *private* royal rituals, sacrifice would have been an element of any Roman imperial state rite.[25] Alternately, if the

---

[23] Suetonius II, trans. J.C. Rolfe, rev. ed., 1930, New York: Putnam (Loeb Classical Library), 185, Nero, 56.

[24] Inez Scott Ryberg, *Rites of the State Religion in Roman Art*, 206–207.

[25] Note, for example, Suetonius comment that on the first day that Tiberius entered the Senate after Augustus' death, 'to satisfy at once the demands of filial piety and of religion, he offered sacrifice after the example of Minos with incense

baraita were directed against private rites, why focus on the kings of East and West? The people were as idolatrous in their private lives. It is true that the king represents his people; but while this is a common conception in the ancient Near East and in the Bible, it is not a prominent feature of rabbinic literature.[26]

The problem does not end there, since even if we assume that the baraita intended to describe the kings as offering sacrifice, why is this not mentioned? Aside from that, its description does not reflect the gestures associated with Roman sacrificial practice, regarding which we are tolerably well informed.

> Traditional Roman animal sacrifice was a lengthy process, involving much more than the killing of the sacrificial victim. There were six main stages in the ritual: (a) the procession (pompa) of victims to the altar; (b) the prayer of the main officiant at the sacrifice, and the offering of wine, incense, etc. (as a 'libation') at the altar; (c) the pouring of wine and meal (mola salsa) over the animal's head by the main sacrificant; (d) the killing of the animal by slaves; (e) the examination of the entrails for omens; (f) the burning of the parts of the animal on the altar, followed normally (except in some cases where the whole animal was burnt) by a banquet taken by the participants from the rest of the meat.[27]

Note that prostration was not a principal part of sacrificial rite, even less was it a rite unto itself. The *victimarius*, the one conducting the sacrifical animal, would stoop in the early Empire, but somewhat later this gesture became more elaborate, so that he would stoop with his right knee bent as he leaned forward to hold down the animal's head. But when the emperor was present, he would stand.[28] In one case we have an illustration of women kneeling with their hands raised in supplication, while offering prayers to Juno, but, here too, the emperor, who officiated, stood near the front corner of the temple steps and dictated the phrases of the prayer.[29] As is well

---

and wine, but without a flute player, as Minos had done in ancient times on the death of his sons' (Suetonius, *Lives of the Caesars*, Loeb Classical Library 31), trans. J.C. Rolfe, III, lxx, 392–393.

[26] See C.R. North, 'The Religious Aspects of Hebrew Kingship,' *ZAW* 50 (1932), 10–11.

[27] See Mary Beard, et al., *Religions of Rome*, vol. 2: *A Sourcebook*, 148. See also the literature referred to on that page, especially Inez Scott Ryberg, *Rites of the State Religion in Roman Art*, to which we have already referred, and to which we will have recourse below.

[28] See Gordon, 206, 209–210, 212–215.

[29] *Ibid.*, 176, and fig. 105f.

known, his reciting of the prayers with their exact wording was much more important than the kneeling or stooping of the *victimarius*.[30] Indeed, prostration was generally considered to be a Persian practice, and was demeaned as such, at least under the Principate and even later.[31] It was only with the absolutism of Diocletian that 'various forms of *proskynesis*—kneeling, kissing the hand and foot—were practiced at the Roman court.'[32]

Underlying these rites is the assumption that the honor paid to the emperor mirrored that paid to the gods, although this was not always the case. Some gestures of respect were reserved, even in pagan cultures, for the gods alone. For example, *labān appi*, a hand gesture by which respect was shown to the deity by neo-Assyrian kings, was never used to pay homage to the kings themselves.[33] When the emperor too was a god, this distinction may have been blurred. But, as we have seen, in the second century, prostration was practice neither before gods *nor* emperors.

The use of crowns is not unknown in Roman ceremonies. Laurel crowns were worn by the participants in a *triumphus* or an *adventus*, or even, on occasion, during a departure sacrifice. Again, gold crowns appear in triumphal processions,[34] but the element of solar worship would be out of place in such a scene. The crown of the baraita is more likely the hat worn by priests on festival days and during

---

[30] See Ryberg, 69 and fig. 36b (pl. XXI); see also 106, 110, 115, 176 and for kneeling, 126 and associated illustrations.

[31] See Liddell-Scott, 1518a–b. s.v. *proskynesis*, sub I.2 for references, and see next note.

[32] See Philip S. Alexander, 'The Family of Caesar and the Family of God: The Image of the Emperor in the Heikhalot Literature,' in Loveday Alexander, ed., *Images of Empire*, 296–297, esp. 288–290, and note that Liddell-Scott, idem, sub II, suggests that it originally meant 'throw a kiss to the god,' and adds that 'the gesture is probably represented in Sumerian and Babylonian art monuments.' The latter probably refers to the gesture called *labān appi*; see Meyer Gruber, 'Akkadian *labān appi* in the Light of Art and Literature, *JANES* 7 (1975), 73–83, and the illustrations there. If so, however, *proskynesis* was *not* originally a sign of respect to a monarch, and it is difficult to understand how Greek historians attribute the introduction of the gesture to Alexander. Alexander notes (290, n. 2) that 'the Greeks (Herodotus, Xenophon, Isocrates) from early on remark, with disapproval, on the Persian practice of prostration before the king; see [F.] Dvornik, *[Early Christian and Byzantine] Political Philosophy* (Washington D.C.: Dumbarton Oaks Center for Byzantine Studies, 1966), I, 117–118.' A perusal of the sources cited by Liddell-Scott will amply confirm this observation.

[33] See previous note.

[34] Ryberg, 152, 154; see also W. Warde Fowler, *The Religious Experience of the Roman People from the earliest times to the age of Augustus*, 1933, 217.

sacrifices, a skin hat ending in a spike of olive-wood which was itself enveloped by a thread of wool.[35] However, gold crowns were an integral part of the imperial cult, and it was sacrilege to knock it off the head of a priest. The wearing of this crown, with the ruler's likeness on it, apparently originated in the East, perhaps as early as Antiochus III in Hellenistic times. Whether the ruler himself wore it in religious ceremonies, and under what circumstances, is uncertain. However, there are representations of a king acting as a priest with a sacrificial bowl and his head covered by his *toga*—and not a crown or headgear of any sort.

Of course, if the baraita deals not with the emperor, but an Oriental king, the uncertainty is even greater, though, as we shall see, Sasanian kings certainly wore elaborate crowns, individually designed (see below). And we know that in the Greek East priests in general wore purple robes, gold crowns and white shoes.[36] If this is so, this would explain why the kings don the crowns before prostrating themselves to the sun; otherwise, we would have expected them to take them off as a gesture of obeisance. Indeed, the scribe of MS Paris 671 (on Berakhot), or his source, obviously felt this problem, and emended the text to read 'the kings place their crowns *on the ground* (*'al gabei qarqa'*) and prostrate themselves to the sun.' Having the kings placing their crowns on their heads is understandable only if the 'crown' were a function of the king's *priestly* office and an integral part of the ceremony.

This raises another possibility, one mentioned in passing above: could the baraita be describing an imperial coronation? The use of

---

[35] See Duncan Fishwick, *The Imperial Cult in the Latin West: Studies in the Ruler Cult of the Western Provinces of the Roman Empire*, vol. II, 1, 475. In all of Ziegler's discussion of the use of crowns in the Roman imperial panoply (*Königsgleichnisse*, 5–11), not one example is to be found of the use of a crown worn on the emperor's head during worship. Indeed, as he points out, quoting Mommsen (q.v), that gold crowns were little used, and were not worn, but held over the emperor's head (6). Moreover, his sources are all late; I list them in order of citation (his numbers IX to XVII, II to IV in the 'Anhang'): Exod R 23:3, Tanh Re'eh, Tanh Buber, 60, bPes 17a (Pes R 39b, Lev R 2:5), Eicha R 3:3, Shoher Tov to Is 49:3, and Exod R 5:14 (Tanh to Exod 5:1–2, and Tan Buber, 19. Still, Hadrian is depicted as a general with a laurel on his head (see Price, *Rituals and Power*, pl. 4d before 199, but compare plates 4a–c. See also Andreas Alföldi, Insignien und Tracht der Römischen Kaiser, *Mitteilungen des Deutschen Archaeologischen Instituts, Roemische Abteilung* 50 (1935), 1–171.

[36] See L. Robert, 'Une vision de Perpetue martyre a Carthage en 203,' *Comptes Rendus de l'Academie des Inscriptiones et Belles-Lettres* (1982), 228–276, at 258f., cited in Fishwick, 477.

crowns as a symbol of kingship was not unknown in Rome. According to Suetonius, when Augustus 'had the sarcophagus and body of Alexander brought forth from its shrine, and after gazing on it, showed his respect by placing upon it a golden crown and strewing it with flowers....'[37] However, this was more in the nature of a gesture of respect than an acknowledgment of kingship, as the end of the anecdote demonstrates. Suetonius goes on to say that, on being asked whether he wished to see the tomb of the Ptolemies as well, he replied: 'My wish was to see a king, not corpses.'

And, indeed, Suetonius' description of the imperial succession contains no mention of crowns as essential elements of the assumption of office; 'donning the purple' was more to the point. In describing Tiberius' assumption of the imperial powers, Suetonius notes that:

> Though Tiberius did not hesitate at once to assume and to exercise the imperial authority, surrounding himself with a guard of soldiers, that is, with the actual power and the outward sign of sovereignty, yet he refused the title for a long time.'[38]

That is, he refused to assume the purple, as the sequel goes on to demonstrate. One of his reasons, again according to Suetonius, was that the army in Germany was reluctant to accept an emperor who was not its own choice. 'With the greatest urgency [the army] besought Germanicus, their commander at the time, to assume the purple....'[39] Suetonius describes the accessions of Claudius and Nero as having been accomplished by acclamation, and by having their litters carried to the Senate.[40] Otho was hailed by his legions and carried on their shoulders.[41] In the case of Vespasian, he notes that 'Tiberius Alexander, prefect of Egypt, was the first to compel his legions to take the oath for Vespasian on the Kalends of July, the day which was afterwards celebrated as that of his accession; then the army in Judaea swore allegiance to him personally on the fifth day before the Ides of July.'[42]

---

[37] *The Lives of the Caesars*, II, xviii, see J.C. Rolfe's translation (Loeb Classical Library 31), 148–149.
[38] *Ibid.*, III, xxiv, 330–331.
[39] *Ibid.*, xxv.
[40] *Ibid.*, V, x, vol. II, 20–21, and VI, vii, 98–99.
[41] *Ibid.*, VII, vi, 236–237.
[42] *Ibid.*, VIII, vi, 294–297. The *Historia Augusta* passes over in silence nearly all details regarding the formal ceremonies which accompanied the change of regime,

In all of these descriptions, crowns play no role. Nevertheless, it may be that coronation, like wearing a purple toga, was so taken for granted as part of the ceremony that it need not have been mentioned. Dio Cassius reports that Julius Caesar was offered the crown (diadem) at the Lupercalia, but refused it. He suggested instead that it be taken to the temple of Jupiter Optimus Maximus who alone deserved it.[43] Shortly before his assassination, however, Caesar seems to have allowed a diadem to be placed on his statue—the Persian symbol of monarchy.[44] Whether the diadem was worn during religious ceremonies—or rather, whether the placement of the crown on the monarch's head was itself part of the ceremony—is far from clear.

Having gotten this far, we may proceed one step further, for there was one Roman institution which combined the rights and rites of king and priest: the *flamen Dialis*, although, unfortunately, here too the element of solar worship is still absent.[45] Fears describes it as follows.

The image of Zeus as the guardian of fertility was well-developed in Greece; and a similar concept lay behind the popular derivation of Jupiter's name from *iuvo quando mortales atque urbes beluasque omnis*

---

although the author does mention in passing that Avidius Cassius had been invested with the imperial insignia (*ornamenta regia*), though 'he had himself proclaimed emperor' (*Scriptores Historiae Augustae*, I (LCL 139), trans. David Magie, Cambridge: Harvard UP, 1991, Avidius Cassius, vii, 244–247. In regard to Maximus and Balbinus, the author writes that 'all the imperial titles and trappings (*insignibus*) having been decreed them, they assumed the tribunican power, the proconsular command, the office of Pontifex Maximus...,' after which they went to the Capitol and made sacrifice (*ibid.*, III [LCL 141], trans. David Magie, Cambridge: Harvard UP, 1993, Maximus and Balbinus, viii, 462–463).

[43] Dio, 3, 11, 44; see Zvi Yaavetz, *Qesar ve-Qasarizm: Massot be-Historia Romanit*, Tel Aviv: Hakibbutz Hameuhad, 1971, 105, and the literature cited there, esp. E. Hohl, 'Das Angebot des Diadems an Caesar,' *Klio* 34 (1942), 71–75.

[44] See Yaavetz, ibid., 108 and the sources cited there, esp. Dio 2, 9, 44 and Plutarch (Caesar, 61). Suetonius describes it as a 'laurel wreath with a white filet tied to it' (*coronam lauream candida fascia praeligata*); Rolfe notes that the ribbon was emblematic of royalty; see his Suetoninius, *Lives of the Caesars*, I, The Deified Julius, lxxix, 102–103. Suetonius also reports the incident at the Lupercalia; see further on, *ibid.*, 104–105.

[45] For a useful survey of various aspects of the institution, see Jens H. Vanggaard, *The Flamen: A Study in the History and Sociology of Roman Religion*; see in particular 24–29, on the fifteen types of *flamines*; the *flamen Dialis* was second in rank. See also the comparative tables on 107–115. The flamen Dialis was permanently cut off from the profane sphere, in contrast to the two other *flamines maiores*. Most important, he was obliged to offer a sacrifice every day, as Vanggaard puts it (see 90, quoting Gellius (X, 15, 16), 'To him, every day is the equivalent of a religious festival' (*Dialis cotidie feriatus est*).

iuvat. In late republican iconography Jupiter's thunderbolt and eagle are associated with the cornucopiae and other symbols of fertility.

Such a view of Jupiter offers the most consistent explanation of the taboos surrounding his special priest, the *flamen Dialis*. Probably originally a king, as well as a priest, the *flamen Dialis* was a relic of sacral kingship at Rome. Embodying in his person the power of the god, the priest-king ensured the temporal prosperity of the community. This charismatic power flowed through him like an electric charge; and if proper care were not taken, it could be diminished with disastrous results for the community. Hence the elaborate set of sacral precautions, which were merely misunderstood relics in the historical period but which were originally intended to protect the sacred representative of Jupiter magical forces which would diminish his giving power.... He [*i.e.*, Jupiter—YE] was the divine magistrate of the Roman People; his servant, the *flamen Dialis*, alone among Roman priests possessed the rights of a magistrate. The *flamen Dialis* was entitled to a *sella curulis* and to a seat in the Senate, and he wore the *toga praetexta*.[46]

The essential point is that the flamen Dialis was required to wear woolen felt cap, the *pilleus* or *pilleum*, made from the fleece or wool of a sacrificial victim, and adorned with an olive branch, fastened to the cap by a band round about it—at all times, and this decidedly includes the time of his performance of the sacrifice; Valerius Maximus notes a case in which the flamen's headgear fell off while he was sacrificing, thus invalidating his role.[47] This is of course the reverse of the baraita's description of this rite, but it may be the exception that proves the rule.

It is however doubtful that a provincial, well informed though he might be in regard to the provincial world around him, would have been aware of the role of a *flamen Dialis* to the point of directing his criticism against that practice as against general idolatry. Nevertheless, it may be that our quest is somewhat misconceived, since paganism eschewed watertight categories of divinity, and syncretistic tendencies were always common. Nevertheless, the almost complete absence of Sol Invictus or Apollo as recipients of *vota* in the second century, as noted above, must be significant. Solar worship fits much more comfortably into the third century.

---

[46] Fears, 26–27, and esp. the literature cited in nn. 95 and 95a.
[47] See Vanggaard, 40–42.

Most forms of solar worship reached Rome from the East, either as a solar god such as Baal of Baalbeck or as Mithra (though probably not the Mithra of the Mysteries; see below), and it would seem that we must seek our king/priest of a solar cult there. R. Meir apparently spent time outside of Palestine, especially in Asia Minor,[48] if Assia is to be identified as such. In any case, it is outside of the Land of Israel.[49] A solar cult flourished in Emesa (Homs) in Syria, dedicated to Elagabal, 'god of the mountains,' who was identified with Sol Invictus. It was a high priest of this god whose daughter married Varius Avitus Bassianus, the man who would become the emperor Marcus Aurelius Antoninus, who was eventually knicknamed 'Heliogabalus,' because of his devotion to this god. In 219 he brought an image of that god to Rome.

> Immediately upon his arrival in Rome, Heliogabalus had a sanctuary (Elagabalium) set up.... Every morning he came out to slaughter bulls and a vast quantity of sheep. On the altars the blood of the victims mingled with exotic aromas and intoxicating wines. The emperor went among hecatombs and libations, with the women of his country playing their cymbals and timbrels. Knights and senators, clad in trailing tunics with long wide sleeves, purple girdles and flaxen footwear 'like the soothsayers of Phoenicia' (Herodian), were not behindhand in participating in the liturgical frolics. On their heads they carried golden vessels containing the entrails of the sacrificed animals and they conformed strictly to the Syrian ritual. The emperor's mother and grandmother danced and sang with them in the language of the Bedouins who had previously installed their cult of the Sun at Emesa. What a spectacle for the old Romans, or at least those who claimed to be![50]

R. Meir's interest in the world around him is evidenced by his friendly relationship with the Cynic Oenomaus of Gadara, who lived

---

[48] See bMeg 18b.
[49] See Louis H. Feldman, *Jew and Gentile in the Ancient World: Attitudes and Interactions from Alexander to Justinian*, 70–72, but see A. Neubauer, *Géographie du talmud: Mémoire couronné par l'Académie des inscriptions et belles-letters*, 1868, 35, and Naomi G. Cohen, 'Rabbi Meir, a Descendant of Anatolian Proselytes: New Light on His Name and the Historic Kernel of the Nero Legend in Gittin 56a,' *JJS* 23 (1972), 51–59.
[50] See Robert Turcan, *The Cults of the Roman Empire*, 176–183. The quote is from 179, and see the bibliography in n. 150. The description is built on that in Augustan History, Life of Heliogabalus, 3, 4–5; 7,1 and 5–6. See also Mary Beard, *et al.*, *Religions of Rome*, vol. I: History, 256. For recent studies of Heliogabalus and his cult, see G.H. Halsberghe, 'Le culte de Deus Sol Invictus à Rome au 3e siècle après J.C.,' in *ANRW* II/1.4, 2181–2201, and Michael Pietrzykowski, 'Die Religionspolitik des Kaisers Elagabal,' *ibid.*, II/16.3, 1806–1825.

during the reign of Hadrian (117–138), and who was known for his mockery of divination and idolatry.[51] Presumably the ceremonies of the early third century at Rome reflected what R. Meir might have seen in a generation or two before in Syria.[52] Still, despite the common element of solar worship, the baraita's description contains none of these elements. Its description of pagan rites is does not have a particularly Roman or Oriental cast, but resembles a generic Jewish description of an idolatrous rite.

Although Dio goes into detail in describing the barbaric plenitude of the sacrificial victims and other aspects of the rites, he does not state that this ceremony took place every day. Still, his description implies that it was not a one-time-a-year occurrence. However, if Heliogabalus had indeed begun his career as high priest at Emesa, he might well have carried out his ceremony daily. But our contention is not that the baraita is based on the particulars of this case of solar worship, but that this description of solar worship mirrors something of the reality of the time. What Heliogabalus practiced in Rome had reflected the Syrian ritual of the generation before. It is likely that solar worship, as opposed to say, the worship of the moon or fertility deities, did indeed take place on a daily basis, at least by professionals. Whether the 'kings of East and West' would have done so is another matter. As far as royal solar worship is concerned, it may well be the case that Heliogabalus was unique.

Beyond that, however, there is another, major impediment to this thesis: the high priest at Emesa was not, as far as we can make out, its ruler, and the baraita is directed against *royal* worship. We are faced with quandary: if the worship was imperial, it was not solar in R. Meir's time; if it was solar, it was not imperial, or, for that matter, royal. Still, even after Emesa lost a good deal of its autonomy under Vespasian, its kings or tetrarchs were still taken from the native Arab dynasty, and some autonomy remained.[53]

> More commonly still [than Zeus], supremacy is concentrated in the sun, natural and visible master of at least the eastern skies [*i.e.*, in

---

[51] See Pauly-Wissowa 17 (1937), cols. 2249–2251. On the relations between the two, see A. Hyman, *Toldot Tannaim va-Amoraim*, III, col. 946b, and Feldman, *Jew and Gentile* 34.
[52] See Javier Teixidor, *The Pantheon of Palmyra*, 47–48 on the identification of Malakbel with Sol Sanctissimus.
[53] See Pietrzykowski, 'Die Religionspolitik des Kaiser's Elagabal,' 1810–1811, and the literature cited in n. 15.

Syria]. So in Mithraism the sun, in hyphenation with Mithra, is the supreme deity. Inscriptions from the western provinces make that clear. They also call the sun 'Helios' more often than 'Sol,' and the dedications are disproportionately in Greek, not Latin, indicating the god's special favor among people of Greek-speaking origin. In western Asia Minor, the sun enjoys favor as a witness to men's oaths, with his all-seeing eye; but that presents him in no regal role. Better, in Egypt, magical papyri invoke the sun in such terms as 'Lord god who grasps the whole, gives life to all, and rules the universe.'

In the Levant, the sun is most at home. In Emesa, and among Arabs generally as Aziz, he reigns uncontested; and as a god great but not supreme, like Apollo, he is worshiped in Palmyra, Baalbek, and other towns and cities.[54]

MacMullen goes on to enumerate many examples of solar iconography and the like throughout the Empire, but especially the East, and not only from the third century, though that is his focus. If the baraita is to be dated to the second century, this would seem to me to be the most likely object of its condemnation.

There may be another possibility along this line, as well, but one subject to several objections. In recent years an influential number of scholars has suggested an astronomical origin for the Mithraic mysteries;[55] this would tend to support another element of Mithra's identity, that of his association with the sun.[56] His sacrifice of the bull (tauroctony) was *ordered* by the sun god, a fact that clearly differentiates him from the sun god himself. However, some Iranists have pointed to a body of evidence that associates him with the sun.[57] To my mind, there are two fatal objections to viewing our baraita as directed against the Mithraic mysteries. First of all, whatever Mithra's relationship to Helios, he was not worshiped as the sun, nor is the sun understood as representative of him. The clear-

---

[54] Ramsay MacMullen, *Paganism in the Roman Empire*, 84.

[55] See David Ulansey, *The Origin of the Mithraic Mysteries: Cosmology and Salvation in the Ancient World.*

[56] See Franz Cumont, *The Mysteries of Mithra*, 95, 121. However, see the trenchant comments of Ilya Gershevitz, 'Die Sonne das Beste,' in John Hinnells, ed., *Mithraic Studies: Proceedings of the First International Congress of Mithraic Studies*, vol. I, 68–89, esp. 75, and the ensuing discussion on 125–134, es 129; they can be applied, *mutatis mutandis*, to our time as well; see below. See also (in the same volume), R. L. Gordon, 'Cumont and the Doctrine of Mithraism,' 215–248, esp. 229. The increasingly accepted interpretation of Mithraic iconography as purely astronomical is really irrelevant to this point.

[57] See A. Herman Lommel, 'Die Sonne das Schlechste?,' *Oriens* 15 (1962), 360–373, which aroused Gershevitch's ire in the first place.

est evidence for that, and proof as well that the description in our baraita cannot refer to the Mithraic mysteries, is that they took place in a subterranean Mithraeum—a cave.[58] 'In principal, the Mithraeum... had the appearance of a grotto (*spelaeum*) or a crypt.... [When half-buried buildings or the like were not available,] Mithraists simply dug into the ground to create the imitation of a crypt and the illusion of descending beneath the level of the ordinary world.'[59] Mithra's initiates hardly prostrated themselves to the sun. Moreover, Cumont's interpretation of the exact significance of the account of Commodus' encouragement of Mithraism in the *Historia Augusta* (Commodus, 9.6) has increasingly been disputed,[60] and the report of that of Nero is, in the word of Robert Trucan, 'suspect,'[61] and so the important element of royal worship is cast in doubt

Again, while Mithra is himself depicted as wearing a Phrygian cap, there is no indication that his initiates did.

Perhaps even more important, the Mithraic mysteries were much more associated with sacrifice than any other of the religions or cults of the Roman world, and the omission of that fact in our baraita, troublesome as it has proved to be in regard to other cults, is that more so in regard to Mithraism.[62]

However, even were we to associate our baraita with the Mithraic mysteries, or any of the other ceremonies current in the Roman

---

[58] See for example Roger Beck, 'Mithraism Since Franz Cumont,' *ANRW* II/17.4, 2001–2115, esp. 2090, who sums up the situation as follows: 'The Mithraeum is ideologically, and sometimes in practice or in décor, a cave.' See the literature cited there; especially, H. Lavagne, 'Importance de la grotte dans le Mithriacisme en Occident,' in J. Duchesne-Guillemin, Études Mithriaques: Actes du 2ᵉ Congrès International, Téhéran, du 1ᵉʳ au 8 Septembre 1975 (Acta Iranica 17). First Series (Actes de congrè), vol. 4, 271–278.

[59] Turcan, *Cults of the Roman Empire*, 218.

[60] See Reinhold Merkelbach, *Mithras*, 108–109, 175, but see Manfred Clauss, *Mithras: Kult und Mysterien*, 35–36; Robert Turcan, *Mithra et la Mithriacisme*, Paris: Le Belles Lettres, 1993, 41, calls Cumont's description as an imperial conversion, as an 'abuse of language.' Robert Turcan notes that 'no coins, no public documents obviously confirm that Commodus was initiated, [though] he granted premises to the Mithraists in his imperial residence at Ostia' (*Cults of the Roman Empire*, 243–244).

[61] Turcan, *Cults of the Roman Empire*, 243.

[62] See Luther H. Martin, 'Reflections on the Mithraic Tauroctony as Cult Scene,' in John R. Hinnells, *Studies in Mithraism: Papers associated with the Mithraic Panel organized on the occasion of the XVIth Congress of the International Association for the History of Religion, Rome 1990*, 217–224. In particular, see his remarks on 218: 'The public perception of Mithraism, according to literary evidence from Herotodus to Pallas, associated Mithra not with a myth, but with rituals of sacrifice,' and see n. 8, where he cites a mass of evidence to that effect.

Empire of the second or third centuries, at least two elements remain to be accounted for—the doffing of the crowns and prostration.

As noted above, prostration does not seem to have been a part of Roman state religion. However, the gesture is so instinctive and universal that it is difficult to deny its pertinence here. Indeed, in Apuleius' *Golden Ass*, Lucius, who has been initiated into Isis' rites in Corinth and is ordered by the goddess to return home to Rome, confesses that 'I fell prostrate at the goddess' feet, and washed them with my tears as I prayed to her in a voice choked with sobs which convulsed my speech.'[63]

This may of course be the exception that proves the rule, since here prostration occurs in private and in connection with an eastern religion, and not the Roman state religion of the second, or even the third, century. Still, despite the Greeks' condemnation of *proskynesis* as a Persian custom,[64] as Alföldi makes abundantly clear, prostration was common enough in Roman court ceremonial even under the Principate, let alone under the empire, and especially after Diocletian.[65] And though its use may have increased under oriental influence in the third century, this would hardly have prevented a Palestinian rabbi from attributing such actions to a Roman emperor even in the second century.

Thus, the baraita may well describe a Syrian or eastern rite, which has been universalized to apply to the kings of both 'East and West.' In any case, it is most likely that this ceremony, whatever its details, was not performed daily, though this is hardly certain.[66] If this is so, we must distinguish the view of the baraita from that of the core-

---

[63] *The Golden Ass*, 11.24.6.

[64] Karl A. Wittfogel, in his classic study, *Oriental Despotism: A Comparative Study of Total Power*, describes *proskynesis* as 'the great symbol of total submission,' and notes its association with Iran, and other 'hydraulic societies,' and the difficulty of its acceptance in Medieval Europe; see his discussion on 152–154.

[65] Alföldi, 'Die Ausgestaltung des Monarchischen Zeremoniells,' 46–48. As Alexander notes, 'Many of [Diocletian's] supposed innovations in ceremonial are attested earlier, as a close reading of Alföldi reveals' (Alexander, 288). Alföldi provides sufficient evidence that, though not originally religious in motivation, prostration was common enough (see *ibid.*, 48–52). Whether a Palestinian rabbi of the second century would have distinguished between its secular and religious use is unlikely.

[66] H.J.W. Drijver's comment in *Cults and Beliefs at Edessa*, 175, is still *apropos*: 'Our sources merely provide us with a superficial knowledge of current religious ideas but do not allow a deeper understanding of the varieties of religious experience as expressed in the formal language of myths and ritual....'

sugya; the Balaam pericope and the story of R. Joshua b. Levi fit the redactor's intentions much better. In addition, the Balaam section fits comfortably within the chiasmic structure outlined above, while the baraita does not. All in all, it would seem that the baraita was added to the core-sugya, much in the same way as the redactional interpretation of R. Joseph's statement in Shab 55a. In both cases, redactional intervention converted statements regarding the all-devouring effects of divine anger, without regard to merit, to ones that fit the prevailing ethos of measure-for-measure divine retribution. In the case of R. Joseph's comment that the men killed were those who had 'fulfilled the Torah from *aleph* to *tav*,' the redactor explained that these elders had failed in their duty to offer reproof to their generation for its idolatrous failings. This was even though they had every expectation that this reproof would not have been effective. In our sugya, there was the danger to the Israelites of Balaam's refocusing of the daily period of divine anger. This could only be countered by God's refraining from any anger during that period; by adding the baraita, this has been converted into a divine anger occasioned by the idolatry of the kings of East and West.

In our case, there is still the possibility that the proof text from Ps 7 was originally part of the baraita, as we suggested originally; if so, we must interpret the sugya as dealing with the possible refocusing of divine anger which is aroused by idolatry. Nevertheless, this very refocusing indicates that the secondary effects of God's anger may not affect only those who merit it. Having limited the measure for measure aspect of divine retribution to this degree, it is hard to see why the redactor would have undercut the message of his sugya with the coda provided by the baraita. On the whole, it would seem that the baraita was not original to the sugya.

Of course, the chiasmic structure itself was an attempt by the original redactor to incorporate a number of heterogenous sources within one statement on divine anger; this is apparent from the duplication of proof texts and questions. The ancedote regarding R. Joshua b. Levi seems to have been motivated by several factors. It demonstrated that the sages of Israel had the same powers as Balaam, on the one hand, but in contrast to the *wicked* Balaam, the *righteous* R. Joshua b. Levi is restrained by Heaven from exercising that power in a less direct way, and one which emphasized his moral standing: It is not proper for punishment to come to the wicked through the agency of a righteous person.

Despite all this, there is yet another possibility that must be examined. The baraita, which appears only in the Babylonian Talmud and not at all in Palestinian sources, may reflect a Babylonian venue and *Sitz im Leben*. Evidence for Zoroastrian worship accounts for nearly all the essential elements we have detailed above, and may account for the attribution to 'the kings of *East* and West' as well. In Zoroastrianism, the sun represents the powers of good, as does holy fire; in addition, Zoroastrianism requires the faithful to pray five times a day, and each prayer must be recited while facing a fire or the sun. The first prayer of the day is offered upon awakening. While animal sacrifices are not unknown, they are theologically problematical, and not necessarily part of the daily rite, and certainly not those performed by laymen (presumably including the king). Here is the description of Mary Boyce, the doyenne of students of Zoroastrianism in our century.

> The symbolism of fire for this struggle [with evil] was very potent, especially at midnight, when, 'awakened' from under its bed of ashes, it leapt up in flames and drove back the 'evil' darkness.... So too at dawn, as they prayed before the again brightly burning fire, they could think that they were thereby helping the glowing light, and with it all the creations of Ača. For the modern Zoroastrian this is pure symbolism; but in Zoroaster's own distant day there would have been no clear distinction made between physical and moral darkness, and the power of prayer was thought to affect both the material and immaterial worlds, the *gaethya* and the *mainyava*. Thus is is said in the Khorčed Niyayeč, the Young Avestan prayer to the sun: 'When the sun with his light brings warmth... the immaterial Yazatas... gather up his glory, they distribute it over the Ahura-created earth, to prosper the world of Ača.... He who worships the Shining Sun, life-giving, bountiful... in order to resist darkness, in order to resist demons born of darkness... he rejoices all the immaterial and material Yazatas.[67]

As Boyce goes on the note, this prayer would have been said daily in every Zoroastrian household, priest and lay.[68]

> When praying in the open (as they often did) Zoroastrians turned towards the sun, since their religion enjoins that they must pray facing fire; and fellow-citizens in Hellenistic Asia Minor, observing this,

---

[67] Mary Boyce, *Zoroastrianism: Its Antiquity and Constant Vigour*, 86–87.

[68] So too in ancient times; see the report of the Armenian historian Eghishe Vardapet, cited in Alessandro Bausani, *Religion in Iran: From Zoroaster to Baha'ullah*, trans. J.M. Marchesi, 61. apud R.C. Zaehner, *Zurvanism: A Zoroastrian Dilemma*, 47.

could be forgiven for assuming that their worship was regularly offered to Mithra as sun god. There is evidence, moreover, of a blurring of the concepts of the luminary and the Ahura among the Zoroastrians themselves in post-Achaemenian times. Strabo's statement that the Persians of Cappadocia called Helios Mithra, taken by itself, might be no more than an accurate recording of the truncated expression '[eye of] Mithra'; but on the coins of the Kučan king Kanička Mithra's name (as MIIRO) replaces that of Helios for the sun-god. Still later, the Sasanian king Shabuhr II[69] is reported to have sworn 'by the Sun, the Judge of the whole earth'; and a minister of Yazdegird II referred to the Sun as one who 'because of his impartial generosity and equal bounty has been called the god Mihr, for in him there is neither guile nor ignorance'. King and minister were both, however, laymen; and it is likely that the laity, not being theologically trained, apprehended the divinities of their worship with less doctrinal clarity than did the priests.[70]

Though Boyce goes on to speculate that even laymen would have discerned the difference between Mithra and Hvar, both sun gods. 'In general, the apprehension of these two divinities, with distinctness tending toward identification but not completely achieving it,

---

[69] That is, the prominent third century Persian monarch Shapur II (309–379), known so well in the Babylonian Talmud; see J. Neusner, *History of the Jews in Babylonia*, vol. III, Leiden: E.J. Brill, 1972. The *Denkard*, the encyclopedic ninth-century work on Zoroastrianism, which contains much early material, credits him with establishing Orthodoxy after a debate between representatives of various opinions: According to Denkard, he 'summoned men from all lands to examine and study all doctrines so that all cause for dispute might be removed. After Āturpāt had been vindicated by the consistency of his argument against all the other representatives of the different sects, doctrines, and schools, he issued a declaration to this effect: 'Now that we have seen the Religion upon earth, we shall leave no one to his false religion and we shall be exceedingly zealous.' And so he did so.' See R.C. Zaehner, *The Dawn and Twilight of Zoroastrianism*, London: Weidenfeld and Nicolson, 1961, 176. Āturpat is Āturpat son of Mahraspand, was high priest in the time of Shapur II, and sayings of his are preserved in the *Denkard*. In particular, he seems to have opposed the doctrine of Zurvanism, which all but replaced free will with what was called 'fatalism.' See Zaehner, 187, though his view is not undisputed. On the theological problem of the source of evil in Ahriman or even within the original creation of Ohrmazd, see Peter Clark, *Zoroastrianism: An Introduction to an Ancient Faith*, Brighton: Sussex Academic Press, 1998, 83–85 ('The Problem of Evil Creatures in the *Vendidad*'). At any rate, this must have occurred early in Shapur's reign, since in 322 he launched a drive against those who 'scorned the sun, despised the fire and did not honour the water' (S.A. Nigosian, *The Zoroastrian Faith: Tradition and Modern Research*, 36).

[70] Mary Boyce and Frantz Grenet, with a contribution by Roger Beck, *A History of Zoroastrianism*, Volume Three: *Zoroastrianism Under Macedonian and Roman Rule* (*Handbuch der Orientalistik*, Achter Band: Religion, Erster Abschnitt, Religonsgeschichte des Alten Orients, Lieferung 2, Heft 2), Leiden: E.J. Brill, 481.

appears not unlike the Greek apprehension of Apollo and Helios, and the Mithraists' of Mithra and Sol.'[71]

Moreover, the baraita's reference to the kings' crowns is entirely appropriate in the case of the Persian kings; it may refer to the Persian tiara. The importance of the crown to Sasanian monarchs is clear; each member of the dynasty had his own particular version of the crown designed for himself, and it is in his crown that each king was depicted on his coinage.[72] The crown was in origin an Iranian horseman's headgear, later on adopted as the 'Phrygian cap' in the iconography of Western Mithra, but when adopted for royal use became quite elaborate.[73] Whether the Persian kings wore their crowns at prayer is not known from literary sources, but the depiction of Darius I in Naqshi-I Rustam, has him praying before a fire altar wearing what appears to be a crown, at least when compared to court scenes of other Persian monarchs.[74]

At any rate, if the baraita is describing something like Persian prayer, we may assume that such prayer, and the divine anger that it inspired, would be a daily occurrence, and the baraita would then fit much better within the core-sugya.

This of course assumes that the baraita is describing conditions in the third and fourth centuries. The Sasanian dynasty came to power in 224, and with it it brought a revived Zoroastrianism; the Parthians

---

[71] *Ibid.*, 482. See also *ibid.*, 479: 'Mithra's association with the sun appears to have been another major factor in his popularity and conspicuousness in the Hellenstic age, and is, notably, a trait he shares with Mithras. Neither Mithra nor Apollo was by origin a solar divinity, and at Commagene, as we have seen, they needed to be linked astrologically through Hermes and Helios.' By R. Meir's time, and certainly later, the identification had long since been established—at least since the fifth century, B.C.E.; see *ibid.*, n. 587.

[72] See the impressive array of crowns depicted on coins and reliefs in Ehsan Yarsheter, ed., *Cambridge History of Iran*, vol. 3(2), *The Seleucid, Parthian and Sasanian Period*, 135.

[73] *Ibid.*, 163.

[74] See Peter Calmeyer, 'Greek Historiography and Achaemenid Reliefs,' in Heleen Sancisi-Weerdenburg and Amélie Kuhrt, eds., *Achaemenid History II: The Greek Sources, Proceedings of the Groningen 1984 Achaemenid History Workshop*, 11–26, especially the plates on 22 (from the tomb of Darius I at Naqshi-I Rustam) and 23 (Xerxes I, from the eastern façade of the Apadana). The the relief of Darius is damaged, but the royal figure is clear, and its headgear resembles the rounded hat that Darius wears in the relief of him standing as crown prince or co-regent before his father Xerxes I in the plate on 23. However, if we take into consideration the damage to the crown in the relief from Darius' tomb, it does quite closely resemble the usual squarish crown. It should be recalled that various types of crowns were common among Persian officials and soldiers; see Calmeyer, 16–17.

were apparently not as concerned with religious matters. And it is unlikely that the baraita's description would apply to them. On the whole, the description would perhaps fit Shapur II (309–379), who did much to establish Zoroastrian orthodoxy and in 324 C.E. at times persecuted those who did not honor the sun, the fire and the water, especially Christians after Constantine's conversion.[75]

In sum, if we are willing to extend our geographical and chronological compass beyond R. Meir's time and/or place, we may assume daily worship of the sun by the 'kings of East and West.' Beyond that, however, at least two problems remain. One indispensable element of Persian prayer is missing—the sacred cord that was tied and untied around the waist during prayer, and one element which is mentioned seems not to have been mandated as accompanying Persian prayer: prostration. Persian prayers were offered while standing.[76] Greek sources are unanimous is attributing the origin of the custom of prostration to Persia, and we have a relatively wide variety and number of such reports.[77] However, these reports refer to the Achaemenian and Parthian dynasties, and not the later Sasanians.

There is some indication that prostration per se was not considered religiously appropriate, though 'bowing,' or other gestures of respect were/are. Most instructive are the comments of a contemporary (and quite conservative!) Parsi priest accompanying the translation of a nineteenth-century Zoroastrian catechism, written in Gujarati, that was itself written by conservative priests in India. In describing the mechanics of prayer, the catechism itself has the following:

> Q. How do you do *bandagi* [= prayer]?
> A. To do *bandagi* we must hold our hands high and reverently. *Yasna* 30[.1] states: 'O God, I praise you and remember you through good mindedness.[78]

On this Dastour Dr. Firoze M. Kotwal writes:

> Every act of bandagi begins with a cleansing of one's hands, face and feet with water, and the tying and untying of the sacred kushti [= cord around the waist]. These religious acts are always accompanied by manthric recitation, *i.e.*, Avestan utterances. It is our firm belief

---

[75] See n. 69.
[76] Boyce, *Zoroastrianism*, 84.
[77] See Liddell-Scott, idem.
[78] Erachji Sobrabji Meherjirana, *A Guide to the Zoroastrian Religion: A Nineteenth Century Catechism with Modern Commentary* ed. Firoze M. Kotwal and James W. Boyd, 53.

> that prayers should always be said in the divine speech of Avestan, and not in translated form. While praying we should concentrate on God alone and should have no bad thoughts in our mind. We should not pray because it is some external obligation imposed upon us by our religion; rather genuine prayer is a deeply natural response of gifts continually bestowed upon us by God. True prayer comes from within. When we say bandagi in front of fire, we first place a white handkerchief over the palm of our left hand. This is a special gesture of reverence which suggests our own submission to God and also our reverent desire to establish a paywand or connection with all spiritual powers. While saying the Avestan phrase 'Homage to thee, O fire, the son of Ahura Mazda', we bow our head, make an upward gesture toward our forehead with our right hand, and then bow deeply, touching our right hand to the ground. After straightening up, we again bow and pay homage to the fire with the gesture of the right hand raised to this forehead.[79]

Here we have several gestures of respect, including bowing, bowing deeply, making an upward gesture, touching right hand to the ground. While a modern description of Zoroastrian prayer can hardly be a firm basis for interpreting a third- or fourth-century text, no one familiar with Middle Persian sources can fail to be impressed by the linguistic and religious conservatism manifested by this survival of the ancient world. Moreover, when changes have been made, we can usually assess the form and direction they took.[80]

Before proceeding, let us compare this description with that of Mary Boyce, in one of the series of such surveys which she authored over the years, and which appeared under the heading 'The times and manner of praying.'

> The five daily prayers were a binding duty on every Zoroastrian, part of his necessary service to God, and a weapon in the fight against evil. The ritual of prayer, as known from living practice, is as follows: first the believer prepares himself by washing the dust from his face, hands and feet; then, untying the sacred cord, he stands with it held on both hands before him, upright in the presence of his Maker, his eyes on the symbol of righteousness, fire. Then he prays to Ahura Mazda, exe-

---

[79] *Idem*, 53–54.
[80] See for example, the remarks of Jamsheed K. Choksy, *Purity and Pollution in Zoroastrianism: Triumph Over Evil*, 15–16, 19. Aside from the ancient Avestan texts and the Middle Persian texts from Late Antiquity and the high middle ages, Zoroastrian priests have preserved later texts, the Persian rivayats, that provide us with data about the ritual and ceremonial aspects of Zoroastrian practice until nearly the nineteenth century.

crates Angra Mainya (flicking the end of the cord contemptuously as he does so), and reties the cord while still praying. The whole observance takes only a few minutes, but its regular repetition is a religious exercise of the highest value, constituting both a steady discipline and regular avowal of the fundamental tents of the faith.[81]

Here, as elsewhere in her writings, Boyce does not take note of any bowing, deep or not. It may be that the discrepancy is due to differences between Parsee and Irani practice. Among the requests made of Atar, the god of fire, in Yasna 62.5–6, is the following: 'May you give me, O Ātar, son of Ahura Mazdā, quickly felicity, quickly protection, quickly life, fully felicity, fully protection, fully life, (and) wisdom, increment, a quick tongue, understanding for (my) soul, moreover, intelligence (which is) great, massive, (and) stable, [5] moreover, (give me) Manly Valor, standing upright, unsleeping, seating in his place wakeful....'[82]

On the other hand, as noted above, in a detail of a relief from the tomb of Darius I at Naqsh-i Rustam, Darius is shown in just such a posture: standing in front a fire altar, right hand upraised.[83] The Parsi community left Iran early in the tenth century, when times were particularly hard for Zoroastrians under Muslim rule. As Boyce puts it, though there was sporadic contact between the two communities, 'clearly most of what the two communities have in common stems from what was general usage for all Zoroastrians in Iran at the time when the Parsis left.'[84] All in all, given the data, it may be that the Greek *proskynesis* describes the Babylonian gesture of *laban appi*, as I suggested above, and that too is the predecessor of both Darius' gesture and that described by Firoze Kotwal. At any rate, it may be that some gesture that could have been interpreted as Hebrew *histahavveh*, was made.

However, there is also the matter of sacrifice. Strabo reports that 'with earnest prayer they offer sacrifice in a purified place, presenting the victim crowned.'[85] Boyce comments that 'it was still the cus-

---

[81] Mary Boyce, *Zoroastrians: Their Religious Beliefs and Practices*, 35.
[82] William W. Malandra, *An Introduction to Ancient Iranian Religion: Readings from the Avesta and Achaemenid Inscriptions* 161.
[83] See fig. 2 (22) of Calmeyer, 'Greek Historiography and Achaemenid Reliefs.' Calmeyer's remark regarding Herodotus is also worth noting: 'But we should try to understand Herodotus rather than convict him' (18).
[84] Boyce, *Zoroastrians*, 157. Compare the discussion in A.V. Williams Jackson, *Zoroastrian Studies: The Iranian Religion and Various Mongraphs*, 195–197.
[85] Strabo, *Geography*, 15.3.13–14, quoted in Boyce and Grenet, 294–295.

tom in the 1960's to tie a garland round the horns or neck of the sacrificial beast,' while Herodotus 'has said that it was the sacrificer himself who wore the crown, 'of myrtle for choice.'[86] The question of whether regular prayers were accompanied by sacrifices is a matter of dispute, and depends in part on whether we give credence to the reports of classical authors that sacrifice was an element of Zoroastrian prayer. If it was, then our baraita does not conform exactly to third- and fourth-century modes of Zororastrian prayer. The most recent discussion of this subject is that of Albert de Jong, who summarizes the situation as follows:

> If we take the Classical accounts of Persian religion seriously—and we are hardly in a position not to—we must conclude that, contrary to more recent practices, animal sacrifice formed a prominent part of Zoroastrian rituals. There are not many descriptions of Iranian rituals, but the most elaborate descriptions frequently and elaborately mention the sacrifice of different kinds of animals: horses, cows and small cattle.[87]

These accounts include those of Herodotus (*Histories* I.132) and Strabo (*Geography* 15.3.14); there are also several mentions of sacrifices, without detail, in Xenophon (*Cyropaedia* 8.7.3 and 8.3.24), and Plutarch (*Life of Lucullus* 24). Still, de Jong notes that Basil, 'in his description of the Maguseans of Cappadocia (Epistle 258.4), writes that the Maguseans reject animal sacrifice altogether, because they consider it a pollution. The animals they need for sustenance are slaughtered 'through the hands of others,' but it is not entirely clear what Basil means with this.'[88]

It would seem that though slaughtering was considered 'pollution,' the results of such slaughter, the availability of meat for consumption, was allowed. The essential point here is that an account closer to the time of our text (Basil's dates are 330–379, making him a younger contemporary of Shapur II) asserts that sacrifice was rejected.

Despite this de Jong argues that earlier accounts that assert that Zarathustra himself opposed sacrifice were based on apologetic motives and rationalistic tendencies, and a consequent overreliance on Parsi

---

[86] Boyce and Grenet, 295.
[87] See Albert de Jong, *Traditions of the Magi: Zoroastrianism in Greek and Latin Literature*, 357–362.
[88] *Ibid.*, 362.

practices. Indeed, Boyce herself has pointed out that even the Indian Parsis still practiced sacrifice at the end of the eighteenth century, as reported by Antquetil du Person.[89]

However, given the long history of Zoroastrianism, and the large geographical area over which its adherents were scattered, it would not be surprising to see a variety of practices competing with one another. Still, whether Basil's report of Cappodician practices is representative of Babylonia or the Persian heartland, must remain moot. On the other hand, if our baraita does reflect Sasanian practice, it may itself serve as evidence for the antiquity of Parsi practice. However, sacrifice was not a daily event, nor was prayer necessarily accompanied by sacrifice. If our baraita is describing daily prayer, this would account for the absence of any mention of sacrifice.

A Babylonian/Iranian venue is the one that would account for most elements of this description: prayer facing the sun, removal or donning of a crown, and the lack of sacrifice, and a monarch whose claim to the monarchy was based in part on his piety. In all, this would seem to be a Babylonian baraita, somehow attributed to R. Meir, whose import may be universal, but whose description is most likely that of the source in which it is found: Babylonia.

However, in a general description of prayer both East and West, we should perhaps not be surprised if the description does not mesh in every detail. Still, no account of ancient rites of R. Meir's time or in the next two centuries fits the baraita's description exactly. Either some elements of the extra-talmudic accounts—such as sacrifice, the sacred-cord, and the like, or elements of the tralmudic account— especially prostration, seem to be missing to some degree.

Whatever the original or originals on which our description is based, the baraita's acount has been assimilated to biblical and rabbinic images of idol worship. It should be borne in mind that, rabbinically speaking, though prostration is an integral part of the Temple service, it was not primary. The four primary acts involving the Temple service were slaughtering, receiving the blood, carrying the blood to the altar and sprinkling it.[90] Indeed, the Talmud itself has difficulty in fixing the exact nature of the prohibition of idolatrous

---

[89] See M. Boyce, 'Miharagān among the Irani Zoroastrians,' in Hinnells, *Mithraic Studies*, vol. I, 106–118, citing Anquetil du Person, *Le Zend Avesta*, vol. II, 577.
[90] See Rashi, Pes 64b s.v. *shema'at minah holakhah*.

prostration.[91] Still, the Mishnah certainly considers idolatrous prostration as a violation of the prohibition of idolatry.[92]

There is yet another possible Zoroastrian connection to consider in this connection: the reification of Anger as a quasi-independent, malevolent force that may be directed against the very people who deserve the most protection. In Zoroastrian dualism, Angra Mainya stands at the head of legions of demons, one of the most prominent of which is Aeshma, Wrath. Generally speaking, Ashmedai, the king of demons in rabbinic lore, is considered, at least linguistically, a reflex of this figure.[93] Within a monotheistic theology there is of course no room for an analoge of Angra Mainya, but Wrath, as a secondary (or tertiary) figure, may have been acceptable, at least to some individuals. Clearly, whoever produced this baraita was familiar with Sasanian practices; it may be that he incorporated some of the elements of the *daeva* of Wrath, into his conception of the Godhead. Thus, the Iranian affinities of this sugya are quite pronounced and important, and that too would tend to support a Zoroastrian venue for the baraita.

Bibliography

Albeck, Hanokh, *Mehqarim ba-Beraita ve-Tosefta ve-Yahasan la-Talmud*, Jerusalem: Mosad Harav Kook, 1969.

Alexander, Loveday, et al., eds., *Images of Empire* (*JSOT SS* 122), Sheffield: Sheffield Academic Press, 1991.

Alexander, Philip S., 'The Family of Caesar and the Family of God: The Image of the Emperor in the Heikhalot Literature, in Loveday Alexander, *et al.*, eds., *Images of Empire*.

Alföldi, Andreas, 'Die Ausgestaltung des Monarchischen Zeremoniells,' *Mitteilungern des Deutschen Archaeologischen Instituts: Roemische Abteilung* 49 (1934), Munich: Verlag F. Bruckmann A.G., 1934, 1–118.

---

[91] See bKer 3b.

[92] See the discussion in B.Sanh 60b–61a.

[93] See Jacob Levy, *Wörterbuch über die Talmudim und Midraschim* I, 179a s.v. *ashmedai*, Alexander Kohut, 'Über die jüdische Angelogie und Daemonolgie in inhrer Abhängigkeit vom Parsismus,' 72–80. See more recently Shlomo Pines, 'Wrath and Creatures of Wrath in Pahlavi, Jewish and New Testament Sources,' *Irano-Judaica: Studies Relating to Jewish Contacts with Persian Culture throughout the Ages*, ed. Shaul Shaked, 76–82., and Shaul Shaked, 'Bagdana, King of the Demons, and Other Iranian Terms in Babylonian Aramaic Magic,' in *Papers in Honour of Professor Mary Boyce*, vol. I, 511–525; his observations on 511 are quite *apropos*. See also his 'The Zoroastrian Demon of Wrath,' in Christoph Elsas, et al., *Tradition un Translation: Zum Problem der interkulturellen Übersetzbarkeit religiöser Phänomene, Festschrift fur Carsten Colpe zum 65. Geburtstag*, 285–291.

———, 'Insignien und Tracht der Romischen Kaiser,' *Mitteilungen des Deutschen Archaeologischen Instituts, Roemische Abteilung* 50 (1935), Munich: Verlag F. Bruckmann A.G., 1–171.
Bausani, Alessandro, *Religion in Iran: From Zoroaster to Baha'ullah*, trans. J.M. Marchesi, New York: Bibliotheca Persica Press, 2000.
Beard, Mary, and John North, eds., *Pagan Priests: Religion and Power in the Ancient World*, Ithaca: Cornell Univ. Press, 1990.
Beard, Mary, et al., *Religions of Rome* (2 vols.), Cambridge: Cambridge Univ. Press, 1998.
Beck, Roger, 'Mithraism Since Franz Cumont,' *ANRW* II/17.4, 2001–2115.
Boyce, Mary and Frantz Grenet, with a contribution by Roger Beck, *A History of Zoroastrianism*, Volume Three: *Zoroastrianism Under Macedonian and Roman Rule (Handbuch der Orientalistik*, Achter Band: Religion, Erster Abschnitt, *Religionsgeschichte des Alten Orients*, Lieferung 2, Heft 2), Leiden: E.J. Brill, 1991.
———, 'Mihragān among the Iraqi Zoroastrians,' in John Hinnells, ed., *Mithraic Studies*, vol. I.
———, *Zoroastrianism: Its Antiquity and Constant Vigour* (Columbia Lectures on Iranian Studies 7), New York: Bibliotheca Persica, 1992.
———, *Zoroastrians: Their Religious Beliefs and Practices*, London: Routledge & Kegan Paul, 1979.
Calmeyer, Peter, 'Greek Historiography and Achaemenid Reliefs,' in Heleen Sancisi-Weerdenburg and Amélie Kuhrt, eds., *Achaemenid History II: The Greek Sources, Proceedings of the Groningen 1984 Achaemenid History Workshop*, Leiden: E.J. Brill, Nederlands Instituut voor Het Nabije Oosten, 1987.
Choksy, Jamsheed,: Triumph *Purity and Pollution in Zoroastrianism: Triumph Over Evil*, Austin: Univ. of Texas Press, 1989.
Clark, Peter, *Zoroastrianism: An Introduction to an Ancient Faith*, Brighton: Sussex Academic Press, 1998.
Clauss, Manfred, *Mithras: Kult und Mysterien*, Munich: C.H. Beck, 1990.
Cohen, Naomi G., 'Rabbi Meir, a Descendant of Anatolian Proselytes: New Light on His Name and the Historic Kernel of the Nero Legend in Gittin 56a,' *JJS* (1972), 51–59.
Cumont, Franz, *The Mysteries of Mithra*, New York: Dover, 1956.
DeJong, Albert, *Traditions of the Magi: Zoroastrianism in Greek and Latin Literature*, Leiden: E.J. Brill, 1997.
Drijvers, H.J.W., *Cults and Beliefs at Edessa*, Leiden: E.J. Brill, 1980.
Duchesne-Guellemin, J., Éudes *Mithraiques: Actes du 2ᵉ Congrès International, Téhéran, du 1ᵉʳ au 8 September 1975* (Acta Iranica 17), First Series (Actes de Congrès), vol. 4, Leiden: E.J. Brill, 1978.
Dvornik, F., *Early Christian and Byzantine Political Philosophy*, Washington, D.C.: Dumbarton Oaks Center for Byzantine Studies, 1966.
Elman, Yaakov, "Is There Then Anger Before the Holy One?' Aspects of the Theology of the Stam,' AJS Twenty-first Annual Conference, Boston, December 19, 1989.
———, 'Righteousness As Its Own Reward: An Inquiry Into the Theologies of the Stam,' *PAAJR* 57 (1991): 35–67.
Elsas, Christoph, et al., in Christoph Elsas, et al., *Tradition un Trnnslation: Zum Problem der interkulturellen Übersetzbarkeit religiöser Phänomene, Festschrift fur Carsten Colpe zum 65. Geburt*stag, 285–291. Berlin: Walter de Gruyter, 1994.
Fears, J. Rufus, 'The Cult of Jupiter and Roman Imperial Ideology,' in *ANRW*, II/17.1, 3–141.
Feldman, Louis H., *Jew and Gentile in the Ancient World: Attitudes and Interactions from Alexander to Justinian*, Princeton: Princeton Univ. Press, 1993.
Ferguson, John, *The Religions of the Roman Empire* (Aspects of Greek and Roman Life), Ithaca: Cornell Univ. Press, 1970.

Fishwick, Duncan, *The Imperial Cult in the Latin West: Studies in the Ruler Cult of the Western Provinces of the Roman Empire*, vol. II, Leiden: E.J. Brill, 1991.

Fowler, W. Ward, *The Religious Experience of the Roman People from the earliest times to the age of Augustus* (The Gifford Lectures for 1901–1910 delivered in Edinburgh University), London: MacMillan and Co., 1933.

Gershevitz, Ilya, 'Die Sonne das Beste,' in John Hinnells, ed. *Mithraic Studies: Proceedings of the First International Congress of Mithraic Studies*, vol. I, 68–89.

Goodman, Martin, ed., *Jews in a Graeco-Roman World*, Oxford: Clarendon Press, 1998.

———, *State and Society in Roman Galilee, A.D. 132–212*, Totowa, NJ: Rowman & Allanheld, 1983.

Gordon, R.L., 'Cumont and the Doctrine of Mithraism,' in John Hinnells, ed. *Mithraic Studies: Proceedings of the First International Congress of Mithraic Studies*, vol. I, 215–248.

Gordon, Richard, *From Republic to Principate: Priesthood, Religion, and Ideology,'* in Mary Beard and John North, eds., *Pagan Priests: Religion and Power in the Ancient World*, Ithaca: Cornell Univ. Press, 1990, 199–232.

Gruber, Meyer, 'Akkadian *labān appi* in the Light of Art and Literature, *JANES* 7 (1975), 73–83.

Halsberghe, G.H., 'Le culte de Deus Sol Invictus à Rome au 3e siècle après J.C.,' in *ANRW*, II/1.4.

Hinnells, John R., ed. *Mithraic Studies: Proceedings of the First International Congress of Mithraic Studies* (2 vols.), Manchester: Manchester Univ. Press, 1975.

———, *Studies in Mithraism: Papers associated with the Mithraic Panel organized on the occasion of the XVIth Congress of the International Association for the History of Religion*, Rome 1990, Rome: L'erma di Bertschneider, 1994.

Kohut, Alexander, Über die jüdische Angelologie und Dämonologie in ihrer Abhängigkeit vom Parsismus, *Abhandlungen der Deutschen Morganländischen Gesellschaft*, IV/3, Leipzig, 1866, repr. Nendeln, Liechtenstein: Kraus Reprint, 1966.

Kraus, Samuel, *Paras ve-Romi ba-Talmud uva-Midrashim*, Jerusalem: Mosad Harav Kook, 5708.

Lavagne, H., 'Importance de la grotte dans le Mithriacisme en Occident, in J. Duchesne-Guillemin, *Études Mithriaques: Actes du 2e Congrès International, Téhéran, du 1er au 8 September 1975* (Acta Iranica 17), First Series (Actes de Congrès).

Levy, Jacob, *Wörterbuch uber die Talmudim und Midraschim*, Berlin and Vienna, 1924, repr. Darmstadt: Wissenschaftliche Buchgeselleschaft, 1963.

Lieberman, Saul, *Tosefta Nashim*, vol. II, New York: Jewish Theological Seminary, 1973.

Liebeschuetz, J.H.W.G., *Continuity and Change in Roman Religion*, Oxford: Clarendon Press, 1969.

Lommel, A. Herman, 'Die Sonne das Schlechste?,' *Oriens* 15 (1962), 360–373.

MacMullen, Ramsay, *Paganism in the Roman Empire*, New Haven: Yale Univ. Press, 1981.

Malandra, William M., *An Introduction to Ancient Iranian Religion: Readings from the Avesta and Achamenid Inscriptions* (Minnesota Publications in the Humanities, Volume Two), Minneapolis: Univ. of Minnesota Press, 1983.

Martin, Luther H., 'Reflections on the Mithraic Tauroctony as Cult Scene,' in John R. Hinnells, *Studies in Mithraism: Papers associated with the Mithraic Panel organized on the occasion of the XVIth Congress of the International Association for the History of Religion*, Rome 1990, 217–224.

Meherjirana, Erachji Sobbrabji, *A Guide to the Zoroastrian Religion: A Nineteenth Century*

Catechism with Modern Commentary (Studies in World Religions 3), ed. and trans. Firoze Kotwal and James W. Boyd.
Merkelbach, Reinhold, *Mithras*, Königstein/Ts.: Hain, 1984.
Millar, Fergus, *A Study of Cassius Dio*, Oxford: Clarendon Press, 1964.
Neubauer, A., *Géographie du talmud: Mémoire couronné par l'Accademie des inscriptionss et belles-lettres*, Paris: Michael Lévy, 1865.
Neusner, Jacob, *History of the Jews in Babylonia*, vol. III, Leiden: E.J. Brill, 1972.
Nigosian, S.A., *The Zoroastrian Faith: Tradition and Modern Research*, Montreal: McGill-Queen's Univ. Press, 1993.
North, C.R., 'The Religious Aspects of Hebrew Kingship,' *ZAW* 50 (1932).
Pietrzykowski, Michael, 'Die Religionspolitik des Kaisers Elagabal,' in *ANRW*, II/16.3.
Pines, Shlomo, 'Wrath and Creatures of Wrath in Pahlavi, Jewish and New Testament Sources,' *Irano-Judaica: Studies Relating to Jewish Contacts with Persian Culture throughout the Ages*, ed. Shaul Shaked, Jerusalem: Makhon Ben-Zvi, 1982, 76–82.
Price, S.R.F., *Rituals and Power: The Roman imperial cult in Asia Minor*, Cambridge: Cambridge Univ. Press, 1987.
Robert, L. 'Une vision de Perpetue martyre à Carthage en 203,' *Comptes Rendus de l'Academie des Inscriptions et Belles-Lettres* (1982), 228–276.
Ryberg, Inez Scott, *Rites of the State Religion in Roman Art* (Memoirs of the American Academy in Rome, vol. XXII), Rome: American Academy in Rome, 1955.
Scullard, H.H., *Festivals and Ceremonies of the Roman Republic* (Aspects of Greek and Roman Life), Ithaca: Cornell Univ. Press, 1981.
Shaked, Shaul, 'Bagdana: King of the Demons, and Other Iranian Terms in Babylonian Mramaic Magic,' *Papers in Honor of Professor Mary Boyce* (Homages et Opera Minora, X), Leiden: E.J. Brill, 1985.
———, 'The Zoroastrian Demon of Wrath,' in Christoph Elsas, et al., *Tradition und Translation: Zum Problem der interkulturellen Übersetzbarkeit religiöser Phänomene*, Festschrift für Carsten Colpe zum 65. Geburtstag, 285–291.
Showalter, Daniel N., *The Emperor and the Gods: Images from the Time of Trajan*, Minneapolis: Fortress Press, 1993.
Stern, Sacha, 'Dissonance and Misunderstanding in Jewish-Roman Relations,' in Martin Goodman, ed., *Jews in a Graeco-Roman World*.
Teixidor, Javier, *The Pantheon of Palmyra*, Leiden: E.J. Brill, 1979.
Turcan, Robert, *Mithra et la Mithriacisme*, Paris: Le Belles Lettres, 1993.
———, *The Cults of the Roman Empire*, Oxford: Blackwell, 1996.
Ulansey, David, *The Origin of the Mithraic Mysteries: Cosmology and Salvation in the Ancient World*, Oxford: Oxford Univ. Press, 1989.
Vanggaard, *The Flamen: A Study in the History and Sociology of Roman Religion*, Copenhagen: Museum Tusculanum Press, 1998.
Wardman, Alan, *Religion and Statecraft Among the Romans*, Baltimore: Johns Hopkins Univ. Press, 1982.
Weiss, Avraham, *He'arot le-Sugyot ha-Shas ha-Bavli veha-Yerushalmi*, Ramat Gan: Bar Ilan University, n.d.
Williams Jackson, A.V., *Zoroastrian Studies: The Iranian Religion and Various Monographs* (Columbia University Indo-Iranian Studies 2), New York: Columbia Univ. Press, 1928, repr. New York: AMS Press, Inc. 1965.
Wittfogel, Karl A., *Oriental Despotism: A Comparative Study of Total Power*, New Haven: Yale Univ. Press, 1957.
Yaavetz, Zvi, *Qesar ve-Qesarim: Massot be-Historia Romanit*, Tel Aviv: Hakibbutz Hameuhad, 1971.
Yarshater, Ehsan, ed., *Cambridge History of Iran*, vol. 3(2), *The Seleucid, Parthian and Sasanian Period*, Cambridge: Cambridge Univ. Press, 1983.

Zaehner, Robert C. *The Dawn and Twilight of Zoroastrianism*, London: Weidenfield and Nicolson, 1961.
———, *Zurvanism: A Zoroastrian Dilemma*, Oxford: Oxford Univ. Press, 1955.
Ziegler, Ignaz, *Königsgleichnisse des Midrasch beleuchtet durch die römische Kaiserzeit*, Breslau: Schlesische Verlag-Anhalf v. S. Schottenlaender, 1903.

THE MEANING OF 'FISCI IUDAICI CALUMNIA SUBLATA' ON THE COINAGE OF NERVA

MARTIN GOODMAN

Between the accession of Nerva in September 96 C.E. and the summer of 97 C.E. the mint in Rome issued a set of distinctive *aes* coins which advertised FISCI IUDAICI CALUMNIA SUBLATA.[1] The coins were produced in two separate issues in 96 C.E., in mid autumn and in December, with a third issue in the first half of 97 C.E.[2] The new emperor evidently intended to impress a wide audience in the city by the changes to the special Jewish tax thus proclaimed, much as he intended to impress by announcing on coins in 97 C.E. PLEBEI URBANAE FRUMENTO CONSTITUTO and ANNONA AUGUST (about the provision of corn to the urban plebs) or VEHICULATIONE ITALIAE REMISSA (the waiving of transport obligations for inhabitants of Italy).[3] These coins have been taken by many scholars as particularly significant evidence of the evolving relationship in the imperial period both between the Roman state and the Jews and, more specifically, between the Roman state and gentiles attracted to Judaism.[4] It thus seems appropriate to dedicate a study on this topic to Louis Feldman, who for many years has contributed so much on these subjects.[5]

The problem to be tackled in this paper is the precise meaning of the Latin legend on the coins. The fact that the Latin formula is unusual and hard to interpret has not been observed as widely as might be expected, primarily because scholars have tended to impose a meaning on the words to make them conform to what they already

---

[1] H. Mattingly and E.A. Sydenham, *The Roman Imperial Coinage* II (1926), 227 (no. 58), 228 (no. 82). I am very grateful to a number of colleagues for their help and advice on the issues raised in this paper, in particular Chris Howgego, Philip Hardie and Fergus Millar. All remaining errors are entirely my responsibility.

[2] D.C.A. Shotter, 'The principate of Nerva: some observations on the coin evidence', *Historia* 32 (1983), 218.

[3] Shotter, 'The principate of Nerva', 218, 222–3.

[4] E.g. P. Schäfer, *Judeophobia: attitudes towards the Jews in the Ancient World* (1997), 133–16.

[5] L.H. Feldman, *Jew and Gentile in the Ancient World* (1993).

expected in the light of other texts, most importantly Suetonius, *Dom.* 12.2, which refers to abuses in the collection of the tax in the time of Domitian,[6] and Cassius Dio, *Hist. Rom.* 68.1.2, which states that under Nerva 'no persons were permitted to accuse anybody of *maiestas* or of a Jewish way of life'.[7]

As will be seen below, the traditional readings of the formula are not impossible, but they require somewhat tortuous construing of the Latin, and occasionally also some odd assumptions. So, for instance, it might be thought just as likely that the linking by Dio of Nerva's prevention of accusations of living a Jewish way of life to accusations of *maiestas* referred to the kind of charge which led to the execution of the consul Flavius Clemens in 93 C.E. (Cassius Dio, *Hist. Rom.* 67.14.1) as to accusations of evasion of an annual tax of two denarii by Jews or Judaizing gentiles.

In any case, the reading of one text in the light of another must always be done with caution. The haphazard survival of evidence from the ancient world permits only occasionally for direct links to be made between the evidence of one source and that of another. It may therefore be preferable to examine the coin issues in their own right without prejudging their historical context and import.

The coins are large bronze sesterces, depicting on the obverse the head of Nerva and his titles and on the reverse the palm tree characteristically used by the Roman state to depict the province of Judaea[8] in the same way as the state used other iconography to depict other provinces, such as Armenia.[9] The main legend, FISCI IUDAICI CALUMNIA SUBLATA, is written round the rim on the obverse, two words on each side of the coin. The initials S C, standard in imperial base metal coinage, are found in larger letter forms, with one letter on each side of the palm tree.

Contemporaries will have been expected to pick up the precise meaning of this imagery and wording without difficulty, in a simi-

---

[6] On the Suetonius passage, see M. Goodman, 'Nerva, the *Fiscus Judaicus* and Jewish Identity', *JRS* 79 (1989), 40–44, with opposing view in M. Griffin, 'The Flavians', in A.K. Bowman, P. Garnsey and D. Rathbone, eds., *The Cambridge Ancient History*, 2nd edn., vol. XI (Cambridge, 2000), 75.

[7] M. Stern, *Greek and Latin Authors on Jews and Judaism*, vol. II (1980), 385.

[8] For other examples, see Y. Meshorer, *A Treasury of Jewish Coins from the Persian Period to Bar Kokhba* (2001).

[9] For coins of Armenia with appropriate depiction, see H. Mattingly and E.A. Sydenham, *Roman Imperial Coinage*, I (1923), 63 (nos. 41 and 45): tiara, quiver and bow (under Augustus).

lar fashion to public appreciation of the messages of advertisements nowadays. In principle the messages proclaimed to Roman users of coins might be an action taken by the emperor, or a quality of the emperor or his entourage, or something about the current state of society, or even perhaps a wish for the future (such as, for instance, the coins celebrating the 'concord of the armies' at times of particular civil strain).[10] It is not at all impossible that those responsible for a coin design might intend to convey one message but the users of the coins might understand the design in quite a different way,[11] though this is perhaps unlikely in the case of coins issued only for a brief period in a single place. But in any case, those who commissioned a design and coin legend will always have meant to say *something*, even if it was banal, and it is therefore always reasonable for historians to try to discover what that message was.

It is particularly likely that FISCI IUDAICI CALUMNIA SUBLATA had a significant meaning because the components of the coin legend are not at all usual. No reference to *fiscus* or *calumnia* can be found on any other coin of the early imperial period, and the use of the verb *tollo*, of which *sublata* is the perfect passive participle used in an ablative absolute construction, is also unparalleled. In 1926 the numismatists Mattingly and Sydenham wrote: 'At first sight the legend on Nerva's coins suggests that the tax was abolished'. They decided not to adopt this interpretation, not as a result of further analysis of the coins themselves but because later documents (literary and epigraphic) showed that the tax was still being collected under later emperors.[12] The possibility of a temporary abolition of the tax, followed by its reinstatement (see below), does not seem to have come into their consideration. In what follows I shall suggest that their first instinct was probably correct, although the precise meaning of each of the four words in the coin legend is by no means wholly clear.

FISCI must refer not to the tax itself[13] but to the treasury or exchequer which dealt with the revenues or expenses of the emperor

---

[10] For examples of other such legends under Nerva, see the list in Shotter, 'The principate of Nerva', 217–18.

[11] See A.H.M. Jones, 'Numismatics and History', in R.A.G. Carson and C.H.V. Sutherland (eds.), *Essays in Roman Coinage presented to Harold Mattingly* (London, 1956), 13–33.

[12] Mattingly and Sydenham, *Roman Imperial Coinage*, II, 221.

[13] Contra C.T. Lewis and C. Short (eds.), *A Latin Dictionary* (1879), s.v. 'fiscus', giving meaning 'tax'.

in his official capacity.[14] Such a reference to the apparatus of government seems to be unique in early imperial coinage and is rather bizarre. It would be like a public statement on a postage stamp about one of the government ministries in a modern state. Something rather remarkable would have to be going on for such a reference to be made.

IUDAICI can mean either 'of the Jews' or 'of Judaea', so that *fiscus iudaicus* could mean either 'the exchequer dealing with Jewish affairs' or 'the exchequer dealing with money from Judaea'. It seems fairly certain that reference to a province would be a more natural reading (as in, for instance, *fiscus Asiaticus*, referring to the province of Asia), but in the city of Rome in the Flavian period the two notions could easily be amalgamated: money extracted from Jews throughout the empire as war reparations (Jos. *B.J.* 7. 218) would be collected into the same exchequer as managed the disbursement of booty from the province of Judaea for the remodelling of the monumental centre of the city to reflect the great victory of Vespasian and Titus.[15]

CALUMNIA is generally a legal term, referring to an act of bringing a false accusation or vexatious proceedings, but it can also have a non-legal, more general, sense of 'a false statement'.[16] At first sight, a legal meaning might seem the most appropriate for a coin issued by the state, but in fact there do not seem to be other cases of the use on coins of precise terminology from the law courts: on the contrary, a certain fuzziness is more characteristic, with reference, for instance, to abstract virtues of the emperor such as *liberalitas*.[17]

SUBLATA could in theory have a positive meaning ('elevate' or 'exalt'), but it is much more likely to refer to the lifting or removal of the *calumnia* in question. Such a term is not at all standard in references on coins to administrative change. The closest terminology may be the use of *abolita* on coins of Hadrian advertising remission of debts (presumably to the state).[18] More common in references

---

[14] See P.G.W. Glare (ed.), *Oxford Latin Dictionary* (1968–82), s.v. 'fiscus'.

[15] M. Goodman, *The Ruling Class of Judaea* (1987), 236. See now F. Millar, 'Monuments of the Jewish War in Rome', in J. Edmondson, S. Mason and J. Rives (eds), *Flavius Josephus and Flavian Rome* (Oxford, 2005, 101–128).

[16] *Oxford Latin Dictionary*, s.v. 'calumnia'.

[17] C.F. Norena, 'The communication of the emperor's virtues', *JRS* 91 (2001), 146–68.

[18] Mattingly and Sydenham, *Roman Imperial Coinage* II, 416 (no. 590): the coin

under Nerva and earlier emperors to changes in the tax regime was *remissa* or *remisso*.[19]

Uncertainty about the meaning of the individual terms is exacerbated by uncertainty about the significance of the genitive case of FISCI IUDAICI. That *calumnia* of some kind has been removed or destroyed is certainly the implication of the ablative absolute, but the relationship of the *calumnia* to the *fiscus iudaicus* is less clear: it could be *calumnia* 'brought to' or 'brought by' the *fiscus iudaicus*.

As a result of these ambiguities, a variety of meanings is possible for the coin legend as a whole. The following four are only the most plausible, or those which have been adopted (explicitly or implicitly) by historians over the years.

A. '[A specific case in which] a false accusation was brought to the treasury for Jewish affairs has been struck out.'
In favour of this meaning, the use of the technical legal sense of *calumnia* would fit well into the atmosphere at the start of Nerva's rule, when a series of attacks was launched by senators against those of their colleagues who were seen as having used the legal system under the previous corrupt regime in order to further their own political careers (cf. Dio 68.1.2: 'many informers were condemned to death'). Against this meaning, however, it is hard to see what cause célèbre could have evoked such a unique response by the new regime specifically in relation to the *fiscus iudaicus*, except perhaps the condemnation in 93 C.E. of the consul Flavius Clemens for 'drifting into Jewish ways' (Cassius Dio 67.14.2). As described in the surviving epitome of Dio's history, the case of Flavius Clemens did not involve the *fiscus iudaicus* in any way, but it is not impossible that the property of a senator condemned on this particular charge would have been forfeited to the treasury for Jewish affairs. On the other hand, it is hard to see why this injustice under Domitian should have received so much more publicity under the new regime than the rest of his reign of terror.

B. '[All bringing of] malicious accusation[s] to the treasury responsible for Jewish affairs has been brought to an end'.

---

types under Hadrian read RELIQUA VETERA HS. NOVIES MILL. ABOLITA. S.C., and depict a lictor standing, holding *fasces*, next to a heap of papers on fire.

[19] Mattingly and Sydenham, *Roman Imperial Coinage*, I, p. 236 (under Galba).

This interpretation is closest to the standard way these coins have been understood by historians, as advertising the cessation of abuses in the collection of the tax on Jews, and, in particular, the prevention of informers who tried unjustly to accuse non-Jews of Jewish practices and thereby render them liable to the tax. The main difficulty with this interpretation (in my view, a problem serious enough to render the standard view implausible) is the use of the singular *calumnia* rather than the plural *calumniis*, and the choice of *sublata* to describe not something which has existed in the past and has now been destroyed but a future state in which malicious accusations will not exist.

C. 'A [specific case in which] a false accusation was brought *by* the treasury for Jewish affairs has been struck out'.[20]

If this meaning, in which the genitive is taken to imply 'by' is correct, responsibility for a grave misdemeanour in the past will be said to lie not at the door of individual informers but at the door of the *fiscus* itself: it will imply that under Domitian the exchequer for Jewish affairs committed some notoriously unjust act which was then overturned by Nerva. This would fit well the description by Suetonius (*Domitian* 12.2) that under Domitian '*iudaicus fiscus acerbissime actus est*', which should mean 'the treasury for Jewish affairs was administered most severely'.[21]

The emperor boasting on a coin about a single act of munificence would not be unusual,[22] but such a prolonged proclamation of apology for maladministration by a government department would be extraordinary. Furthermore, it would be most odd, if the case celebrated by the coins was so well known, for Suetonius to have chosen to refer in his discussion of the collection of the Jewish tax under Domitian (*Dom.* 12.2) not to this infamous case but to a personal anecdote about an event he had witnessed in his youth, when an anonymous man aged ninety was examined before a court to see if he was circumcised.

D. 'The false accusation [against all Jews made by] the treasury for Jewish affairs has been wiped away'.

---

[20] This meaning was suggested to me by Michael Winterbottom.

[21] Not as in the Loeb translation by J.C. Rolfe: 'Besides other taxes, that on the Jews was levied with the utmost vigour'.

[22] E.g. Mattingly and Sydenham, *Roman Imperial Coinage* II, 195 (no. 323): coin of Domitian advertising ANNON.AUG.S.C

This interpretation depends on taking the genitive as subjective, meaning 'made by' or 'brought by', and on assuming an implied expansion of the whole concise slogan to mean something like: 'The false accusation [against Jews of disloyalty to the Roman state] brought by the treasury for Jewish affairs has been wiped away'. The whole process of collection of two denarii from each Jew by the *fiscus*, which implied that all Jews after 70 C.E. were by definition opposed to Rome and required to pay reparations for the Judaean revolt even if, like most of the diaspora communities, they had played no part in the war of 66–70 C.E., is here described as the product of a falsehood. The coins will therefore have advertised the abolition of that process.

As I have already indicated, I find this interpretation of the coin slogan attractive, even though it is not entirely without problems: most obvious, if the coins proclaimed the abolition of the specific tax collected by the *fiscus iudaicus*, why did they not state this directly? One possible simple explanation may have been that there does not seem to have been a single noun in Latin to refer to the tax, equivalent to *didrachmon* in Greek (cf. Cassius Dio 66.7.2), so that the tax could have been described as abolished rather than the *calumnia* brought by the special treasury.

It might also be objected that the new emperor could hardly proclaim as a *calumnia* the collection of a tax which had been inaugurated not by the acknowledged tyrant, Domitian, but by a predecessor, Vespasian, who was officially recognised as divine. With hindsight it is indeed clear that the condemnation of Domitian was not at all carried over into hostility to the older Flavians, to whom too many of the governing class too patently owed their political advancement, but in the autumn of 96 C.E. matters may have been less clear-cut: in the early months of his principate, Nerva's coins emphasised his link not with the 'good' Flavians, whom he ignored, but with the Julio-Claudians, and especially Augustus.[23] In the highly-charged atmosphere of September 96 C.E., when the monuments of Domitian were being ostentatiously and violently destroyed,[24] only a brave (or foolish) inhabitant of Rome would have objected to the abolition of

---

[23] Mattingly and Sydenham, *Roman Imperial Coinage*, II, 232–3, nos. 126–37; cf. Griffin, 'Flavians', 85.

[24] Griffin, 'Flavians', 86.

a tax favoured by Domitian on the grounds that its original inspiration had been not Domitian himself but his revered father.

To recapitulate the possibilities: the coins may have been intended to advertise the end of some type of abuse of the legal system through which either one individual in a notorious case or many in many cases might be reported unfairly to the treasury for Jewish affairs and compelled to pay money to the treasury against their wills; or the coins may proclaim the end of a practice under which one or more individuals may have been subjected to maladministration by the treasury itself; or, most convincingly in my view, the coins may advertise a decision by the emperor to do away with the hated Jewish tax altogether. Each of these interpretations raises some difficulty for construing the Latin of the slogan so as to make historical sense while obeying the rules of Latin grammar. This will have mattered less at the time than it does for historians now, since contemporaries will have picked up meaning from a context, which they knew but at which we can only guess.

In practice the precise meaning of the words may have mattered less than might be assumed, since, even if the formal reform was only to claim the preventing of specific false accusations, this could only be so conclusively achieved (c.f. the resounding term *sublata*) by terminating the whole procedure, which had been abused. So long as a law existed under which Jews were required to pay a certain tax, it was inevitable that there would be a question as to who should pay the tax and who was trying to evade payment. Under the Roman system, which relied on private initiative for prosecutions to be brought, malicious accusations of any kind were always possible so long as accusations were possible, and so long as there was a tax to administer there was always a danger of maladministration.[25]

If the suggestion is accepted that the special two-denarii tax collected by the *fiscus iudaicus* was abolished for a while at the start of Nerva's rule, the historical implications would be considerable. I have argued elsewhere that Nerva's initial policy reversing the anti-Jewish policy of the Flavians was abruptly halted in autumn 97 C.E. when, under pressure from the praetorians, he adopted Trajan, whose father, Traianus *pater*, had made his name and established his career along-

---

[25] I owe this observation to Alex Yakobson and Hannah Cotton.

side Titus in the Judaean war.²⁶ The optimism of Jews in late 96 C.E. will have been much enhanced if all signs of the uniquely hostile discrimination of the past twenty six years had been swept away with the ending of the special Jewish tax.²⁷ The ensuing disappointment, as the tax was reimposed at the latest by mid 98 C.E.,²⁸ will have been proportionately bitter and its effects dire.²⁹

---

²⁶ M. Goodman, 'Trajan and the origins of the Bar Kochba War', in P. Schäfer, ed., *The Bar Kochba War Reconsidered* (2003), 23–29.
²⁷ On this as the date for the composition of Josephus' last work, *Contra Apionem*, see M. Goodman, 'Josephus, *Against Apionem*', in M. Edwards, M. Goodman and S. Price, eds. *Apologetics in the Roman Empire: Pagans, Jews and Christians* (1999), 45–58.
²⁸ See V.A. Tcherikover, A. Fuks and M. Stern, *Corpus Papyrorum Judaicarum* vol. II (1960), 194: ostracon receipt dated to 28 June, 98 C.E.
²⁹ It may be worth stating explicitly at the end of this article that if the suggestion presented here is correct, the hypothesis which I put forward in *JRS* 79 (1989), 40–44, that Nerva's coins advertised a reform in the way individuals were defined by the state as liable to the Jewish tax, will be wrong. There is no doubt that at least by the time of Cassius Dio in the early third century the tax was levied from those Jews who still observed their ancestral customs (cf. Dio 66.7.2), and probably only from them, and the disapproval of practices under Domitian to be found in the writings of Suetonius in the 120s suggests that such practices had ended by his time (*Dom.* 12.2); but reform towards defining Jewish identity by religious practice may have been more gradual than I implied in 1989.

THE ABUSE AND MISUSE OF JOSEPHUS IN EUSEBIUS' *ECCLESIASTICAL HISTORY*, BOOKS 2 AND 3[1]

Gohei Hata

The history of Christianity in the western world seems to have been a history of the abuse and misuse of the Bible. Likewise, the reception history of Josephus in the western world seems to have been a history of the abuse and misuse of Josephus. This is at least true of Eusebius of the fourth century. In his *Ecclesiastical History*, Eusebius abused and misused Josephus to express his anti-Jewish message, which seems to have paved a way for Christian anti-Judaism in subsequent generations.

The gist of Eusebius's anti-Jewish message in his *Ecclesiastical History* is as follows:

(1) Jews put the Saviour on the cross.
(2) This is the crime against Christ.
(3) The Jewish people, to whom the above-mentioned Jews belong, must be accused as a race.
(4) The penalty of God pursued the Jewish people for their crimes against Christ.
(5) At the same time, God postponed his decisive punishment upon the Jewish people until the year 70 in an attempt to give them an opportunity for repentance.

---

[1] The sections I and II in this paper are partly based on the lecture which I gave on 2 November, 1999, at the Tuesday seminar on Jewish History and Literature in the Greco-Roman world at Wolfson College, Oxford. I am very grateful to Prof. Martin Goodman for giving me this opportunity. I am also grateful to Profs. Averil Cameron and Sebastian Brock who attended the lecture and gave me some useful comments.
I want to express my thanks to the following four works which gave me an insight into the reception history of Josephus and the abuse and misuse of Josephus by Eusebius: (1) Heinz Schreckenberg, *Die Flavius-Josephus-Tradition in Antike und Mittelalter* (Leiden: E.J. Brill, 1972): (2) Michael E. Hardwick, *Josephus as an Historical Source in Patristic Literature through Eusebius* (Atlanta, Georgia: Scholars Press, 1989); (3) Heinz Schreckenberg and Kurt Schubert, *Jewish Historiography and Iconography in Early and Medieval Christianity* (Assen/Maastricht: Van Gorcum; Minneapolis: Fortress Press, 1992); and (4) Steve Mason, *Josephus and the New Testament* (Peabody, Massachusetts: Hendrickson Publishers, 1992), especially Chapter 1 (The Use and Abuse of Josephus).

(6) However, the Jewish people did not repent. Therefore, God punished them by destroying both Jerusalem and the Temple in the year 70.

The works of Josephus are utilized in the form of citation in the above (4), (5), and (6). We will see how Eusebius used Josephus in his *Ecclesiastical History*, Books 2 and 3.[2]

I

The second book of the *Ecclesiastical History* starts with descriptions of the missionary activities of the apostles after the ascension of Christ. On the basis of Acts and some other sources, Eusebius narrates how the gospel spread all over the world, though it didn't reach Japan until the seventeenth century. In the process of this narrative, the pogrom that befell the Alexandrian Jews in 37 C.E. at the time of Gaius Caligula plays an important role for Eusebius's theological purpose. He refers to Philo, an Alexandrian philosopher and quotes a long passage from the *Antiquities* 18.257–60. Then, after making a short remark that 'I shall pass over the greater part and cite only those points which plainly demonstrate to students the misfortunes which came upon the Jews, all at once and after a short time, in consequence of their crimes against Christ' (2.5.6), Eusebius, on the authority of Philo, states that Sejanus in Rome in the time of Tiberius took relentless measures to destroy the 'whole nation' of the Jews and in Judaea Pilate, 'under whom the crime against the Saviour' was perpetrated, made an attempt on the Temple, contrary to the privileges granted to the Jews, and harassed them to the utmost' (2.5.7). Eusebius then changes the flow of the narrative and returns

---

[2] According to Lawlor and Oulton in their *Eusebius: Ecclesiastical History*, vol. 2 (London: SPCK, 1928) 19, 'in the *History* we find nearly 250 passages transcribed from early sources.... In addition to these there are 90 or 100 indirect quotations or summaries...' In the first three books of the *History*, 16 passages from the *War*, 13 passages from the *Antiquities*, one passage from *Against Apion* and one passage from *Vita* are cited. This means that more than 12 percent of 250 passages cited in the entire *History* is from the works of Josephus. Thus, we may rightly point out that citations from Josephus in the *History* are overwhelming. However, in this paper, citations from Josephus in the first book of the *History* will not be discussed because they are not related to the anti-Jewish message of Eusebius. Quotations from the *History* are from *Eusebius* in the Loeb Classical Library and quotations from Josephus are also from *Josephus* in the same library.

to the Alexandrian pogrom. Eusebius is here surprisingly skilful in the construction of his narrative for his specific purpose. As is clear from his remark placed in the beginning of this narrative, in an attempt to give an impression to his readers that God punished the Jews swiftly because of their crimes against Christ or their crimes against the Saviour, Eusebius refers to the Alexandrian pogrom of 37 C.E. as if it had taken place soon after the death of Christ, and, before quoting Philo's report on this pogrom, Eusebius adds the following preface to it: 'after the death of Tiberius, Gaius... inflicted many injuries on many, but more than all did the greatest harm to the whole nation of the Jews' (2.6.1). Eusebius's theology of punishment is now playing its greatest role here. The scope of the harm the local Jews, that is Alexandrian Jews, suffered is now expanded to the size of the whole nation of the Jews and the number of misfortunes of the local Jews, that is Alexandrian Jews, suffered is likewise expanded to the 'innumerable' number.

After quoting Philo, Eusebius narrates the commotion in Jerusalem caused by Pilate when he attempted to set up the images of Caesar in the Temple. Eusebius's story is based on the *War* 2.169–170 and 2.175–177. Since Pilate was the Roman governor at the time when Jesus was crucified, the readers of Eusebius are bound to believe that the Alexandrian pogrom of 37 C.E. is without doubt one of the 'innumerable' misfortunes which fell on the Jews soon after the death of Christ. Eusebius concludes the narrative about Pilate by saying: 'the same writer [*i.e.* Josephus] shows that besides this, innumerable other revolts were started in Jerusalem itself, affirming that from that time risings and war and the mutual contrivance of evil never ceased in the city and throughout Judaea, until the time when the siege under Vespasian came upon them as the last scene of all. Thus the penalty of God pursued the Jews for their crimes against God' (2.6.8). Despite the statement of Eusebius, the fact is that Josephus does not report in his narratives 'innumerable' commotions in the city and throughout Judaea. This exaggeration is on the same level with the preceding one. The repetition of exaggeration may add a touch of truthfulness to Eusebius's statement. Here we should pay special attention to such phrases as 'the penalty of God pursues without delay.' This expression, and these kinds of expressions are repeatedly used hereafter (*War* 2.7.1, 2.10.1, 3.5.4, 3.5.6, 3.5.7). When ancient writers say in their narratives that the penalty of God fell on some nation or some city, we understand that their statements suggest nothing more than the 'once-ness' of an event, but when they say that the penalty of God pursued, we understand that their statements intend to create the continuity of the event. We also know that if an adverb or an adverbial phrase such as 'without delay' or 'promptly' is inserted after the verb 'pursue' in the narrative of the punishment of God, that inserted adverb or adverbial phrase will certainly heighten the tension between the event and any possible audience of the narrative. And the repeated use of the phrases such as 'the penalty of God pursued' also gives an impression to his audience that the whole nation of the Jews is destined to destruction.

Acts 12.21–3 reports on the sudden death in Caesarea of Agrippa I who is referred to as 'Herod the King.' This Herod was involved in the killing of James, the brother of John, and the imprisonment of Peter (Acts 12.1–4). After emphasizing the 'agreement' between Josephus's report on Herod, though this Herod seems to be Agrippa II, and the 'divine Scripture' (2.10.2), Eusebius quotes a long passage from the *Antiquities* 19.34–51. In quoting Josephus, however, Eusebius changes the owl perched on the head of Herod as a portent of death to the angel to make the description of Josephus agree with that of Acts 12.23. Although some critics are uncertain about the authenticity of the text, to us it is evident that the text is forgery. We should bear in mind that Eusebius is the kind of person who changes words or phrases in the text for his own theological purposes. He is not strict, but loose in his treatment of the sources. In a place where he concludes this narrative, after emphasizing an agreement between Josephus and the divine Scripture by stating that 'I am surprised how in this and other points Josephus confirms the truth of the divine Scripture' (2.10.10), Eusebius, as a further proof of agreement between the two, refers to the revolt of Theudas in Acts 5.36 and cites a passage from the *Antiquities* 20.97–98. Acts reports the words of Gamaliel that 'Theudas arose, saying that he was somebody', but it does not specify when he arose. According to the *Antiquities* 20.97, Theudas appeared when Fadus was the governor of Judaea, that is, somewhere between 44 C.E. and 45/46 C.E. As is clear from this instance, if the names of the two persons are identical in the two different sources, Eusebius naively regards those sources as referring to the same persons and as belonging to the same period. What is important for Eusebius is not the critical analysis of the two sources he uses, but the agreement that seems to exist at first sight between them. A serious famine took place in the time of Claudius (41–54 C.E.). So with a naïve belief that it 'agrees with' Acts (11.29–30), Eusebius quotes a passage from the *Antiquities* 20.101 about the purchase of corn and its distribution by Queen Helena of Adiabene (2.12.2).

Both the *War* 2.227 and the *Antiquities* 20.112 report on the commotion at the time of the feast of the Passover in Jerusalem, when Cumanus was the governor of Judaea (48–52 C.E.). Eusebius refers to this commotion as one of the incidents which occurred towards the end of the rule of Claudius (2.19.1), and by so doing he brings the description therein closer to the time of the emperor Nero (52–60 C.E.). He then refers to the narrative of the *Antiquities* 20.180–1 about the power struggle among the priests in Jerusalem when Felix was governor (52–60 C.E.) and the report in the *War* 2.254–6 about the Sicarii, a group of assassins, which appeared in Jerusalem in those days, and quotes a passage from the *War* 2.261–3 about a so-called false Egyptian prophet who appeared when Felix was governor. This passage about the Egyptian prophet who, according to Josephus, went into the wilderness with a group of 4,000 Sicarii, Eusebius juxtaposes with the passage in Acts 2.27–38. Eusebius then, by this juxtaposition, tries to imply that there is an agreement between the two sources. As we have already pointed out, an agreement between the two sources, no matter how superficial it may look, is a sure guarantee of historical accuracy for Eusebius or, should I say a blessing of God for Eusebius.

Eusebius claims (2.23.1ff.) that it was because of 'the crimes' of the Jews against James, the brother of the Lord, that Jerusalem was besieged by the Roman army. So, after citing a long passage about the death of James from the fifth book of Hegesippus's *Hypomunemata*, Eusebius emphasizes that the siege of Jerusalem took place 'soon' after his martyrdom. Eusebius first states: 'Of course, Josephus did not shrink from giving written testimony to this, as follows.' And then he says: 'And these things happened to the Jews to avenge James the Just, who was the brother of Jesus the so-called Christ, for the Jews killed him in spite of his great righteousness' (2.23.20). Although this passage is quoted in Origen's *Against Celsus* 1.47 as coming from Josephus, we cannot find it in the text of Josephus. We should also point out here that according to the *Antiquities* 20.197ff., James died around the year 62 C.E., that is, eight years before the actual siege of Jerusalem in 70 C.E. Eusebius also quotes a long passage from the *Antiquities* 20.197–203 by saying that 'the same write [*i.e.* Josephus] also narrates his death in the twentieth book of the *Antiquities*' (2.23.21).

Eusebius, toward the end of the second book of the *Ecclesiastical History*, narrates a situation into which the Jews were placed before the Jewish war. In doing so he summarizes Josephus' report in the *War* 2.306ff. and concludes his narrative by quoting a passage from the *War* 2.465. Before citing this passage, however, Eusebius makes the following comment: 'Josephus in the course of his extremely detailed description of the catastrophe which overcame the whole nation of Jews, in addition to many other things explains exactly how many thousand Jews of his rank in Jerusalem itself were outraged, scourged, and crucified by Florus...' (2.26.1–2). Here again, not only the phrase 'the whole nation of Jews', but also an exaggeration inherent in Eusebius's all-inclusive way of describing the crimes of the Jews must be pointed out. Firstly, since the population of Jerusalem at that time is said to have been somewhere between 50,000 and 100,000, according to modern archaeologists, such as M. Broshi[3] in Israel, and secondly, since, according to the *War* 2.307, the number of the citizens who were scourged and then crucified before Florus was evidently less than 'three thousand six hundred,' the statement that many thousand Jews of high rank were scourged is nothing more than an exaggeration of grotesque kind. The exaggeration of the figure makes a contribution in heightening the tragic element of the incident which fell on 'the whole nation of Jews.' In concluding the second book of the *Ecclesiastical History*, Eusebius cites a passage from the *War* 2.465. It says: 'Everywhere the Gentiles mercilessly attacked the Jews in the cities as though they were foes, so that the cities could be seen full of unburied bodies, thrown out dead, old men and children, and women without covering for their nakedness; the whole province was full of indescribable misery and the strain of the threats for the future was worse than the crimes of the present' (2.26.2). When Josephus says 'the strain of the threats for the future', he refers to the anti-Jewish attacks which occurred in Scythopolis, Ascalon, and Alexandria, but the quotation detached from the context can be a good prelude to the catastrophe which is to be told in the next book.

---

[3] Magen Broshi, 'La population de l'ancienne Jerusalem' in *Revue Biblique* 82 (1975) 5–14.

II

The third book of the *Ecclesiastical History* moves on to the narrative of the siege of Jerusalem by Titus. The descriptions of the siege are a highlight for the anti-Jewish theological purpose of Eusebius. He interprets the siege as the verdict of God upon the crimes of the whole race of the Jews. Thus, he declares: 'Now after the ascension of our Saviour in addition to their crime against him the Jews at once contrived numberless plots against his disciples' (3.5.2). After this declaration, as concrete examples Eusebius cites only three out of what he called 'numberless plots': They are the death of Stephen (Acts 7.58–60), the death of James, the son of Zebedee and brother of John (Acts 12.2), and the death of James, the brother of the Lord and the first bishop in Jerusalem. Eusebius then states without citing any examples that 'the other apostles were driven from the land of Judaea by thousands of deadly plots' (3.5.2). Although Eusebius emphasizes the countlessness of plots, there is no mention whatsoever either in Josephus or in Acts of what he wishes to call 'numberless plots.' Since the audience of Eusebius does not necessarily test the accuracy of each of his statements or remarks, it is quite safe for him to exaggerate here and there the number of the crimes or plots of the Jews. And the repetition of a simple slogan is most effective in giving an impression to his readers that the siege of Jerusalem in the year 70 was a sure result of the verdict of God upon the crimes of the Jews.

After exaggerating the number of plots, probably on the basis of Hegesippus, Eusebius narrates a story concerning a group of Christians in Jerusalem who fled to the land of Perea just before the Jewish war. In doing so, he makes the following comment: 'when holy men had altogether deserted the royal capital of the Jews and the whole land of Judaea, the judgement of God might at last overtake them for all their crimes against the Christ and his apostles, and all that generation of the wicked be utterly blotted out from among men' (3.5.3). No one knows whether those Christians who fled to Perea were 'holy men'—they might have been simply timid—but Eusebius defines them as such, perhaps in contradistinction with the 'generation of the wicked'.

As we have already seen, in the theology of Eusebius, the judgement of God began to chase after the Jews soon after they put Jesus on the cross. This personified judgement of God, like the avenging spirit or deity, is indeed a stalker. This stalker, which, according to the description of Nicolaus of Damascus in the *War* 1.596, drove Herod to his corner in his domestic troubles. Thus, this judgement of God chases after the Jews until it drives them to a corner.

In narrating the destruction of the Temple and Jerusalem in the year 70 C.E., Josephus becomes the only source for Eusebius. He mentions that 'those who wish can retrace accurately from the history written by Josephus how may evils at that time overwhelmed the whole nation in every place and especially how the inhabitants of Judaea were driven to the last point of suffering...' (3.5.4). He continues to state: 'But it is necessary to point out how the same writer [*i.e.* Josephus] estimates at three millions the number of those who in the days of the Feast of the Passover thronged Jerusalem from all Judaea and, to use his words, were shut up as in prison. It was indeed right that on the same day on which they had perpetrated the passion of the Saviour and benefactor of all men and the Christ of God they should be, as it were, shut up in prison and receive the destruction which pursued them from the sentence of God' (3.5.5–6).

Eusebius is evidently saying this on the basis of the *War* 6.423–8. Comparison with the actual words of Josephus, however, immediately reveals the purpose of Eusebius in using Josephus here. In the *War*, Josephus refers to the number of casualties from the start of the war to the end of war. According to him, the number of those who were captured is ninety-seven thousand and the number of those who were killed or died during the siege is one million and one hundred thousand. The number of casualties Josephus gives here is of course nothing more than an exaggeration to please Vespasian and Titus, his Roman patrons, but Eusebius here is fabricating the number for his own purpose. To do justice, Josephus is here responsible because it is his exaggeration that has helped Eusebius' fabrication for his theological vandalism. By stating that the three million Jews who thronged Jerusalem were shut up and killed at the Feast of Passover, that is, at the time of the Passion of Christ, Eusebius is successful in creating the impression that God rightly punished the whole Jewish nation.

Josephus states in the *War* 6.435 that Jerusalem fell to the Romans 'in the second year of the reign of Vespasian, on the eighth day of Gorpiaios'. According to the calculation of Benedictus Niese who established the Greek text of Josephus in the 19th century, that day was 26 September in the year 70. The incident, which Josephus refers to with the above-mentioned exaggerated figure, is the one which occurred just before the fall of Jerusalem, not in the week of the Passion of Christ. As H. Schreckenberg has rightly pointed out,[4] we can see here the arbitrary use of the source by Eusebius.

Although he omits the details of the misfortunes which overcame the Jews, Eusebius states that he [*i.e.* Josephus] 'adduces only their sufferings from famine in order those who study this work may have some partial knowledge of how the punishment of God followed close after them for their crimes against the Christ of God' (3.5.7) and then he cites four long passages from the *War* (5.424–5, 5.512–9, 5.566, 6.193–213). Although we cannot go into the details of these four passages, we may point out here that in a story of Mary who roasted and devoured her son during the famine (*War* 6.193–213), there is a possibility that Eusebius changed the Greek name of Mariamme (Hebrew name Miriam) found in the original text into Mary (Greek name Maria) in an attempt to demonstrate to his readers that the Christian Mary, the mother of Jesus, was a benevolent woman while the Jewish Mary was an evil woman. Eusebius concludes this series of quotations with a remark that 'such was a reward of the iniquity of the Jews and of their impiety against the Christ of God' (3.7.1). He then says: 'it is worth appending to it the infallible forecast of our Saviour in which he prophetically expounded these very things' (3.7.1) and quotes a passage of Matthew 24.19–21. According to the report of Josephus which Eusebius cites, the number of those who were destroyed by famine and the sword during the Jewish war was one million and one hundred thousand (War 6.420). Eusebius also cites a passage from the *War* 6.420, which refers to the fate of those Jews who were taken to Rome for the victory parade of the Roman soldiers.

Eusebius then emphasizes that the prophecy of 'our Saviour' concerning the whole war does agree with the other narratives of Josephus, and he states that anyone who compares both cannot 'avoid surprise and a confession of the truly divine and supernaturally wonderful character both of the foreknowledge and of the foretelling of our Saviour' (3.7.6). And finally Eusebius says, as if he were making a recollection of the misfortunes which overtook the Jews, that

---

[4] Heinz Schreckenberg, *Jewish Historiography and Iconography in Early and Medieval Christianity*, 69.

'there is no necessity to add to the narratives of what happened to the whole nation after the passion of the Saviour' (3.7.7). He then goes on to claim that 'for forty whole years it [*i.e.* God's mercy] suspended their destruction, after their crime against the Christ, and during all of them many of the apostles and disciples, and James himself, who is called the Lord's brother, the first bishop of the city, still survived in this world. By their dwelling in Jerusalem, they afforded, as it were, a strong protection to the place: for the government of God had still patience, if haply they might at last by repenting of their deeds, be able to obtain pardon and salvation: and in addition to such great long-suffering it sent wonderful tokens from God of what would happen to them if they did not repent. These things have been thought worthy of mention by the historian already quoted, and there is nothing better than to append them for the readers of this work' (3.7.8–9). After saying this, Eusebius quotes a long passage from the *War* 6.288–304 concerning the various portents which, according to Josephus, were seen in the last phase of the siege. According to Eusebius, the reason why the punishment of God did not fall upon the Jews immediately after the death of the Saviour was to give the Jews an opportunity for repentance (3.7.8). This is certainly a new interpretation of history, but this does not fit in the framework of his previous statements in which he kept quoting the instances which he thought overcame the Jews soon after the death of the Saviour. At this point, however, Eusebius's use of Josephus for his anti-Jewish message comes to an end.

III

Frequent citations of Josephus by Eusebius suggest that he felt sympathy or affinity with Josephus and that he could share with Josephus his understanding of God or his application of the concept of God to the actual history, especially in the interpretation of the sovereignty of the Roman empire.

The Greek word *theos* appears 192 times in the *War*, and in each instance it is used in the singular form. According to Josephus, this *theos* stays in the Temple of Jerusalem as long as both the Temple and Jerusalem are not polluted. Conversely, if the hands of Jews contaminate the Temple in Jerusalem, the *theos* moves out of it and stays away from it. The *theos*, with or without mobility, is also used to designate the God who governs the actual human history. It is this *theos* who has built up so vast an empire of the Romans (*War* 2.390, 5.367–8). It is this *theos* who has placed the sovereignty of the world in the hands of the Roman emperor (*War* 3.404, 5.2. Cf. 4.622). From this basic cognizance, the following understandings seem to be derived: (1) God or divine providence is on the side of the Roman army (*War* 3.484, 4.366, 5.378, and 6.38–40, 6.411. Cf. 2.390) and thus assists the Roman army in various ways during the war (*War* 3.293, 3.494, 4.104, 362, 366, 573, 5.39, 60, 343, 7.318–19), and; (2) God, who is already away from the Temple for its pollution (*War* 5.412–3, 6.127. Cf. 2.239), hopes to condemn Jerusalem to destruction and purge the Temple by fire (*War* 4.323, 6.110), and wishes the Jews to be delivered to the Romans (*War* 4.370). Besides this understanding of God in history, Josephus also shows his unique understanding of the fated day when he refers to the burning of the Temple. Here he tries to find some meaning in the coincidence between the tenth of the month Lous in the year 70 on which the Temple was burnt down and the same day of old on which the first Temple was burnt down by the king of Babylon, and interprets this coincidence as the 'fated day', that is, the day that God had long sentenced the Temple to the flames (*War* 6.250–1). According to Josephus, God sentenced the verdict not only on the fate of the Temple, but also on His whole people. Thus, in the mouth of Titus, Josephus says: '... but here God and no other had condemned His whole people and was turning every avenue of salvation to their destruction' (*War* 5.559. Cf. 7.327).

IV. Summing up

The salvation history in Christian theology regards the history of human kind as completed with the advent of Christ and his Second Coming. As long as that man called Jesus is regarded as Christ and as long as the Jewish people do not accept such a Christian faith, this understanding of history can be seen as anti-Jewish. What the *Ecclesiastical History* of Eusebius teaches us is what kind of an anti-Jewish stance this can become in practice. With this kind of interpretation of history, together with the repetition of oversimplified slogans such as 'crime against Christ' (2.5.6, 2.6.8, 3.7.8), 'crime against the Saviour' (2.5.7, 2.6.3), 'plots against the apostles' (2.10.1), 'plots against Paul' (2.23.1), 'crime against James, the brother of Jesus' (2.23.1, 2.23.19), 'crime against the Lord' (3.5.2), 'plots against the apostles of the Lord' (3.5.2), 'most lawless acts against Christ and his apostles' (3.5.3), 'lawless acts against the Christ of God' (3.5.7, 3.7.1), and the application of labels such as 'Lord-killers' to the Jewish nation, an impression will certainly be given to the audience of his work that the whole Jewish nation is indeed responsible for the death of the Saviour and therefore the Jews are doomed to destruction. This impression in turn creates grave anti-Jewish feelings or sentiments which certainly have paved a way for Christian anti-Judaism. To do justice, however, Josephus's understandings of God and his naïve application of the concept of God to the sovereignty of the Roman empire seem to be regrettably responsible for creating such a message. Yet, what is more regrettable is in the reception history of Eusebius because the *Ecclesiastical History*, which is far from anything that could be called a 'history' in the modern sense of the word, was regarded as a kind of an authoritative book on the history of the church in the Christian circles. No one, therefore, criticized Eusebius's abuse and misuse of Josephus, his way of descriptions, his way of forgering, his slogans, and his theological vandalism. Indeed, the subsequent ecclesiastical historians like Philostorgius of Constantinople (368–433), Socrates Scholasticus (380–450), Sozomen (376–447), and Theodoret (393–458) of Cyrrhus did start their narratives from the place where Eusebius had ended his narratives.

JUSTUS OF TIBERIAS AND THE SYNCHRONISTIC CHRONOLOGY OF ISRAEL

CHAIM MILIKOWSKY

Of the many Jewish authors who lived between Alexander the Great and the beginnings of rabbinic literature and whose works have been lost, Justus of Tiberias is to my mind the one whose works are the most sorely missed. Though he is best known today because of his (lost) history of the Jewish war against Rome and his concomitant dispute with Josephus about the course of that war, that perspective is a skewed one and simply derives from the fact that Josephus is our basic source for this entire period and thereby establishes the focal point for all of our discussions. Whether in his own day Justus was more known for this work or for other works we know he authored, a history of Israel from Moses to Agrippa and commentaries on Scripture, is of course impossible to determine.[1]

---

[1] The testimonia about and fragments of Justus were identified and collected by Felix Jacoby, *Die Fragmente der griechischen Historiker* (= FGrH), Part IIIC: Nos. 608a–856, II, Berlin 1958, No. 734, pp. 695–699. An overlapping but not identical identification and collection of the fragments, with English translation, was made by C.R. Holladay (ed. and transl.), *Fragments from Hellenistic Jewish Authors*, Vol. 1: *Historians*, Society of Biblical Literature Texts and Translations 20, Pseudepigrapha 10, Chico, California 1983, pp. 382–387. A generally excellent discussion of Justus, with bibliography, can be found in E. Schürer, *The History of the Jewish People in the Age of Jesus Christ*, revised and edited by G. Vermes, F. Millar and M. Goodman, 3 volumes in 4 parts, Edinburgh 1973–1987, Vol. 1, pp. 34–37, Vol. 3, Part 1, p. 546. Schürer doubts the veracity of Jerome's statement (in *de viris illustribus* 14) that Justus composed small commentaries on Scripture, 'since no other author knows anything of it' (p. 35). I am unconvinced by this argument: a moment's reflection should be sufficient to persuade us that there are extant no other authors who would necessarily be expected to know anything of it. The Judaeo-Greek cultural synthesis, which Justus exemplified and which is discussed below, seems to have come to its end—in Israel—soon after the time of Justus, and what has been preserved, transmitted, discovered, or excavated are the rabbinic writings and some reworked pseudepigraphal works. Jerome, of course, is that early Church Father who made a special effort to establish contact with Jewish teachers in order to facilitate his study of Holy Scripture, and so if one were to ask of which Church Fathers would it be the most plausible that he would know of a Judaeo-Greek commentary on the Bible written in Israel, Jerome is the obvious answer. Also F. Jacoby in Pauly-Wissowa's *Realencyclopädie*, s.v. Iustus (9), col. 1344, rejects Schürer's skepticism regarding the

In a seminal article published fifteen years ago, Moshe David Herr argued that Justus of Tiberias was the only Jew living in Israel who wrote original compositions in Greek.² Herr presents this claim in a consciously polemical context—countering the too-facilely accepted claim of Martin Hengel and others that the level of Greek acculturation of the Jews in Israel was similar to that of Jews in Alexandria, Rome and other capitals of the empire.³ Whether or not Herr is correct that Justus was so unique—and of course both possible responses are unverifiable and unrefutable—his emphasis upon Justus as a uncommon exemplum of the penetration of Hellenistic culture among the Jews living in Israel is surely accurate.

More recently, Gregory Sterling listed under the heading 'Graeco-Jewish Literature in Jerusalem' five original compositions.⁴ Regarding three of the five he himself notes that their attribution to Jerusalem is questionable, or even very questionable; regarding a fourth, what he calls the Alexander Romance (Josephus, *Antiquities* 11.304–5, 313–47), his sole reason for attributing it to a Jerusalem author is the fact that the high priest and the temple in Jerusalem are the focus of the story, a very dubious justification.⁵ Only with regard to the fifth, the history of Eupolemos composed, it seems, in the second century B.C.E., can a good case be made for the claim that the work was composed in Israel,⁶ and so Justus, if not an unicum, is close to being one.⁷

---

commentaries mentioned by Jerome. It should be noted that some scholars have claimed that Justus only composed one work of history (see Schürer and the discussion of Rajak below), but I do not think that position can stand.

² '*Hashpaʿot hizoniyyot be-olamam shel hakhamim be-ʾerez yisraʾel—qlitah ve-dehiyya*,' in *Hitbolelut ve-temiʾah: Hemshekhiyut u-temurah be-tarbut ha-ʿamim u-be-yisraʾel* (= *Acculturation and Assimilation: Continuity and Change in the Cultures of Israel and the Nations*), ed. Y. Kaplan and M. Stern, Jerusalem 1989, p. 84.

³ See his appendix, pp. 103–105, where he cites the extremely important, but unfortunately rarely cited, review of Martin Hengel's *Judentum und Hellismus* published by Menahem Stern in *Kiryat Sefer* 46 (1970–71), pp. 94–99 (republished in the posthumous collection of his essays *Mehkarim be-toldot yisraʾel bi-yemi ha-bayit ha-sheni* [= *Studies in Jewish History: The Second Temple Period*], ed. M. Amit, I. Gafni and M.D. Herr, Jerusalem 1991, pp. 578–586).

⁴ G.E. Sterling, 'Judaism between Jerusalem and Alexandria,' in *Hellenism in the Land of Israel*, ed. J.J. Collins and G.E. Sterling, Notre Dame 2001, pp. 263–301, at p. 279.

⁵ See what Sterling writes on pp. 271–272 and in note 55.

⁶ This is of course related to the question if Eupolemos the historian is the same as Eupolemos the Maccabean diplomat; see Herr, '*Hashpaʾot hizoniyyot*,' p. 103; B.Z. Wacholder, *Eupolemos: A Study of Judaeo-Greek Literature*, Cincinnati 1974, pp. 1–5.

⁷ Sterling does not mention Justus because he only lists extant compositions. True

Herr further suggests that Justus attained a broad Greek education only after he became the secretary of Agrippa II.[8] This to me seems implausible: does it not make more sense that Agrippa chose him as secretary because he already had an extensive Greek education, assuredly a sine qua non for the secretary of a petty monarch in the eastern Roman Empire? True Josephus tells us that he began his study of Greek only at a relatively advanced age, and also tells us that the education he received was the norm in Judea,[9] but it surely does not follow that no social groupings in Judea or Galilee educated their children in the classic Hellenistic mode.[10]

I suspect therefore that Justus should be seen as the representative of a not-insignificant number of Jews in first-century Israel who combined a passion for both Jewish and Greek learning. This attempt to synthesize two venerable cultural heritages seems to have petered out in the ensuing centuries, at least we have no evidence which indicates that it continued.[11]

Justus was from Tiberias, but Sterling does list Greek documents from the Dead Sea area. The extremely small number of compositions he lists which are definitively from Jerusalem renders his conclusion—'[o]ur overview of the evidence confirms Hengel's argument that Judea was hellenized' (p. 278)—very dubious. Were he working with an all-inclusive denotation of 'hellenism', which would include data of a linguistic and material nature, perhaps this conclusion could stand, but inasmuch as he specifically emphasizes cultural and educational contexts (p. 264), it would seem more accurate to conclude that though no doubt Judea was hellenized, the extent of hellenization was quite limited. The question of the interconnectivity of a specific society in the eastern Roman Empire, *i.e.* its use of the same language, utensils, material artifacts and designs as those used by its neighboring societies, should not be conflated with the question of the extent of cultural hellenization in that society.

[8] '*Hashpa'ot hizoniyyot*,' p. 84, note 5.

[9] *Antiquities* 20:263–5; upon which see my article 'Josephus Between Rabbinic Culture and Hellenistic Historiography,' *Shem in the Tents of Japhet: Judaism in Hellenistic Garb*, ed. J. Kugel, Supplements to the Journal for the Study of Judaism 74, Leiden 2002, pp. 159–161.

[10] On education in the Hellenistic world, see in addition to the classic and still very useful H.I. Marrou, *A History of Education in Antiquity*, translated by G. Lamb, Madison 1956, two monographs which have been published recently, T.J. Morgan, *Literate Education in the Hellenistic and Roman Worlds*, Cambridge 1998, and R. Cribiore, *Gymnastics of the Mind: Greek Education in Hellenistic and Roman Egypt*, Princeton 2001.

[11] If we accept, as I do, that elite rabbinic culture steadily became more dominant during these centuries, then the discontinuation of this attempt at synthesis should be attributed to the rabbinic disapproval, at best, or possibly rejection of Greek learning. The alternative narrative, which rejects any major influence of rabbinic culture upon the Jewish polity during the second and third centuries C.E.— a narrative ably presented by Seth Schwartz in his *Imperialism and Jewish Society, 200 B.C.E. to 640 C.E.*, Princeton 2001—would presumably suggest that works synthesizing the two cultures continued to be composed, but were lost, just as were lost

The history of Israel from Moses to Agrippa authored by Justus is just about completely unknown, indeed the very fact that he authored a history of non-contemporary Israel is mentioned only once, by Photius in *Bibliotheca* 33:

> A chronicle of Justus of Tiberias was read. It is entitled *On the Jewish Kings by means of Genealogical Tables*, by Justus of Tiberias. He came from Tiberias in Galilee, from which he took his name. He begins his history with Moses and carries it down to the death of Agrippa, the seventh of the house of Herod and the last of the Jewish kings.... It has a very concise style and passes by the majority of the most important events.[12]

This work of Justus is referred to by (partial) name one more time. The Greek words in Photius translated above as 'by means of Genealogical Tables' are ἐν τοῖς στέμμασιν, and Diogenes Laertius 2.41 refers to a story about the trial of Socrates reported by Justus of Tiberias ἐν τῷ στέμματι (in his Genealogical Table). The similarity in title leaves no doubt that Photius and Diogenes Laertius are referring to the same work.

As Tessa Rajak has noted, the very fact that a historian of the Jewish kings relates a story about the trial of Socrates is of the utmost importance;[13] presumably Justus has created a chronological context for relating together crucial events in Jewish history and in Greek history.[14]

Rajak attributes great importance to Photius's statement that Justus's history was very concise, and consequently has a serious difficulty with the citation from Diogenes Laertius, for surely it makes no sense to include such an anecdote about Socrates's trial in such a short work. Rajak therefore suggests as one possibility that the anecdote appeared in a preamble or as a rhetorical aside—which does not really resolve convincingly her objection. She prefers therefore her

---

the vast majority of works written in Jewish Alexandria, indeed as were lost all Judaeo-Greek works other than those preserved by the church.

[12] The Greek text is available in Jacoby (FGrH 734 T2); the translation is my own, having consulted the J.H. Freese translation of codices 1–165 (*The Library of Photius*, Vol. 1, London 1920), available online at http://www.ccel.org/p/pearse/morefathers/photius_03bibliotheca.htm, and Shaye Cohen's translation of this passage (S.J.D. Cohen, *Josephus in Galilee and Rome*, Columbia Studies in the Classical Tradition 8, Leiden 1979, p. 142). For a recent spirited defense of Photius, see N. Kikkonis, 'Justus, Josephus, Agrippa II and his Coins,' *SCI* 22 (2003), pp. 163–180.

[13] T. Rajak, 'Justus of Tiberias,' *CQ* N.S. 23 (1973), pp. 345–368, at 364.

[14] This is my presumption; Rajak disagrees, as I will shortly point out.

second suggestion, that Justus only wrote one work, his history of the Jewish War; originally, the genealogical tables of the Jewish kings were included in this work, but were later extracted, and this extraction is what Photius saw. In a longer work, Rajak argues, an anecdote about Socrates's trial fits more easily.

Aside from the inherent implausibility of Justus including a chronology of Jewish kings in a history of the Jewish War, especially not a chronology which continues until the death of Agrippa II, who outlived the war,[15] this suggestion cannot explain the identity of names between the reference in Photius and the reference in Diogenes Laertius. For if only the extract had the (partial) title 'Genealogical Tables', how did Diogenes Laertius, who used the larger work, come to know that name?

These points can, of course, be argued back and forth without coming to any clear conclusion. Two other points are more important. As noted above, on the basis of Photius's comment, Rajak is convinced that the work was very concise. It is true that Photius emphasizes the conciseness of Justus's composition (συντομώματος), but if we note that also regarding Julius Africanus Photius tells us that his style is concise,[16] and yet a few lines later tells us that his *History* is in five volumes, and further point out that 'the most important events' which Justus skipped and thereby aroused Photius's ire, are his non-mention of Christ, as Photius tells us explicitly in his next sentence, then there is no reason to conclude that the work was a short extract. The terms history (ἱστορίας) and chronicle (χρονικόν) also imply a book-length composition, not a miniscule tome of a page or two.

The other important point which lies behind Rajak's disinclination to accept the most obvious interpretation of the evidence, *i.e.* (1) that Justus wrote a short history of Israel which focused upon

---

[15] The list of high priests beginning from Aaron which Josephus includes in *Antiquities* (20:224–251), cited by Rajak (op. cit.), cannot serve as an analogy. Josephus is not listing the high priests 'when he has reached Claudius' reign,' as Rajak puts it—Claudius's reign is reached already in middle of Book 19, but rather when Josephus arrives at the destruction of the Temple and the concomitant end of high priesthood, he presents a short history of that institution from its beginnings (and not even a complete listing of all those who occupied that office). The kingship, as Justus presents it, did not end with the war, and so a listing of all kings, short as it may have been according to Rajak's suggestion, would very much be out of place in a history of that war.

[16] He uses the same Greek root as he does in his description of Justus's composition.

chronological matters and had chronological-genealogical tables (Photius), (2) that Diogenes Laertius saw this work (similarity of names between Photius and Diogenes Laertius), and (3) that this work contained non-Jewish material also (Diogenes Laertius), is her conviction that no evidence indicates that Justus 'strayed beyond Jewish history.'[17]

On the face of it, this assertion is dubious: if we have a grand total of two references to a named work of Justus, and one of them does indeed stray beyond Jewish history, then ipso facto there is such evidence. Possibly it can be explained away, but evidence there is.

Perhaps Rajak means to affirm that there is no other evidence. In theory, the point should be irrelevant, for fifty percent of the available evidence should be more than sufficient to conclude that Justus did not limit himself to Jewish history. In fact, I would like to suggest now that such an affirmation is also incorrect.

Jacoby, in collecting the fragments of Justus, assigns three fragments to Justus's work on the Jewish kings.[18] The first fragment is that passage from Diogenes Laertius just discussed, and it is now time that we give the other two fragments the attention they deserve.

The second fragment stems from the preface to Eusebius's *Chronological Canons*:

> Moses, a Hebrew by lineage, the first of all the prophets, who committed to scripture oracles and divine precepts both about our Saviour, I mean the Christ, and the knowledge of God made possible to the Gentiles through him, flourished in the same time as Inachos. This is what is said by men who are well known for their learning—Clement, Africanus, and Tatian, men of our doctrine, as well as those of the circumcision, Josephos and Justus. Each of them separately produced proof from ancient history.[19]

---

[17] Op. cit., p. 363.

[18] See note 1; Jacoby, p. 699; Holladay, p. 382. Holladay follows Jacoby completely on this point.

[19] Eusebius's *Chronological Canons* are not extant, but a Latin translation-adaptation made by Jerome, as well as an Armenian translation, have survived; see R. Helm (ed.), *Eusebius Werke*, VII, *Die Chronik des Hieronymus*, Griechische christliche Schriftsteller 47, Berlin 1956; J. Karst (ed. & transl.), *Eusebius Werke*, V, *Die Chronik des Eusebius aus dem Armenischen übersetzt mit text-kritischen Commentar*, Griechische christliche Schriftsteller 20, Leipzig 1911. The eighth-ninth century Christian chronographer George Synkellos cited a large section of Eusebius's preface to the *Canons* in direct quotation in his *Chronography*, and it was this Greek text which was used by Jacoby and Holladay (see previous note) in their presentation of the fragment; for Jerome's Latin translation, see Helm, p. 7; the preface was not preserved in the Armenian translation. The most recent edition of Synkellos is that of Mosshammer: *Georgii*

Eusebius is quite explicit. He cites five authors, two Jewish and three Christian, and says they each prove 'on their own account' (ἰδίως) that Moses lived at the same time as Inachos. The clear conclusion should be that Eusebius saw a work of Justus which contained this synchronization.[20]

Though Eusebius does not tell us the name of Justus's composition from whence he drew his information, Jacoby's decision to include this passage among the fragments of Justus's work *On the Jewish Kings by means of Genealogical Tables* is eminently understandable. A synchronization between Moses, who was in Justus's eyes the first Jewish king,[21] and Inachus, often considered the first Greek king,[22] is precisely what we would expect to find in a history of the Jews which has chronological-genealogical tables and which also deals with non-Jewish matters.

The third putative fragment ascribed by Jacoby (and in his wake Holladay) to Justus's history of the Jewish kings is taken from Synkellos's *Chronography*:

Syncelli Ecloga chronographica, ed. A.A. Mosshammer, Leipzig 1984; for this quotation from Eusebius see p. 73; the translation is taken from *The Chronography of George Synkellos: A Byzantine Chronicle of Universal History from the Creation*, translated with introduction and notes by W. Adler and P. Tuffin, Oxford 2002, pp. 93–94. The impression one gets while reading this passage is that Eusebius is quoting this synchronism approvingly; accordingly, it should be noted that Eusebius does not actually follow it in his *Canons* (Inachus is synchronized with Jacob, see Jerome's *Chronicle*, ed. Helm, pp. 27a–27b), as indeed Eusebius tells us explicitly further on in his preface, pp. 9–10; see W. Adler, 'Eusebius' Chronicle and Its Legacy,' *Eusebius, Christianity, and Judaism*, ed. H.W. Attridge and G. Hata, Studia Post-Biblica 42, Leiden 1992, p. 471; idem, 'The Origins of the Proto-Heresies: Fragments from a Chronicle in the First Book of Epiphanius' Panarion,' *JThS* 41 (1990), pp. 479–481. On Eusebius's *Chronological Canons* see A.A. Mosshammer, *The Chronicle of Eusebius and Greek Chronographic Tradition*, Lewisburg 1979, 29–83; T.D. Barnes, *Constantine and Eusebius*, Cambridge and London 1981, pp. 111–114; W. Adler, *Time Immemorial: Archaic History and its Sources in Christian Chronography from Julius Africanus to George Syncellus*, Dumbarton Oaks Studies 26, Washington 1989. An excellent discussion of the complicated transmission history of this work is found in Mosshammer, and a short adequate summary in Barnes; see also W. Adler, 'Eusebius' Chronicle and Its Legacy,' pp. 481–484.

[20] It is of course possible that Eusebius is basing himself upon a report given by someone else about Justus's synchronization, but his language and his grouping of Justus with four other authors, all of whose compositions he definitely did see, render this supposition rather implausible. Note also that Eusebius includes a mention of Justus in his *Chronological Canons*, that he was a Jewish author during the reign of Nerva (anno Abraham 2113).

[21] This can be inferred from the description of the book in Photius quoted above.

[22] See discussion below.

For all those of the circumcision, Josephos and Justus, and those of the Greeks, I mean Polemon and Apion, Poseidonios and Herodotos, have recorded the Exodus of Israel from Egypt at the time of Phoroneus and Apis the kings of the Argives, while Amosis was king of Egypt.[23]

Several scholars have claimed that that these two synchronizations attributed to Justus (and Josephus) contradict each other:[24] fragment 2 makes Moses the contemporary of Inachus, while according to fragment 3 he was the contemporary of Phoroneus and Apis.

Some information about the Greek figures mentioned here will be useful. There was a wide-spread tradition in the Hellenic world that Argos was the mother-city of all of Greece.[25] Thus, in the Iliad Homer constantly uses the term Argives when referring to the entirety of what we would call the Greeks; *i.e.* the two adversaries in the war are generally the Trojans and the Argives.[26] Variant traditions abound about the beginnings of Argos, and several of them focus upon Inachus and Phoroneus. These two figures were not necessarily related in the oldest attestations of their names, but many strands of the tradition know that Phoroneus was the son of Inachus. At times, Inachus is called the first king; alternatively, Phoroneus is the first king, and Inachus a river-god.[27]

It is of course obvious why someone would want to place Moses at the time of the first Greek king: the Jewish nation, defined by the exodus, is thereby seen to be as ancient as the Greeks, and the

---

[23] Ed. Mosshammer, p. 70; transl. Adler and Tuffin, pp. 88–89 (with some minor modifications).

[24] Wacholder, *Eupolemos*, pp. 123–124; Holladay, *Fragments*, p. 388, note 8.

[25] See, e.g., Dionysius of Halicarnassus who asserts that the history of Argos, from Inachus downward, is older than any Hellenic history (apud Clement, *Stromata* 1, 21, 101, 5–102.1).

[26] Another geographic-ethnic term used in a similar manner is Achaians, though it is my impression that the term most often contrasted to the Trojans is the Argives.

[27] See, e.g., Pausanias 2.15.4: 'The oldest tradition in the region now called Argolis is that when Inachus was king he named the river after himself and sacrificed to Hera. There is also another legend which says that Phoroneus was the first inhabitant of this land, and that Inachus, the father of Phoroneus, was not a man but the river' (translation from Pausanias, *Description of Greece*, ed. and transl. W.H.S. Jones, Loeb Classical Library, London and Cambridge 1964, Vol. 1, pp. 325–327); see also Hyginus, *Fabulae* 143. The basic parameters are set out succinctly by F. Jacoby, *Die Fragmente der griechischen Historiker*, Part IIIb (Supplement), *A Commentary on the Ancient Historians of Athens (Nos. 323a–334)*, Vol. 2, p. 279: 'Akusilaus (a Greek historian from approximately 500 B.C.E.–C.M.) began the Argive history with Phoroneus..., whereas Kastor (a chronographer of the 1st century B.C.E.–C.M.) made Inachos precede him.'

ancestors of the Jews, the Patriarchs, lived even earlier. Quite plausibly, the source which correlated Moses to Inachus held that the Inachus was the first king of the Greeks, while those who originally correlated Moses to Phoroneus, or alternatively, to Apis, his son, did not know of (or did not accept) the alleged kingship of Inachus. In the final analysis, however, as a result of the amalgamation of the two traditions, there is not that much of a disparity between the two passages Jacoby attributes to Justus: after all, Moses could have flourished in the days of all three: Inachus, father, Phoreneus, son, and Apis, grandson.[28]

Disparity, however, there still is, and it would extremely unsatisfactory to be compelled to resort to this explanation to explain why Justus synchronizes Moses and the Exodus with both Inachus and Phoroneus. Happily, we have not the slightest need to resort to this explanation.

I noted above that the third fragment ascribed by Jacoby to Justus's history of the Jewish kings is taken from Synkellos's *Chronography*, and indeed Jacoby's superscription reads 'Synkell. p. 116, 17 (= Africanus).'[29] Unfortunately, Jacoby never published a commentary on this volume of the *Fragmente*, and so we do not know what exactly he meant by the notation '(= Africanus).' A comparison of this superscription to the superscription of the previous fragment—'Euseb. *Chron.* p. 7b Helm (Synkell. p. 122, 3 Ddf; ....)'—makes it clear that he does not mean to attribute the entire quotation to Africanus. In the previous fragment, he is also quoting Synkellos, but inasmuch as the passage in Synkellos is a direct quote from Eusebius and appears in the edition of Eusebius's *Chronological Canons* only in Jerome's Latin translation, Jacoby decided to quote the passage in Greek from Synkellos, presuming, quite logically, that this secondary witness remained true to the original Greek text of Eusebius, and to attribute it to Eusebius. Since Jacoby does not attribute the third passage to Africanus, but only indicates '(= Africanus),' he clearly does not consider it to be a direct quote from Africanus.[30]

---

[28] And indeed, this harmonization is found explicitly in Synkellos; see below.
[29] The page reference is to the W. Dindorf edition of Synkellos, 2 vols., Bonn 1829.
[30] But this unclear indication led Wacholder (*Eupolemos*, pp. 123–124) and Holladay (*Fragments*, p. 382) astray. According to Wacholder, Africanus said that Justus made Moses the contemporary of Phoroneus and Apis, and Holladay places in the superscription to the third passage 'Julius Africanus apud Georgius Syncellos.'

The justification underlying Jacoby's cryptic association of this passage to Africanus is easily discernible. Just prior to this passage Synkellos attacked Eusebius's chronological reconstruction, and praised Africanus for presenting a 'reckoning [which] does not square entirely with his own arguments; but it was because of the truth that he preferred to align himself with the majority opinion.'[31] Then comes the sentence Jacoby quotes which indeed cites many authorities—'the majority opinion' according to Synkellos—that the Exodus was at the time of 'Phoroneus and Apis the kings of the Argives... when Amosis was king of Egypt.' From the context it is at least plausible that the references to all these historians was made by Africanus himself, for, after all, if he did not know that all these historians held this position, why would he present a reckoning which disagrees with his own arguments?

This is the impression which Synkellos wished his readers to receive, but a closer examination will demonstrate that the list of historians, as well as the assertion which is attributed to them, were generated solely by Synkellos, who however did use—in a reformulated and embellished form—something Africanus had written.

Two points in the passage immediately arouse our suspicions: (1) What is the logic of writing that the Exodus occurred 'at the time of Phoroneus and Apis the kings of the Argives'; the Exodus occurred at a specific point in history, and so cannot have occurred during the reign of two different kings, even if they are father and son. (2) The inclusion of Herodotus among the historians who 'recorded the Exodus of Israel from Egypt' is of course an egregious error; as is well known, Herodotus never mentioned Israel or the Jews. It is implausible in the extreme that Africanus, a careful and judicious scholar, would write such a sentence.[32]

Fortunately, we do not have to guess what Africanus did write about these matters; we have his words. The following passage is a direct quote of Africanus by Eusebius:[33]

---

[31] Synkellos, transl. Adler and Tuffin, p. 88.

[32] For a notable encomium to Africanus by a nineteenth century Protestant scholar generally very critical of the Church Fathers, see F.W. Farrar, *History of Interpretation*, New York 1886, pp. 207–208. A good characterization of Africanus is found in W. Adler, 'Julius Africanus and Judaism in the Third Century,' in *A Multiform Heritage: Studies on Early Judaism and Christianity in Honor of Robert A. Kraft*, ed. B.G. Wright, Scholars Press Homage Series 24, Atlanta 1999, pp. 123–138.

[33] *Praeparatio evangelica* 10.10.15–18 [490a–c], transl. E.H. Gifford, Oxford 1903,

From Ogyges therefore to Cyrus there were as many years as from Moses to the same date, namely one thousand two hundred and thirty-seven. And some of the Greeks also relate that Moses lived about those same times; as Polemon in the first book of his Hellenic histories says, that 'in the time of Apis son of Phoroneus a part of the Egyptian army was expelled from Egypt, who took up their abode not far from Arabia in the part of Syria called Palestine,' being evidently those who went with Moses.

And Apion, the son of Poseidonius, the most inquisitive of grammarians, in his book *Against the Jews*, and in the fourth Book of his *Histories*, says that in the time of Inachus king of Argos, when Amosis was reigning in Egypt, the Jews revolted with Moses as their leader.

Herodotus also has made mention of this revolt and of Amosis in his second Book; and, in a certain way, of the Jews themselves, enumerating them among those who practice circumcision, and calling them the Assyrians in Palestine, perhaps on account of Abraham.

And Ptolemaeus of Mendes, in writing the history of the Egyptians from the beginning, agrees with all these; so that the variation of the dates is not noticeable to any great extent.

Africanus never wrote that 'Herodotos recorded the Exodus of Israel from Egypt', but only that he mentioned a revolt and Amosis in his second book, and indeed Herodotus does so, in chapter 162 of that book.[34] It was Africanus, critically combing Gentile historians to find some basis for relating secular history to biblical history, who connected the revolt mentioned by Herodotus to the story of the Exodus.[35] And it was Synkellos, reading Africanus in an outstandingly uncritical manner, who falsely attributed a mention of the Exodus to Herodotus.[36]

Note also that Africanus does not synchronize Moses with Phoroneus. He quotes Polemon as saying that in the time of Apis son of Phoroneus part of the Egyptian army was expelled and Apion that in the time of Inachus king of Argos, when Amosis was reigning in Egypt, the Jews revolted with Moses as their leader. Synkellos, however, has his own chronological agenda, made explicit in the following passage:

---

pp. 525–526. Much of this passage from Africanus is also quoted by Synkellos himself, ed. Mosshammer, pp. 173–174, transl. Adler and Tuffin, pp. 213–214.

[34] The name given is Amasis, but that is of course a trivial distinction.

[35] The rationale for this connection is of course the mention of a revolt by the previous authors Africanus cites there.

[36] This point was well emphasized by Rajak, *Justus*, pp. 360–361. Her criticism of Africanus, on the other hand, is not justified: his use of Herodotus fits well into the general thrust of the Hellenistic-Roman synchronizations used by Jewish and Christians writers of that period.

> All the historians, both those of the circumcision and those living under grace—Josephos and Justus, the blessed Clement, author of the *Stromateis*, and Tatian and Africanus—are in agreement that Moses was born at the time of Inachos, that he was in his prime at the time of Phoroneus, the son of Inachos and Niobe, and that at the time of Apis he was in command of Israel's Exodus from Egypt; the proof for this they also furnish from those historians who are held in repute among the Greeks.[37]

Note well the harmonizational move made by Synkellos, based upon a conscious creative misreading of the Africanus passage cited above. Two unrelated passages in Africanus, stemming from different historians, one mentioning Apis the son of Phoroneus and the other mentioning Inachus, have been combined to create the triple synchronization: Moses born—Inachus; prime of his life—Phoroneus; Exodus—Apis. Now of course it is clear why in the earlier passage Synkellos's synchronization included both Phoroneus and Apis: in order to synchronize Moses with both Inachus and Apis, he must also be synchronized with Phoroneus, the son of Inachus and father of Apis.

Comparing again the Africanus passage with the earlier Synkellos passage, we can see that his list of Greek historians in Synkellos, Polemon, Apion, Poseidonios, and Herodotos, is taken directly from the Africanus passage.[38] There is however no mention of Josephus or Justus in this passage of Africanus, so from where did Synkellos take their names?

The solution is obvious, though nonetheless astonishing. Above we cited the passage from the preface of Eusebius's *Chronological Canons* within which he tells us that according to both Josephus and Justus Moses flourished at the same time as Inachus.[39] Synkellos, as just noted, connects together Inachus, Phoroneus and Apis for the purpose of synchronization, and therefore did not hesitate to amalgamate the list of Greek historians, upon whom Africanus draws upon for an Inachus synchronization and an Apis synchronization, and the list of Jewish historians, upon whom Eusebius draws upon for

---

[37] Ed. Mosshammer, p. 140; transl. Adler and Tuffin, p. 175.

[38] Note that Apion the son of Poseidonius has become Apion and Poseidonius. One cannot but suspect that that Synkellos wishes to allude to the Hellenistic historian Posidonius. True the latter's history only begins in the second century B.C.E., but quite possibly Synkellos was not aware of this fact, or alternatively, was convinced that his readers would not be aware of this fact.

[39] The second fragment of Justus in Jacoby's collection.

an Inachus synchronization.[40] What is astonishing is that, as outlined above, the rhetorical context of this passage in Synkellos is that of polemic against Eusebius: Synkellos creatively revises data taken from Eusebius and then uses it to attack Eusebius himself.

Leaving then our delineation of Synkellos's (creative and irresponsible) historical method and returning to Justus, we conclude that the third fragment Jacoby adduced should be excised, and so we are left only with the Moses—Inachus synchronization, which Eusebius attributes to three Christian authors, Clement, Africanus, and Tatian, and to two Jewish authors, Josephus and Justus.

Regarding the Christian authors Eusebius's assertion is easily substantiated. The relevant compositions of Tatian and Clement are extant, and the Moses—Inachus synchronization is found in both: Tatian, *Oratio ad Graecos* 38;[41] Clement, *Stromata* 1, 21, 101, 2–5.[42] Africanus's *Chronography* is not extant, but, as we have already seen, the Moses—Inachus synchronization appears in that Africanus passage cited by both Eusebius and Synkellos and quoted above.[43]

Regarding Josephus and Justus the matter is not so simple. Rajak states bluntly 'that the attribution to Josephus is certainly false,' and therefore we should also 'suspect the attribution to Justus.'[44] I do not quite see the logic of this argument: were we to grant that the attribution to Josephus is false, does it not make at least as much sense to argue that Eusebius wished to add the illustrious Josephus to the relatively unknown Justus as to claim that both are the fabrication of Eusebius?[45] At the very least, such an accusation against Eusebius

---

[40] So already A. von Gutschmid, *Kleine Schriften*, Vol. 2, Leipzig 1890, p. 196.
[41] Ed. and transl. M. Whitaker, Oxford 1982, pp. 68–71.
[42] Ed. O. Stählin, revised by L. Früchtel, Berlin 1960, pp. 64–65.
[43] P. 113. Immediately after his citation of this Africanus passage in *Praeparatio evangelica* 10.10.15–18 [490a–c], Eusebius also cites the passages from Tatian (10.11.13–14 [493d]) and Clement (10.12.2–4 [496d–497b]).
[44] Op. cit., p. 360. S. Schwartz, 'Georgius Syncellus's Account of Ancient Jewish History,' *Proceedings of the Tenth World Congress of Jewish Studies*, Division B, Vol. 2 (Jerusalem, 1990), pp. 1–2, note 4, accepts Rajak's skepticism concerning the authenticity of the fragments. (Though Schwartz refers to 'Syncellus' 'citations", he gives a reference to only one fragment and ignores the Eusebian citation; nonetheless, I assume he means to accept Rajak's skepticism regarding both of them).
[45] W. Christ, 'Philologische Studien zu Clemens Alexandrinus,' *Abhandlungen der koeniglichen Akademie der Wissenschaften*, Philos.-philol. Klasse, 21.3 (1901), p. 506, agrees with Rajak that not a hint of the Moses—Inachus synchronization can be derived from Josephus and arrives at a conclusion directly opposed to that of Rajak: the synchronization must derive from Justus. Also J. Sirinelli, *Les vues historiques d'Eusèbe de Césarée durant la période prénicéennee*, Paris 1961, p. 501, note 1, asserts that the Moses—Inachus synchronization cannot be found in the works of Josephus; for his hesitations regarding Justus, see p. 503, note 3.

should have been grounded in an analysis of his historiographical methodology and an attempt to show that mendaciousness is not uncommon in his work.[46]

But the attribution to Josephus is not false; indeed, Eusebius was a better reader of Josephus than many. Rajak cites Josephus claiming that Moses lived a very long time ago, and adduces *Contra Apionem* 2.156.[47] Josephus did indeed believe that Moses lived a very long time ago, and did make that statement in *Contra Apionem* 2.156, but of course the appearance of such a statement does not prove that Josephus nowhere else dated Moses more concretely and precisely. This can only be determined by scrutinizing all of Josephus's references to Moses which may have a chronological referent.

Though the names Inachus and Amosis are never mentioned by Josephus, it can nonetheless be shown that Eusebius is basically correct in citing Josephus in support of the datum that the Exodus was at the same time as Inachus.

Josephus deals with date of the Exodus in two place in *Contra Apionem*. In *Contra Apionem* 1.85–103 he cites Manetho at length, and states that the 'shepherds' (Hyksos) of Manetho's account, who departed from Egypt to Jerusalem in the time of Tethmosis,[48] were the ancestors of the Jews.[49] He clearly takes this position as his own,

---

[46] I can do no better than quote what Timothy Barnes wrote about Eusebius in a slightly different context, that 'the evident care and honesty of his scholarship' should not 'be assumed to guarantee the accuracy of his results' (*Constantine and Eusebius*, p. 141). We should not confuse his methods with those of the modern academy, but he did not fabricate sources.

[47] Op. cit.

[48] This king is called Thoumosis in 1.88, and again Tethmosis in 1.231 and in 2.16.

[49] The text of Manetho cited by Josephus does not say that Hyksos were the ancestors of the Jews, but it does say that they came to country presently called Judea and built a city called Jerusalem (*Contra Apionem* 1.90). For our purposes the question of the original text of Manetho and the question of his original intention are irrelevant, for all that concerns us is what later authors deduced on the basis of the text which was in front of them. The literature on these matters is quite large; for bibliography until 1993 see M. Pucci Ben Zeev, 'The Reliability of Josephus Flavius: The Case of Hecataeus' and Manetho's Accounts of Jews and Judaism; Fifteen Years of Contemporary Research (1974–1990),' *JSJ* 24 (1993), pp. 215–234; see also P. Schäfer, 'The Exodus Tradition in Pagan Greco-Roman Literature,' in *The Jews in the Hellenistic-Roman World: Studies in Memory of Menahem Stern*, ed. I.M. Gafni, A. Oppenheimer, and D.R. Schwartz, Jerusalem 1996, pp. 9*–38* (and his book, *Judeophobia: Attitudes toward the Jews in the Ancient World*, Cambridge 1997); E.S. Gruen, 'The Use and Abuse of the Exodus Story,' *Jewish History* 12 (1998), pp. 93–122 (and his book, *Heritage and Hellenism: The Reinvention of Jewish Tradition*, Hellenistic Culture and Society 30, Berkeley 1998); L. Raspe, 'Manetho on the Exodus: A Reappraisal,' *JSQ* 5 (1998), pp. 124–155; J.J. Collins, 'Reinventing Exodus:

as can be seen from paragraph 103, and also from *Contra Apionem* 1.230–232, where he uses this putative dating of the Exodus by Manetho to the reign of Tethmosis to discredit what he considers to be a second account of the Exodus in Manetho, during the reign of the Egyptian king Amenophis 518 years later.

At first glance this assertion of Josephus, that the Exodus occurred during the reign of Tethmosis, appears to preclude the possibility that anyone would use Josephus's composition to support the Moses—Inachus synchronization, which as we saw above in the passage quoted from Africanus,[50] is really a Moses—Amosis—Inachus synchronization.[51] In truth, however, a close reading of Josephus and other relevant sources will indicate that Tethmosis is nothing but an alternative name for the Egyptian king Amosis.

Josephus took the name Tethmosis from the version or adaptation of Manetho which he used throughout the first section of *Contra Apionem*. It appears in a direct quote from his source (1.94) and following upon the mention of this king there comes immediately a list of his successors. The next eight names are: Chebron, Amenophis, Amesses, Memphres, Mephramuthosis, Tethmosis, Amenophis, Orus, Acenchres. Turning now to the passages of Manetho quoted by Africanus and Euesebius and looking at the list of Egyptian kings who succeeded Amosis, we have no choice but to conclude that Josephus's Tethmosis is Eusebius's and Africanus's Amosis.[52] The following chart presents all the relevant evidence.[53]

Exegesis and Legend in Hellenistic Egypt,' *For a Later Generation: The Transformation of Tradition in Israel, Early Judaism, and Early Christianity; Festschrift for George W.E. Nickelsburg*, ed. R.A. Argall, B.A. Bow, and R.A. Werline, Harrisburg 2000, pp. 52–62; J. Assmann, 'Antijudaismus oder Antimonotheismus? Hellenistische Exoduserzählungen,' in *Das Judentum im Spiegel seiner kulturellen Umwelten: Symposium zu Ehren von Saul Friedländer*, ed. Dieter Borchmeyer und Helmuth Kiesel, Neckargemünd 2002, pp. 33–54.

[50] P. 113.

[51] This point, though obvious, must be made explicit. All these historians and chronographers knew that is no possibility of establishing contact between the history of Israel at the time of Exodus and the history of Greece, so when Eusebius says that Moses flourished at the same time as Inachus, he is presupposing the Amosis—Inachus synchronization we saw in Africanus.

[52] In Synkellos's citation of this Egyptian dynasty list from Africanus the reading is Amos, but inasmuch as Africanus writes here explicitly that Moses left Egypt during the reign of this king and in the passage of Africanus quoted above (p. 113), which appears in both Eusebius and Synkellos, the king in whose time Moses left Egypt is called Amosis, the obvious conclusion is that 'Amos' is a scribal error from an original 'Amosis.'

[53] All of these lists are presented conveniently next to each other in W.G. Waddell's *Manetho, with an English Translation*, Loeb Classical Library, London and Cambridge

Josephus	Africanus (Synkellos)	Eusebius (Synkellos)	Eusebius (Armenian)
Tethmosis	Amos	Amosis	Amoses
Chebron	Chebros	Chebron	Chebron
Amenophis	Amenophthis	Ammenophis	Amophis
Amesses	Amensis		
Memphres	Misaphris	Miphres	Memphres
Mephramuthosis	Misphragmuthosis	Misphragmuthosis	Mispharmuthosis
Tethmosis	Tuthmosis	Tuthmosis	Tuthmosis
Amenophis	Amenophis	Amenophis	Amenophis
Orus	Orus	Orus	Orus
Acenchres	Acherres	Achenchrses	Achencheres

True that Josephus probably never saw or heard the name Amosis used for any Egyptian king and may very well never have heard of the Argivian Inachus, but nonetheless Eusebius's statement, that according to Josephus Moses flourished at the time of Inachus, is an eminently reasonable conclusion to draw from his writings.[54]

Regarding four of the five historians mentioned by Eusebius to support the Moses—Inachus synchronization we know that Eusebius is correct. A priori therefore this should lead us to the conclusion that he is correct also with regard to the fifth, Justus.

Before however we turn to the implications of this conclusion I wish to interrogate the passage from Eusebius's preface quoted above from another perspective. It was obviously important for Eusebius to show just how many historians accept the Moses—Inachus synchronization, and so he mentioned the two Jewish authors, Josephus

---

1956. The passage from Josephus appears on pages 100–107; the passage from Africanus apud Synkellos on pages 110–113; the passage from Eusebius apud Synkellos on pages 115–117; and the passage from the Armenian translation of Eusebius on pages 116–119. In Synkellos's *Chronography* the dynasty lists are not all adjacent to each other—because Synkellos often inserted his own comments, and thereby broke the continuity: the Africanus list appears in the Mosshammer edition of Synkellos on pp. 69, 76, 77–78, 80, and in the Adler and Tuffin translation on pp. 88, 99, 100, 102; the Eusebius list appears in the Mosshammer edition on pp. 69, 77, 79, 80–81, and in the Adler and Tuffin translation on pp. 88, 89, 102, 103. The dynasty list appears in the Armenian translation of Eusebius on p. 68.

[54] After all, the Amosis (Tethmosis)—Inachus synchronization is found in the writings of several Hellenistic-Roman chronographers (see below for further discussion), and there is no reason to entertain the possibility that Josephus would not accept it.

and Justus, and the three Christian authors, Tatian, Clement, and Africanus. Above we cited the relevant Africanus passage,[55] and we saw there that Apion—a non-Jewish and non-Christian author—is quoted as saying that in the time of Inachus king of Argos, when Amosis was reigning in Egypt, the Jews revolted with Moses as their leader. Africanus further seems to imply—what is explicit in the Tatian and Clement passages[56]—that Ptolemy of Mendes also knows of this synchronization. Why then does Eusebius not add these figures to his list of those who attest to the Moses—Inachus synchronization?[57]

Let us therefore turn to the relevant passages in the works of these three early Christian Fathers, and see what can be deduced about the earlier Hellenistic-Roman attestations of this synchronization. The historical order of the three Christian Fathers is Tatian, Clement, and Africanus,[58] and so we shall quote them in that sequence.[59]

Tatian writes:

> Egyptian chronological writings are accurate, and their records were translated by Ptolemy, not the king, but a priest of Mendes. This writer, narrating the acts of the kings, says that the departure of the Jews from Egypt to the lands they entered under the leadership of Moses occurred in the time of Amosis king of Egypt. He thus speaks: 'Amosis lived in the time of king Inachus.' After him, Apion the grammarian, a man most highly esteemed, in the fourth book of his *Aegyptiaca* (there are five books of his), besides many other things, says that Amosis

---

[55] P. 113.
[56] See citation below.
[57] The Ptolemy of Mendes fragment is presented and translated by M. Stern, *Greek and Latin Authors on Jews and Judaism*, Vol. 1, Jerusalem 1974, pp. 380–381; the Apion fragment is on pp. 391–392; see there for references to the earlier publication in Jacoby's *Fragmente der griechischen Historiker*.
[58] According to the *Oxford Dictionary of the Christian Church* (third edition, Oxford 1997), the *floruit* of Tatian was c. 160, that of Clement was c. 150–c. 215, and that of Africanus was c. 180–c. 250.
[59] Tertullian (c. 160–c. 225), *Apologeticus* 19.3, and Origen (c. 185–c. 254), *Contra Celsum* 4.11, also mention the Moses—Inachus synchronization, but insofar as they only mention the basic datum and cite no sources, they add nothing to the discussion. In *Cohortatio ad Gentiles* 9, a work attributed in ancient times to Justin (c. 100–c. 165), Apion is cited as saying 'that during the reign of Inachus over Argos the Jews revolted from Amasis king of the Egyptians, and that Moses led them.' Were this work actually composed by Justin, then the entire analysis I present below, based upon the conclusion that only Tatian's account of what Apion said should be taken into account, would be fallacious. There is however no doubt that this work was not authored by Justin, that it made use extensive use of Tatian throughout, and that it also used Africanus; see M. Stern, *Greek and Latin Authors on Jews and Judaism*, Vol. 3, Jerusalem 1974, pp. 38–41.

> destroyed Avaris in the time of the Argive Inachus, as Ptolemy of Mendes wrote in his *Chronicles*.[60]

Several points are noteworthy in this passage. First of all, the quotation from Ptolemy is strange in that the first part is indirect quotation and the second part direct quotation. Note especially that Moses is not mentioned in the direct quotation, which only deals with the Amosis—Inachus synchronization. Also strange is that Tatian cites Apion citing Ptolemy, but only for the one specific fact that Amosis destroyed Avaris in the time of the Argive king Inachus. No mention is made of Moses, or of any part of the indirect quotation of Ptolemy.

Following Tatian closely, Clement writes:

> This has been discussed with accuracy by Tatian in his book *To the Greeks*, and by Cassian in the first book of his *Exegetics*. Nevertheless our treatise demands that we too should treat summarily what has been said on the point. Apion, then, the grammarian, surnamed Pleistonikes, in the fourth book of his *Egyptian History*, although of so hostile a disposition towards the Hebrews, being of lineage an Egyptian, that he wrote a book *Against the Jews*, when referring to Amosis king of the Egyptians and his activities, adduces, as a witness, Ptolemy of Mendes. And his remarks are as follows: Amosis, who lived in the time of the Argive Inachus, utterly destroyed Avaris, as Ptolemy of Mendes relates in his *Chronology*. Now this Ptolemy was a priest; and setting forth the deeds of the Egyptian kings in three entire books, he says that the exodus of the Jews from Egypt, under the leadership of Moses, took place while Amosis was king of Egypt, from which it is seen that Moses flourished in the time of Inachus.[61]

Clement has switched the order of the Ptolemy and Apion passages, and has also reworked both of them in such a way that the two problematic points in the Tatian passage noted above have disap-

---

[60] The reference was cited above, but for the sake of simplicity we shall give it again here: Tatian, *Oratio ad Graecos* 38, ed. and transl. M. Whitaker, Oxford 1982, pp. 68–71. The translation is my own, having consulted the Whitaker translation and the J.E. Ryland translation, which originally appeared in volume two of the multi-volume series *Ante-Nicene Fathers* (originally edited by A. Roberts and J. Donaldson, Edinburgh 1867–1872, with additional material and notes provided in the American edition by A.C. Coxe 1885–1896), and which is widely available on the internet, e.g. at <www.earlychristianwritings.com/tatian.html>.

[61] *Stromata* 1, 21, 101, 2–5, ed. O. Stählin, revised by L. Früchtel, Berlin 1960, pp. 64–65; the translation is primarily that of W. Wilson, which originally appeared in volume two of the multi-volume series *Ante-Nicene Fathers* (see previous note) and which is widely available on the internet, e.g. at <www.earlychristianwritings.com/clement.html>, with some modification.

peared. In Clement's reworking there is no indirect quote of Ptolemy followed by a direct quote, and the moving of Apion to precede Ptolemy implies that Apion also affirms the Moses—Amosis—Inachus synchronization.

There is no information in Clement which is not already present in Tatian, other than two bibliographical details, that Apion wrote a book *Against the Jews*, a detail which is incorrect,[62] and that Ptolemy wrote a history of the Egyptian kings in three books, and the additional information that Apion was hostile to the Jews. Consequently, even though Clement mentions Cassian and his composition *Exegetics*, there is no reason to suppose that Clement had information about these passages from Ptolemy and Apion which did not derive from Tatian.[63] In tabular form the comparison between the major points of Tatian and Clement is as follows.

Tatian	Clement
Ptolemy... says that the departure of the Jews from Egypt to the lands they entered under the leadership of Moses occurred in the time of Amosis king of Egypt.	Apion... his remarks are as follows: Amosis, who lived in the time of the Argive Inachus, utterly destroyed Avaris, as Ptolemy of Mendes relates in his Chronology.
He thus speaks: 'Amosis lived in the time of king Inachus.'	Ptolemy... says that the exodus of the Jews from Egypt, under the leadership of Moses, took place while Amosis was king of Egypt,
Apion... says that Amosis destroyed Avaris in the time of the Argive Inachus, as Ptolemy of Mendes wrote in his Chronicles.	from which it is seen that Moses flourished in the time of Inachus.

---

[62] See M. Stern, *Greek and Latin Authors on Jews and Judaism*, Vol. 1, p. 389; Schürer-Vermes-Millar-Goodman, *History*, Vol. 3.1, Edinburgh 1986, p. 606.

[63] I find it hard to accept that Clement cites this unknown author Cassian only because he took from him the fact that Ptolemy wrote a history of the Egyptian kings in three books, and prefer the possibility that Cassian quoted Tatian and was therefore adduced in turn by Clement. Christ ('Philologische Studien zu Clemens Alexandrinus,' pp. 504–505) suggests that Cassian was the source of more than I am willing to grant him. I simply see nothing in Clement which is not a quote or a direct reworking of Tatian. See also A. von Gutschmid, *Kleine Schriften*, Vol. 2, pp. 197–198. Also N. Walter, 'Der angebliche Chronograph Julius Cassianus: Ein

The passage from Africanus was cited above;[64] we will repeat the relevant part here:

> And Apion, the son of Poseidonius, the most inquisitive of grammarians, in his book *Against the Jews*, and in the fourth book of his *Histories*, says that in the time of Inachus king of Argos, when Amosis was reigning in Egypt, the Jews revolted with Moses as their leader.... And Ptolemaeus of Mendes, in writing the history of the Egyptians from the beginning, agrees with all these; so that the variation of the dates is not noticeable to any great extent.

Africanus's discussion of Ptolemy and Apion is clearly based directly upon Clement. Clement did not directly affirm that the Apion passage mentioned Moses, but his change of order would lead to that conclusion, and so indeed Africanus explicitly attributes the Moses—Amosis—Inachus synchronization to Apion. Once everything has been attributed to Apion, a more famous figure, there is hardly any need for Ptolemy, and so Africanus merely lists him at the end as also agreeing to what was already said. Furthermore, Clement only mentioned the (imaginary) work authored by Apion *Against the Jews* as a means of identifying that grammarian; but in Africanus this work also contains the synchronization, clearly a reworking or a creative misreading of Clement.

In the light of this analysis then, any attempt to determine what exactly Ptolemy and Apion said should base itself solely upon Tatian. The two later Christian Fathers simply reworked the materials he cited.

Given the fact that the Tatian citation of Apion contains no mention of the Jews, Moses or the Exodus, that Ptolemy himself is quoted by Apion only in relation to Amosis and Inachus and for nothing else, and that Tatian contains a direct quote from Ptolemy with the same basic information (though without the mention of the destruction of Avaris), and that only the paraphrase contains a reference to Moses and the Jews, we are faced with two possible interpretations of the evidence: (1) Ptolemy and Apion both explicitly dated the Exodus to the time of Inachus, by chance or by error this fact

---

Beitrag zu der Frage nach den Quellen des Clemens Alexandrinus,' *Studien zum Neuen Testament und zur Patristica: Erich Klostermann zum 90. Geburtstag dargebracht*, Berlin 1961, pp. 177–192, rejects the hypotheses of von Gutschmid and Christ and concludes (p. 180) that Clement himself changed the citations of Ptolemy and Apion that he found in Tatian.

[64] P. 113.

was left out of Tatian's quote from Apion (this is clearly how Clement and many modern scholars have understood the passage), and there is no significance to the distinction between direct quote and indirect quote; or (2) neither explicitly dated the Exodus to the time of Inachus, and the indirect quote passage in Tatian does not stem from Ptolemy himself but from a mediating source who used Ptolemy's (and Apion's) Amosis—Inachus synchronization to create the Moses—Amosis—Inachus synchronization.[65]

To my mind the second interpretation is intrinsically more probable: the inexplicable change from indirect quote to direct quote and the absence of the Jews and Moses from Apion are sufficient grounds to conclude that neither Ptolemy nor Apion, who used Ptolemy, mentioned them. In addition, only this reconstruction allows us to understand one specific aspect of the Apion quote not yet touched upon. If Ptolemy and Apion both mentioned the Jews or Moses explicitly, the mention of Avaris in the quote from Apion is inexplicable. After all, Amosis did other things also while Inachus was king in Argos, so why mention specifically the destruction of Avaris?[66] But if neither Moses nor the Jews were mentioned by Ptolemy and Apion, then the mention of the destruction of Avaris in this quote is crucial. Avaris is the city of the Hyksos-shepherds at the borders of Egypt, as can be seen from several of Josephus's citations of Manetho.[67] Consequently, Apion's reference to the destruction of this city would cause an astute reader, for whom the identification of the Hyksos-shepherds with the Jews is a given, to use Apion's (and Ptolemy's) Amosis—Inachus synchronization to create the Moses—Amosis—Inachus synchronization.

In *Contra Apionem* 2.17 Apion is cited as explicitly dating the Exodus to the first year of the seventh Olympiad (= 752 B.C.E.), and, as Louis Feldman, among others, has pointed out, this contradicts the attribution of the Amosis (= Tethmosis) Exodus date to Apion.[68] It

---

[65] The possibility that Ptolemy mentioned Moses or the Jews, and that Apion, who cited Ptolemy, did not, is implausible in the extreme.
[66] Africanus clearly did not understand the importance of Avaris and therefore excised it from his citation of Apion.
[67] See *Contra Apionem* 1.78, 86–87, 237, and passim.
[68] See L.H. Feldman, *Jew and Gentile in the Ancient World*, Princeton 1993, p. 181, and also his article 'Origen's Contra Celsum and Josephus' Contra Apionem,' *VC* 44 (1990), p. 132, note 14. Inasmuch as Josephus in the next paragraph strongly rejects the chronological datum he attributes to Apion, it cannot be that he purposely

is far-fetched to suppose that Apion gave two dates for the Exodus, and so in the light of the previous analysis of the Tatian passage, I think we can conclude quite definitively that neither Ptolemy of Mendes nor Apion dated the Exodus to the days of Amosis.[69]

We are missing then a crucial link in the chain. On the one hand, though the materials for the Moses—Amosis—Inachus synchronization are already found in the works of Ptolemy of Mendes and Apion—if one accepts the identification of the Hyksos with the ancestors of the Jews (an identification which we have no reason to suppose was accepted by Ptolemy and Apion), that synchronization is not there. On the other hand it is clear that Tatian already has this synchronization in the source from which he is quoting. Who was this crucial link?

Josephus cannot be the source. He nowhere mentions Inachus, has never heard of Ptolemy of Mendes, and knows of Amosis under the name Tethmosis.

---

chose this datum of Apion to present. See also Wacholder, *Eupolemos*, pp. 125–126, and Rajak, 'Justus,' p. 360.

[69] A. von Gutschmid, *Kleine Schriften*, Vol. 4, Leipzig 1893, p. 362, asserted that Apion never dated the Exodus to Amosis, but did not deal with Ptolemy of Mendes. The conclusion that Apion did not mention the Jews or Moses in the context of Amosis and Inachus also solves another problem for us, a problem of a more minor nature. On page 395 of *Greek and Latin Authors on Jews and Judaism*, Vol. 1, Menahem Stern pointed out that Josephus in *Contra Apionem* 2.10 quotes a reference to Moses from the third book of Apion's *History of Egypt*, yet according to Africanus (Stern is referring to the passage cited above, p. 000). Apion dealt with the Exodus in his fourth book. (The reference to the fourth book of Apion's *History of Egypt* is also found in Tatian and Clement; interestingly, also in a discussion of the same problem by Schürer-Vermes-Millar-Goodman, *History*, Vol. 3.1, Edinburgh 1986, p. 606, note 126—a problem not discussed in the original German edition, E. Schürer, *Geschichte des jüdischen Volkes im Zeitalter Jesu Christi*, Vol. 3, fourth edition, Leipzig 1909, pp. 538–544—only Africanus in mentioned, and not his predecessors Tatian or Clement). There is no need for either of the solutions Stern proposes (also proposed—with a slight distinction—by Schürer-Vermes-Millar-Goodman, op. cit.), for in truth, as von Gutschmid asserted, Apion dealt in the fourth book with Amosis and Inachus, but not with the Exodus. Wacholder (*Eupolemos*, pp. 106–128) not only accepts the attribution of the Moses—Amosis—Inachus synchronization to Ptolemey of Mendes (as do all scholars I have seen), but also suggests that these synchronizations of Jewish history were already part of the universal world chronicle in the first century B.C.E. Clearly, various Hellenistic authors did synchronize Moses to parallel events, but to jump from a handful of synchronizations (if that many) to the claim that Hellenistic and Roman authors of the first century B.C.E as a matter of course regularly synchronized biblical and post-biblical Jewish history with Greek and Roman events is to go much further than the evidence indicates; see the criticism of Wacholder by H. Conzelmann, *Gentiles, Jews, Christians: Polemics and Apologetics in the Greco-Roman Era*, transl. M.E. Boring, Philadelphia 1992, pp. 144–145.

Returning now to the passage from Eusebius's preface to his *Chronological Canons*,[70] the answer is obvious. Even without this just-presented analysis of the citations of Ptolemy and Apion in the works of the three Church Fathers, we saw no reason to doubt Eusebius's clear and unambiguous statement that according to Justus, Moses flourished in the days of Inachus; consequent to this analysis the matter is even more certain. It was Justus who scrutinized the works of the Hellenistic-Roman historians and chronographers who preceded him, and generated this synchronization.

We can now also offer a conjecture why Eusebius does not include Ptolemy and Apion among those who attest to the Moses—Inachus synchronization. Eusebius, who had Justus's composition in front of him, and was not dependent upon Tatian, knew that Ptolemy and Apion did not contain that synchronization, and it was only Justus who had generated it, and so could only cite the two Jewish and three Christian authors.

With this conclusion we have come to the end of the conclusions which can be drawn from the very limited evidence available to us. Nonetheless, a few more, rather speculative suggestions are in place.

Seth Schwartz has shown that Synkellos has preserved material which stems from a pre-Christian non-Josephean source. He adds that though the nature of the sources makes it difficult to prove that this material stems from Justus by means of Africanus, this is his inclination.[71]

Another text worth looking at in greater detail in this context is the twenty-first chapter of Clement's *Stromata*.[72] I think it quite possible

---

[70] Quoted above, p. 113.
[71] Schwartz, 'Georgius Syncellus's Account of Ancient Jewish History,' pp. 1–8. According to Adler ('Julius Africanus and Judaism in the Third Century,' p. 136, note 60) the claim that Africanus's source for some of his Hasmonean and Herodian history is Justus is 'groundless.' If by groundless he means 'unsubstantiated', then his point is both correct and obvious; if he means 'implausible', I see no reason—nor does he give any—to acquiesce in this judgment. See also H. Gelzer, *Sextus Julius Africanus und die Byzantinishe Chronographie*, Vol. 1, Leipzig 1880, pp. 19–21, 246–265, whose study is the starting point for Schwartz's article and the probable referent of Adler's objection.
[72] This is that chapter of the Stromata which contains the Moses—Amosis—Inachus synchronization cited above (p. 113). Clement definitely used Jewish sources extensively in this chapter; he is only very parsimonious in his explicit citations (pace A.J. Droge, *Homer or Moses? Early Christian Interpretations of the History of Culture*, Hermeneutische Untersuchungen zur Theologie 26, Tübingen 1989, p. 8). Thus he writes that that 410 years passed from 'the restoration of the people into their own land until the captivity in the time of Vespasian' (*Stromata* 1,21,140,7), an assertion

that Clement has preserved for us a long quote from Justus. A 'chronography of the Greeks from Moses' (*Stromata* 1.21.136.3) begins with the birth of Moses, continues with the exodus which is synchronized to the reign of Inachus—already connecting us to Justus—and from then on only mentions events (from our perspective both mythical and historical) of first the Greek world, and then, at the end, also the Roman world. This long passage ends with the death of Commodus (1.21.139.3), an event mentioned many times in this chapter of Clement, an event which took place during Clement's lifetime, and therefore a natural end for his chronological calculations. However, the immediately preceding event mentioned is the establishment of athletic games in Rome by Domitian,[73] an important institution in subsequent Roman history, and a significant event in its own time. It is difficult however to suppose that their foundation was such an epochal event that it would be used for chronological calculations made a century later.[74] Since these games were instituted in the middle of the ninth decade of the first century, when Justus of Tiberias was active as an historian, and since this list begins with Moses, just as Justus's history is reputed to do, as reported by Photius, and since it contains the Moses—Inachus synchronization attributed to Justus by Eusebius, it is at least worth suggesting that Clement took this entire passage from Justus.

Whether this last suggestion is accepted or rejected, I think we can conclusively affirm that Justus was an accomplished scholar of both Jewish and Hellenistic learning and in his *On the Jewish Kings by means of Genealogical Tables* desired to merge the histories of both into one well-wrought chronological framework.

---

radically at odds with other chronological calculations in this chapter, and which doubtlessly reflects the tradition found in Seder Olam and in other rabbinic works that the Second Temple stood 420 years ('410' being a scribal error for '420'); see already H. Grätz, 'Hagadische Elemente bei den Kirchenvätern,' *MGWJ* 3 (1854), p. 315. Also noteworthy is Clement's claim that the 490 years of Daniel 9:24 end at the destruction of the Second Temple (1,21,126,3), a chronological claim fundamentally at odds with the general early Christian interpretation of this verse, but basic to rabbinic literature.

[73] These are generally called the Capitoline Games, and like the Olympic Games, were to be held every four years.

[74] They are nowhere else mentioned in this very chronological chapter of the *Stromata*.

'WOMEN ARE (NOT) TRUSTWORTHY'—TOWARD THE RESOLUTION OF A TALMUDIC CRUX*

Leib Moscovitz

[1]

A much discussed,[1] but extremely problematic passage in PT (yPes 1.1, 27b) states:[2]

1. Everyone is believed about searching[3] for leaven [ביעור חמץ], even women, even slaves.[4]
2. R. Jeremiah said in the name of R. Ze'era: [The expression] 'even women' isn't here [לית כאן, *i.e.*, is incorrect].[5]
3. Women themselves are trustworthy,
4. because they are lazy [עצילות],
5. and they check every little bit.

This passage has perplexed generations of commentators, although we do not find any of their interpretations of this *sugya* convincing.

---

* It is a pleasure to dedicate this article to my teacher, Prof. Louis H. Feldman. While the subject matter of this paper is perhaps somewhat removed from Prof. Feldman's principal areas of research, I trust that he will find it of interest: *Iudaici nihil a se alienum putat*.

[1] See most recently A. Grossman, *Ḥasidot U-Moredot* (Jerusalem, 2001), pp. 328–331, with references to earlier literature.

[2] I translate the text of MS Leiden of PT (the only direct witness to this text extant, to the best of my knowledge); for variants from medieval testimonia see below. The Hebrew-Aramaic text of this passage reads: הכל נאמנין על ביעור חמץ אפי' נשים אפי' עבדים ר' ירמיה בשם ר' זעירה לית כאן אפי' נשים נשים עצמן הן נאמנות מפני שהן עצילות והן בודקות כל שהוא כל שהוא.

[3] I translate 'searching,' rather than 'destroying,' as the former meaning is clearly called for by the context (cf. 5 below, where the term *bodeqin* is used to describe this action). For *bi'ur* (*ḥamez*) in the sense of 'searching,' see E.S. Rosenthal, 'Toledot Ha-Nosaḥ U-Va'ayot 'Arikhah Be-Ḥeqer Ha-Talmud Ha-Bavli,' *Tarbiz* 57 (1998), pp. 12–13, especially n. 33.

[4] This statement is anonymous, and hence it is impossible to determine its chronological provenance with certainty. However, from the parallel in BT (bPes 4a, where this statement is introduced by the term *tenituha*), it would appear that this is a baraita.

[5] On this expression see generally J.N. Epstein, *Mavo Le-Nosaḥ Ha-Mishnah* (Jerusalem, 1948), pp. 262–268 (and elsewhere); S. Lieberman, *Tosefta Ki-Fshutah*, 8 (New York, 1973), p. 820. For its meaning in our passage, see below.

We accordingly consider the difficulties in this passage, both ambiguities and contradictions, and continue with a critique of earlier interpretations of this passage. This survey is followed by the suggestion of a new, though admittedly tentative and highly conjectural, solution to this crux, a solution whose broader implications are considered at greater length in the conclusion of this paper.

[2]

We begin with the ambiguities: What is the meaning of R. Ze'era's assertion in 2 that "even women' isn't here'? Theoretically, this statement can be interpreted in two ways, although both are problematic: (1) R. Ze'era might have rejected the ruling in 1 and claimed that women are not believed about searching for leaven. However, this explanation seems to be contradicted by 3, which asserts that women are trustworthy, and by 5, which stresses their diligence in searching for leaven (for 4 see below); (2) R. Ze'era might have disagreed with the wording rather than the contents of 1. For 1, as presently formulated, seems to imply that women are somehow inferior to men ('*even* women').[6] Thus, R. Ze'era maintained that there is no reason to treat women differently from men with regard to searching for leaven. According to this interpretation, then, there seems to be no practical difference between the original ruling in 1 and R. Ze'era's statement in 2: both of these comments assume that women are believed about searching for leaven. This explanation accords with 3 and 5 (see above), although it is problematic for another reason: the Yerushalmi term לית כאן is generally used to reject the contents of statements and not just their wording.[7]

---

[6] This explanation assumes that R. Ze'era's statement reads '*even* women' is not here,' as in our text of PT. However, virtually all medieval citations of our passage omit the word 'even' here (the only exception is Ra'avyah; see below, n. 42). Of course, it might be argued that the reading without 'even' is simply an abbreviated citation of or reference to the words '*even* women' in 1 (according to this possibility, this citation might have been abbreviated either by the medieval commentators who cited this passage or by the *sugya* itself); thus, the presence or absence of the word 'even' in 2 would not affect the interpretation of this statement. Indeed, some commentators whose Yerushalmi text apparently did not include the word 'even' here interpret this text as if it did; see e.g. below at n. 24.

[7] See examples in M. Kosovsky, *Ozar Leshon Talmud Yerushalmi* (Jerusalem, 1980–2002), 4:495–496, and cf. the literature cited above, n. 5.

The next sentence (3) is also problematic: what does the Yerushalmi mean by the words 'women *themselves* are trustworthy'? In other words, what exactly is the point of the word 'themselves'? This word fits a context in which women are contrasted with another group of people, but this is not the case here.[8]

The next clause ('because they are lazy,' 4), too, is problematic, because it seems to contradict both the previous and following clauses.[9] For we are told in 3 that women are trusted about searching for leaven and in 5 that they check carefully; but how can this be reconciled with the Yerushalmi's assertion in 4 that women are lazy?

[3]

Our passage was already discussed by medieval commentators, one of whom, R. Zerahiah Halevi (Ba'al Ha-Ma'or), commented on it in a responsum:[10]

> Some explain: 'since they are lazy' [עצלניות] they have nothing else to be bothered with, [so] they check everything, even what is not necessary, and [hence] it is not justified [lit. 'customary,' דרך] to say '*even* women,' since their checking is better than men's checking.[11]

According to this interpretation, the word translated here as 'lazy' (עצלות or עצלניות) really means 'unpressured, carefree'; thus, the upshot of the Yerushalmi is that women check more carefully than men! This view was adopted by some later commentators as well.[12]

---

[8] Likewise, it is difficult to explain that the Yerushalmi means that *even* women are believed (or not believed; see below) about searching for leaven, as some commentators suggest (see below); had this been the case, a word denoting 'even' would presumably have been used, rather than the word 'themselves' (*'azman*).

[9] A similar objection was raised by Sheyarei Qorban ad loc., s.v. *let kan* (in connection with Rosh's interpretation of the Yerushalmi; see below, n. 19). Sheyarei Qorban resolves this objection by suggesting that Rosh had a different reading in PT, or by adopting an alternative interpretation of PT, proposed (in his view) by R. Nissim of Gerona (see below).

[10] Published (inter alia) in *Ozar Pisqei Ha-Rishonim 'Al Hilkhot Pesah*, ed. G. Zinner (Brooklyn, 1985), p. 199.

[11] Interestingly, similar views have been espoused (apparently without knowledge of R. Zerahiah's comments or similar interpretations of PT) by modern halakhists—presumably, based on their personal experience. See e.g. R. Yehiel Michel Epstein, *'Arokh Ha-Shulhan, Orah Hayyim*, 437:7: 'Nowadays our wives [or: women] check better and ferret out even the slightest quantities of *hamez* ... more carefully than men.'

[12] See R. Menahem b. Shlomo Ha-Meiri, *Beit Ha-Behirah* on bPes 4a, s.v. *u-ve-Talmud ha-ma'arav* (ed. Klein, p. 14); R. Manoah of Narbonne, *Sefer ha-Menuhah* on

However, it seems problematic, since this usage of the word עצל is not attested anywhere else in rabbinic literature (to the best of my knowledge): this word invariably means 'lazy'![13] Indeed, the usual meaning of this word ('lazy')—in connection with women!—is evidently attested by another, very similar PT passage, yPes 2.7, 29c:[14]

1. We may not knead matzah ... in lukewarm water ...
2. But we have learned [mMen 5:2]: 'All meal-offerings may be kneaded in lukewarm water, although one must guard them so they do not become leavened'!
3. R. Ammi said in the name of R. Simeon b. Laqish: There [with regard to kneading meal-offerings] the matter is entrusted to the priests, and priests are diligent [זריזין]; here [with regard to kneading matzah] the matter is entrusted to women, *and women are lazy* [עצילות].

The context here, and particularly R. Ammi's dichotomy between priests and women, clearly indicates that the word עצלוח means 'lazy,'[15] strongly suggesting that R. Zerahiah Halevi's interpretation of our passage should be rejected as lexically untenable.[16] Likewise, the use of the term לית כאן here is problematic, as indicated earlier. Precisely what prompted this interpretation remains to be determined, although this explanation might stem from a desire to reconcile PT with BT[17] (bPes 4a–b), according to which women are trusted about searching for leaven (albeit for a slightly different reason— because the search for leaven is a rabbinic precept; see below), and,

---

Hilkhot Ḥameẓ U-Maẓẓah, 2:17 (is this a distinctively Provençal interpretation?). This interpretation was also adopted by Radbaz (below, n. 25) and Sedei Yehoshua. Interestingly, Meiri remarks that 'some explain [the Yerushalmi] in the opposite way [see the sources cited in ed. Klein, n. 158], but their remarks are worthless!'

[13] Cf. the lexica and concordances of rabbinic literature, s.v.

[14] Cf. also yPes 1.4, 27c = ySan 5.3, 22d.

[15] Theoretically, one might be tempted to explain the problematic mention of women's laziness in yPes 1.1 as an erroneous transfer (*'ashgara*) from yPes 2.7. However, this suggestion seems unlikely for two reasons: (1) there is no link to yPes 2.7 in yPes 1.1 which would justify such an *'ashgara*; (2) the text of our passage is confirmed by numerous medieval testimonia, suggesting that this text is correct (although it goes without saying that neither of these considerations is decisive).

[16] It might be argued that *'azelot* here means 'slow' rather than 'lazy' (in contrast to *zerizin* ['quick'], the term used to describe the priests), and slowness might accordingly be associated with thoroughness. However, the context here, as well as the use of this word in other contexts, suggests that the women described by Resh Laqish as *'azelot* are careless rather than diligent.

[17] Alternatively, this interpretation might have been prompted by some sort of proto- or quasi-feminist leanings, although this possibility seems unlikely to me.

consequently, with accepted custom, which also seems to have regarded women as trustworthy about searching for leaven.[18]

An alternative interpretation was proposed by R. Shlomo ibn Aderet (Rashba) and adopted by a number of other medieval commentators.[19] According to Rashba, the seeming contradiction between 2 and the later parts of the *sugya* is due to the fact that the Yerushalmi executes an abrupt *volte face* after 2:

> 'Women are not here' [in 2] means that women are believed about ritual matters [*issurin*] like a single witness, even with regard to Torah [prohibitions] . . . but [the Yerushalmi] rejects this[20] [*pariq*] well: 'Women are here,'[21] for since they are lazy, they check little,[22] and if searching for leaven was [required by] Torah law, they would not have been believed.[23]

According to Rashba, R. Ze'era (2) did not disagree with the contents of 1, but with its wording ('*even* women' are believed), since women are ordinarily just as trustworthy about ritual matters as men. In the final analysis, however, the Talmud justifies use of the expression 'even'[24] on the grounds that women are lazy, and hence would not have been believed about searching for leaven if not for the fact

---

[18] See the discussions of the medieval commentators on our passage and related contexts (e.g., bHul 10b and bKet 72a) about the trustworthiness of women concerning various types of ritual precepts.

[19] See e.g. R. Yom Tov b. Abraham Ishbili, *Hiddushei Ha-Ritba* on bKet 72a, s.v. *u-meshammashto* (ed. Goldstein, cols. 577–578); R. Nissim of Gerona, *Hiddushei Ha-Ran* on bPes 4b, s.v. *himninhu* (ed. Lichtenstein, p. 22); and cf. Pisqei Rosh, Pesahim, 1:3, and see generally on these sources S. Lieberman, *Ha-Yerushalmi Ki-Fshuto* (Jerusalem, 1935), p. 375. Cf. also R. Yechiel Michel Epstein, *Mikhal Ha-Mayim* ad loc.

[20] Other commentaries who follow Rashba's interpretation describe the relationship between the two parts of the Yerushalmi as a dispute between different opinions, rather than as a thesis and its rejection; see Rosh and R. Nissim, cited in the previous note.

[21] No such assertion appears in our text of PT or in Rashba's citation from that work, and there is no reason to assume that Rashba had a different reading here; Rashba presumably just paraphrased PT's contents as he understood them. Cf. Lieberman, *Ha-Yerushalmi Ki-Fshuto*, p. 375.

[22] This assertion contrasts with that in our text of the Yerushalmi in 5, according to which women check 'every little bit' (*kol she-hu kol she-hu*). Cf. below, n. 44.

[23] R. Shlomo b. Abraham ibn Aderet, *Torat Ha-Bayit*, Hilkhot Shehitah, Sha'ar 1, 7b. Cf. also idem, *Hiddushei Ha-Rashba* on bHul 10b, s.v. *we-nashim* (ed. Ilan, p. 89).

[24] Rashba does not cite the words '*even* women,' although it is clear from his remarks that these words were the focus of R. Ze'era's remarks. Cf. the more explicit formulation of this viewpoint in R. Moshe b. Nahman, *Hiddushei Ha-Ramban* on bHul 10b, s.v. *u-mazati ha-'iqqar* (ed. Reichman, p. 30).

that the requirement to search for leaven is of rabbinic origin. According to this interpretation, then, all parts of our passage agree that women may search for leaven; the disputes in this passage, whether in the beginning of the *sugya* (between 1 and 2) or towards the end (the *volte face* after 2), focus on the theoretical underpinnings of this ruling rather than on its practical application. Nevertheless, the dispute between 2 and the end of the *sugya* does have practical ramifications (even though these are not spelled out explicitly in our passage): according to R. Ze'era, women are treated no differently than men, whereas the end of the *sugya* assumes that women are not believed about Torah prohibitions, at least those prohibitions concerning whose fulfillment women are assumed to be lazy.

However, this explanation, too, is far from satisfactory. As noted earlier, interpreting ליה כאן in 2 as an objection to the wording rather than the content of 1 is terminologically problematic. Indeed, this interpretation seems to run counter to the whole thrust of the argumentation here, which appears to be practical rather than theoretical or phraseological. Second, and perhaps more important, in order to sustain this interpretation Rashba is compelled to introduce a distinction between rabbinic and Torah prohibitions into the text, even though this passage provides not the slightest allusion to the existence or applicability of such a distinction.[25] The grounds for assuming that such a distinction exists, of course, are clear—the parallel *sugya* in BT (bPes 4b) distinguishes between women's credibility about rabbinic and Torah prohibitions—but this certainly does not justify adopting such an assumption to explain PT. Indeed, even if PT agrees that the requirement to search for leaven is of rabbinic

---

[25] This difficulty can be avoided by adopting a variation of Rashba's interpretation proposed by R. David b. Zimra (*Teshuvot Radbaz Ha-Ḥadashot*, § 51) and attributed by that scholar to R. Yom Tov b. Abraham Ishbili (although it is highly questionable whether the latter commentator really entertained such a view—in fact, he seems merely to have paraphrased Rashba, as is frequently the case). Radbaz explains R. Ze'era's statement the same way as Rashba, although he maintains that the conclusion of the *sugya* sets forth a theoretical possibility (*hawah 'amena*) which is rejected (and which aims to account for a view not explicitly cited in the passage, namely, that it was necessary to mention women explicitly): since women are lazy and do not check carefully, one might think that they should not be believed about searching for leaven, although in fact they are believed. Needless to say, this suggestion is even more problematic than Rashba's own explanation, as it requires us to radically rewrite the Yerushalmi, or, at the very least, to read into the Yerushalmi assumptions of which there is not the slightest allusion in its text.

origin—and this assumption is highly questionable, to say the least[26]—this does not make Rashba's interpretation any more plausible. For the text of PT gives no indication that any sort of distinction should be drawn between different types of precepts, and certainly not that women are believed about searching for leaven despite their alleged laziness. On the contrary, the plain sense of the assertion 'women are lazy' is that women are not believed at all about searching for leaven! One more (admittedly inconclusive) objection to Rashba's interpretation may also be raised: the sudden and abrupt transition between R. Ze'era's view and the Talmud's rejection of that view seems rather awkward, stylistically speaking: had the Yerushalmi executed such a *volte face*, we should have expected it to have been introduced by appropriate terminology, e.g., אפילו תימר[27] ('even if you say').

A minor variation on Rashba's interpretation is suggested by Qorban Ha-'Edah.[28] He too assumes the existence of an abrupt transition in the Yerushalmi, albeit in a manner slightly different from that proposed by Rashba. According to Qorban Ha-'Edah, our passage cites two opposing views:

(1) "Women are not here' [*i.e.*, there is no reason to say that 'even' women are believed, as women are no different from men], because women themselves are believed';
(2) [Women are not believed at all], 'because they are lazy, and they check every little bit.'

This interpretation avoids one of the principal difficulties with Rashba's explanation—the introduction of an implausible distinction between rabbinic and Torah laws with regard to women's trustworthiness—although it is untenable for other reasons. For it requires us to assume

---

[26] See generally Y.D. Gilat, 'Bittul Ḥameẓ Be-Fesaḥ,' *Bar-Ilan* 11 (1973), pp. 17–25, especially p. 22, and see now S.Y. Friedman, *Tosefta 'Attiqta, Massekhet Pesaḥ Rishon* (Ramat-Gan, 2002), pp. 336–351.

[27] For use of this term in such contexts, see pro tempore the examples in Kosovsky, *Oẓar*, 1:930–931.

[28] He attributes this interpretation (see Sheyarei Qorban ad loc., s.v. *let kan*) to R. Nissim of Gerona; cf. R. Nissim's remarks in *Ḥiddushei Ha-Ran* ad loc. (above, n. 19) and in R. Nissim's commentary on Alfasi Pesaḥim, §689 (ed. Vilna, 1b), s.v. *we-ameri[nan]*. In fact, however, R. Nissim's comments on our passage seem to be little more than an abbreviated paraphrase of Rashba (see above). Similarly, this interpretation is attributed by Radbaz (above, n. 25) to Tosafot (and, apparently, Rosh), although there is not the slightest indication from the wording of Tosafot that they interpreted the Yerushalmi this way.

that the latter part of the *sugya*, which speaks of women's laziness, refers not to the part of the *sugya* immediately preceding, but to an assumption which is nowhere explicitly or even implicitly made in this passage, viz., that women are not believed at all! Thus, this explanation too must be rejected.

One final interpretation of our passage may be considered, the interpretation proposed by Penei Moshe (cf. also Tuv Yerushalayim),[29] who emends the text of 3 from 'women are trustworthy' to 'women are *not* trustworthy.'[30] According to this interpretation, R. Ze'era's statement in 2 means that women are not trusted about searching for leaven (as suggested by the plain meaning of the term *let kan*), and 3, 4, and 5 all explain this statement. The principal problem with this interpretation is that it requires emendation. To be sure, this emendation is relatively trivial, graphically and phonetically—it entails alteration of הן (נאמנות) to אין (נאמנות)—although the fact that all witnesses to the text (MS Leiden and numerous medieval commentators; see below) oppose this emendation (note that the medievals did not even suggest such an emendation!) suggests that this reading is textually untenable, though not logically or exegetically unreasonable.

Summarizing, then, all of the interpretations proposed by earlier commentators seem problematic.[31] We are accordingly justified in considering a new solution to this crux.[32]

---

[29] An interesting variation on this interpretation is found in Qorban Netan'el on Pisqei Ha-Rosh, Pesaḥim 1:6, who suggests that 3 should be interpreted as a question ('are women themselves believed?'—after all, they should not be!), while 4 presents the answer to this question—'since [women] are lazy, they check a little bit,' and hence are not believed. However, this explanation is extremely forced: there is no indication in the text that the beginning of this passage should be interpreted interrogatively. Moreover, according to this interpretation, the main point of the Talmud's supposed reply—that women are believed—is missing from the text.

[30] Such a reading seems to be attested by the citation of our passage adduced by a questioner of Radbaz (*Teshuvot Radbaz Ha-Ḥadashot*, § 51, *nashim 'ein 'azmam [!] ne'emanot*). However, from the content of this responsum (q.v.) it would appear that this reading is a fortuitous (and felicitous) error, and that the word *'ein* should be emended to *hen*, as in our text of PT.

[31] Another rather ingenious explanation of our passage was once suggested to me (orally; I do not recall by whom): the word *'azelot* ('lazy') should be emended to *'amelot* ('working'; see below). According to this emendation, the last three parts of the *sugya* cohere nicely with one another—'women are trustworthy, since they work [at searching for leaven], and they check every little bit.' However, the exact relationship between this statement and R. Ze'era's comment remains somewhat problematic, as indicated earlier, unless we assume that 3–5 refers back to 1 and justifies it (of course, on this assumption it is difficult to understand why 3–5 follows 2 rather than 1).

[4]

Virtually all of the medieval commentators who cite our passage[33] (I do not refer to commentators who paraphrase or otherwise comment on this text) preserve a different reading from that found in our text of the Yerushalmi (the numeration of the stages of the *sugya* here follows that in the beginning of this paper):

Our text	Medieval commentators' text
2. [The expression] 'even women' isn't here	[The expression] 'women' isn't here.
3. Women themselves are trustworthy	
4. because they are lazy	Since they are lazy,
5. and they check every little bit [כל שהוא כל שהוא].	they check a little bit [כל שהוא].

There are three principal differences between these readings:[34]

1. According to the medievals' citation, the beginning of our passage (2) speaks of 'women,' and not '*even* women.' The absence of the word 'even' seems to suggest that R. Ze'era disagreed with the contents and not just the wording of 1 (contra Rashba etc.), although it might be argued that the omission of this word reflects abbreviated citation of 1 rather than a bona fide textual variant.[35]

Nevertheless, further scrutiny suggests that this suggestion, too, is untenable, for two reasons. First, it requires emendation; and while this emendation is relatively minor, it is contradicted by the readings of all the medieval commentators who cite our passage (see below). Moreover, the word '*amel* in rabbinic literature apparently does not mean 'careful' or 'diligent'—these meanings are denoted by words such as *zahir* and *zariz* (see e.g. above, at n. 14, and note additional examples in Kosovsky, *Ozar*, 3:460)—but rather 'engaged' (in activity): '*amel* seems to denote activity (see e.g. m'Av 2:2, 14; tMen 13:22 [ed. Zuckermandel, p. 534]; yBer 4.2, 7d), unlike '*azel*, which describes one's character or disposition, and it is clearly the latter meaning which is called for by the context here.

[32] Interestingly, while Lieberman discusses our passage at some length (*Ha-Yerushalmi Ki-Fshuto*, pp. 374–375)—primarily, in the course of analyzing the remarks of medieval commentators who comment on or paraphrase it—he gives no indication of how he thought this text should be interpreted.

[33] R. Zerahiah Halevi, R. Shlomo ibn Aderet, R. Manoah of Narbonne, Maharam Halawah, R. Nissim of Gerona; see above (and cf. below, n. 41). The Hebrew-Aramaic text of this citation reads לית כאן נשים מתוך שהן עצלות בודקות כל שהו (I do not cite trivial variants between the citations adduced by different authorities, e.g., *kol she-hen* instead of *kol she-hu*).

[34] In addition, some medievals read *mi-tokh* (here translated 'since,' to distinguish it from *mippenei*, 'because,' as in MS Leiden), although this difference is not critical for purposes of the present discussion.

[35] Cf. above, n. 6.

2. In the end of 5, the medievals read 'because they check a little bit' (כל שהוא),[36] in contrast to our text, which repeats this expression. To be sure, the medievals' reading might be attributed to haplography, or to intentional hypercorrection of the repetition in our text of the Yerushalmi, which scribes might have erroneously construed as a dittography. Alternatively, this reading might be attributed to abbreviation of the Yerushalmi citation, a phenomenon frequently attested in medieval Yerushalmi citations. However, as we shall see below, this reading too seems to be authentic.

3. The most striking difference[37] between the medievals' reading and that of our text of PT is the absence of the Yerushalmi's assertion that 'women themselves are trustworthy' (3).[38]

Taken together, these variants allow for[39] a rather radical revision of our understanding of PT. For according to this reading, the last parts of the *sugya* (4–5) cohere perfectly not only with one another, but also with the previous part of the *sugya*. Thus, R. Ze'era's statement that "even women' isn't here' (*i.e.*, isn't correct, in accordance with the usual meaning of לית כאן) is explained by the following sentence (4–5): 'Since [women] are lazy, they check only a little bit,' so all of the interpretative difficulties noted earlier in connection with our text disappear. (This interpretation is substantively equivalent to Penei Moshe's, although these interpretations differ on textual grounds; see below.) So interpreted, R. Ze'era and the following part of our *sugya* agree that women are not trusted about searching for leaven, in contrast to the view of most commentators, who maintain that

---

[36] This reading is also attested by R. Eliezer b. R. Joel Halevi, *Sefer Ra'avyah*, §428 (ed. Aptowitzer, 2:60), although the Yerushalmi text he cites is otherwise essentially identical to that of MS Leiden (cf. below, n. 42).

[37] This point was already noted by B. Ratner, *Ahavat Ziyyon We-Yerushalayim, Pesaḥim* (Vilna, 1912), p. 9, although Ratner failed to consider the possible implications of this reading for the exegesis and textual history of our passage.

[38] It might be argued that the omission of 3 in the medieval citations is not attributable to a different *Vorlage*, but to abbreviated citation: only those parts of the text directly relevant to the talmudic argument or in need of explanation were cited. However, this suggestion seems unlikely: (1) if the medievals had the reading found in our text of PT, it seems strange that they did not attempt to explain it, since this reading is extremely problematic; (2) the reading without 3 seems to be attested by all medievals who cite our passage, and it seems extremely unlikely that all of these commentators fortuitously decided to omit exactly the same words.

[39] Although they do not *necessitate* such an interpretation of the Yerushalmi; note that many commentators who had this reading interpreted it differently (although their interpretation, as noted above, is extremely forced). See below.

R. Ze'era, the end of the passage, or both maintain that women are trusted about searching for leaven.

This reading admittedly solves all of the difficulties in our passage, but is it authentic? I suggest that it might be, as this reading, with trivial variations,[40] is corroborated by all medieval commentaries who cite our passage in its entirety,[41] with only one seeming exception, Ra'avyah.[42] If, however, this reading is correct, two important questions remain: how did our presumably corrupt reading of PT originate? Moreover, why didn't those commentators who attest this reading[43] (as evidenced by their interpretations of PT and not just by their citations of that work), interpret it as suggested here?

---

[40] Thus, some commentaries read *mippenei* in 4 rather than *mi-tokh*, although all of these commentaries seem to be dependent on the Yerushalmi 'citation' of Nahmanides, which in fact seems to be a paraphrase rather than a verbatim citation. See Nahmanides (above, n. 24); Maharam Halawah on bPes 4b, s.v. *kewan* (15a); R. Nissim of Gerona (above, n. 24; but note that this same commentator, both in his novellae and his comments on Alfasi on bPes, reads [?] *mi-tokh*, as he does in his comments on Alfasi Hullin, § 682, s.v. *we-khullan* [p. 1a]: apparently, the reading in his *hiddushim* on bHul reflects the influence of Nahmanides' *hiddushim* [cf. also below, n. 42]).

[41] See the sources cited above, n. 33. To be sure, many of these commentaries apparently cited the Yerushalmi secondhand, based on the citations found in other commentators, as is frequently the case with medieval Yerushalmi citations (see e.g. Y. Sussmann, 'Ketav Yad Leiden Shel Ha-Yerushalmi: Lefanaw U-Le-Aharaw,' *Bar-Ilan* 26–27 [1995], pp. 204, 216). However, the fact that this reading is attested by scholars from different countries (Provence, Spain), some of whom apparently did cite this passage directly from the Yerushalmi, suggests that this reading should be taken quite seriously.

In this connection, one final medieval testimonium to our passage should be mentioned, that of Nahmanides in his novellae on bHul 10b (above, n. 24). Nahmanides fails to distinguish the actual text of PT (which in any case he seems to have cited paraphrastically and not verbatim) from his own comments, rendering it impossible to determine exactly what reading this scholar had in the Yerushalmi. Nevertheless, careful scrutiny of his remarks suggests that he had the same reading as the other medievals, and this conclusion is supported by the fact that this reading (without 3) is attested by other scholars who were apparently dependent, directly or indirectly, on Nahmanides, such as Rashba and Maharam Halawah.

[42] I say 'seeming exception' because it is possible (though not likely) that the citation of 3 in Ra'avyah is really Ra'avyah's own comment, rather than a direct citation from the Yerushalmi. See *Sefer Ra'avyah*, §428 (ed. Aptowitzer, 2:60), whose text is almost identical to that of MS Leiden (although Ra'avyah reads *kol she-hu* only once; our reading in Ra'avyah is confirmed, with insignificant variants, by MS London Beth Din 11, the best MS of Ra'avyah [as I learn from Prof. S. Emanuel], which was not used in Aptowitzer's edition of this work). Of course, the value of this citation is limited: the extant MSS of Ra'avyah's work are all rather late (the London Beth Din MS, [one of?] the earliest of these MSS, dates to the fifteenth-sixteenth centuries!), and thus might have been influenced, directly or indirectly, by the reading of MS Leiden and/or the *editio princeps* of PT (for similar phenomena

Beginning with the textual question, duplication of the expression כל שהוא, which altered the meaning of 5 from 'they search a little' to 'they search every little bit,' could be attributed to dittography or to *'ashgara* from other parts of this halakhah in the Yerushalmi, where the phrase כל שהוא is duplicated, and justifiably so.[44] The first variant ("women' is not here,' rather than "*even* women' is not here'), too, might be due to *'ashgara* from the words 'even women' in 1, although this reading might have arisen under the influence of the commentators' interpretation of our passage.[45]

The critical issue, therefore, is how the statement that women are believed (3) entered the text of PT (assuming, of course, that the medievals' reading is authentic). I suggest that this sentence might be a post-talmudic interpolation,[46] based on, though not copied directly from, the parallel passage in BT—or, perhaps (and these two possibilities are so closely related as to be almost inseparable), based on exegesis of PT in light of BT. Thus, the parallel *sugya* in BT (bPes 4a–4b) states:[47]

> Everyone is believed about searching[48] for leaven [ביעור חמץ], even women, even slaves, even minors... [One might think] the rabbis should not have believed [such people. Therefore the baraita] teaches

---

in connection with other medieval Yerushalmi citations, see Y. Sussmann, 'We-Shuv Li-Yerushalmi Neziqin,' *Meḥqerei Talmud* 1 [1990], p. 120).

[43] I refer primarily to Nahmanides/Rashba and their school; for the motivations behind R. Zeraḥiah Halevi's interpretation of our passage see above, n. 17, and the accompanying text. (At first sight it might appear that the interpolation in 3 is also attested by *Ḥiddushei Ha-Ran* on bḤul 10b, s.v. *'ed eḥad*, although further scrutiny reveals that R. Nissim's 'citation' of the Yerushalmi here was not taken directly from the Talmud [cf. also above, n. 40], but from Nahmanides' comments on this passage [above, n. 24]—and, actually, from an inaccurate interpretation of these comments.)

[44] See yPes 1.1, 27a, line 53 (in ed. Venice); the same reading should also be adopted ibid., line 46, where one instance of the expression *kol she-hu* was apparently omitted through haplography. Cf. Lieberman, *Ha-Yerushalmi Ki-Fshuto*, p. 368.

[45] See below, n. 54.

[46] Such phenomena are extremely rare, though not wholly unattested, in standard texts of PT. See generally L. Moscovitz, 'Kiflei Girsah Bi-Yerushalmi,' *Tarbiz* 66 (1997), pp. 216–219 (= idem, 'Double Readings in the Yerushalmi,' *The Talmud Yerushalmi and Graeco-Roman Culture*, 1, ed. P. Schäfer [Tübingen, 1998], pp. 123–125).

[47] This passage discusses the question of women's trustworthiness in an entirely different context—whether a house rented on the fourteenth of Nisan may be assumed to have been checked for leaven—although this contextual change is not very significant for our purposes here. See further D. Halivni, *Meqorot U-Masorot, Pesaḥim* (Jerusalem, 1982), pp. 279–280.

[48] Cf. above, n. 3.

us [that] since searching for leaven is [a] rabbinic [requirement], for according to Torah law mere nullification [of leaven, ביטול] is sufficient, the rabbis believed [such people] about [a] rabbinic [legal requirement].[49]

This passage disagrees with the conclusion of PT (2–5) as explained earlier: according to BT, women are believed about searching for leaven (because this is a rabbinic precept), whereas PT disagrees. Note that this dispute between the two Talmuds is normative and not just interpretative: acceptance of PT's conclusions would have dire halakhic ramifications.

If our suggestion that 3 is an interpolation is correct, we may offer two (possibly complementary) explanations of how this material entered our text of PT. This sentence might have been added to indicate the accepted halakhic 'bottom line' (as articulated by BT), namely, that women themselves—as opposed, perhaps, to slaves, who are also mentioned in the beginning of PT—are believed about searching for leaven. Alternatively, this material might serve an exegetical function, explaining R. Ze'era's statement that "even women' is not here' in conformity with BT's view that women are believed about searching for leaven. The exegetical function of this material is clear from the remarks of medieval commentaries on our *sugya*, especially those who adopt Rashba's (etc.) interpretation. Thus, Rashba wrote:[50] "Women are not here,' *since women are believed...*,' and similarly (and more explicitly) in the remarks of R. Nissim of Gerona:[51] 'There is an authority[52] who says there [in PT] that 'Women are not here,' for *they themselves are believed* [דהן עצמן נאמנות], just as in our text of PT!]...'[53] Is it possible, then, that 3 in our text of PT was taken

---

[49] The Hebrew-Aramaic text of this passage reads: הכל נאמנים על ביעור חמץ אפילו נשים אפילו עבדים אפילו קטנים... מהו דתימא לא להימנינהו רבנן, קא משמע לן כיון דבדיקת חמץ מדרבנן הוא מדאורייתא בביטול בעלמא סני ליה הימנוהו רבנן בדרבנן (no variants of significance are found in the MSS here).

[50] See above, at n. 23.

[51] *Hiddushim* on bPes (above, n. 19).

[52] R. Nissim construes the alleged *volte face* between 2 and the next part of the *sugya* as a dispute, rather than as an assertion and its subsequent rejection; cf. above, n. 20.

[53] This entire passage is clearly a paraphrase of PT, while the italicized phrase seems to be R. Nissim's own explanation of PT and not a verbatim citation of that source (as indicated, inter alia, by the Aramaic *de-hen* in the middle of the Hebrew context). Accordingly, I see no reason to assume that R. Nissim's Yerushalmi *Vorlage* included 3, as in our texts of PT (besides, R. Nissim's comments on the Yerushalmi were almost certainly based on Rashba's citation and interpretation of that work, rather than on direct citation from or analysis of the Yerushalmi).

from the comments of scholars who interpreted the Yerushalmi here the same way these scholars did?[54] In any event, it is clear why Rashba (etc.) interpreted our passage as they did, even though their text of PT apparently did not include the statement in 3: this way these scholars were able to avoid head-on conflict between BT and PT.

* * *

Summarizing, we have suggested that the difficulties in the brief passage from yPes 1.1 considered here might be resolved by assuming that this passage contains a post-talmudic interpolation which contradicts the rest of the *sugya*. This reading, we conjecture, might reflect the influence of BT (and, presumably, of accepted halakhic practice, which was also based on BT), mediated through the interpretation of our *sugya* suggested by various Spanish medievals. (The only claim we can make with certainty about the provenance of this reading is that its terminus ad quem is 1289, when MS Leiden of PT, the earliest source for this reading, was written.) This suggestion, if correct, has implications more wide-ranging than just clarifying the meaning of our passage: it illustrates the complex interaction between different works of rabbinic literature, showing how the texts of these works were affected and their contents transformed by students and interpreters who read these sources as one, thereby giving them new life, form, and meaning.

---

[54] In light of the seeming dependence of the interpolation on Rashba's (etc.) interpretation of our passage, it is possible that the word '*afilu* in 2 ('*even* women'), which does not appear in most medieval citations of our passage (see above, n. 6), was added to support this interpretation.

JOSEPHUS AND THE BOOKS OF SAMUEL

ETIENNE NODET

In the *Jewish Antiquities*, the paraphrase by Josephus of 1–2 Samuel covers the end of book 5 and the whole of books 6 and 7, the latter including the beginning of 1 Kings until the death of David; some portions of 1 Chronicles are used, too. This papers aims at dealing with Josephus' Biblical sources, as a by-product of a French translation and extensive commentary of his narrative.[1] The topic is complicated by the fact that several forms of 1–2 Samuel are extant: the Massoretic text (MT), which is admittedly difficult; in Greek, there are very different versions; the Latin and Syriac also have significant variant readings. Moreover, interesting fragments of 1–2 Samuel have been discovered in some Qumran caves, which have noteworthy contact points with 1 Chronicles, with the Greek (against the MT) and with Josephus.

Josephus himself tells us that he has 'translated' (μεθηρμηνευμένην) from the Hebrew Scriptures, as stated in the prologue of the *Antiquities* (1:5). The same claim is sometimes made within the narrative, even more clearly. About Jonas, he feels compelled to tell of the miracles as written 'in the Hebrew books' (9:208). Later he insists (10:218): 'In the beginning of this history, I have said that I intended to do no more than translate (or 'paraphrase' μεταφράζειν) the Hebrew books into the Greek language..., without adding to, or removing from, them anything of my own'.[2] In *Ag. Ap.* 1:54 he states: 'I have translated (μετηρμήνευκα) the *Archaeology* from the holy books'. It is obvious, however, that he has many contacts with the Septuagint (LXX) against the MT, therefore many commentators have not taken these statements seriously, out of the assumption that the only Hebrew Bible extant in his time was the MT, supposed to have been fixed

---

[1] Étienne Nodet, *Les Antiquités juives de Josèphe, livres VI et VII*, Paris, Éd. du Cerf, 2001.
[2] About the book of Daniel, which Josephus uses extensively, he warns his reader that should he want to know the secrets of the future, he must scrutinize the text by himself, a difficult task he has done privately (*Ant.* 10:210). We may surmise that he does not refer to a Greek book, which suggests that he addresses the Jews.

at the Yabneh academy and immediately diffused everywhere. But things have not been that easy. In a previous study of Josephus' Pentateuch, I concluded that the best hypothesis to explain the pecularities of his text was that he had not used a Greek Bible, but paraphrased a much altered Hebrew source including marginal glosses or variant readings. In other words, this was a perused reference copy, most probably the one taken by Titus when he plundered the Temple archives in 70 C.E. This is suggested by Josephus in *Vita* § 417, but unfortunately the passage is corrupted.[3]

Now, in the same prologue of the *Antiquities*, he alludes, as a precedent to his own work, to the story of the Greek translation of the Pentateuch made in Alexandria upon a request of king Ptolemy II. Then he adds (1:12-13): 'But [the king] did not obtain all our writing at that time: those who were sent to Alexandria as translators gave him only the books of the Laws, while there are a vast number of other matters in our sacred books, for they contain the history of five thousand years'.

So Josephus utters three statements: 1. he translated or paraphrased from the Hebrew; 2. he is the first to render into Greek the historical books (former Prophets), at least in connection with an official request, which implies some protection of the works in public libraries; 3. he adds or omits nothing. The third point is easy to check: unlike what he did to the Pentateuch, he follows faithfully the Samuel narrative, only adding some speeches and personal comments and removing some inconsistencies in detail. As for the first two claims, this paper will conclude that we may trust him, too.

The progression will be in five stages: 1. it is necessary to show first that here Josephus follows closely his sources; 2. the significance of his relationship to the so-called 'Lucianic recension' of the LXX; 3. specific contacts with Qumran fragments; 4. the incidence of the additions and parallels of 1 Chronicles; 5. Josephus and the Greek Bible. We may add that the text of the *Antiquities*, only witnessed by medieval manuscripts, is not very well preserved, but the actual effect of this problem for an assessment of its sources is minimal, except in some cases in the spelling of proper names.[4]

---

[3] See Étienne Nodet, 'Josephus and the Pentateuch', *JSJ* 28 (1997), pp. 154–194.
[4] See Étienne Nodet, 'Le texte des *Antiquités* de Josèphe (livres 1–10)', *RB* 94 (1987), pp. 323–376.

I. Josephus and His Sources

Frequently the various forms of the Bible differ in minute detail. Thus, for the contacts of Josephus to any variant to have a meaning, we must first check the way he follows his sources. The general conclusion to be extracted from the sample below is that he is rather scrupulous, sometimes at the cost of inconsistencies. There are some mistakes, maybe out of casual sloppiness, but in general the difficult style and uncertain meanings can be explained away by an effort of the author to put together contradictory sources, for he never discards any information he has, if it does not contradict his personal biases.

For instance, according to 2 Samuel-1 Kings, David at the end of his life has only built an altar on Arauna's threshing-floor, while in 1 Chronicles he prepares everything for the Temple building and for Levitical worship. These sources are difficult to reconcile, but Josephus makes a clumsy combination without much editing of the sources; moreover, he leaves Solomon with almost nothing to do. The apparent reason for this change is that he was still very young (12 or 14) when his father died.

The same phenomenon can be seen in minor details:

– in *Ant.* 6:110, Jonathan arrives close to the Philistine encampment, and says to his armour-bearer: 'Now let us attack the enemy and, if on seeing us they bid us to climb up to them, take that for a presage of victory'. This is not very clear, but can be explained by a conflation of readings. 1 Sam 14:8–10 MT has 'We will show ourselves (ונגלינו, from גלה) to them... If they say: Come up to us, &c.' But the LXX puts 'We will roll down to them. If they say, &c.' The verb has been understood after the root גלל 'roll', which implies a reading ונגלנו. Josephus, who speaks of 'attack' and 'show up', reads and combines both forms, and the result is confused.

– In 6:128, Jonathan is condemned for his transgression, but the Israelites do not accept this, and 'snatched him from his father's curse, and offered prayers for the young man'. 1 Sam 14:45 MT has 'The people redeemed (or 'rescued' ויפדו) Jonathan', but the LXX reads 'The people interceded (προσηύξατο)'; the underlying Hebrew can be restored ויפלל (as in 1 Sam 2:25), which differs by a little shape alteration of the Hebrew letters. Here, too, Josephus combines the two meanings.

– In 7:259, after Absalom's death, the Israelites blame themselves because they have not appealed to David to abate his anger and resume his throne as before. 2 Sam 19:11 MT has 'Why are you silent to bring back the king (להשיב את המלך)', but the LXX is different '...silent to bring back (the people) to the king', which comes from להשיב אל המלך, with one slightly altered letter. Again, Josephus combines both.

– In 7:299, David is threatened by a Giant, who has 'a spear, the haft of which was said to weigh three hundred shekels'. 2 S 21:16 MT only mentions this heavy haft (קינו), which could be of a sword, but the LXX only speaks of a heavy spear, and does not mention the haft. And Josephus has both.

– In 7:324–327, Josephus reports that God sent pestilence unpon the Hebrews. He describes a dramatic plague; some die suddenly, others after a painful illness, others while burying a parent, etc. He adds that from early morning until noon seventy thousand perished, and then the evil angel proceeded toward Jerusalem, till David put on a sackloth and interceded. It is not clear whether the plague lasted one day or more. 2 Sam 24:15 MT has 'from the morning till the appointed time (עת מועד)... Seventy thousand died'. The 'appointed time' could match the three-day punishment announced before (v. 13), but the LXX reads 'till the time of the noon meal', corresponding to a variant עת סועד, with a slight alteration. Josephus combines both, hence some confusion about the length of the plague.

This brief sample, which represents such frequent features, suggests a comment: either Josephus had before his eyes two different copies of the Bible, one Greek and one Hebrew, and he carefully checked both, without being influenced by Greek terminology; or he was using a Hebrew Bible which had in the margins some variant readings as glosses, something like the *qeré-ketib* in the MT, and he 'chose not to choose', *i.e.* added together everything he found.

Sometimes, Josephus' faithfulness to his source, which could be termed a lack of distance, leads him to a degree of nonsense:

– In 7:213–216, when Absalom arrives at Jerusalem, David flees, and Ahitophel advises first the former to lie with his father's concubines, so that the people can see that no reconcialition is possible. He follows the advice in a tent pitched on the roof of the palace, in the sight of the people. Then Ahitophel's second advice is to let him run immediately after David with ten thousand men, but David's friend Hushaï, who recommends that Absalom himself do it after levying an army of all Israel—and so plays with his vanity—wins his approval. This is stupid, for David will have time to escape. For the first advice Josephus follows 2 Sam 16:21–22, but in 17:1, Ahitophel's second advice is to let him 'pursue David *this very night*'; speed is essential. But Josephus has explained the first with realism, which implies some degree of length, so that he cannot speak of speed any more for the second piece of advice. As a result, he adds clumsy and tasteless remarks to explain why Absalom preferred Hushai's suggestion (§§ 217–221).

– In 7:346, when Adonias tries to be proclaimed king, the opponent party includes the best warriors, the high priest Zadok, the prophet Nathan,

Benaya and 'Shimei, David's friend (φίλος)'. This wording, which sets Shimei at the rank of Hushai, is strange, for in the sequel, David in his last speech to Solomon advises him to punish Shimei, who had badly cursed him during his flight. In 1 Kings 1:8 MT, the opponents are Zadoq, Benayah 'and Shimei and Rei and the mighty men (והנבורים וֹרעי)'. For 'and Rei', the LXX has a transcription καὶ Ρησει, but the Antiochian version (or 'Lucianic', see below) translates 'Shimei and his fellows, these being the mighty'. This version depends on a reading וֹרעיו הנבורים, where the ו of the first word is attached to the second. Josephus saw neither version, but we can restore his ultimate Hebrew source: it read רעו after 'Shimei', hence the obvious meaning 'and Shimei his fellow', which fits poorly in this context. Incidentally, this example shows that Josephus may have had a Biblical text of his own.

However, in spite of his general faithfulness, Josephus sometimes introduces his own bias. For instance, during the secret visit of David to Ahimelek, the priest of Nob, he omits the story of the 'hallowed bread' and the ritual purity which allowed David and his servants to eat it, although they were not priests (6:243). Josephus, who was a priest and favoured a priestly leadership over any monarchy, certainly viewed this affair as a bad precedent, not one to be published. In the same way he had omitted the story of the golden calf, when he paraphrased Exodus, to avoid fueling any criticism against the Jews.

2. Josephus and the 'Lucianic Recension' (or Antiochian Bible)

Eusebius of Cesarea mentions favorably Lucian, a priest from Antioch, who was martyred in 312 C.E. (*HE* 8.13.2 et 9.6.3). Around 390, in the prologue to his translation of Chronicles, Jerome states that there are three authorized version of the Greek Bible: 'Alexandria and Egypt praise Hesichius as the author of their LXX; from Constantinople to Antioch, the copies of the martyr Lucian have approval; the intermediate provinces read the Palestinian books prepared by Origen and published by Eusebius and Pamphilus.'[5]

---

[5] Migne, *PL* 28, 1932A; later (*ca.* 392), in *De viris inlustribus* § 77, he praises Lucians, who is so outstanding that 'until now some copies of the Scriptures are called Lucianic'. See Bruce M. Metzger, *Chapters in the History of New Testament Textual Criticism* (New Testament Tools and Studies, 4), Leiden, Brill, 1963, pp. 1–41.

For many centuries this 'Lucianic version' (hereafter $\mathcal{L}$) seemed to have disappeared. But in 1863 it was observed that a small group of medieval manuscripts did have the same text-type as the quotations of the main Antiochian Fathers, especially Theodoret of Cyr and Chrysostom,[6] as well as contacts with some hexaplaric fragments marked with the letter λ (for Λουκιανός 'Lucien'). Later, A. Mez showed that from Joshua through 2 Samuel Josephus' paraphrase has a significant relationship with $\mathcal{L}$.[7] Thus Josephus used a 'proto-Lucianic' Greek Bible almost three centuries before Lucian. This conclusion, generally followed, was based on two assumptions: first, the only Hebrew Bible extant by Josephus' time was the MT, fixed by the rabbis at Yabneh some years before; secondly, the contacts with $\mathcal{L}$ proved that Josephus used a Greek Bible.[8]

H. St. J. Thackeray, who had prepared the Loeb edition of the *Antiquities* and who had studied the LXX a great deal, concluded boldly that from 1 Samuel through 1 Maccabees Josephus had used, besides a semitic source, a $\mathcal{L}$-type scroll of the Greek Bible.[9] Indeed, for 1-2 Samuel, Josephus' contacts with $\mathcal{L}$ are innummerable.[10] But we may ask whether this is valid proof that Josephus used a Greek text, and not a Hebrew Bible close to the source of $\mathcal{L}$. This ques-

---

[6] The minuscules 19, 82, 93 et 108 of the *editio maior* of Robert Holmes et James Parsons, Oxford, 1798-1827. After A. Ceriani et F. Field independantly discovered the fact, Paul de Lagarde added to the group ms. 118.

[7] Adam Mez, *Die Bibel des Josephus, untersucht für Buch V-VII der Archäologie*, Basel, 1905.

[8] Dominique Barthélemy, *Les Devanciers d'Aquila* (VT Sup., 10), Leiden, Brill, 1963, pp. 126-127, concludes that the phrase 'Lucianic recension' is misleading, for this text-type was extant centuries before. Emanuel Tov, 'Lucian and Proto-Lucian. Toward a New Solution of the Problem', *RB* 72 (1979, pp. 101-113), has the same reluctance and states, with interesting arguments, that there was no 'proto-Lucianic recension', but a full-scale ancient Greek translation, which was later revised by the Antiochians (Lucian). This paper will have the same conclusion, but with a totally different approach. Anyway, it is better to keep using the terms 'Lucianic' or 'Antiochian', in order to avoid useless confusions.

[9] Henry St. John Thackeray, *Josephus: The Man and Historian* (Stroock Lectures, 1928), New York, 1929, p. 85. But he gives very few example to justify his claim; more are to be found in the footnotes of his translation (Loeb Classical Library).

[10] For a good critical edition of $\mathcal{L}$, see Natalio Fernândez Marcos y José Ramón Busto Saiz, *El texto antioqueno de la Biblia griega. I-1-2 Samuel*, Madrid, Instituto de Filología (CSIC), 1989. The previous edition, without annotation, was by Paul de Lagarde *Librorum Veteris Testamenti canonicorum pars prior graece*, Göttingen, 1883, who invited somebody else to refine his work, for he was convinced that $\mathcal{L}$ had its roots before Origen's hexaplaric texts.

tion is prompted by a fact easy to check: Josephus' spelling of the proper names is often independant from both £ and LXX.

To begin with, it should be noted that Josephus' relationship with £ does not mean identity, which can be seen in different ways. First, he has several contacts with LXX againts £ and MT:

– in 1 S 19:22, when the messengers sent three times by Saul were unable to find David, 'he also went', according to MT and £; but before this phrase the LXX adds καὶ ἐθυμώθη ὀργῇ. These very words render ויחר אף in 20:30 'his anger was aroused'. Likewise, Josephus has (6:222) ὀργισθεὶς αὐτὸς ἐξώρμησεν 'in a rage he set out himself', which is close to the LXX. This minor contact is interesting, for £, which has many doublets owing to revisions, is seldom shorter than the LXX.
– In 1 S 17:43, after Goliath's words 'Am I a dog, that you come to me with sticks?' the LXX adds a reply of David ignored by MT, £ and Origen καὶ εἶπεν Δαυιδ Οὐχὶ ἀλλ᾽ ἢ χείρω κυνός 'and David said: No, but worse than a dog'. Josephus (6:186) has this addition, with a wording almost identical οὐχὶ τοιοῦτον ἀλλὰ καὶ χείρω κυνός 'not even so, but worse than a dog'. It should be noted that the comparative χείρω, frequently used by Josephus, is a *hapax legomenon* in the LXX.

Second, Josephus has contacts with MT against LXX and £. Most cases concern proper names. Here is one example:

– in 2 S 4:4 f. and 9:6 f., £ names Jonathan's son Μεμφιβααλ and Saul's son Μεμφιβοσθε. Josephus distinguishes them, too (7:9), but follows the MT spelling, respectively מפיבשת 'Mephiboshet' and אישבשת 'Ishboshet'. LXX is somewhat confused, as is the main Qumran witness (*4 QSam^a*, discussed below). Here £, or more probably its Hebrew source, reflects an old tradition, for it is largely admitted that the ancient component *-baal* of pagan theophoric names has been subsequently replaced with *-boshet* 'shame', in a disparaging way.

Third, Josephus sometimes diverges from £, and follows simply the text common to MT and LXX:

– in 1 S 28:19, at the meeting with the witch in En-Dor, Samuel says to Saul 'Tomorrow you and your sons will be with me'. So Josephus (6:336) but £ has 'you and your son Jonathan'. This variant stands alone, for in 31:2, when Saul's three sons die, £ does not diverge from MT and LXX.
– According to 2 S 5:4–5, David reigned forty years, in Hebron seven years and six months and thirty-three years in Jerusalem. So Josephus (7:389), but £ puts 'thirty-two years and six months in Jerusalem', which improves the calculation. Here Josephus has just told of David's death according to 1 Kings 2:10, but he does not follow the next verse, which corrects the calculation in another way, by putting only seven years in Hebron. Thus Josephus' copy of 1 Kings had a reading like 2 S 5, but

more probably as a marginal gloss than in the main text, so we cannot conclude that he witnesses a real variant.

– In 1 Kings 1:6 f., the name of Adonias, the third son of David, is spelled אדוניה in the MT, and Ἀδωνίας by both the LXX and Josephus, but 𝓛 reads Ορνια, which implies a Hebrew form ארניה, with a slight alteration.

– Let us now examine a more complex case. According to 2 Sam 8:9–10 Toi (MT תעי) king of Hamath sent Yoram (MT יורם) his son to David. For Toi, LXX gives Θοου and 𝓛 Ελιαβ (probably a mistake), while Josephus has Θαῖνος (7:108), which is independant from both and seems to imply a source such as תעין. In the parallel passage of 1 Chron 18:9, we read תעו and Θωα; here, תעו agrees with Θοου of 2 Sam LXX, while Θωα implies תעה or תועה. Now תעו and תעי have almost the same shape, and we may imagine a correction of ו into י (or the opposite), and a mistaken result of תעיו or תעין. The former is close to תעה of 1 Chron 18, the latter may have evolved in תעין of Josephus, who stands thus between LXX and MT. We may note incidentally that the *vorlage* of 2 Sam LXX is close to 1 Chron TM. Many other instances of this pattern will be seen below.

As for Yoram, 2 Sam LXX and 𝓛 read Ιεδδουραν, which cannot be reconciled with Ἀδώραμος of Josephus (7:107). The missing link is to be found in 1 Chron, which has הדורם (the source of Josephus) and Ιδουραμ. The forms are corrupted, but it seems that an original *hadad-ram* (הדדרם, see 1 Chron MT) a pagan theophoric name, has been changed into *yoram* (2 Sam MT). If so, 1 Chron would reflect an earlier stage. Here, Josephus does not follow any known Greek Bible, but we cannot conclude that he looked at 1 Chron, for it is possible that his copy of 2 Sam was close to its source. We shall see that the Qumran fragments of 2 Samuel help clarify this question.

This sample by no means denies the close relationship between 𝓛 and Josephus, but another possibility emerges, that both eventually depend on the same Hebrew source. Another set of case strengthens such a hypothesis:

– in 1 S 8:12, when the Israelites want a king, Samuel warns them of the 'rights of the king'; he will turn them into slaves, and they will have, according to the various versions:

MT	to plow his ground	to reap his harvest	~
Hebrew (restored)	לחרש חרישו	ולקצר קצירו	ולבצר בצירו
LXX	~	to reap his harvest	harvest his grapes
𝓛	to plow his ground	to reap his harvest	harvest his grapes
AJ 6:40	craftsmen, husbandmen	tillers	diggers of vineyards.

The MT omits the third component, which may have been a doublet of the second. Josephus has: '(The kings) will make of them craftsmen ... husbandmen, tillers of their estates, diggers of their vineyards'. He gives four terms: the last two are extant in LXX and ₵, but the first two correspond to 'plowing' alone (omitted by LXX). The explanation is simple: the same Hebrew root חרש can mean either 'to forge (smith)' or 'to plow' (homonyms), and Josephus renders both. In other words, he agrees with ₵ against the others, but more precisely both have the same Hebrew source, understood in different ways.

– In 1 S 23:25 David, aware that Saul pursues him, hides 'in the wilderness of Maon' (מעון). The LXX transcribes τῇ Μααν (from מעו), but ₵ has a strange translation τῇ ἐπηκόῳ 'in the obedient desert'. Josephus puts τῇ Σίμωνος ἐρήμῳ 'in the desert of Simon' (from שמעון, *Ant*. 6:280), which gives a clue to restore the *vorlage* of ₵ as שמע[11] 'attentive, obedient', or maybe the same שמעון.[12] One may observe that the latter form may have resulted of an addition and fusion of מעון and שמע, which would be typical of Josephus' handling of variant readings. As for the genealogy of this doubling, the simplest way is to suppose an original מעו (like the LXX), then a correction of ו- into ן- as a gloss; later a copyist would have misread and/or wrongly inserted ש for ן.

The same name appears a little later. In 25:2 Nabal, Abigail's husband is introduced thus: 'There was a man in Maon (מעון)'. The LXX has the same Μααν, but ₵ reads 'in the desert', which might be the result of a misleading influence of the passage discussed. But the verse before (25:2) allows a better explanation: 'David arose and went down to the wilderness of Paran (פארן)', but the LXX has 'the wilderness of Maon (Μααν)', and ₵ again 'the obedient desert' as above. So the origin of the ₵ reading in v. 2 becomes clear: a corrector saw 'obedient' and added 'desert' as a gloss after the previous verse, and later a copyist replaced the word, instead of adding the gloss. This way we may restore under ₵ a Hebrew form שמע or שמעון as above. This reasoning is confirmed by Josephus, who says that Nabal was ἐκ πόλεως Εμμα (6:295, 'of the city of Emma'). It suffices to admit that one s dropped (haplography), and we can restore Σεμμα, i.e. שמע. Here too Josephus is close to ₵, but both stem independently from the same Hebrew.

– Other cases lead us to the same conclusion. For instance, in 2 S 17:27 a friend of David's is mentioned: 'And Shobi (ושבי) son of Nahash from Rabbah of the sons of Ammon'. The LXX sloppily transcribes Ουεσβι, but ₵ reads καὶ Σεφεει, from a variant ושפי. Josephus puts Σειφαρ (7:230), which is connected to ₵, but not directly. We may surmise that he depends on שפר, where ר- erroneously comes from י- too long. In fact, Σειφαρ rather suggests שיפר, *i.e.* שפר together with a misplaced correction י, in the usual Josephan way.

---

[11] To be vocalized שָׁמֵעַ or שֵׁמַע.
[12] Concerning Simeon, Jacob's second son (spelt Συμεών in *AJ* 1:304, by the influence of the LXX), Leah explains 'Yhwh has heard (שמע) that I am unloved' (Gen 29:33). However Philo, *De somniis* 2:34, states that this name indicates an ability to listen (and obey), which suggests that שמעון as a noun may have existed with this meaning, but it is not witnessed by the extant sources.

This sample prompts us to search out other passages where Josephus did not have a Greek Bible before his eyes (either LXX or £), while it could have helped him in transcribing proper names or rendering peculiar phrases. In these cases, it is immaterial whether LXX and/or £ agree or not with MT.

– In 1 S 7:11 a place in Judea is mentioned whose name is בית כר 'Bet-Kar', (or 'place of pastures'), perhaps to be identified with *Ain Karīm*. LXX and £ transcribe Βαιθχορ, but Josephus reads Κορραῖα (6:28), quite independently; for him this is a locality (τόπος τις) and not a city, which better fits the context.

– In 1 S 9:13, Samuel has to bless the sacrifice (for the feast), then the 'invited ones' (קְרֻאִים) will eat. So Josephus, very literally, renders κεκλημένων 'summoned' (6:48), but both LXX and £ translate ξένοι 'guests'. This felicitous rendering would have improved Josephus' style.

– In 1 S 16:2 God advises Samuel, in order that he remain unnoticed with his oil horn for the anointing of David, to take a heifer (עגלת בקר, MT and £ δάμαλιν βοῶν) and to say he has to go to Bethlehem and perform a sacrifice. The device seems to be obvious, but Josephus only says vaguely that 'God provided him a way of safety' (6:157). He has not understood that the heifer is meant to camouflage the horn, which the Greek makes plain. In fact, the Hebrew is ambiguous, for עגלת בקר means also 'ox cart' (homonyms); in this case, the trick is not apparent, and Samuel's safety should have necessitated an armored cart ! So Josephus' vagueness proves that he only read the Hebrew, all the more that עגלה 'cart' occurs much more frequently than עגלה 'heifer'. A couple of chapters before (1 S 6:7–14) the Ark was carried back to Beth Shemesh on a cart (עגלה).

– In 1 S 19:18 f. MT David fled and stayed with Samuel 'in Nawit' (*Ketib* בנוית) or 'in Nayot' (*Qeré* בניות). The LXX transcribes ἐν Ναυιωθ, (ms. B), and £ ἐν Αυαθ, to be restored ἐν Ναυαθ (a form witnessed by ms. V). There is a hesitation between ו and י, which are very similar letters, but all the versions understood the -ב as a preposition. For Josephus, the mss. give variant readings which derive from a form Βαλγουαθ. The initial B-, viewed as a part of the name, indicates that he did not see the Greek Bible. As for the letters -λγ- we may conjecture an uncial error ΛΓ for ΝΙ and restore ΒΑΝΙΟΥΑΘ, a transcription of MT *Qeré*.

– In 2 S 3:26, Joab has sent messengers to Abner, to bring him back 'from the cistern of Sirah' (מבור הסירה). LXX and £ translate ἀπὸ τοῦ φρέατος Σειρα(μ) 'from the well of Sirah', which implies a reading מבאר הסירה. Josephus has Βησηρα (7:34), which depends on the same reading, but independently.

– In 7:377, Josephus writes that David has secured much material for the building of the Temple, including 'emeralds (σμαράγδου) and precious stones of every kind'. His source is 1 Chron 29:2 'onyx (שהם) stones and stones &c.' LXX gives a transcription λίθους σοομ, but £ translates λίθους ὄνυχος 'onyx stones'. Josephus observed neither version, though he is not at home with the names of precious stones.¹³ In Exod 28:9, the *ephod* of the high priest is adorned with the same stone שהם, but the LXX understands 'emeralds', while Josephus speaks of 'sardonyxes' (3:165), which is inconsistent. So we may safely exclude the idea that he wanted to emend the Greek rendering of either passage.

The various cases discussed above—which are only a small sample—suggest the best hypothesis is that for 1–2 Samuel Josephus only used a Hebrew copy sharing many peculiarities with the source of the specific £ readings. More precisely, this copy had some marginal glosses, including variant readings. So its origin should have been from an official library. But two important topics which have surfaced above remain to be discussed: first, the agreements of Josephus, Chronicles and some Qumran fragments of 1–2 Samuel against 1–2 Samuel MT; secondly, Josephus and LXX (and/or £) use in some instances the same Greek words, which may imply that he actually glanced at a Greek Bible!

3. Josephus and the Qumran Fragments (DSS)

The excavations at Qumran have unearthed fragments of four different copies of 1–2 Samuel. Their datings have been established around the Herodian period, somewhere after 50 B.C.E.:¹⁴

1 QSam (1 Q7), with seven small fragments; three passages have been restored to date, 1 Sam 18:17–18, 2 Sam 20:6–10 and 21:16–18. The copy is marred by scribal errors, but the text-type is close to MT and has no specific contact with Josephus.

4 QSam^a, with hundreds of fragments scattered over the whole books. It has some outstanding agreements with Josephus and £, as

---

¹³ This is made plain in other places. In *War* 5:324 and *Ant.* 3:168, he has given twice the names of the twelve precious stones of the *hoshen* of the high priest, according to Exod 28:17–20 (or 39:10–13, with slight changes); among them, he renders שהם with 'beryl' and 'onyx' respectively (like £ here), but he may have read the list in different orders. The same list appears elsewhere, see the discussion by Louis H. Feldman, 'Prolegomenon' of the reprint of Montague R. James, *The Biblical Antiquities of Philo*, New York, Doubleday, 1971, p. cxiii.

¹⁴ The official edition of these fragments (DJD) still awaits publication, because of the complexity of the problems involved. A preliminary view is given by Martin Abegg Jr., Peter Flint & Eugene Ulrich, *The Dead Sea Scrolls Bible*, Edinburgh, T&T Clark, 1999, pp. 213–259, with bibliography.

well as 1 Chronicles against 2 Samuel. The main features of this copy are discussed below.[15]

4 QSam^b, with one large fragment and seven smaller ones; four passages have been restored, 1 Sam 16:1–11, 19:10–17, 20:26–42, 21:1–9 and 23:9–17. The text has numerous contacts with the LXX and £, sometimes with the LXX against £ (and MT), but never with £ against the LXX. It has some readings of its own, including one contact with Josephus in a difficult passage (1 Sam 21:3, see below).

4 QSam^c, with one fragment which gives a part of 1 Sam 25:30–31 and numerous small ones, from which 2 S 14:7–33 and 15:1–15 have been restored. The text has some peculiarities, several scribal errors and a couple of contacts with £ and with *4 QSam^a*, but it has nothing in common with Josephus.

Before discussing *4 QSam^a*, lets us present first the only significant contact of *4 QSam^b* with Josephus:

– in 1 Sam 21:3 David tells the priest Ahimelek of his secret mission and explains why he does not have an escort: 'And I let the servants know (יודעתי) to such and such a place'. The sentence is awkward, even if we understand the strange יודעתי as a *po^{a}el* of ידע with a *hif^{a}il* meaning (instead of הודעתי). The LXX and £ have 'And I witnessed (διαμεμαρτύρημαι) to the servants, &c.' This points to a Hebrew source העדתי, which hardly improves the sense. *4 QSam^b* reads יעדתי 'I rendezvoused the servants', which gives the expected meaning. So there is a confusing of the roots יעד, עוד and ידע (metatheses, a frequent feature). Josephus writes that David ordered (προσέταξα) his servants to join him (6:243); so he depends on either יעדתי like *4 QSam^b* or העדתי like the LXX (but read as *hif^{a}il* of יעד). Here, *4 QSam^b* helps assessing an indirect relationship between Josephus and LXX-£.

---

[15] Concerning *4 QSam^a*, the main peculiarities are given and discussed by Eugene Ulrich, *The Qumran Text of Samuel and Josephus* (Harvard Semitic Monograph, 19), Missoula (Mont.), Scholars Press, 1978; Id., 'Josephus' Biblical Text for the Books of Samuel', in: Louis H. Feldman & Gohei Hata, *Josephus, the Bible, and History*, Leiden, Brill, 1989, pp. 81–96, where the author summarizes his previous discussions, but adduces no further evidence. This paper, slightly revised, is published again in Eugene Ulrich, *The Dead Sea Scrolls and the Origins of the Bible* (Studies in the Dead Sea Scrolls and Related Literature, 1), Grand Rapids (Mich.), W.B. Eerdmans & Leiden, Brill, 1999, pp. 184–201. Ulrich's main thesis, that Josephus used a Greek Bible close to £ and reflecting a Hebrew source close to *4 QSam^a*, is discussed below. It should be noted that Edward D. Herbert, *Reconstructing Biblical Dead Sea Scrolls: A New Method Applied to the Reconstruction of 4 QSam^a* (Studies on the Texts of the Desert of Judah, 22), Leiden, Brill, 1997, has developed a statistical method which allows an assessment of difficult readings and helps locate isolated fragments.

As for *4 QSam^a*, its agreements with Josephus are really impressive:

– in 1 Sam 1:22, after Samuel's birth, Hannah tells her husband Elkanah she wants to consecrate their son to God. *4 QSam^a* adds [ונת]תיהו נזיר עד עולם '[and I shall] make him a *nazir* for ever'. Now Josephus says that Hannah 'delivered [Samuel] to Eli, dedicating him to God to become a prophet' (ἀνατιθεῖσα τῷ θεῷ προφήτην γενησόμενον, 5:347). He summarizes the passage, but he certainly read like *4 QSam^a*, because for him the status of *nazir* is only temporary (see 4:72, following Num 6:4–21), and he calls 'prophet' a permanent *nazir* (see 5:278). Incidentally, we may remark that in Lk 1:15 John the Baptist is presented as a new Samuel; he is to become a permanent *nazir* (or prophet): 'For he will be great in the sight of the Lord, and shall drink neither wine nor strong drink'. The connection with the MT as it stands is rather loose, for even in v. 11 the precepts of the *nazir* are not alluded to (see below).

In 1:11, *4 QSam^a* is longer the the MT; in Hannah's prayer, the following word sequence ונתתיו ליהוה כל ימי חיו 'I shall give him to YHWH all the days of his life' is replaced by a longer phrase, which is poorly preserved, but has been restored after LXX and 𝓛 καὶ δώσω αὐτὸν ἐνώπιν σου δοτὸν ἕως ἡμέρας θανάτου αὐτοῦ καὶ οἶνον καὶ μέθυσμα οὐ πίεται 'and I shall give him before you as 'donated' until the day of his death and he shall drink neither wine nor strong drink'. The word δοτός 'donated' is a *hapax legomenon* in LXX and 𝓛. It might render נזיר *nazir* in the source, but in Judg. 13:5 (Samson), this word is simply transcribed ναζιρ; more probably it corresponds, together with δώσω, to a typical emphatic doubling of the verb with an infinitive נתון נתתיו, and the latter can be read נתון 'donated, given'. Joesphus' text confirms this possibility (5:344): in her prayer, Hannah promised 'that her first-born should be consecrated to the service (καθιερώσειν ἐπὶ τῇ διακονίᾳ) of God and that his manner of life (δίαιταν) should be unlike that of ordinary men'. The 'manner of life' indicates that he had the longer reading, and the 'consecration to the service' refers to an absolute donation.

– After the word מנחה in 1 Sam 10:27a, *4 QSam^a* leaves a blank end to the line *(petuḥa)*, than adds three and a half lines about Nahash, the Ammonite king. No other version knows this passage, but Josephus read this long plus, which he faithfully paraphrased, adding only some personal comments (6:68–69): 'A month later, [Saul] began to win the esteem of all by the war with Nahash, king of the Ammonites. The latter had done much harm to the Jews who had settled beyond the river Jordan . . . By force and violence he secured their subjection in the present . . . He cut out the right eyes of all . . .' The table below shows in details the closeness of *4 QSam^a* to this text:[16]

---

[16] E. Ulrich, *The Qumran Text of Samuel*, pp. 166–170, deals at length with these passages, but his hypothesis, discussed below, that Josephus depends on an old Greek Bible, introduces intricate elements.

Josephus	4 QSam^a (translation)
Μηνὶ δ' ὕστερον ... (a month later ...)	
Ναάσην ... τὸν Ἀμμανιτῶν βασιλέα·	[נ]חש מלך בני עמון Nahash king of the sons of Ammon
οὗτος γὰρ πολλὰ κακὰ	הוא לחץ he had oppressed
τοὺς πέραν τοῦ Ἰουδάνου ποταμοῦ	את בני גד the sons of Gad
κατῳκημένους τῶν Ἰουδαίων διατίθησι ...	ואת בני ראובן and the sons of Ruben
ἰσχύι μὲν καὶ βίᾳ ...	בחזקה with strength.
τῶν ... λαμβανομένων πολέμου νόμῳ	וינקר להם כ[ול] He had pierced to them
τοὺς δεξιοὺς ὀφθαλμοὺς ἐξέκοπτεν.	[ע]י[ן] ימין every right eye.

MT

| v. 27b | ויהי כמחריש | and he was silent. | ויהי כמו חדש | There was about a month (= LXX) |
| v. 28 | ויעל נחש | And Nahash came up, &c. | ויעל נחש | and Nahash came up, &c. |

Josephus differs from *4 QSam^a* in one detail: in the former, the phrase 'a month later' comes before the addition, while the latter puts it afterward. This may have been a difference of texts, which would indicate that the passage dropped and then was later wrongly reinserted in one of the copies. It is possible, too, that Josephus himself made the change, if he understood that the oppression of Gad and Ruben occurred much before the Saul story. But in view of the general faithfulness of Josephus to his source, the first possibility is probably better.

– In 1 Sam 28:1, King Akish invites David to join with him against Saul: 'Know assuredly that you will go out with me to battle, you and your men'. *4 QSam^a* adds יזרעאל 'to Jezreel', where Saul's encampment stands (see 29:1 MT 'by a fountain which is in Jezreel). Josephus explains (6:325) that the Philistines summon all their allies to join them 'to fight at Rega' εἰς τὸν πλεμον εἰς 'Ρεγάν. This place name, spelled by the mss. Ρıγαν, Ρεγγαν, *Rella* (Lat), cannot be found in the Bible and has elicited various conjectures, but *4 QSam^a* helps in finding a tolerable solution in four steps: first, Ιεζραηλ 'Jezreel' is often changed by sloppy copyists into Ισραηλ 'Israel' (see 1 Sam 29:1 LXX [B], variant readings of *Ant.* 8:346 f. and 8:105 f.), hence various intermediate forms: second, 'at Rega' of Josephus is EICPE-ΓAN in uncials; third, one may view Λ as a slight alteration of L (a frequent confusion), and obtain EICPEΛAN; fourth, it is possible to surmise a haplography of the preposition EIC, and to restore EIC (E)ICPEΛAN, which is quite close to 'at Jezreel' of *4 QSam^a*. The feminine form probably comes from the direction suffix (יזרעאלה), for Josephus sometimes takes it as a feminine mark (e.g. *Ant.* 1:336, where שעירה 'to Seir' of Gen 33:16 is rendered with a feminine 'hairy'). This analysis can be summarized briefly: a casual haplography of EIC, has been followed by several corrections (prior to the archetype), which have made things worse.

– In 2 Sam 5:6, David arrives at Jerusalem, but the Jebusites say: 'You shall not come in here unless you repel (הסירך אם כי) the blind and the lame'. The meaning is ambiguous: either David has first to win over the disabled who defend the city, or he must remove the disabled from his own army.[17] The parallel of 1 Chron 11:5 does not mention the disabled. LXX and £ have 'for the blind and the lame will expel you', which implies a reading הסירך כי; in other words, the city walls are so strong that even the disabled can defend it. Here, 4 *QSam*^{a} has a peculiar reading הסית כי (ת- and ך- have a similar shape), which can be rendered 'for the blind and the lame will stir'. Josephus explains (*Ant.* 7:61) that the Jebusites 'shut their gates against him and placed on the wall the blind, the lame and all the disabled to mock at the king; they said that these cripples would prevent him from entering ... David's wrath, however, was aroused, and he began to besiege Jerusalem'. Josephus understands like the LXX and £ against MT (*i.e.* without אם), but he adds the mocking at David and his wrath, *i.e.* a stir or incitement. This indicates that he also had the 4 *QSam*^{a} reading, probably as a marginal gloss, and as usual he strove to combine all the available data.

– In 2 Sam 11:6, at the time of his affair with Bathsheba, David orders Joab to send him her husband, Uriah the Hittite. 4 *QSam*^{a} alone adds נושא כלי יואב 'Joab's armour-bearer', a qualification unknown elsewhere (the name Uriah occurs 26 times). But Josephus too tells us (7:131) that David summoned Uriah, who was 'Joab's armour-bearer' (τὸν Ἰωάβου μὲν ὁπλοφόρον). There is no reason to surmise that he invented this detail.

These pluses common to Josephus and 4 *QSam*^{a} are impressive. Unfortunately, it is impossible to check the minuses they may have in common, because both 4 *QSam*^{a} is too fragmentary and Josephus' minor omissions may be due to his style.

4. Josephus, 1 Chronicles and 4 *QSam*^{a}

After this assessment of the relationship between Josephus and 4 *QSam*^{a}, we may discuss the question raised above of the agreements of Josephus and 1 Chronicles against 2 Samuel in their parallel passages. Some 4 *QSam*^{a} readings allow to determine the significance of these contacts:

– According to 2 Sam 3:3 MT, the name of the second son of David, or more precisely the firstborn of his second wife was 'Kileab, from Abigail'

---

[17] Lev 21:18 forbids the disabled to take part in the worship. This prohibition is extended here, as if the whole city were like a shrine (2 Sam 5:8 'the lame and the blind are hated by David').

(כלאב לאביניל). The name is strange, and some suspect a dittography of לאב. The LXX and 𝓛 have Δαλουια, which agrees with *4 QSam*ᵃ דלויה or דליהו (the last three letters are uncertain). The parallel in 1 Chron 3:1 has דניאל, LXX Λαμνιηλ or Δαλουια (as 2 Sam LXX); the MT form is contaminated by the more frequent 'Daniel'. All this allows a restoration of the double form of a theophoric name דלויה/דליאל as the source of the various readings (outside 2 Sam MT), including Josephus, who writes Δαλουίηλος (7:21, with some variants contaminated by Δανιηλ, too). The latter seems to have combined the two forms (Δαλουια + ηλ + ος), which would imply that he read both: like *4 QSam*ᵃ in the text, and a marginal gloss דליאל, or maybe only a correction אל-, as witnessed by 1 Chron MT. Now we may ask whether such a variant has been imported from 1 Chron (Hebrew), or belongs to the 2 Sam textual tradition. The following cases suggest an answer.

– In 2 Sam 6:7, after Uzzah has taken hold of the Ark, 'God struck him for insolence (על השל) and he died'. This word is an *hapax legomenon* of uncertain meaning. The ancient versions connect it to the Aramaic verb שלו 'to be careless'. The parallel 1 Chron 13:10 is longer (and clearer) על אשר שלח ידו אל הארון 'God struck him because he put his hand to the Ark', but these very words are to be read in 2 Sam 6:7 according to *4 QSam*ᵃ. Josephus says plainly (7:83) that Uzzah died 'because he had stretched out his hand toward [the Ark]'. This agrees perfectly with 1 Chron, but the *4 QSam*ᵃ variant shows that Josephus may have found it in a copy of 2 Sam. Thus the latter would be closer than MT, LXX and 𝓛 to the ancient source of the excerpts quoted in 2 Chron.

But there are further complications, for Josephus does not insert this longer reading at its normal place (2 Sam 6:7, with Uzzah's death), but a little later, when he paraphrases v. 9 'David was afraid of YHWH that day'. When Uzzah touched the Ark he explains (7:81, corresponding to v. 7): 'Because he had touched [the Ark] though not being a priest, God caused his death'. So, according to Josephus, the Levite Uzzah had been careless, insolent or presumptuous; this is not properly an addition, but corresponds to the difficult words על השל of v. 7, which Josephus understood as a specific carelessness, probably after the same Aramaic שלו. We may add that Josephus was not aware of 1 Chron 15:22, which grants the Levites the right to handle the Ark; as above, he did not check details against 1 Chron.

The conclusion is that Josephus has read the two variants: the shorter at its place (v. 7) but the longer with a subsequent verse, though it would have been easy to combine both into one statement, as he usually does. This indicates that he did not read the latter at its proper place (in 2 Sam or 1 Chron) but as a marginal gloss in his copy of 2 Sam, but poorly aligned with the relevant verse. Thus the *4 QSam*ᵃ witness has its full value: the gloss has not been borrowed from 1 Chron, but is indeed an alternate reading of 2 Sam Hebrew.

– In 2 Sam 24:17a, during the plague, we find 'And David said to YHWH when he saw the angel who was striking the people, and he said &c. (see below)' Both *4 QSam^a* and 1 Ch 21:16 have a longer text: 'And David lifted his eyes and saw the angel of YHWH standing between earth and heaven, having in his hand a sword stretched out toward Jerusalem. And David and the elders, clothed in sackcloth, fell on their faces'. LXX and £ have no significant variant. Josephus faithfully follows this longer form (7:327), but omits the elders, probably because they are not mentioned in the context. Again, the *4 QSam^a* witness suggests that Josephus found this very text in his copy of 2 Sam, and did not have to check it against 1 Chron. It is not to be ruled out, however, that Josephus did read both forms, and that the shorter one, which does not speak of elders, was his starting point. But the following discussion will show that this is rather unlikely.

Here is the continuation of 2 Sam 24:17a: 'and he said: Behold, I have sinned, and I (LXX, £ and *4 QSam^a* add 'the shepherd') have acted wickedly, but these sheep, what have they done ?' Again, the 1 Chron 21:17 parallel is different: 'And David said to God: Was it not I who commanded the people to be numbered ? I am the one who has sinned and done evil indeed, but these sheep, what have they done ?' It is instructive to compare these texts on a table, after restoring the source of LXX and £ after *4 QSam^a*. The part under discussion is set between two vertical bars.

2 S MT	מה עשו	ואלה הצאן	העויתי	|חטאתי ואנכי| הנה אנכי
2 S LXX(-£)[18]	מה עשו	ואלה הצאן	הוא הרעה הרעיתי	|חטאתי ואנכי| הנה אנכי
4 QSam^a			הרעה הרעיתי ו[...]	[...]נכי	
1 Ch MT-LXX	מה עשו	ואלה הצאן	והרע הרעותי	חטאתי	ואני הוא אשר

The difference between MT העויתי 'I have acted wickedly' and *4 QSam^a* הרעתי 'I have done evil' may be explained with a metathesis ער/רע and a confusion ו/ד. 1 Chron has a doubling of the root רעע 'to be bad' (*hif^a il*, see 1 Sam 12:25), while LXX-£ and *4 QSam^a* put together similar roots (רעה 'shepherd' and רעע). However, the spelling difference between *4 QSam^a* and 1 Chron MT is slight: one ה before another ה. 1 Chron is probably secondary, resulting from a haplography, for it seems to have lost the symmetry 'shepherd' vs. 'sheep'. Josephus follows LXX-£ and *4 QSam^a* against MT and 1 Chron (7:328): '[David] said to God that it was he, the shepherd who was rightly to be punished, but the flock, which had committed no sin, should be saved'. Then he continues 'And he entreated him to cause his anger to fall upon him and all his line, but to spare the people'. Here he seems to depend on 1 Chron 21:17 'Let your hand be against me and my father's house, *but not against your people that they should be plagued*', for the part in italics is omitted by 2 Sam 24:17. *4 QSam^a* is destroyed here, but in the previous example, which belongs to the same context, it agreed

---

[18] For the part between the bars, the LXX has καὶ ἐγώ εἰμι ὁ ποιμὴν ἐκακοποίησα, but £ and Origen omit εἰμι, a rendering of הוא, in the *vorlage* of LXX (nominal sentence). The same way Deut 6:4 LXX has κυρίος εἷς εστιν against MT יהוה אחד; the *vorlage* of LXX did have an additional הוא at the end, as we find in the Nash papyrus (יהוה אחד הוא).

with the longer text of 1 Chron. So we may conclude that here too he did not run to 1 Chron in the middle of a verse, but read the longer form in his copy of 2 Sam. Another case in the same passage will confirm this. – In 2 Sam 24:20, the prophet Gad has sent David to Arauna's threshing floor, and the latter 'looked, and saw the king and his servants coming across to him'. *4 QSam^a* adds 'covered with sackcloths, and Arauna was threshing (דש) wheat'. The parallel in 1 Chron 21:20 is difficult: 'And Arauna turned and saw the angel (המלאך, LXX 'the king', from המלך) and his four sons with him who were hiding (מתחבאים, LXX transcribes μεθαχαβιν), and Arauna was threshing (דש) wheat'. It is unclear whose are the sons, but their hiding may be connected to the 'servants covered with sackcloths' of *4 QSam^a*. Josephus says plainly (7:330): 'Arauna was threshing his grain, and when he saw the king approaching with all his servants (or 'children', παῖδας, like LXX)'. He ignores 1 Chron 21, and agrees with *4 QSam^a*; the sackcloth is omitted here, but mentioned before (§ 327, see 2 Sam 24:17 above). His use of παῖδας is ambiguous, and may have been a compromise between 2 Sam 'servants' and 1 Chron 'sons'; unfortunately, the word cannot be read on *4 QSam^a*. Here, two conclusions can be drawn: first, Josephus used a copy of 2 Sam close to *4 QSam^a*; second, the same text type was the source of 1 Chron, which was was subsequently altered.

In order to conclude on Josephus' use of 1 Chronicles, we must distinguish its two very different components: its own portions, unparalleled elsewhere, and the passages in common with 2 Samuel. It is obvious that Josephus had included whole chapters of the first category in his narrative, especially at the end of book 7, when he portrays David as preparing everything for the future Temple.

As for the passages parallel with 2 Samuel, they show many discrepancies. They are excerpts from a specific Hebrew copy we can term 2 Sam*, and subsequently had a history of their own within 1 Chronicles (editing and/or alteration). For this book, LXX and £ do not shed useful light, for their *vorlage* was almost identical to MT. The discussions above, albeit limited to a sample, allow us to build a general hypothesis in three parts:

1. 2 Sam* is close to *4 QSam^a*, and has many agreements with LXX and especially £. There is no reason to suppose that *4 QSam^a* is the result of an attempt to harmonize MT-type texts of 2 Sam and 1 Chron.

2. When Josephus agrees with 1 Chron against 2 Sam, they come from readings of his copy of 2 Sam, which is close to 2 Sam* and displays some marginal glosses.

3. From 1 Chron Josephus paraphrases specific chapters, but never uses isolated readings in the passages parallel to 2 Sam. It should

be noted that we cannot be sure that he had 1 Chron in its actual form. Of course, this statement has to be tested for 1–2 Kings.

The previous analyses have shown that in many cases Josephus follows a Hebrew source. Even his relationship with £ makes more sense if both depend on a common Hebrew source, because of some pecularities of transcriptions and translations. The next step is to look for his possible dependance on a Greek Bible.

5. Josephus and the Greek Bible

Before discussing specific cases, let us first outline a logical synthesis of the previous conclusions.

We saw above (§ 2) that Thackeray stated that besides a semitic source Josephus had used à £-type Greek Bible. We may name it £*. Now if we take into account the features of *4 QSam^a*, we must conclude, first that the Hebrew source of £* was close to *4 QSam^a*, and second that £ was the outcome of revisions posterior to Josephus which made it closer to MT, but without losing its own character. Now another set of data must be introduced, which show that some of these revisions were made long before Lucian; indeed numerous features of £ (but not of £*) are to be found in various witnesses, prior to Lucian: ancient papyri, fragments of the *Vetus latina*, Armenian version of the Bible, quotations of the *Biblical Antiquities* of Ps.-Philo, quotations by ancient Fathers (Clement of Alexandria, Origen, Theophilus of Antioch, Tertullian, Hippolytus, &c.).

This impressive diffusion of the £ text-type, which is obviously 'protolucianic', lead E. Tov to claim that it was not a revision of an Old Greek Bible, but a full-scale translation that was widely used.[19] This statement is really interesting, but the combined witnesses of Josephus and *4 QSam^a* prompt us to refine it. The ancient translation is necessarily £*, which was subsequently revised (or altered) in the 2nd century, the result being a 'protolucianic' £ that was widely spread. This seems to be quite possible, but we must add that the similarity of Josephus and £ is due to their having a common

---

[19] E. Tov, 'Lucian and Proto-Lucian...' (see n. 8), pp. 104–105. He rightly refutes the usual explanation, that the ancient witnesses mentioned would have been revised by some 'lucianic' scholars or copyists.

Hebrew source. In other words, $\mathcal{L}$ and $\mathcal{L}^*$ are two independent translations of the same Hebrew text-type, which means that $\mathcal{L}^*$ is only a Greek proto-Josephus (his Greek source). Thus two conclusions appear:

1. Thackeray's hypothetic text $\mathcal{L}^*$, unknown otherwise, never existed. Josephus used a Hebrew copy close to *4 QSam^a*, which itself is close to the source of the 1 Chron excerpts. These were not used by him.

2. Tov's hypothesis of a true 'protolucianic' translation is notably strengthened. It is the ancient layer of $\mathcal{L}$. Moreover, it should be stressed that nothing suggests that it was already extant by Josephus' time. It cannot be ruled out, thus, that the translator took advantage of his work, since it was protected in official libraries (as was the official Septuagint in Alexandria, according to the *Letter of Aristeas*).

After these reasonings, some detailed discussions are appropriate. First, we may observe that Thackeray's conclusion, that Josephus used a protolucianic Greek $\mathcal{L}^*$, was in fact based upon a hidden principle: if Josephus diverges from the MT, he necessarily follows a Greek source or an Aramaic *targum*. The root of this principle was the received view that the MT had been authoritative of old, so that the disagreements over the Greek translations were due to a kind of *targum*-like paraphrasing. Thus all the recensions of the Bible, including Origen's works, were just attempts to get closer to the MT. But things have become much less self-evident since the discovery of other forms of the Hebrew text.

E. Ulrich's arguments[20] have to be carefully scrutinized, for after a detailed study of *4 QSam^a* he concludes, even more definitely than Thackeray, that Josephus used almost exclusively a Greek text for 1-2 Samuel. Here is his main evidence:

– In 1 Sam 10:4 Samuel announces to Saul that he will meet three men 'who will give you two 'breads' (or 'of bread' שתי לחם), and you shall receive from their hands'. LXX-$\mathcal{L}$ renders καὶ δώσουσίν σοι ($\mathcal{L}$ omits σοι) δύο ἀπαρχὰς ἄρτων (= *4 QSam^a* שתי תנופות לחם) καὶ λήμψῃ. Josephus has a similar wording (6:55): δώσουσί σοι ἄρτους δύο, σὺ δὲ λήμψῃ. Ulrich concludes that Josephus has copied the Greek, but this view is not very well founded: first, the words used are precise but quite common, which cannot preclude independent translations of the same source; second, Josephus omits ἀπαρχάς 'first fruits, offerings', which agrees with MT against the others; third,

---

[20] E. Ulrich, *The Qumran Text*... (see n. 15), pp. 183–187.

𝓛 omits σοι against Josephus and LXX, so that his Greek source is not clear. Ulrich gives other inconclusive examples of agreements of Josephus and LXX and/or 𝓛 for usual words. They may well be the result of independant translations. It is unnecessary to repeat here this kind of evidence.

In the previous verse (10:3) LXX, 𝓛 and Josephus (6:55) translate נבל יין 'skin of wine' with ἄσκος οἴνου. The compound נבל יין occurs in MT another three times, and only in 1–2 Sam. In 1 Sam 25:18 LXX and 𝓛 put, more vaguely, ἀγγεῖον 'vessel'; in 1 Sam 1:24 and 2 Sam 16:1 both transcribe νεβελ. (In theses three places, Josephus summarizes the narrative and does not render the locution.) This indicates that it was rather unfamiliar to the LXX translators. Moreover, the only place where the translation is accurate has a parallel in Josephus, which may suggest that the latter was indeed the source. In any case, it is unsound to conclude that Josephus has copied a Greek source (LXX or 𝓛), all the more that in the same verse the three ככרות לחם 'loaves of bread' are plainly rendered 'three breads' by Josephus, while LXX and 𝓛 have ἀγγεῖα ἄρτων 'vessels of bread' (probably from כלי לחם). Incidentally it is significant to observe that in this passage Josephus has two minor agreements with the MT against the others (including *4 QSam^a*).

– In 1 Sam 25:3 Nabal, Abigail's husband, is introduced as a wicked individual, and MT *ketib* concludes והוא כלבו 'and he was like his heart'; the *qeré* is 'and he was a Calebite' (from the house of Caleb); this makes sense, since Nabal is from Maon and 1 Chron 2:42–49 says that the house of Caleb includes Ziph, Hebron and Maon. One may understand, also, that he was 'dog-like' (from כלב 'dog'). LXX and 𝓛 put καὶ ὁ ἄνθρωπος (as *4 QSam^a* והאיש) κυνικός 'and the man was dog-like', which may mean 'churlish' or 'a Cynic'. They follow the *qeré*, but did not recognize a clan name. Josephus states more clearly (6:296) that Nabal 'was a hard man of a bad character, who lived according to the practices of the Cynics'. Ulrich concludes that he depends on LXX-𝓛, but this is unproven if he does not show that this LXX-𝓛 reading antedates Josephus. In fact, κυνικός is a *hapax legomenon* in the LXX, which gives a strange meaning without explanation. On the contrary, it is not inconceivable that a translator or revisor of the Greek Bible, being at a loss with the difficult word כלבו/כלבי, has looked at Josephus' paraphrase. As for Josephus, who had noteworthy training in Greek literature, he may well have glossed his translation and introduced a special hint of Greek philosophy as he did elsewhere.

– In 1 Sam 26:11 f. צפחת מים 'flask of water' occurs three times; LXX and 𝓛 put τὸν φακὸν τοῦ ὕδατος, which is a stange translation: צפחת is rendered otherwise elsewhere, and conversely φακός renders other words. In the paraphrase of this passage (6:313 f.) Josephus uses the same expression three times ὁ φακὸς τοῦ ὕδατος, which does not occur elsewhere. Ulrich rightly remarks that Josephus and LXX-𝓛 cannot have arrived at the same translation independently. But, again, it is not proven that this LXX-𝓛 reading antedates Josephus. Moreover, other details in this passage are rendered independantly by Josephus and LXX-𝓛.

– In 1 Sam 28:1 King Akish invites David to join with him against Saul: 'Know assuredly that you will go out with me to battle, you and your men'. *4 QSam*ᵃ adds יזרעאל 'to Jezreel', and Josephus 'to Rega' (6:325), which has been explained as an uncial error for 'to Jezreel' (§ 3 above). Ulrich claims that this was already an error of the Greek source of Josephus, for if he had recognized the name 'Jezreel' he would have added πόλις to identify it as a city, which was for a time the capital of the Northern kingdom (8:346 f.). But the present context hardly hints at a city. 1 Sam 29:1 MT mentions the encampment 'by the fountain (בעין) which is in Jezreel'; the wording seems to indicate a region rather than a city. LXX has 'by Ain-Dor which is in Jezreel', and ℒ 'by Ain', a transcription of MT. So, for LXX-ℒ the city is Ain or Ain-Dor, and Jezreel is a region.

– In 2 Sam 6:13, when the Ark was being transferred to Jerusalem, those bearing it went 'six paces' (צעדים) before the sacrifice. LXX and ℒ have a different text: 'with them were the ark bearers, seven choirs (χοροί), and a sacrifice, &c.' It is unclear whether the choir are to be identified with the bearers. Josephus is unambiguous (7:85): '[The Ark was carried by the priests, who were preceded by seven choirs' (ἑπτὰ δὲ χορῶν ... προαγόντων). Josephus and LXX-ℒ obviously agree against MT (and against the parallel 1 Chron 15:26, which is much shorter), but may have been independent renderings of the same Hebrew, for they do not display agreements for odd Greek words (as in the case of the 'flask' above). Unfortunately, *4 QSam*ᵃ is lacking here, but Ulrich's conclusion, that Josephus followed LXX-ℒ, seems to be unwarranted.

– In 2 Sam 10:6, in a passage discussed above (§ 4) 'the sons of Ammon sent and hired Aram (of) Beth Rehob (את ארם בית רחב), &c.' LXX has '... and hired Syria (τὴν Συρίαν) and Beth Rehob'; 'Syria' for ארם is normal, but ℒ replaces it with Σύρον, which can be 'one Syrian' or a proper name, but does not improve the meaning. The underlying Hebrew has ובית instead of בית. The parallel 1 Chron 19:6 is different: 'And the sons of Ammon ... sent a thousand talents to hire for themselves from Aram Naharaim (מן ארם נהרים, LXX ἐκ Συρίας Μεσοποταμίας) and from Aram Maakah, &c.' Beth Rehob is not mentioned. Josephus says (7:121) that they sent 'a thousand talents to Syros, the king of the Mesopotamians, and invited him to become their ally, &c.' So he agrees with 1 Chron (*4 QSam*ᵃ is lacking), with a minor discrepancy: he read 'to hire for themselves Aram' with the accusative (את ארם like 2 Sam, instead of מן ארם); so he took 'Aram' as a man, hence a translation 'Syros'. Ulrich affirms that Josephus copied 'Syros' from ℒ. This is hardly possible, for he follows a 1 Chron-type text against 2 Sam. Now, we may observe that 'Syros' in ℒ is strange: first, he is introduced as a king, and seems to have been hired alone; second, Σύρος is an *hapax legomenon* in LXX and ℒ, while Josephus uses it frequently. So the best hypothesis would be that a ℒ revisor took this name from Josephus.

This discussion shows that Ulrich's conclusions need a serious reassessment, all the more if one compares them with the facts which suggest that Josephus followed a Hebrew source. The only case which is not easily dismissed is the 'flask of water' of 1 Sam 26:11. The next step, then, is to examine other places where Josephus and LXX-£ have similar Greek phrases:

– In 1 Sam 20:30 Saul calls his son Jonathan a 'son of a perverse, rebellious [woman]', with a difficult expression נַעֲוַת הַמַּרְדּוּת. LXX and £ have κορασίων αὐτομολούντων 'son of renegade maidens', and similarly Josephus (6:237) ἐξ αὐτομόλων γεγεημένον 'offspring of renegades'. But, again, the LXX-£ translation is strange: first, the root מרד is almost always rendered with ἀφιστάναι or a related noun; second, the word used is rare, while it is usual under Josephus' pen. It is possible that a LXX-£ reviser, facing the awkward Hebrew words, borrowed it from him. As for Josephus' Hebrew source, it suffices to add a ר to MT, hence נערות המרדות 'rebellious maids'.
– In 1 Sam 22:6 and 31:13 we read תחת האשל 'under the tamarisk tree', an expression which is not found elswhere. LXX and £ render ὑπὸ τὴν ἄρουραν 'under the field', a strange meaning, for in the first occurrence this is the place where Saul sits, and in the second his burial place. In both places Josephus puts an invariable name (without article) Αρουρης: Saul sits on 'Aroures' (6:251), then is buried 'in a place called Aroures' (6:377). The origin of the name is unknown, but it does not come from LXX-£, for Josephus would not have removed the declension, of which he is fond (see *Ant.* 1:129).
– In 2 Sam 2:21, the rare word חליצה 'armor' is translated πανοπλία by LXX-£ and Josephus (*Ant.* 7:15). It occurs only once elsewhere, in Judges 14:19, translated στολάς by LXX (A) and ἱμάτια by (B), which indicates that the word is not properly understood. Moreover, the word πανοπλία, frequently used by Josephus, is an *hapax legomenon* in LXX-£. So the agreement in 2 Sam suggests that LXX-£ borrowed from Josephus, and not the other way around.
– We saw above (§ 2) the strange addition to 1 Sam 17:43 LXX (but not £) 'No, but worse (χείρω) than a dog', that Josephus knows. The comparative χείρω, frequent in Josephus' works, is an *hapax legomenon* in LXX, and has no exact Hebrew counterpart. So again, a Josephan influence may be suspected. As for the origin of the sentence, it may have been a mere paraphrasing expansion by Josephus, with no specific source.

In any case, LXX and £ have many expressions and spellings that Josephus renders otherwise, as well as many words transcribed and not translated, a feature which never occurs in Josephus. This weakens even more Ulrich's conclusion, and shows that any influence of Josephus' paraphrase upon LXX and/or cannot have been more than sporadic and somewhat casual.

6. Conclusions

Let us first summarize the results of each step of this study:

1. In his paraphrase of 1–2 Samuel, Josephus follows more and more faithfully his sources. Consequently, it is legitimate to scrutinize the details and inconsistencies of his narrative, all the more that the Biblical text has been preserved in many different versions.

2. The affinity of Josephus with £ is obvious, but it is better understood if both come independently from a Hebrew source. This confirms Tov's view, that the earliest form of £ was a full-scale translation, and not a mere revision.

3. Josephus has impressive agreements with *4 QSam^a*, a scroll which is not later than the Herodian period (second half of the 1st century B.C.E.). This fact is very significant, for Josephus' Hebrew source was an official, glossed copy, most probably the one taken in 70 C.E. by Titus from the Temple archives (or library). If we combine the conclusions of Barthélemy and Ulrich,[21] we may add that when £ reflects the most ancient Greek translation, it has many more agreements with *4 QSam^a*. It should be stressed that no external evidence proves that £ antedates Josephus.

4. *4 QSam^a*, which is very different from 1–2 Sam MT, has obvious affinities with the text type from which the parallel passages of 1 Chron were taken. The available evidence suggests that Josephus' knowledge of 1 Chron was limited to its specific chapters, unparalleled in 2 Sam. In other words, it is unclear whether he knew this book as it stands now. Of course, this problem needs further consideration.

5. The agreements of Josephus with LXX and/or £ (Greek expressions) fall into two classes: for common words, they may be a mere result of independent translations; for peculiar phrasings, especially when the underlying Hebrew is difficult, the better hypothesis is that a LXX-£ translator or reviser made spot checks in Josephus' paraphrase. The *Antiquities*, protected and available in official libraries, was most probably known as a reference work.

As for the dating of the earliest form of £, we must now look for any evidence of an *official* Greek translation of 1–2 Samuel before Josephus.

---

[21] E. Ulrich, *The Qumran Text*... (see n. 15), pp. 115–117; D. Barthélemy, *Les devanciers*... (see n. 8), pp. 110–127.

First, it is interesting to observe that the New Testament, which frequently cites the Biblical history, quotes only two passages from the historical books (besides pieces of poetry which may come from the Psalms): 2 Sam 7:8.12.14 (Nathan's prophecy) and 1 Kings 19:14–18 (Elijah at Horeb). These well-known, short passages may have been a kind of *ad hoc* translation or come from *testimonia*. In other words, this does not imply that an approved translation of all the historical books was available. Philo's testimony is interesting, too: for him, David was only a poet (Psalms), Solomon a sage (Proverbs, Wisdom); moreover, there was no exile, but voluntary emigration in order that Moses' Law be known everywhere, for only it had the power to overcome wars.

Second, we cannot conclude that there was nothing. Some fragments of the Prophets in Greek were found in the Qumran caves. In his prologue dated 132 B.C.E., Ben Sirah's translator complains that the (Greek) translations of the Law and Prophets seriously differ from the Hebrew original (ll. 22–25, Rahlfs). These were not approved translations.[22] The same way, the *Letter of Aristeas* explains (§ 30) that Demetrius, the Alexandrian librarian, was complaining that he had inaccurate copies of the Jewish laws; they were *marked*, *i.e.* did not meet the standard requirements of the royal library. As a result, the king launched the project of an official translation of the Pentateuch by the Seventy-Two experts (Septuaginta). The story tells us that this was done with an outstanding accuracy.

To sum up, there is no positive evidence of an official translation of the former Prophets (historical books) before Josephus. As for 1–2 Samuel, the ancient layer of $\mathcal{L}$ displays less affinity than Josephus with *4 QSam^a*, the latter being quite close to an authorized Jerusalem copy. So $\mathcal{L}$ as a translation depends on a later form of the Hebrew text, hence a probable dating after Josephus. It can still be called a 'forerunner of Aquila', for the latter's translation can be dated around 120 C.E. In view of the vast diffusion of $\mathcal{L}$-type readings since the 2nd century, Tov's claim that $\mathcal{L}$ was an official translation makes a great deal of sense, and if we follow Barthélemy's remarks, it was the earliest one. All this should have noteworthy consequences for

---

[22] See Marguerite Harl, Gilles Dorival et Olivier Munnich, *La Bible grecque des Septante* (Coll. 'Initiation au christianisme ancien'), Paris, Cerf, 1988, pp. 100–111.

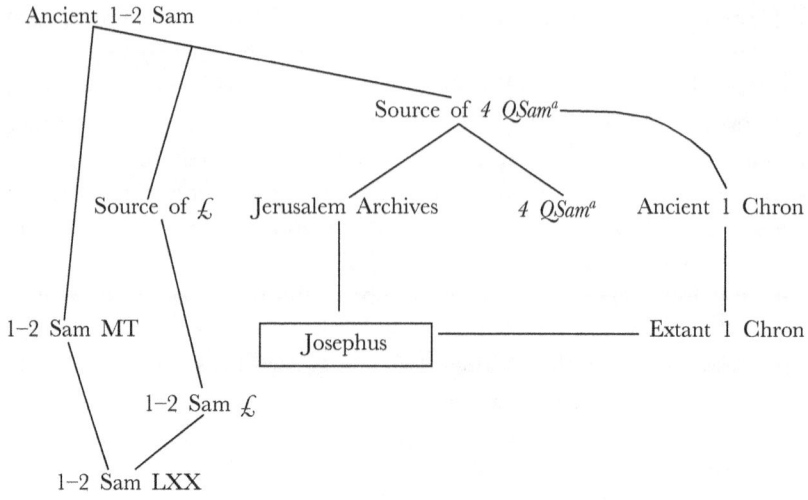

Outline of a stemma of the main text types of 1–2 Samuel

the history of the Biblical text before Origen's Hexapla[23] and the appearance of the rabbinic protomassoretic Bible.[24]

So Josephus' claim, that he was the first to render into Greek the historical books of the Bible, is not necessarily a fiction, but only under the condition that we follow carefully his justification for having done it. He sets as a precedent the permission granted by the high priest Eleazar to make an official translation at the request of the Gentile authorities, an allusion to the story of the *Letter of Aristeas*. He too introduces himself as a priest accepting the request of the Roman authorities, and the work will be protected in official library, as Eusebius reported later.

The conclusions arrived at, summarized in the table above, should still be called a working hypothesis, or an interpretive pattern for further investigation of Josephus' paraphrase of the Biblical history, from Joshua through Esther (books 4–11).

In any case, we may conclude that Josephus holds a respectable position among the Bible translators, and even among the witnesses

---

[23] See Sebastian Brock, *The Recensions of the Septuaginta Version of Samuel* (Quaderni di Henoch, 9), Torino, S. Zamorani, 1996.

[24] There should also be some methodological consequences upon the relationship between lower and higher criticisms, see Julio Trebolle Barrera, *Centena in libros Samuelis et Regum. Variantes textuales y composición literaria en los libres de Samuel e Reyes* (Textos y Estudios 'Cardinal Cisneros', 47), Madrid, Instituto de Filología (CSIC), 1989.

of the Biblical text, because his work is well dated. Of course, a major question remains: Why and for whom did he write such a detailed history, quite faithful to the Biblical source ? In the prologue, he says he addresses the Gentile readers. But this can be a mere literary device, for we may ask who would be interested in such a complicated work, with such a parochial scope. It stands far away from the brilliant polemicist's style of *Against Apion*, where Josephus skillfully addresses the Gentiles to defend his religion and nation. I have discussed elsewhere[25] some facts which suggest that Josephus has written the *Antiquities* for his countrymen, to help restore after the war a Jewish identity from Rome. This argument is further fueled by this paper: he strove to present them with a detailed account of the Bible in Greek, somewhat adorned by speeches and comments of his own. But he seems to have failed, for no external evidence indicates that he was welcomed by the Jews.

---

[25] É. Nodet, *Flavius Josèphe*... (cf. n. 2), pp. 7–17. Id., 'Un nouveau commentaire des œuvres de Josèphe', *RB* 108 (2001), pp. 161–188 (a review of Feldman's new translation of books 1–4 of the *Antiquities*).

LYSIAS—AN OUTSTANDING SELEUCID POLITICIAN

URIEL RAPPAPORT

Antiochus' persecution of Judaism is a well known historical episode, for which various explanations have been proposed. It was so exceptional in the framework of the polytheistic, Hellenistic, world within which it happened, that it attracted the attention of many scholars. We will not discuss this theme at present, but we will try to follow and to scrutinize the career of one personality among the Seleucid politicians, who took part in the military and political efforts to put down the Judean revolt. His activity was also linked to the struggles which were taking place between various groups within Judean society regarding their cultural and political position, and their familial affiliations.

In our discussion we will accept two assumptions: First, that there were disagreements among Seleucid high officials about the policy that should be adopted by the Seleucid government towards the Jews (i.e., which of the various Jewish parties should they support). Second that the religious persecution in Judaea implicated both the king Antiochus Epiphanes and a part of the Judean aristocracy, which we will henceforth call the Hellenizers, who were lead by the Hellenized High Priest Menelaus.

Both these assumptions are accepted in some form or another by many scholars. The former is substantiated by the careers of Ptolemy Macron and Ptolemy the son of Dorymenes, as well as by the careers of some other Seleucid officials.[1] The latter was convincingly presented by Bickerman and Tcherikover (although disagreeing on some points, they both saw the initiative for the religious persecution originating from within Jewish society), who were followed, with variations of course, by many others.[2]

---

[1] For Macron's attitude toward the Jews see 2Macc., X, 12–13. About opposition to such a sympathetic attitude see implicitly in loc. cit. and and in 2Macc., XII, 2. Further discussion and bibliography see J. Kampen in *The Anchor Bible Dictionary*, s.v. (IV, 461–462).

[2] M. Hengel follows basically Bickerman's understanding of the religious persecution, which he developed further on, and which was considered by other scholars

Among the Seleucid officials who were involved in Judean affairs Lysias is singled out as the most important and tenacious opponent to the policy which was dictated by his king, Antiochus IV. This is not evident from a superficial reading of the sources. So we will first assemble them all, and then try to analyze them critically, following Lysias' activity and policy, and then propose our conclusions on the basis of a general evaluation of his career (as much as we know of it).

The first time Lysias name is mentioned in 1&2 Maccabees is when he was appointed by Antiochus IV as 'over the affairs of state' (*o epi ton pragmaton*, 1Macc. III, 32), and was also entrusted with the guardianship of the young son and successor of Antiochus IV (III, 33). An additional piece of information about Lysias position at court should also be looked at, though it is less accurate. 1Macc., III, 32, tells that Lysias was of royal lineage. This datum is not substantiated by any other source and is not at all reasonable, but it can be explained by what is told about Lysias in 2Macc., XI, 1. There we are informed that Lysias was guardian (*epitropos*) of the young son of Antiochus IV, and 'relative' (*syngenes*) of the king. It is evident then that his being of the royal lineage in 1 Macc. is a misunderstanding of the meaning of *syngenes*, taking it to mean literally a relative, that is a member of the same family, when in the present context it is an hierarchical designation.[3]

It is clear then that, though we do not know Lysias' ancestral or political background, he was an important member in Antiochus IV's court and administration, and was entrusted by him with both the office of 'Prime Minister' (*o epi ton pragmaton*) and the confidential task of guardian of the young crown prince.

Being in charge of the western part of the Seleucid kingdom, after Antiochus IV left for an expedition to the East, Lysias first conducted the war against the Judean rebels through the agency of

---

as being brought *ad absurdum* (See M. Stern's review of the first German edition (Tübingen, 1969) of Hengel's *Judaism and Hellenism*, Philadelphia, 1974 (In *Qiriath Sepher* 46 (1970/71), 94–99). Stern himself follows in Tcherikover's footsteps, though with different emphases (See e.g. his 'The Hasmonean Revolt and its Place in the History of Jewish Society and Religion', *Cahiers d'histoire mondiale* 11 (1968), 92–106 (= *Jewish Society through the Ages*, eds. H.H. Ben-Sasson and S. Ettinger, NY, 1969, 92–106), esp. 98.

[3] See D. Gera, *Judea and Mediterranean Politics, 219 to 161 B.C.E.*, Leiden, 1998, 240, n. 58; Bikerman, *Institutions des Séleucides*, Paris, 1938, 42.

others, and later personally. 1Macc. mentions three men as the commanders charged by Lysias to put down the rebellion (1Macc., III, 38). At this stage of the rebellion 2Macc., X, 11 mentions Lysias for the first time in a somewhat depreciating way ('a certain Lysias'). This is rather strange, as later on he is described properly (cf. XI, 1 and XIII, 2), according to his formal title and tasks. In any case, Lysias is not looked on favorably also in 2Macc., XI, 12, where he is said to be saved 'by shameful flight', after being routed by the rebels,. But more important information about Lysias is his involvement in the famous letters cited in 2Macc. XI, 16–38. He is named the executioner of Menelaus (XIII, 3–8); and he pleads before the citizens of Akko-Ptolemais to gain support for his conciliatory policy toward the Jews. These acts of Lysias will be dealt with below.

1Macc. mentions Lysias a few times more. He was regent for Antiochus V, Antiochus IV's son, who was nine years old when his father died,[4] and thus formally became the *de facto* ruler of the Seleucid empire (1Macc., VI, 17). In this position he had to cope with Philip (*ibid.*, 55–63), who was appointed by the dying Antiochus IV to replace Lysias.[5] This appointment of Philip to replace Lysias is doubtful. We must assume that Antiochus repented his appointment as *epitropos* of his son, and that he was ready to open an internal war within his kingdom between the two generals, not to speak about his son being in the hands of Lysias, not under the guadianship of his new nominee. We may than doubt the truth of this appointment and suppoose that it is more of a conspiracy by Philip to take over the government from Lysias. The appointment of Philip may be then either a fictitious story propagated to strengthen Philip's bid for power, or an appointment squeezed from a not fully conscious Antiochus on his deathbed. It is also interesting to note how late Lysias reacted to the threat from Philip and how easily it was crushed.[6] He would have been reacted differently was it a real act initiated by Antiochus.

---

[4] A. Houghton and G. Le Rider, 'Le deuxième fils d'Antiochos IV à Ptolemais', *RSN* 64 (1985), 79, note 29.

[5] On Antiochus' death see D. Gera and W. Horowitz, 'Antiochus IV in Life and Death: Evidence from the Babylonian Astronomical Diaries', *JAOS* 117 (1997), 240–252.

[6] See 1Macc., VI, 55–56. Was Lysias aware of a royal appointment to remove him from office and still went to Judea and lingered in Jerusalem till he heard about Philip's arrival to Antioch? Or was he unaware of this appointment, which was invented by Philip and his supporters, and took action only when they tried

His peace agreement with the rebels is also related, and his supposed infringement of the agreement is criticized. Here the act of tearing down the wall of Mount Zion is blamed on the boy-king, but it must have been accomplished by Lysias.[7]

> In Lysias' relations with the Jews we can single out those points, which may illuminate a political position which reflect his personal approach toward the events in Judea: His role in the negotiations with the rebels according to the correspondence in 2Macc. XI, his order to execute Menelaus (XIII, 4–8), and his harangue to the citizens of Acco-Ptolemais (25–26). Analyzing these three occurences in which Lysias was involved may reveal a consistent political approach, which confirms Lysias as an independent politician, who had reservations about the policy of religious persecution, probably initiated by Menelaus and adopted by Antiochus IV.[8]

The correspondence in 2Macc., XI, shows Lysias to be the first Seleucid high official to negotiate with Judean rebels, who were under the leadership of Judas Maccabaeus or perhaps someone else. Lysias was ready to accept some rebels' demands, but was obliged to get the king's agreement to any change in the king's decrees against the Jewish religion. As a result of Lysias' message, Antiochus IV annulled the more extreme part of his decree about the persecution of the Jewish religion, although the Temple was not restored to its former situation; Menelaus stayed in the office of High-priest. Soon afterwards Antiochus IV passed away, and in a letter by his son,[9] the boy-king Antiochus V, the religious persecution was completely can-

---

their coup d'état, under the pretext of a royal appointment by the late king? I tend to agree with Habicht, *CAH*, 2nd edition, VIII, 354, note 1, who doubts the veracity of the information about Philip's appointment, given by 1Macc., VI, 14–15. And see the detailed analysis of D. Gera, op. cit. (in note 3), 255–259, who dismisses 2Macc.'s version on these events. He is undecided about the veracity of Philip's appointment, but refers to scholars who accepted or doubted its veracity (ibid., 259, note 16).

[7] It is difficult to ascertain if it really was an infringement of the agreement by Lysias, or an unsubstantiated accusation by our Jewish sources. Similar censure of the Seleucid authorities, either right or wrong, can be found elsewhere. See 1Macc., VII, 27–30; Also Josephus' story about Antiochus VII Sidetes accepting the surrender under agreement of Hyrcanus I includes the pulling down of the walls, which can be interpreted as going beyond the agreement or within its stipulations (*Antiquities*, XIII, 248; Diodorus, XXXIV–XXXV, 1, 5).

[8] This is basically Bickerman's thesis, which we accept with some reservations, agreeing that the idea and initiative of religious persecution originated in Judean-Hellenized circles.

[9] 2Macc., XI, 23–26.

celled. This decision was formally taken by the boy-king, but in reality it was Lysias's own decision. This radical change in policy can be explained either as a realistic step resulting from the Seleucid failure to subdue the rebels, or, as an a priori position of Lysias, which finally became the policy adopted by the Seleucid government. This policy begins when Antiochus IV was convinced by Lysias to partially repeal his decree and fully operative when Lysias himself became the de facto head of state and cancelled it completely.

Lysias was consistent in this policy when he concluded a peace agreement with the rebels, who were besieged in the Temple Mount. We may even doubt the claim that he withdrew the siege only because of Philip's arrival in Syria. But, be that as it may, he continued in this policy when he executed Menelaus, the one who represented the opposite policy and had at the very least contributed to the entanglement of the Seleucids in the war in Judea. Lysias was forced to defend this radical change in policy in Akko-Ptolemais, where the citizens were ardent supporters of the anti-Jewish policy of his predecessors in the Seleucid government.[10]

What motivated Lysias to change the Seleucid policy in Judea? Leaving aside for the moment the supposition that he may have opposed the religious policy of Hellenization in Judea as a matter of principle (a supposition that cannot be neither proved nor disproved), or that he did not belong to the same group of courtiers who supported Menelaus' ambitions and cooperated with him,[11] we have to look first at some realistic political considerations which may have influenced his decisions.

After about three years of unsuccessful efforts to subdue the Judean revolt Lysias must have considered the reasons for the failure of the Seleucid government. The most evident reason was no doubt the failure of the policy, put forward by Menelaus, that his party, the Hellenized Judean aristocracy led by the Balgean and Tobiad families, had the power to quench any inner opposition in Judea, rule securely over the country and provide a faithful base of support

---

[10] On Akko-Ptolemais' attitude towards Antiochus IV's policy in Judea see U. Rappaport, 'Akko-Ptolemais and the Jews in the Hellenistic Period', *Cathedra* No. 50 (Dec., 1988), 31–48, esp. 43–44.

[11] For Ptolemy son of Dorymenes, see 2Macc,. IV, 45–49; About Andronicus and the murder of Onias IV by him see 2Macc., 32–34; See also note 1 above concerning 2Macc., X, 12–13 and esp. XII, 2 and K. Bringmann, 'Die Verfolgung der jüdischen Religion durch Antiochus IV . . .', *Antike und Abenland* 26 (1980), 186.

for its Seleucid overlord. The assumption on which this policy rested proved to be wrong. Neither Menelaus nor the Seleucid government correctly assessed the relative power of the various 'parties' in Judea and the power that religious motivation would exert on an important segment of the Judean population. This miscalculation turned the expectations of both Menelaus and the Seleucid government upside down. Instead of having a sound base of support in Judea, Judea became an unstable province, that demanded military resources needed elsewhere. The political and military problem shifted to how to terminate this investment of useless military resources, replacing the expectation of having in Judea a sound and supportive base on the southern border of the Seleucid empire. Such miscalculation by an imperial overlord about his native subordinate population is not very rare.[12] It seems that Lysias understood this situation quite soon, since he drew the right conclusions from it and probably succeeded, in convincing a probably reluctant Antiochus IV to change his policy.

The full repudiation of the religious persecution by Lysias aroused criticism from various quarters, and at least one such disagreement with Lysias' policy came from the *Polis* of Akko-Ptolemais. The opposition in Akko-Ptolemais should be taken as an expression of protest by other *Poleis* in Eretz-Israel as well. In 2Macc., V, 15 Ptolemais is mentioned as attacking, in cooperation with Tyre and Sidon, the Jews of Galilee. This attack is to be understood as a reaction to unrest among Jews in the Galilee, which in turn was caused by the religious persecution and the revolt in Judea. This unrest endangered the interests of the three Phonician cities, for whom the Galilee was their hinterland on which they depended for food supply, and from which they benefited by commerce. In part it may have belonged to their *chora*.[13]

These three neighboring important Phoenician cities were acting in concert according to 2Macc., V, 15. But enmity towards the Jews was also harbored by other cities, either *Poleis* or Hellenized towns

---

[12] See for example the French in Algeria and, *mutatis mutandis*, the Americans in Vietnam.

[13] See U. Rappaport, 'The Hellenistic Cities and the Judaizaion of Eretz-Israel in the Hellenistic period', in The Hasmonean State, eds. U. Rappaport and I. Ronen, Tel-Aviv, 1993, 231–242, esp. 235 (Heb.); Id., 'Phoenicia and Galilee: Economy, Territory and Political Relations', *Studia Phoenicia* IX (1992), *Numismatique et histoire économique phéniciénnes et punique*, eds. T. Hackens et G. Moucharte, 262–268.

which had not yet attained the formal status of *Polis*; among them Jamnia, Gaza, Marissa, Jaffa etc. may be mentioned.[14]

We do not know and cannot restore Lysias' speech in Akko-Ptolemais. Did it contain only *reapolitik* arguments in favour of the repeal of Antiochus IV's decree against Judaism and the new policy of Lysias towards the Jews, or did it also include conceptual and moral considerations? It looks to me that Lysias' position was not based exclusively on ephemeral oportunistic reasons, as our sources, 1 and 2Macc., depict. Rather it seems to me that he opposed the Menelaus-Antiochus policy consistently and as a whole. In Antiochus IV's life time Lysias could not express his opposition openly, but he cautiously adhered to it, taking advantage of Antiochus' departure to the east, and implemented it when he became the real ruler of the Seleucid kingdom.

---

[14] See U. Rappaport, 'The Hellenistic Cities', cited in note 13 above.

DOCUMENT AND RHETORIC IN JOSEPHUS: REVISITING THE 'CHARTER' FOR THE JEWS

Tessa Rajak

It is a pleasure to dedicate to Louis Feldman, whose enormous pioneering contribution has done so much to bring about the current flourishing of interest in Josephus, the fruits, however slight, of my own pleasant return to territory of old acquaintance.[1]

In recent years research on Greek and Roman historiography has in various ways emphasized the role of rhetoric.[2] The newer writing on Josephus has to an extent reflected this interest and scholars have begun to pay attention to his manifold rhetorical strategies: much work remains to be done. Speeches, letters, narrative structure and authorial comments can all fall under this rubric.[3]

The decrees concerning Jewish communities, especially those which appear in *Antiquities* book XIV (185–267; 305–22) and XVI (160–78), seem at first sight to be something rather different: they appear as raw insertions into the text, clumsily produced and lacking in verbal polish. Marcus in his Loeb translation conveys the flavour admirably with the phrase 'of which we subjoin copies', used to render the author's formalistic *hypetaxamen ta antigrapha* at *AJ* 16.161. Yet even the un-literary handling of the *acta* is susceptible to analysis in terms of rhetorical strategy. In an important new study, Claude Eilers suggests Josephus tampered with the name in a superscription in order to be able to bring a bunch of texts together in his Caesarian narrative.[4] In a paper presented, like that of Eilers, to the SBL Josephus

---

[1] I am grateful to Professors Steve Mason and Honora Chapman for inviting me to participate in a session of the SBL Josephus Seminar on the subject of the *Acta pro Iudaeis* in Josephus, held in Atlanata in November 2003. I thank our perceptive respondent, Professor Erich Gruen, together with all the participants in the session, for a valuable discussion, which enabled me to turn the thoughts I adumbrated there into the present paper.

[2] A good discussion in Fornara 1983, chaps 4 and 5.

[3] As recently studied in the Oxford University DPhil thesis (2003) of Tamar Landau, *Out-Heroding Herod: Josephus, Rhetoric and the Herod Narratives* (publication forthcoming).

[4] Eilers 2004: 4 and n. 21.

seminar's 2003 session on Josephus's *Acta*, Miriam Ben Zeev pinpointed the author's use of half-truths and ambiguities, ever the stock-in-trade of rhetoricians. She also argued that the split presentation of the various blocks of documents in the *Antiquities* is designed as an attempt to save the reader from boredom. Already in 1984, I talked about Josephus's symbolic use of the decrees, suggesting that, for him, their importance lay less in their specific content than in the general conclusions that could be drawn from them as manifestations of enduring official respect for urban Jewish communities, evinced by a succession of regimes. This was linked to a hypothesis about the earlier functioning of those official documents *qua* documents: from the beginning, they appear to have been deployed as instruments in an ongoing political struggle for status, rather than serving as exact records of the specific rights contained in each and every one separately. As such, they depended upon beneficent maintenance and reaffirmation, and they were subject to local civic vicissitudes, and in their very nature they were never securely established. This too might be described as a rhetorical deployment, already present at the origins of the documents.

From Plato's attacks on the sophists onwards, rhetoric and truth have been set up in opposition to one another. The distinctive ways in which fact and fiction intersect in discourse has been another topic of particular concern to modern critics, who have brought to bear on ancient literary genres a more nuanced understanding of conceptions of historicity, informed undoubtedly by post-modern sensibilities. Obviously, the implications for historiography are particularly important. In her newly-published book on the letter of Aristeas, which she considers to have been heavily influenced by the canons of history-writing in the broad sense, Sylvie Honigman (2003) considers under one heading the deployment of speeches, of letters and of documentary material in narrative works, stressing that it was within the rules for ancient authors not only to recast where necessary and even to invent.

One might object that Honigman has failed to observe carefully enough distinctions between various types of insertion in histories: the speeches of ancient historians particular have their own rules and raise their own kinds of problems. She also takes a radical view of how the ancients drew the line between truth and fiction: not only, she claims, was this line located in a different position from the point where positivist modern thinking might put it, but, she seems to be saying, the line itself was generally disregarded, even by historians. There is much to debate here. But this new study undoubtedly brings a welcome sophistication to our reading of Greek-Jewish literature. And there is some relevance for Josephus and his decrees.

Not that we are likely to be seriously tempted, at least for more than a moment, to assert that Josephus simply invented the documents he purported to cite, reverting to that old view, of which Horst Moehring in 1975 (in a paper which is still of interest) was probably the last exponent. We can comfortably accept not only that Josephus had a real dossier or dossiers in front of him when he wrote, but that, if we look behind Josephus, there is genuine archival material present in those dossiers going back to the late republican, triumviral and early imperial periods. The point is rather that there is no simple choice between true or false, genuine or forged. Authorial strategies are likely to comprise the use of both.

In thinking harder about authorial strategy, we are taken back to the question I posed in 1984, a question which to my mind was unanswered in my own study and has remained unanswered in the nearly twenty years that have since elapsed. What did Josephus think he was doing when he inserted these scrappy, defective, disorganized dossiers—'verstummelt', to use Laqueur's term,[5] 'half-digested', in Eilers' words—into what he presented as a text polished to the best of his ability? The opening formulae to the individual documents are, to say the least, erratic: dates are often missing, names need correction to an extent which cannot entirely be ascribed to the latter copyists of Josephus' works, and contexts for specific decisions are not supplied. At the same time, some features which are perhaps less expected have been preserved: Troiani has signaled the survival in two cases of the names, Dositheus son of Cleopatrides of Alexandria and Prytanis son of Hermas, of individual complainants who surely displayed an admirable zeal in bringing the Jews' case to the Roman proconsul's assizes.[6] It is not necessary to reopen here the question of where and how Josephus might have found these groups of texts, nor to tackle the problem of what reordering the historian might have brought to the material he received—or indeed

---

[5] See the account in Laqueur 1920: 221–30, which is highly critical of Josephus.
[6] At Ephesus and Tralles respectively. See Ben Zeev no. 15, l. 4 and no. 18, l. 3. Ben Zeev points out that Dositheus and Prytanis need not, however, have been Jewish: see pp. 183 and 201.

what confusion he might have sown by his placing of them or even by verbal changes (such as the one suspected by Eilers by which the patronymic and titulature of Hyrcanus were altered in the decree of the Athenians, *AJ* XIV.149). Whatever the case, it is scarcely conceivable that what was received by the historian was not already seriously defective; and it is indisputable that he chose to insert these free-standing documents directly into his text, as a scarcely alleviated succession, leaving them, moreover, in the form of direct speech. We are faced by a literary decision which has to be viewed as a device of some kind; but how should we categorize it? If this too is rhetoric, what kind of rhetoric is it?

Arnaldo Momigliano's brief discussion (1977) of the role of documents in ancient historiography, whether Greek, Greek-Jewish or Roman was followed up only very slowly. M.I. Finley offered some typically trenchant observations in the 1980s,[7] commenting, again with brevity, on the connection between the sheer paucity of documents produced during almost all periods of classical history and the inability of ancient historians to give what we would consider due weight to written evidence. Later came an excellent, but again very brief discussion by John Marincola (1997: 103–5). Today, however, two large-scale projects are underway, in Italy and in England.[8] The question of documentary citations is of course related to the larger question of the nature of a historian's sources, and particularly of the balance between oral and written evidence. Until now, one has looked in vain for a comprehensive study of the connection between the two.

Momigliano's claim played a role in my 1984 analysis of Josephus' procedure.[9] It is worth citing Momigliano's *ipsissima verba*:

> The Persian state was bureaucratic, and took care of its archives. The documents quoted in the books of Ezra and Nehemiah are of Persian

---

[7] Chapter 3 of the book of 1985 adds some pages to the version in the article of 1983.

[8] A multi-university Italian project on precisely this theme, 'I'uso dei documenti nella storiografia antica' directed by Paolo Desideri of Florence, will publish the proceedings of an important colloquium held in Gubbio, 2001. I am grateful to Professor Desideri for this information, to Professor Glen Bowersock for leading me to the project and to Professor Lucio Troiani for allowing me to read his forthcoming contribution on Josephus's dossier in *AJ* 14. In England, Professor John Davies is engaged in a major study funded by the Leverhulme Trust on the documents and 'documents' in Greek literary sources: see Davies 1996.

[9] Cf. Ben Zeev 1998: 2.

origin and presuppose archives in some sort of order, but not too well-ordered (Ezra 6.1–2)... It is also probable that in the matter of quoting documents the Books of the Maccabees followed the example of the Books of Ezra and Nehemiah. Just as Flavius Josephus was later to follow the example of the Books of the Maccabees (p. 31).

There are various problems in this compressed paragraph which can merely be mentioned now but which do deserve further scrutiny. To what kind of Persian documentation does Momigliano refer—bureaucratic archives, autocratic, self-aggrandizing decrees of the King, or perhaps both? More specifically, what Persian material of the relevant period does he have in mind?[10] What evidence is there of Persian influence on any aspect of the writing of their subjects, beyond enigmatic passages about women as causes of the wars between east and west in the prologue of Herodotus. And how far was the Thucydides, not an oriental but the most Greek of writers, stepping out of line when he inserted the unmodified text of the treaties of 421 B.C. into book V of his narrative, if there are reasons for this other than lack of completion of his history?

Here my concern is simply the insertion of Josephus into this supposed tradition. If the tradition crumbles in our hands, so does our leverage on what Josephus is up to. And even if something of Momigliano's proposed lineage were to remain intact, the Josephus who inserted the charters into his narrative does not fit particularly well into it. It is true that a somewhat mysterious remark in Josephus's introductory comment to the first block of documents appears to testify in support of the Persian connection: at *AJ* 14.186, Josephus speaks about the numerous people who

> out of enmity to us refuse to believe what has been written about us by Persians and Macedonians because these writings are not found everywhere and are not deposited even in public places but are found only among us and some other foreign peoples.

Presumably this comment by Josephus is indeed meant as an oblique allusion, not just to his own inclusion of such documents, but to the incorporation of Persian material into Jewish writing, as well as of Seleucid material into the Maccabaean books (though Momigliano does not seem to refer to the passage). In any case, in important

---

[10] On the deficiencies in Persian documentary evidence, see the succinct statement in Briant 2002: 5–9.

respects, neither Ezra-Nehemiah's decrees nor the Maccabaean letters offer good parallels for the blocks of archival material found in *Antiquities* XIV and XVI. In the instances prior to Josephus, the material is deployed with considerably more care: literary effort is put into the framework and the texts of the documents themselves read agreeably. They lead on naturally from reported transactions between the protagonists in the story and they serve as a visible enhancement. This is the case with Artaxerxes' decree in Ezra 7, significantly placed after we have learned of the departure from of Ezra's group of Jews from Babylon and his own resolve to study and teach Torah in Jerusalem. The decree is followed by an extremely portentous blessing: 'blessed be the Lord, the God of our fathers, who put such a thing as this into the heart of the king, to beautify the house of the Lord which is in Jerusalem, and who extended to me his steadfast love ... and I gathered leading men from Israel to go up with me' (Ezra, 7.27). There is also some artistry, even if not quite as much, in the presentation of the much-discussed sequence of communications from Lysias, from Antiochus V and from the Romans, in chapter 11 of II Maccabees. Whatever their historical value, they serve to make the circumstances described there concrete and real; by reproducing the language of the rulers or of the government they convey not only an air of veracity but something of the 'feel' of the transactions, the spirit of the age, just as such quotations do when modern historians incorporate them. At the same time they are able to offer the reader welcome *variatio* through a change of pace. There may even be genuine drama. A good example of the latter effect is provided by the repentant deathbed letter of Antiochus IV in which, far too late, he accords honours to the Jews, and recommends his son and heir to them. This is framed between a graphic description of his loathsome disease, and a concluding few lines which tell of his lonely, and deserved death in the mountains (II Macc. 9).

The Maccabaean documents have often been held to be on a par with those of Josephus. From the sixteenth century onwards, scholars brought to both their extraneous theological motivations and they became prey to disputation between Protestants and Catholics.[11] And there is at least one group of governmental pronouncements included by Josephus in the *Antiquities* which may indeed be compared in its

---

[11] Moehring 1975: 126–7, drawing on Bikerman 1953.

deployment to the colourful use of letters in II Maccabees. From an earlier period than our decrees, this is the group which contains the proclamation and letters of Antiochus III (*AJ* 12.129–53), where, admittedly, three documents are cited in succession, but only in the wake of an emotive account of the troubles of the Jews of Coele-Syria during the wars between Antiochus and Ptolemy Philopator, of a strong statement about the motives of Antiochus who felt it right to reward the zeal and the *philotimia* of the Jews on his behalf, and of a rather elaborate invocation of seemingly supportive passages of Polybius.[12]

Our documents, by contrast, fall into line only insofar as, like the Ezra-Nehemiah documents and the Maccabaean ones, they are citations of favourable pronouncements from the ruling power. For in literary terms they do different work in relation to their narrative contexts, into which they have not been adequately integrated. Miriam Ben Zeev has attempted to give Josephus the benefit of having created a sort of 'literary continuum' through his grouping of the documents into blocks, with his sporadic introductory sentences and conclusions to those blocks. But, we note that scrupulously honest as her scholarship is, she has not allowed herself here to dispense with those tell tale words 'sort of' and they make all the difference.

In what respects, then, can the decrees of books XIV and XVI be regarded as an aspect of Josephus' rhetoric? I suggest that there are at least two ways. One is obvious, and general—he has an overriding apologetic purpose, the aim of 'reconciling the nations', as is made abundantly clear in the programmatic statements Josephus offers both in book XIV and in book XVI. But the second aspect of rhetoric which I have in mind is perhaps less obvious. Here the term 'rhetoric' applies in fact in a more precise meaning than that in common literary critical use. My suggestion is that such recitation of bare legal, or would-be legal, provisions is at home in one particular context. That context is broadly-speaking forensic, belonging to the forum or to the law courts, or possibly also to other locations of public speech-making. Marincola (1997: 103–5) goes some

---

[12] We cannot, on the other hand, include in this list the Roman warning inscription affixed to the Temple barrier, a document is only referred to by Josephus and not cited (*BJ* V.194, *AJ* XV, 417), so that it was left to Clermont-Ganneau's famous archaeological discovery of 1871 to present us with its wording. The crude presentation of the two Claudian edicts of book XIX.278–90 looks more like that of the book XIV decrees.

of the way towards my interpretation, in his discussion of why ancient historians do not feature documents prominently. He points to the way documents were used in Athenian courts from the time of Demosthenes onwards: they were not seen as impartial evidence, but as witnesses to support whichever pleader invoked them. They were used, he says, to build a case. This would diminish their usefulness to a compiler of history and may account for the caution of historians in drawing on them.

My point is that those who read the published versions both of public orations and of law-court speeches, from fourth century B.C.E. Athens to imperial Rome (less so it seems in the Athenian fifth century), are familiar with interruptions to the flow, where they are meant to imagine someone being brought on to declaim the text of a law, decree, or provision, or some substantial extract. Similar interruptions were made for the citation of relevant personal evidence, such as snatches of correspondence. Even in a court of law, the purpose of this practice is likely to be at least as much symbolic as real. Judge, jury and spectators will hardly be able to attend to the minute detail—perhaps not even to hear the crucial words adequately. Certainly, they were not going to dissect them. But they are subject to the persuasive power of hearing a ruling which apparently supports the case being made, to the introduction of something seemingly authoritative, neutral, irrefutable; and to a different voice, as though the voice of officialdom itself. Needless to say, such cited documents could perfectly well be forgeries (Thomas 1989: 83–5).

To understand how this practice might have a bearing on written history, we have to remember that literature, whether verse or prose, at Rome as in the Greek world, was for the most part recited, usually in sections and sometimes in different versions, before the completion of composition and before the occurrence of anything that might be termed publication, that is to say the distribution of a limited number of a complete written texts.[13] Dramatic moments could occur during such recitations, as in the famous case of the collapse of Octavia, sister of Augustus, when Virgil's tragic passage in Aeneid book VI referring to the death of her son Marcellus was recited in her presence.[14] And even finalized texts, in the privacy of

---

[13] Mason (forthcoming) effectively places the production of Josephus' *Jewish War* in the context of a full account of our understanding of this literary process.

[14] *Vit.Don.* 32; Servius on *Aeneid* IV.323 and VI.861.

an individual's own environment, may well have been read aloud. Thus the circumstances in which Josephus' *Antiquities* were first presented to the public were in some significant respects not so far removed from those in which an oration was delivered or the scene in a court of law where a case was argued. Both were performances and both needed to be good theatre. It is worth reflecting on the possibility that Josephus too might have deployed a separate reader to offer a recitation, with suitable gravity, of the decrees in favour of the Jews.

This last suggestion is of course speculation. But I think my interpretation overall serves well to explain the way in which Josephus' inclusion of the charters could have originated. It can also explain why Josephus left the charters in the state that he did, why, although he felt free to tamper, and probably did tamper here and there, he did not do a thoroughgoing job of tidying them up, of filling gaps or ironing out anomalies. Still under the Romans, when documentation and archival practice had advanced greatly over even the most developed of Greek states, attention to the accuracy of texts, to the maintenance of a complete record after the immediate need for it had passed, to systematic storage in one central location, to accessibility, to consultation, to precision of reading, left a lot to be desired. There is a good discussion of the tendency to a 'casual approach to accuracy' in the epilogue to Thomas (1992), where the author concludes her survey of Greek literacy with observations on the practice of the Roman state.[15] So the state of the texts given us by Josephus was not far from what people were used to in the case of certain real documents in real contexts. Honigman speaks of inaccuracy perpetrated for the 'literary improvement' of documents and embedded in literary texts (2003: 169, n. 28). We are dealing here with almost the opposite. Literary advantage, in this case, might lie precisely in the absence of literary finish.

The intimate connections between classical historiography and ancient rhetorical principles form the background to what Josephus is doing here. But they still do not serve fully to explain the technique involved in the citations of documents in *Antiquities* XIV and XVI. If I am right, then I need to explain why our historian should be adopting a technique borrowed from law courts. What does he

---

[15] And see especially 168, n. 29; cf. Ben Zeev 1998: 16, on the tendency of surviving *senatus consulta* to lack key formulaic elements.

have to gain? It is scarcely enough to remind ourselves yet again that Josephus is engaged in a major apologetic enterprise, that his avowed purpose is to show how Jews had constantly been respected by those who ruled them (*AJ* 14.86) and to remove the causes of hatred between ethnic groups (*AJ* 16.175).[16] I propose a further step. I should like to link, even more tightly than before, Josephus' purpose in making the citations with the original role of the documents. Possession of them, whatever their shape, was crucial to Jewish communities. We know that the onus was on the recipients, in this case the Jewish communities in the cities, and not on the Roman governors to preserve communications sent to them (Thomas 1992: 168). Habits of documentation have been interpreted as an arm of imperialist exploitation (Thomas 1992: 128, on Lévi-Strauss), but there is also the other side of the coin. Documentation was indispensable in defending such concessions or benefits (we should perhaps not speak of rights) as were accorded by sovereign powers to subjects. For minority groups within subject populations, this was *a fortiori* the case.

Such documentation took visible form, and the display copy, on bronze or stone had a special importance. Callie Williamson (1987) examines how and why bronze was often material of choice to achieve 'grandiloquence'. Thomas has made the important observation that the displayed text, even if by no means always easily legible, had an overwhelming symbolic importance as an object. Its removal could be read as the removal of the provision contained in it. The inscription was in a sense the law itself, irrespective of the quality of the text. In such a spirit the Greek inhabitants of Antioch urged Titus, as he came through the city after the fall of Jerusalem, to remove the bronze tablets on which Jewish privileges had been inscribed. He refused, says Josephus, thereby confirming the existing status of the Jews (*BJ* 7.110).[17] We may compare *AJ* 12.122 where we hear also of a similar and contemporaneous local conflict and a similar Flavian intervention in Alexandria, though there is no mention there of the bronze tablets.[18] The evidence for the existence of such bronze tablets setting out the privileges of individual groups is by no means

---

[16] Sterling 1992, claims apologetic history as a distinct genre and offers a full analysis of Josephus' apologetic motivations and methods.

[17] A relevant case not mentioned by Thomas, *loc. cit.*

[18] The existence of such tablets there can probably be accepted, even if Josephus misunderstood their content: see Ben Zeev 1998: 386.

exclusively confined to Jewish groups, and it is very well set out by Miriam Ben Zeev (1998: 381–7). They probably had to be erected at private expense (Williamson 1987: 181–2). Their quality then will have inevitably depended upon the resources of the community involved.

Obviously, the inscribed texts had somehow to remain in existence if they were to continue being invoked. We are fortunate to have at least a snippet of evidence revealing the care with which the actual tablets of bronze were guarded; but transcription and distribution also had a role to play. Through what, to my mind, was a particularly difficult period for much of Mediterranean Jewry, the three-quarters of a century following 66 C.E.,[19] such testimonies will have been found to be more than ever necessary for Jewish communities. Troiani has suggested that, from the Jews' point of view, they served also the purpose of emphasizing the possibility of continuing to maintain a Torah-observant Judaism within a mixed civic environment. Yet, of the actual inscriptions, some, we must suppose, were indeed successfully removed; some had perhaps simply faded from view or even from consciousness. In some places, again, the Jews may never previously have entered into direct confrontation with their fellow citizens or with the authorities, and so they may never have acquired or maintained any material of specific application to themselves or any copies of material from other communities. If they did, they may have had nowhere to display them. And even to make and store an archival copy required ownership of premises and some resources. This will have been considerably harder for a small body of Jews in a small or middle-sized city, say Tralles or Laodicea, than for a major Jewish community in a significant centre, such as Pergamum, where, in Eilers' view, Josephan material from a different city (Athens) can be shown to have received its 'archival tag'.

Josephus came into the picture at this juncture. There is good reason, as we have seen, to think that the material available to him was not in good shape. He seems to have depended on local collections, probably consolidated before his time. Though he refers to a display at Rome, he does not specifically claim to have seen the

---

[19] For a maximalist account of Roman post-war hostility, see the concluding section of Goodman 1987. Cf. Ben Zeev: 5; and Troiani forthcoming.

material there, and it is unlikely that there was much to be seen.[20] It was by then a very late stage in the history of the decrees: between the age of Julius Caesar and the composition of Josephus' *Antiquities* some one and a half centuries elapsed.[21] But that did not matter. They still had value. And in a paradoxical way their very inadequacy made them all the more expressive. So the historian's role was, as it were, to inscribe the texts into history. Publication gave them a new lease of life. On this interpretation, Josephus is seen as an integral continuation of a transmission process whose earlier stages can only be approximately surmised. It emerges that he was putting the material to the same kind of service as previous users. He was personally re-activating the case for the defence of Jewish observances in the face of hostile or potentially hostile Greek elites, wherever they might be, and of a not necessarily supportive Roman government. Furthermore, in his *Antiquities*, the documents, however damaged, would be made accessible, and there they would remain. The material could be drawn upon for support and sustenance of various kinds by Jewish future readers (or any of their backers and friends). History, via rhetoric, was engaging with life. The *Antiquities*, if circulated, would disseminate the decrees within them, just as those decrees had previously been spread around. If my reading of what is happening here is correct, then necessity was indeed the mother of invention. Through pressure of circumstances, Josephus was led to break the old bounds of genre, to mix the genres, and to evolve a type of performative writing which embodied a new relationship between documents and historiography.[22] Here historical narrative is politics continued by other means.

---

[20] The possible routes by which the preserved material may have reached Josephus are explored with acumen by Ben Zeev 1998: 388–408.

[21] And almost another century if Eilers' backdating of the supposedly Caesarian material to Hyrcanus I be accepted.

[22] The practice of drawing freely on cited documents was be put to good use in Christian historiography of the first centuries, notably the *Ecclesiastical History* of Eusebius.

Bibliography

Ben Zeev, M. Pucci 1998 *Jewish Rights in the Roman World: the Greek and roman documents quoted by Josephus Flavius* (Tübingen).
Bikerman, E. 1953 'Une question d'authenticité : les privilèges juives', *Annuaire de l'Institut de philologie et d'histoire orientales et slaves* 13, *Mélanges Isidore Lévy* = E. Bickerman, *Studies in Jewish and Christian History* II, (Leiden 1980): 24–43.
Briant, P. 2002. *From Cyrus to Alexander: a history of the Persian empire*, transl. P.T. Daniels (Winona Lake, Indiana). In French as *Histoire de l'empire perse*, Paris, 1996.
Davies, J.K. 1996 'Documents and "Documents" in Fourth-Century Historiography', in P. Carlier ed., *Le IVème siècle av. J.C.* (Nancy), 29–39.
Eilers, C. 2004 'Josephus' Caesarian *Acta*: history of a dossier', *SBL Seminar Papers 2003*, 189–213.
Finley, M.I. 1983 'The Ancient Historian and his Sources', in E. Gabba, ed. , *Tria Corda: scritti in onore di Arnaldo Momigliano* (Como), 201–14.
——. 1985 *Ancient History: evidence and models* (London).
Fornara, C.W. 1983 *The Nature of History in Ancient Greece and Rome* (Berkeley, London, Los Angeles).
Goodman, M. 1987 *The Ruling Class of Judaea: the origins of the Jewish revolt against Rome, A.D. 66–70* (Cambridge).
Honigman, S. 2003 *The Septuagint and Homeric Scholarship in Alexandria: a study in the narrative of the Letter of Aristeas* (London).
Laqueur, R. 1920 *Der jüdische Historiker Flavius Josephus; ein biographischer Versuch auf neuer quellenkritischer Grundlage* (Giessen).
Marincola, J. 1997 *Authority and Tradition in Ancient Historiography* (Cambridge).
Mason, S. forthcoming 'Of Audience and Meaning: reading Josephus' *Bellum Judaicum* in the context of a Flavian audience', in J. Sievers, ed., *Flavius Josephus between Jerusalem and Rome* (Leiden).
Moehring, H.R. 1975 'The *Acta pro Iudaeis* in the *Antiquities* of Flavius Josephus', in J. Neusner ed. *Christianity, Judaism and Other Greco-Roman Cults* III (Leiden), 133–57.
Momigliano, A.D. 1977 'Eastern Elements in Jewish, and Greek Historiography', in *Essays in Ancient and Modern Historiography* (Oxford).
Rajak, T. 1984 'Was There a Roman Charter for the Jews?', *JRS* 74, 1984, 107–23, also in *The Jewish Dialogue with Greece and Rome: studies in cultural and social interaction* (Leiden, Boston, Köln 2001), 301–34.
Sterling, G.E. 1992 *Historiography and Self-Definition: Josephos, Luke-Acts and Apologetic Historiography* (Leiden, New York).
Thomas, R. 1989 *Oral Tradition and Written Record in Classical Athens* (Cambridge).
——. 1992 *Literacy and Orality in Ancient Greece* (Cambridge).
Troiani, L. forthcoming 'Il dossier prodotto da Giuseppe nel libro XIV delle *Antichità Giudaiche*', in P. Desideri ed., *L'uso dei documenti nella storiografia antica: convegno di Gubbio 2001*.
Williamson, C. 1987 'Monuments of Bronze: Roman legal documents on bronze tablets', *Classical Antiquity* 6, 160–83.

ADNOTATIONES CRITICAE AD FLAVII JOSEPHI *CONTRA APIONEM*

Heinz Schreckenberg

Vorbemerkung: Contra Apionem, das wahrscheinlich letzte der vier erhaltenen Werke des Flavius Josephus (37/38 Jerusalem—nach 100 Rom), ist nur in einer (unvollständigen) griechischen Handschrift, im Laurentianus 69.22 (11. Jh.), erhalten, dazu in einer mangelhaften lateinischen Übersetzung des 6. Jahrhunderts und in etlichen Zitaten bei Eusebius (4. Jh.) und anderen. Sowohl die lateinische Version wie die einzig relevante griechische Handschrift—alle anderen sind wertlose Abschriften—tradieren den genuinen Wortlaut in oft entstellter Form, so daß die Schrift 'Gegen Apion' als die am schlechtesten erhaltene des Josephus gelten muß. In dieser schwierigen Situation kann Konjekturalkritik helfen, wie sie im Folgenden versucht wird. Philologische Bemühungen sind hier auch deshalb besonders gerechtfertigt, weil '*Contra Apionem* can be regarded as the key to all of Josephus' writings' (Per Bilde).

Omnes qui supersunt libri Graeci operis *Contra Apionem* ad unum redeunt codicem Laurentianum LXIX 22 saeculo fere undecimo exaratum (L a Niesio notatum), quem multis locis corruptum interpolatumque esse constat. Versio Latina antiqua (*Lat.* notatum) a Cassiodori senatoris amicis saeculo sexto facta, quamvis sit ad textum emendandum graecum necessaria utilisque, secuta est exemplum graecum tot multis iam locis corruptum, ut interpretes (vel interpres) saepenumero insana traderent. Accedit quod frequenter, quae sana invenerunt, neque recte intellegere neque accurate vertere potuerunt.

At Eusebius (vel loci eius ad Iosephum spectantes) neminem arbitror dubitaturum esse, quin sit librorum *Contra Apionem* et antiquissimus et optimus testis. Neque tamen, ut iam Niesio persuasum fuit, ab omni vitio liber putandus est et sunt nonnullae corruptelae ab eo traditae communes cum ceteris testibus, quae iam antiquitus corrupta esse Iosephi verba demonstrant.

Verum et Carolus Boysen, qui anno MDCCCXCIII versionem Cassiodoream edidit, id libellum pessime traditum esse maximeque arte critica indigere iudicavit. Quae res similiter et ad textum Graecum et ad versionem Latinam antiquam pertinet. Iam nemo non concedet, usque ad hunc diem parum factum esse, ut huic malo remedium inveniretur. Itaque non alienum videtur, aliquot observationes proferre fortasse usui futuras ad Josephi verba restituenda.

Contra Apionem I 46 *peri tou ... polemou tines historias epigrapsantes* traditum est in codice *L(historias conscribentes* Lat.). Fortasse legendum est *historias syngrapsantes* (vel *grapsantes*), nam *epigraphein* desiderat *ti tini, epi ti, eis ti, en tini, ti ti* (id est *signo afficere*) vel simile. Iosephus dicit, ut exempla afferam, *syngraphein tas historias* (*C.Ap.* I 7.13.57) et *ten historian (syn)graphein* (*C. Ap.* I 18.55.73.213.288); confer etiam *ten historian anagraphein* (Vita 40), *ten pragmateian graphein* (Vita 336). Non contradicit Bell. Iud. I 7 *historias autas (sc. tas kolakeias) epigraphein tolmosin*.

Contra Apionem I 162 traditur *Pythagoras ... ou monon egnokos ta par hemin delos estin, alla kai zelotes auton ek pleistou* (*ek pleistou* L, apparet Lat., Text probably corrupt Thackeray, suspectum Reinach) *gegenemenos*. Legat quis *pleiston* (id est *valde*) pro *ek pleistou*. Exempli causa confer Ant.Jud. XX 263 *pleiston diapherein* (i.e. *valde praestare*). Quomodo orta sit haec textus depravatio, fortasse apparet ex Ant. Jud.XI 79 (*Omega* mutatum in *Epsilon* in codicibus PW; cf.codices SPA Ant. Iud. VIII 42). Saepe etiam *Ny* mutatur in *Kappa* (e.g. codices MSP Ant. Iud. III 321 et OE Ant. Iud. IV 118). Ita per duplicationem ex *auton* oriri potuit *auton ek*, quo factum est, ut *pleiston* in *pleistou* transformaretur.

Contra Apionem I 198 *peribolos lithinos, mekos hos pentaplethros* (*hos pentaplethros* L et Eusebius, *lapidea quadriporticus* Lat.). *Hos* delendum esse puto, quia mensurae accurate dari solent, si templa vel loca sancta describuntur. Confer exempli causa emendationem in *C. Ap.*I 58 *pepoiekos hoti* (*pepoiekos hos hoti* L, *quia* Lat., *hos* del. Gutschmid) ab omnibus operum Iosephi editoribus in textum receptum.

Contra Apionem I 210 *diaterounton ten anoian* (L: *stultitiam observantibus* Lat.) traditum est. Pro *anoian* legendum est *argian*. Nam non dubium mihi videtur *anoian* esse glossema ad *argian* adscriptum. Qua adnotatione lectoris urbis incolas vituperantis genuinum verbum *argian* expulsum esse videtur. Nam lector, vel librarius, Hierosolymitas reprehendit, quippe qui contra hostes inter sabbati otium invadentes non se defenderint, sed solitum otium observaverint. Confer textum praecedentem (I 209): *argein eithismenoi di' hebdomes hemeras*. Similiter invenitur *argia* Ant. Iud. XII 4 (*ten hemeran en argia tynchanonton*) et XVIII 319 (*sabbaton, argias hemera*).

Contra Apionem I 211 *henika an tois anthropinois logismois peri ton dia-*

poroumenon exasthenesousin. Hic gravem offensionem habet *diaporoumenon* (sic L et Eusebius, *dum circa res necessarias ratio nihil valet humana* Lat.), nam magnopere desideratur *ton aporoumenon*, fortasse simili modo depravatum ac e.g. in codicibus *auton nemetai* mutatum in *auton dianemetai* (Ant. Iud. I 212), *proteron nemetheisi* in *proteron dianemetheisi* (Ant. Iud. III 284), *ten koreian* in *ten diakorian* (Ant. Iud. VII 170).

Contra Apionem I 260 *kathareusai* (L, *iurgare* Lat., *katharisai* Cobet, Naber, Reinach; cf. Guilelmum Schmidt, De Flavii Iosephi elocutione observationes criticae, Lipsiae MDCCCXCIII, p. 534, qui *kathareuein* apud posteriores transitivam notionem accipere notat) *ten Aigypton*. Pro *kathareusai* legendum esse mihi videtur *katharai*. Confer C. Ap. I 257 *(katharai ten choran)*, C. Ap. I.289 *(ean ... kathare ten Aigypton)*, C. Ap. I 306 *(ta hiera katharai ap' anthropon anhagnon kai dyssebon)*.

Contra Apionem I 269 traditur *ouk an eis* (*pros* Schmidt, l.c., p. 392) *tous auton theous polemein etolmesan* (sic codex L, *non tamen contra deos impietatem gerere praesumebant* Lat.). Offendit *polemein eis* inusitatum et apud scriptores Graecos et apud Flavium Iosephum. Qui semper scribit *polemein tini, polemein pros tina, polemein tina* (cf. exempli causa Ant. Iud. VII 100.280; X 173; XII 229; XIII 196). Praestare Schmidtii coniecturae mihi videtur delere *eis*. Nam saepe in codicibus antecedens littera N a librariis depravatur in (E)IS. Ex eo fit, ut e.g. Ant. Iud. III 182 Naberus cum codicibus RO *eis* (post *eniauton*) deleat. Item Ant. Iud. I 227 Ernesti et Naberus delent *eis* post antecedentem *onton*.

Contra Apionem I 309 (Moses Hebraeis persuadet, ut forti animo ex Aegypto proficiscantur) traditum est *paraballomenois mian hodon temnein achri an elthosin eis topous oikoumenous* (*ut properantes unam viam secarent, donec ad loca habitabilia pervenirent* Lat.). Nullo modo *mian* intellegi potest. Id, quod Iosephus scripsit, fortasse ex simili loco Ant. Iud. II 341 (narratio Exodi ex Aegypto) patet: *idian hodon Hebraiois gegenemenen*. Ergo videtur Moses Ant. Iud. I 309 Hebraeis suasisse, ut viam propriam facerent, id est *idian hodon temnein*. In aperto est, a librario neglegenti *idian* et *mian* facile permutari potuisse.

Contra Apionem II 291 de legibus Hebraeorum in codice Graeco (L) dicitur *oud' epi misanthropian, all' epi ten ton onton koinonian parakalountes* (*non ad humanum odium, sed ad rerum communionem potius invitantes* Lat). Quid sibi vult *onton* ? Nescio an *anthropon* legendum sit. Fortasse in hoc loco intelligendo aliquot loci similes adiuvant: Bell. Iud. VII 264 *ten pros anthropous hemeroteta kai koinonian.*—C. Ap. II 146 *pros koinonian ten met' allelon kai pros ten katholou philanthropian.*—C. Ap. II 196 *epi koinonia gegonamen.*—Confer C. Ap. II 208 et II 281 *ten pros allelous koinonian.*—Praeterea, extra Iosephi opera, comparandum est Plato, *Politicus* 276 b, *anthropine sympasa koinonia* et idem, *Symposium* 188 b–c, *he peri theous te kai anthropous pros allelous koinonia)* et ad extremum Philo (Fr. 71 H.): *ton anthropon he physis kateskeuase koinonikotaton.* Ex locis talibus colligere potest, Iosephum *C. Ap.* II 291 spectare ad unum hoc tantummodo, quemadmodum omnes homines concorditer et familiariter vitam agant. Itaque non *onton*, sed *anthropon* Iosephum scripsisse conicio.

Zusammenfassung: Es werden Vorschläge gemacht zur Wiederherstellung des vermutlich entstellt überlieferten Textes *Contra Apionem* 1.46; 1.162; 1,198; 1,210; 1,211; 1,260; 1,269; 1,309; 2,291.

JOSEPHUS ON HIS JEWISH FORERUNNERS
(*CONTRA APIONEM* 1.218)*

Daniel R. Schwartz

Josephus' first goal in *Contra Apionem* is to demonstrate, against the claims of skeptics, the antiquity of the Jews. Given the fact that one of the skeptics' major arguments derived from the general failure of Greek literature to mention the Jews, Josephus opened his response with general remarks on the late origin and lack of reliability of Greek evidence on antiquity, and on the greater credence to be given to oriental records (§§ 6–28). Josephus argues that the Jews' chronicles are no less credible than the latter (§§ 29–43), and then—after some more disparaging remarks about Greek historians—he presents his own credentials for writing about the Jews and their history (§§ 47–56).

Following this prefatory material, Josephus offers in §§ 58–59 a brief outline of what's to come. He promises (i) to reply briefly to those critics who argue, from the silence of Greek historians concerning the Jews, that the Jews are of only recent origin (κατάστασις); (ii) to cite statements by others (παρ' ἄλλοις) that do testify to the Jews' antiquity; and then (iii) to show the absurdity of calumnies against the Jews. As H.St.J. Thackeray noted on 1.59 in the Loeb Classical Library edition, the second of these sections runs from 1.69 to 1.218, a point reflected clearly by Josephus' notice in the very next paragraph (1.219) that he has only one task left of those promised at the outset, namely, the rebuttal of calumnies against the Jews. The second section neatly and explicitly divides the evidence adduced from 'others' between that of 'barbarians' (Egyptians, Phoenicians and Babylonians—§§ 69–160) and that of Greeks (§§ 161–217 or 218 [see below!]). In what follows, we will focus on § 218, a passage in which, according to most scholars, Josephus made two egregious mistakes.

---

* This paper began as a lecture given in May 1997 at the 26th Annual Conference of the Israeli Society for the Promotion of Classical Studies, Jerusalem.

The passage comes after Josephus finished assembling his citations of Greek writers on the Jews, to which he appended a complaint that some writers, such as Hieronymus of Cardia, deliberately ignored the Jews (§§ 213–214). He then continues as follows, according to Thackeray's translation, which we shall use as a point of departure:[1]

> (215) However, our antiquity is sufficiently established by the Egyptian, Chaldaean and Phoenician records (ἀναγραφαί), not to mention the numerous Greek writers. (216) In addition to those already cited, Theophilus, Theodotus, Mnaseas, Aristophanes, Hermogenes, Euhemerus, Conon, Zopyrion, and, may be, many more—for my reading has not been exhaustive—have made more than a passing reference to us. (217) The majority of these men have misrepresented the facts (τῆς μὲν ἀληθείας ... διήμαρτον) of our primitive history, because they have not read our sacred books (βίβλοις); but all concur in testifying to our antiquity, and that is the point with which I am at present concerned. (218) Demetrius Phalereus, the elder Philo, and Eupolemus are exceptional in their approximation to the truth (οὐ πολὺ τῆς ἀληθείας διήμαρτον), and [their errors] may be excused on the ground of their inability to follow quite accurately the meaning of our records (μετὰ πάσης ἀκριβείας τοῖς ἡμετέροις γράμμασι παρακολουθεῖν).

Now to our problem. According to the consensus of scholarship, Josephus made a minor error and a major one in § 218.[2] The minor

---

[1] I made two corrections. (a) On the one hand, at the end of § 215 Thackeray gave 'historians' for συγγραφεῖς, but I give 'writers'. True, 'historians' is a frequent meaning. But here Josephus is alluding to the case he began in § 161, which was based upon citations not only from historians, but also from Pythagoras, Theophrastus, Choerilus and Clearchus. Similarly, we really don't know that all of the writers mentioned in § 216 were historians. Hence, I would stick with the literal translation, just as Josephus himself, who sometimes uses ἱστοριογράφος when he specifically means 'historian' (*C. Ap.* 1.2; *Ant.* 1.133, 16.183), uses—at *C. Ap.* 1.72, 161, 215; 2.288—συγγραφεύς with reference to the Greek writers assembled in §§ 161–217. For more on the translation of συγγραφεῖς here, see B. Bar-Kochva in *Zmanim* 61 (Winter 1997/98), p. 113 and my response *ibid.*, 67 (Summer 1999), p. 90 (both in Hebrew). (b) On the other hand, at the outset of § 217 Thackeray translated ἀνδρῶν 'authors' but I turned it into plain 'men'.

[2] See, inter alia, the notes ad loc. in Thackeray's 1926 Greek-English Loeb edition, in Th. Reinach's 1930 Budé Greek-French edition (with translation by L. Blum), and in F. Calabi's 1993 Greek-Italian edition, also: N. Walter, 'Zur Ueberlieferung einiger Reste früher jüdisch-hellenistischer Literatur bei Josephus, Clemens und Euseb', *Studia Patristica* VII/1 (1966), pp. 318–319; A.-M. Denis, *Introduction aux pseudépigraphes grecs d'Ancien Testament* (Leiden 1970), pp. 248–249, 251, 271; C.R. Holladay, *Fragments from Hellenistic Jewish Authors* (Scholars Press, 1983–), I, pp. 98–99, n. 2; H.W. Attridge, 'Historiography', in: *Jewish Writings of the Second Temple Period* (ed. M.E. Stone; Assen – Philadelphia 1984), p. 169; A.J. Droge, 'Josephus Between Greeks and Barbarians', in: *Josephus' Contra Apionem: Studies*... (edd. L.H. Feldman & J.R. Levison; Leiden 1996), pp. 124–125.

error is that he referred to Demetrius *of Phalerum*, although that famous intellectual is not known to have written anything about the Jews. Josephus, it is assumed, in fact meant to refer to a Jewish Demetrius, who wrote about biblical history.[3] The major error is that Josephus evidently took Demetrius, Philo and Eupolemus to be Greeks, not Jews. That these three writers were in fact Jews is clear from the contents and tone of the fragments of their works and stated explicitly by Eusebius.[4]

The minor error, however egregious, is indeed easy to posit: it is easy to imagine that a *lapsus* or learned *Verschlimmbesserung* by Josephus or by one of his copyists turned plain 'Demetrius' into 'Demetrius Phalareus' (who is in fact mentioned at *C. Ap.* 2.46 and *Ant.* 12.12–114 *passim*). But as for the major error, it is in fact quite difficult to imagine that Josephus did not recognize that Demetrius, Philo the Elder and Eupolemus were Jews. Whether or not Josephus read their works,

---

[3] For the famous Demetrius' works, see F. Wehrli, *Demetrios von Phaleron (Die Schule des Aristoteles*, 4; Basel 1949); on our text see p. 87, where Wehrli opines that it more probably reflects confusion than the existence of an otherwise unknown work falsely ascribed to this Demetrius. For the fragments of the Jewish Demetrius, see F. Jacoby, *Die Fragmente der griechischen Historiker*, IIIC (Leiden 1958), no. 722; A.-M. Denis, *Fragmenta pseudepigraphorum quae supersunt graeca*... (Leiden 1970 [published together with M. Black, *Apocalypsis Henochi graece*]), pp. 175–179; Holladay (above, n. 2), I, pp. 51–93 (along with introduction, English translation and notes). There is also an annotated English translation by J. Hanson in *The Old Testament Pseudepigrapha*, II (ed. J.H. Charlesworth; Garden City, NY 1985), pp. 843–854, and one in German by N. Walter in *Jüdische Schriften aus hellenististisch-römischer Zeit*, III/2 (Gütersloh 1975), pp. 280–292.

[4] For the fragments of Philo (presuming the reference is to the epic poet) and Eupolemus see, respectively, Jacoby (above, n. 3), nos. 729 and 723; Denis (above, n. 3), pp. 203–204 and 179–186; Holladay (above, n. 2), II (1989), pp. 205–299 and I, pp. 93–156; H. Attridge (pp. 781–784) and F. Fallon (pp. 861–872) in Charlesworth (above, n. 3); Walter (above, n. 3), IV/3 (1983), pp. 139–153 and I/2 (1976), pp. 93–108. Philo's texts and testimonia may also be found in *Supplementum Hellenisticum* (edd. H. Lloyd-Jones and P. Parsons; Berlin – New York 1983), nos. 681–686, and English translations of Eupolemus' texts and testimonia may be found in B.Z. Wacholder, *Eupolemus: A Study of Judaeo-Greek Literature* (Cincinnati 1974), pp. 307–312. Concerning Eusebius' explicit identification of Demetrius, Philo and Eupolemus (along with Aristobulus and Josephus) as Jews, in *Hist. Eccl.* 6.13.7, it should be noted that he does not specify which Philo he means; perhaps he refers to the famous philosopher. Moreover, it has been argued that *C. Ap.* 1.218—as also Clement of Alexandria, *Stromata* 1.141, which similarly refers to Demetrius, Philo and Eupolemus and implies they're all historians—refers not to the epic poet but, rather, to a Jewish historian from whom no fragments have survived. See Walter (above, n. 3), I/2, pp. 112–113; M. Goodman in E. Schürer, *The History of the Jewish People in the Age of Jesus Christ* III/1 (edd. G. Vermes et al.; Edinburgh 1986), pp. 556, 560; Holladay (above, n. 2), II, pp. 216–217 (bibliography).

in the original or via an intermediary such as Alexander Polyhistor, it is reasonable to sympathize with Th. Reinach, who once put the matter quite roundly: 'Josèphe n'a pu ni ignorer la nationalité de ces trois auteurs, ni prétendre la dissimuler'.[5] Hence, some scholars have sought other ways of dealing with our passage. I know of three, none of which is very satisfactory:

a. In 1895 Reinach (*ibid.*), building upon the premise quoted in our preceding paragraph, suggested that §218 is an interpolation. However, this hardly solves the problem; it only rolls it over from Josephus to some interpolator. Moreover, the suggestion itself has little to recommend it. Accordingly, it is not surprising to find that although Reinach repeated it (and accordingly bracketed § 218) in the 1902 Société des Études Juives publication of L. Blum's translation of *Contra Apionem*, in his notes to the 1930 Collection Budé republication of that translation Reinach omitted the suggestion and the brackets, observing instead only that Josephus was wrong.[6]

b. A few scholars have suggested, gingerly, that Josephus is in fact referring to non-Jewish writers, otherwise unknown to us.[7] This, however, is hardly more than a counsel of despair.

c. B.Z. Wacholder suggested Josephus did indeed recognize that Demetrius, Philo and Eupolemus were Jewish, but that his comment on them is to be understood as deliberately cryptic: the unitiated

---

[5] Th. Reinach, *Textes d'auteurs grecs et romains relatifs au judaïsme* (Paris 1895), p. 217, n. 1. As for the question, whether Josephus read Alexander Polyhistor, see Walter (above, n. 2), pp. 315–319; Wacholder (above, n. 4), pp. 52–57; and Denis (above, n. 2), pp. 248–249.

[6] For the sake of completeness, we note that although Reinach died in 1928 and the publisher's notice on the back of the title page of the Budé edition says Isidore Lévy completed the 'annotation', that same notice says the volume was in proofs when Reinach died, and A. Puech specifically says that Reinach himself completed the manuscript; see 'Une edition nouvelle du 'Contra Apion' de Josèphe', *Bulletin de l'Association Guillaume Budé* 27 (Avril 1930), p. 30. Reinach's original suggestion, that § 218 is an interpolation, received little attention, although lately Denis (above, n. 2: p. 248, n. 22 and p. 271) leaned toward it. In the margin of his copy of Reinach's *Textes*, which is now in my possession, Hans (Johanan) Lewy wrote 'überprüfen' alongside of Reinach's suggestion that the passage is interpolated, but I do not know of any publication of his, or of anyone else, which deals with this issue in any detail.

[7] See esp. L.H. Feldman, *Jew and Gentile in the Ancient World* (Princeton 1993), p. 29 (on Eupolemus), quoted below, n. 12. A. Kasher, in the commentary to 1.218 in his 1996 Hebrew translation of *Contra Apionem* (vol. I, pp. 221–222), defended Josephus' presumption that our trio were non-Jews (noting, in connection with Eupolemus, that he 'found encouragement' in Feldman, loc. cit.).

could read it as if they were Greek, while those in the know would realize that they were Jewish and that Josephus was criticizing them for depending upon the Septuagint.[8] But Wacholder did not explain why Josephus would have wanted to be cryptic, and Wacholder's importation of the Septuagint into this passage, which nowhere mentions it, seems to complicate the issue unnecessarily.

* * *

Nevertheless, it seems that Wacholder's basic premise, that Josephus knew these authors were Jewish, may be bolstered.

To begin with, an external argument. At *Praeparatio evangelica* 9.42.2–3 (ed. Mras, pp. 553–554), Eusebius quotes *C. Ap.* 1.215–218 *verbatim* with no comment, although elsewhere, as noted (n. 4), he explicitly labels all three of our writers as Jews. It seems, therefore, that Eusebius was not troubled by the common interpretation of our passage. Perhaps he assumed another one.

More important, however, is the argument from structure. The placement of § 218 requires some comment, for it reads as an afterthought, the opening μέντοι sounding quite clumsy after its appearance in the final clause of § 217. Moreover, if we recall the breakdown of section ii of Josephus' case between the evidence from barbarians (§§ 69–160) and that of Greeks (§§ 161ff.), it seems that it should have ended with § 217. Josephus' argument is very well-built and to the point: in § 215 the reference to the Egyptian, Babylonian and Phoenician records shows that he has finished the Greek part of this section and is summarizing, § 216 promises the reader (whom he addresses like a jury) that he could have brought much additional evidence, and § 217 reiterates what the issue at stake is. After § 217 all we need is 'I rest my case'. The addition of § 218, which refers to some more or less accurate but non-quoted writers and attributes their mistakes to their less than perfect knowledge of Hebrew, contributes nothing to Josephus' case against Greek skeptics, and seems rather to arise out of some other Josephan agenda, to which we will revert at the conclusion of our study. In the meantime, what is important is to underline that once we note the isolation of § 218 we may consider the possibility that the three writers it mentions are not to be understood as more examples of Greek writers who mentioned the Jews.

---

[8] Wacholder (above, n. 4), pp. 2–3. Wacholder's position seems to be adopted by M. Goodman (above, n. 4), p. 519.

Indeed, the usual reading of § 218 entails a grave difficulty. For it assumes that the structure of §§ 216–218 is as follows: § 216 defines the universe of additional Greek writers about the Jews, § 217 says most of them were not accurate and § 218 says three of them, in contrast, were relatively accurate. But although such a structure is a natural one,[9] here it cannot be posited, for the simple reason that the three mentioned in § 218 were not included in the universe specified in § 216. Moreover, Josephus' purpose in § 216 was to give as long a list as possible. If he took Demetrius, Philo and Eupolemus to be Greeks, why didn't he include them in the list in § 216, and then proceed to single them out via the contrast in §§ 217–218?

Next, what is implied by the identification of Philo as ὁ πρεσβύτερος? There are two ways of translating this: 'Philo the Elder' or 'the elder Philo'. The former option, that Josephus meant Philo held the position of 'elder' in some Jewish community, is not very likely, inasmuch as Josephus makes no reference to any Jewish community here and anyway the title πρεσβύτερος seems to have been rare in Jewish communities.[10] Hence 'the elder Philo' is more likely. But what is important here is that this latter option, no less than the former, implies that Philo was a Jew. For it shows that Josephus wants the reader to be careful not to think of another, more recent, Philo. Now, although 'Philo' was a very common name, borne even by a number of philosophers who lived prior to Josephus,[11] the use of the mere comparative, 'elder', seems to imply that Josephus feared only that his readers would think of only one other possibility. The only reasonable explanation for that is the assumption that Josephus was worried only about the famous Alexandrian Jewish philosopher, and that, in turn, means that Josephus assumed his readers knew that he was referring to a Jew. If not, why wouldn't he be afraid they'd think of Philo of Athens (fifth century B.C.E.), Philo of Megara (fourth), Philo of Herakleia (third), or even Philo of Larissa (first)?

---

[9] For two examples in *Contra Apionem*, see 1.38–40 (the canon includes 22 books, of which five are by Moses, thirteen are by other prophets, and four contain hymns and precepts) and 1.220–222 (of the four authors named in § 221, some were moved by envy and ill will, while others hoped that the novelty of their writings wuld make them famous).

[10] See Schürer (above, n. 4), p. 102.

[11] For the data on the widespread occurrence of the name Philo, including among individuals prominent in the arts, literature or philosophy, see D.T. Runia, 'Philonic Nomenclature', *Studia Philonica Annual* 6 (1994), pp. 1–3.

Finally, four points of Josephus' diction in §218b seem also to indicate that Josephus took our trio to be Jewish.

a. First, what is implied by τοῖς ἡμετέροις γράμμασι, which Thackeray translated by 'our records'? Some have built upon 'our', inferring that it means 'ours but not theirs', seeing here an indication that Josephus indeed viewed the writers as non-Jews.[12] However, it is just as easy to understand it as meaning 'belonging to us, i.e. to Jews, including them and me'.

But if arguments from ἡμετέροις lead nowhere certain, γράμμασι seems to be of more use. Does it really mean the same as ἀναγραφαί, which too Thackeray frequently rendered as 'records' (as in § 215, cited above)?[13] True, γράμματα can mean merely 'books', 'records'; so, for example, *C. Ap.* 1.21, 42, 160. However, its basic meaning is 'letters' (of the alphabet), and that is all it means in such passages as *C. Ap.* 1.10–11 (bis) and many other Josephan passages.[14] But although 'letters' and 'books' (or 'records') are different words in English, the fact that one Greek word is used must be given its due. Namely, even when γράμματα is used of books and records, it seems that—as opposed to ἀναγραφαί, which refers to the fact of having been written, and as opposed to βιβλία (§ 216) or βίβλοι (§ 217), which, if anything, allude to the material (βύβλος or βίβλος = papyrus) from which the book is made or to its being a 'volume' of a given size (as in *C. Ap.* 1.320)[15]—γράμματα retains something of its basic meaning and so alludes particularly to the letters in which the text is written. So, for example, at *C. Ap.* 1.12 Josephus notes that there is no Greek γράμμα earlier than Homer's poetry, and that

---

[12] Note especially Holladay (above, n. 2), who after stating that Josephus referred to Eupolemus as a pagan adds only '(Wacholder, *Eupolemus*, 2–3, notwithstanding; N.B. τοῖς ἡμετέροις γράμμασι)'. So too Feldman (above, n. 7): 'Josephus cites him [= Eupolemus] together with Demetrius of Phalerum and the Elder Philo, apparently as non-Jews, because he speaks of them as not accurately following the meaning of "our" records'.

[13] For ἀναγραφαί as 'records' in Thackeray's translation, see also *C. Ap.* 1.9, 11, 20, 29, 36, 38, etc. Other translations of γράμμασι in 1.218 are essentially similar to Thackeray's 'records'. So, for example: 'writings' (Wacholder [above, n. 4], p. 307), '*sepharim*' (= 'books', Kasher—above, n. 7), 'annales' and 'scritti' (Blum and Calabi—above, n. 2).

[14] See H. St. J. Thackeray, *A Lexicon to Josephus* (Paris 1930–1955), p. 117, s.v. The ancient Latin translation of our passage has 'nostras litteras' (Corpus Scriptorum Ecclesiasticorum Latinorum, 37; ed. C. Boysen; Vienna 1898; p. 48).

[15] See Thackeray, ibid., pp. 34, 105 s.vv. For the differing nuances of γράμματα and the like ('Schrift') as opposed to βιβλίον ('Buch'), see also: W. Schubart, *Das Buch bei den Griechen und Römern* (Berlin – Leipzig 1921²), p. 34.

even the latter is said to have been first transmitted by memory and not ἐν γράμμασι.

More particularly, however, note that since the Greek and Hebrew alphabets differ from one another, Josephus' reference to reading 'our γράμματα' implies reading them *in the original*. For this sense of γράμματα, note especially *C. Ap.* 1.73, where Josephus begins his proof of the Jews' antiquity from the Egyptian γράμματα. Immediately after that opening Josephus adds that he cannot read *them*, and so depends on Manetho, who, Josephus says, *translated* (μεταφράσας) the Egyptian sources into Greek. That is, presenting a translation does not constitute presenting γράμματα. The same is indicated by *C. Ap.* 1.54 (ἐκ τῶν ἱερῶν γραμμάτων μεθηρμήνευκα), where—just as at *Ant.* 1.5 (ἐκ τῶν Ἑβραϊκῶν μεθηρμηνευμένην γραμμάτων), Josephus says his *Antiquities* is a *translation* from the Jews' γράμματα. And the same conclusion emerges also from *C. Ap.* 1.116, where Josephus notes that Menander diligently learned the history of Greek and barbarian kings from the 'native' γράμματα of each country (τῶν παρ' ἑκάστοις [or: ἐκείνοις] ἐπιχωρίων γραμμάτων). Since it is clear that the natives of barbarian countries did not write in Greek, but also that it would not require special diligence on Menander's part to read Greek translations of such native works, the implication is that Menander read them in the original—here termed γράμματα. Indeed, at *Ant.* 8.144 Josephus quotes the same passage from Menander and explicitly notes that Menander *translated* records from the Phoenician language into the Greek language (ὁ μεταφράσας ἀπὸ τῆς Φοινίκων διαλέκτου . . . εἰς τὴν Ἑλληνικὴν φωνήν).

Accordingly, a better English translation for γράμματα in *C. Ap.* 1.218 would be 'letters' or 'texts'. What Josephus means is that the three authors mentioned here could not read Hebrew with complete accuracy. Why did he make no such statement concerning the Greek writers mentioned in § 216? Evidently because in their case it was clear that they could not read Hebrew at all, since they were termed (at the end of § 215) 'Greeks'. The implication is that the three writers listed in § 218, of whom the inability to ready Hebrew could not be taken for granted, were Jews.

b. Correspondingly, note that while Josephus says the Greek writers of §§ 216–217 *did not* read (μὴ . . . ἐνέτυχον) the Jews' holy books, of our trio he says that they *could not* (οὐ γὰρ ἐνῆν αὐτοῖς) follow them with total accuracy. That apparently means that they wanted to. Now, if all were assumed to be Greeks, the reader should expect some comment on or explanation for our trio's exceptional interest. But there is no such comment or explanation. The likeliest explanation, I believe, is that Josephus supposed his readers would know, or infer, that Demetrius, Philo and Eupolemus were Jewish. That, in and of itself, would explain their interest in reading the Jews' writings and in presenting the truth about them.

c. Third, note that Josephus specifies that the three writers in question could not follow our texts *with complete accuracy* (μετὰ πάσης ἀκριβείας). This means they could read them with some accuracy—which certainly implies they were Jewish. For it is only among Jews that it makes sense, and that Josephus was wont, to distinguish between those who know the Bible somewhat and those who know it with complete accuracy. The latter capacity was one which he ascribes to priests (*C. Ap.* 1.36, 54; *Vita* 9; *War* 3.352)[16] and to Pharisees (*War* 1.108-9; 2.162; *Ant.* 17.41; *Vita* 191);[17] since Josephus was himself a proud priest (*War* 1.3, 3.352; *Vita* 1–6; *C. Ap.* 1.54; *Ant.* 16.187), it is not surprising to find that he claims that he too, as a priest, could interpret the Bible accurately (*C. Ap.* 1.54; *War* 3.352).

d. Finally, we note that Josephus' usage, in referring to these three writers' competence in our γράμματα in a negative context ('could not follow with complete accuracy'), is apparently playing with the so very standard notice in ancient documents, known from hundreds of papyri, that so-and-so does not know γράμματα i.e., is illiterate (and hence needs an agent to read and sign for him or her). But in that notice it is clear that γράμματα retains its most rudimentary meaning: 'letters'.[18] Here, then, is another reason to retain this meaning for Josephus here as well: what he means is that while Demetrius, Philo and Eupolemus—as opposed to the non-Jewish authors mentioned

---

[16] See S.N. Mason, 'Priesthood in Josephus and the 'Pharisaic Revolution'", *Journal of Biblical Literature* 107 (1988), esp. pp. 658–659.

[17] See A.I. Baumgarten, 'The Name of the Pharisees', *Journal of Biblical Literature* 102 (1983), pp. 413–417, who also refers to Acts 26:5 and 22:3 for the Pharisees—ἀκρίβεια connection.

[18] On this phrase, see H.C. Youtie, "Because they do not know letters", *Zeitschrift für Papyrologie und Epigraphik* XIX (1975), pp. 101–108; J.C. Greenfield, "Because he/she did not know letters': Remarks on a First Millennium C.E. Legal Expression', *Journal of the Ancient Near Eastern Society* XXII (1993), pp. 39–44; and H.M. Cotton, 'Subscriptions and Signatures in the Papyri from the Judaean Desert: The XEIPOXPHCTHC', *Journal of Juristic Papyrology* XXV (1995), pp. 37–38. See also E.J. Goodspeed, *Problems of New Testament Translation* (Chicago 1945), pp. 102–104, on John 7:15.

in §216—were not totally illiterate in Hebrew, neither were they fully competent in it.

* * *

Thus, rather than seeing in *C. Ap.* 1.218 only a bipartite contrast, between those many Greeks who 'deviate from the truth' (§ 217) and those three (wrongly thought to be) Greeks who 'did not deviate greatly from the truth' (§ 218), we should see here a tripartite comparison: Greeks, whose accounts are often far from the truth; some Greek-writing Jews who came nearer to the truth but were not totally accurate due to their inability to read Hebrew with complete accuracy; and Josephus himself, who, as he told us at *C. Ap.* 1.54, was able to do just that, as we would expect from a priest from Jerusalem.[19] His condescending attitude toward his colleagues ('it is proper to excuse them...' [οἷς συγγιγνώσκειν ἄξιον]) is just like that which he adopts elsewhere toward another colleague, Nicolas of Damascus, whom Josephus similarly accuses of falling far below his own level as an historian: ἔχοι τὴν συγγνώμην (*Ant.* 16.186).

In conclusion, we would suggest the following translation of § 218:

> But Demetrius Phalereus and Philo the Elder and Eupolemus did not deviate greatly from the truth. (And) it is proper to forgive them (their errors), for they (—in contrast to me—) were not able to follow our texts with complete accuracy.

If this interpretation of *C. Ap.* 1.218 is indeed correct, then a further observation is in order. It concerns Josephus' continuing education between the seventies of the first century, when he wrote his *Jewish War*, and the nineties, when he wrote the *Jewish Antiquities* and *Contra Apionem*,[20] and is occasioned by the similarity of *C. Ap.* 1.218 and *War* 1.17. In the latter, Josephus had explained that there is no need for him to retell the Jews' ancient history, for that had quite accurately been done by numerous Jews before him, and their writings had already been translated into Greek by some Greeks 'who

---

[19] Perhaps it would not be out of line to note that if Eupolemus was indeed a priest from Jerusalem, as is often assumed on the basis of his identification with the individual mentioned in in I Maccabees 8:17 and II Macc 4:11, the fact that he too made errors about basic points of biblical history would undercut Josephus' claim that Jerusalemite priests are infallible in this realm.

[20] On Josephus' reading between the seventies and the nineties, see especially S. Schwartz, *Josephus and Judaean Politics* (Leiden 1990), pp. 45–57.

did not deviate greatly from the truth' (οὐ πολὺ τῆς ἀληθείας διήμαρτον). In other words, writing in the seventies Josephus knows only of Jews who write Hebrew (or Aramaic) and Greeks who write Greek. He doesn't know of, or take into account, Jews who wrote in Greek. Moreover, he assumes—whether naively or merely politely—that there were Greeks who read the Jewish writings and more or less accurately wrote in Greek on their basis.[21] But during the following two decades, years in which his reading and proficiency in Greek grew so much that he could now dispense with assistants 'for the Greek language' (see *C. Ap.* 1.50), Josephus changed his mind about the need to write the Jews' ancient history (although he would claim he had it in mind all the time—*Ant.* 1.6) and, correspondingly, about the value of his predecessors' work. On the one hand, he discovered that the Greeks among them were frequently inaccurate, in large measure because they in fact hardly related to the translations of the Jews' sacred scriptures.[22] On the other hand, he also discovered that those predecessors included Jews as well as Greeks. Accordingly, he had to reassure his readers that they all still left room for him.

---

[21] I see no reason to assume—*pace* Thackeray (Loeb) and Pelletier (Budé) ad loc.—that the writers termed 'Greeks' in *War* 1.17 are in fact Demetrius, Philo and Eupolemus and that, hence, Josephus already made in *War* precisely the same error usually imputed to him in *C. Ap.* 1.218. Thackeray points to the recurrence of οὐ πολὺ τῆς ἀληθείας διήμαρτον in both passages—in *War* of the 'some Greeks' and in *C. Ap.* 1.218 of Demetrius, Philo and Eupolemus. But the phrase is banal enough, recurring at 1.287 in connection with Manetho; cf. *Ant.* 4.303 (μηδὲν ἐκείνου διημαρτηκότος τῆς ἀληθείας—of Moses) and 7.103 (οὐ διήμαρτε δὲ τῆς ἀληθείας—of Nicolas of Damascus). Hence, the similarity of the passages need indicate only that Josephus was used to applying similar categories to historians, not that he always applied them to the same historians. On the other hand, I am not convinced by T. Rajak's suggestion that the writers of *War* 1.17 were 'manifestly Jews' and Josephus knew it; see her 'The Location of Cultures in Second Temple Palestine: The Evidence of Josephus', *The Book of Acts in its Palestinian Setting* (ed. R.J. Bauckham; Grand Rapids, Mich.—Carlisle, Cal. 1995), p. 12. Josephus clearly distinguishes here between 'Jews' who accurately wrote our ancestors' history and 'Greeks' who translated those records, more or less accurately, into their native tongue; for 'Jew' and 'Greek' as mutually exclusive categories for Josephus, see Rajak, pp. 11–12 (*War* 1.17 is the only putative exception she cites). In the immediate vicinity of *War* 1.17, note esp. § 16, which begins with Josephus presenting himself as a foreigner (ἀλλόφυλος) in contrast to the Greeks and Romans, and ends by saying that 'we' should respect historical truth although 'the Greeks' disregard it.

[22] On Greek and Roman reading of the Septuagint, see Feldman (above, n. 7), pp. 311–314; he cites several pessimistic assessments (add M. Radin, 'Roman Knowledge of Jewish Literature', *Classical Journal* 13 [1917/18], pp. 149–176), and even his own more optimistic dossier doesn't have very much. See also D. Rokéah, 'The Jewish Bible and the New Testament in the Pagan World', *Tarbiz* 60 (1990/91), pp. 451–464 (in Hebrew).

This he does, especially on the background of his first-hand experience in a Diaspora community, which taught him that—at least on the basis of Jerusalemite standards—Jews of the Greco-Roman Diaspora frequently did not know Hebrew very well.[23] This seems to be the point he was making, perhaps too subtly, at *C. Ap.* 1.218.

---

[23] On even Philo's lack of Hebrew, see idem, 'A New Onomasticon Fragment from Oxyrhynchus and Philo's Etymologies', *Journal of Theological Studies* 19 (1968), pp. 70–82. Cf. N.G. Cohen, *Philo Judaeus: His Universe of Discourse* (Frankfurt am Main 1995), pp. 14–18.

ARE THE 'HALACHIC TEMPLE MOUNT' AND THE 'OUTER COURT' OF JOSEPHUS ONE AND THE SAME?

Joshua Schwartz and Yehoshua Peleg

Introduction

The 'Temple Mount' is the modern term for Mt. Moriah on which the Temple in Jerusalem stood. This walled compound constitutes the archaeological *temenos* of the Temple. The *temenos* compound went through various incarnations, growing over the years from Solomon's time, through the Persian period and the Hasmonean expansion, and until the Herodian period, when the present boundaries were set. During the Herodian period, the *temenos* contained several elements, such as porticoes bounding the outer court on the east, north, and west. The Royal Portico, built in the southern side of the *temenos*, was unparalleled in size and grandeur in the entire Roman Empire (map 1). Located within the boundaries of the outer court was the '*Azarah*' of the rabbis, or as Josephus refers to it, the 'Second Court' or the 'Second Sanctified Precinct'. The Outer Court surrounded the *Azarah* on all sides.

The term 'Temple Mount' as used in rabbinic literature reflects the reality of the late first century and second century C.E., after the destruction of the Second Temple.[1] The rabbis used the term in specific ways in the rabbinic literature of the time, knowing exactly what area was meant by the term when they used it. The halachic Temple Mount is the area defined in Mishnah Middot (2:1) and is much smaller than the Herodian *temenos*.

Many scholars have pointed out contradictions between Josephus's two books regarding the perimeter of the Temple Mount. These contradictions are summed up by the archaeologist and historian Lee I. Levine:

> Although a number of sources describe the physical dimensions of this building complex, the contradictions among them are many and far

---
[1] Y.Z. Eliav, *A Mount without a Temple*, unpublished doctoral dissertation, Hebrew University of Jerusalem, 1998, p. 10.

> from trivial ... the discrepancies among the sources (= Mishnah Middot, *The Jewish War, Antiquities*) touch on nearly every aspect of the Temple complex.... M *Middot* notes that the Temple Mount had a circumference of two thousand cubits ... whereas Josephus records four stades (= in *The Jewish War*) and six stades (= in *Antiquities* 223–224).²

A look at *The Jewish War* (5.192) proves that when Josephus says six stades, he is referring to the perimeter of the Outer Court:

> And the complete circuit of them (= porticoes), embracing the tower of Antonia, measured six furlongs (= stades).³

We shall return to this matter later on. In contrast, in *Antiquities* (15.400) he seems to be discussing the perimeter of the rabbinic *Azarah*, or the Josephan 'Second Sanctified Precinct':

> When this work reached the top of the hill, he [Herod] leveled off the summit, and filled in the hollow spaces near the walls, and made the upper surface smooth and even throughout.⁴ Such was the whole enclosure, having a circumference of four stades, each side taking up the length of a stade.⁵

It should be noted that this explanation eliminates the apparent contradiction between the two sources by Josephus regarding the description of the Outer Court, since in reality the smaller figure refers to the internal court and thus there is no contradiction. Although we shall make occasional reference to the 'Internal', 'Upper', 'Second' court, the present paper, for the most part, deals with the 'Outer',

---

² L.I. Levine, *Jerusalem: Portrait of the City in the Second Temple Period (538 B.C.E.–70 C.E.)*, Philadelphia 2002, pp. 223–224. Cf. *idem*, 'The Second Temple of Jerusalem: Josephus' Description and Other Sources,' *Cathedra*, 77 (1995), 3–16 and esp. 4 (Hebrew).

³ The translations from Josephus, unless indicated otherwise, are from the Loeb Classical Library edition of Josephus. See H.St.J. Thackeray *et al.*, *Josephus: with an English Translation, I–IX (LCL)*, London and Cambridge, MA, 1926–1965.

⁴ Josephus lists two 'surfaces' in the Temple Mount complex, i.e. a lower one and a higher one. Josephus refers to the lower one as 'the first sanctified precinct' (*tou hierou propedontes*) in *War* 4.196. In *War* 5.193 he refers to the upper surface as the *deuteron hieron* (5.193), or the second sanctified precinct. The sentence from *Antiquities* cited above, as does the rest of the paragraph there, refers to the upper surface.

⁵ Here Josephus is describing the *pan peribolos* ('whole enclosure') when the supporting walls of the Temple Mount had been completed and the builders were working on the hilltop fortifications. The term *pan peribolos* here technically refers to an area surrounded and protected by a wall, which in the case described above is the wall of the *azarah*. See K.H. Rengstorf (ed.), *A Complete Concordance to Flavius Josephus, III*, Leiden 1973, p. 387, s.v. *peribolos*.

'Lower' and 'First' court of Josephus in relation to the dimensions of the 'halachic' Temple Mount as stated in M Middot (2:1) and in relation also to the dimensions of the present archaeological Herodian *temenos*.[6]

The basic problem is that the perimeter of the Temple Mount based on archaeological evidence is 8.14 stades (or 1514 meters based on 186 meters per stadium) and this is inconsistent with Josephus's description of the 6 stades perimeter of the porticoes surrounding the outer court as mentioned in *War* 5.192.[7] Moreover, it is not clear how the three sources, the two of Josephus and the Mishnah relate to one other as well as to the archaeological evidence.

The purpose of this paper is to propose a way of reconciling the supposed contradictions between Josephus, the rabbis and archaeology. We shall attempt to show that the area of the Temple Mount as given in M Middot corresponds to the area of the outer court as described by Josephus and also corresponds to the size of the present *temenos*.

The Temple Mount of Mishnah Middot

M Middot (2:1) gives the dimensions of the Temple Mount as 'five hundred cubits by five hundred cubits.' There are two main schools of thought as to how to approach this text.

Most scholars, from Hollis to Ritmeyer, understand the Mishnah as saying that the Temple Mount was a square with a length and width of 500 cubits each.[8] However, so far no geometric solution has been found that would accommodate this approach with Josephus and the archaeological remains. We shall not re-hash the vast amount of literature and scholarship devoted to this approach.

---

[6] The literature on Mishnah Middot is voluminous. Much of Tractate Middot is attributed to the first century C.E. sage R. Eliezer b. Jacob, who theoretically provides eye-witness testimony. See, for example, Middot 2:5.

[7] See Levine, *Jerusalem*, p. 224. Levine solves discrepancies between the two works of Josephus by claiming that *The Jewish War* describes the Temple as viewed by Titus in 70 C.E. and *Antiquities* describes Herod's original construction. The Mishnah, according to Levine is similar in many aspects to *War* and thus reflects the last years of the Second Temple period. As seen above, and as will be shown in detail, the authors of this study have a different approach.

[8] See, for example, F.J. Hollis, *The Archaeology of Herod's Temple*, London 1934 and L and K. Ritmeyer, *Secret's of Jerusalem's Temple Mount*, Washington D.C. 1998, pp. 57ff.

The second school of thought maintains that the Mishnah is stating the area of the Temple Mount, but does not describe its shape. In the Mishnah period, measurements of area were expressed based on the measurement of a square of the length.[9] Thus, the Mishnah is giving the area of the halachic Temple Mount without stating whether it was a square, a trapezoid, or a rectangle. The very fact that the Mishnah does not specify the length and width of the Temple Mount indicates that the intention was to define the area and the shape need not be a square.[10]

The Size of the Stade and Cubit used by Josephus and Middot

Understanding the units of length used in the Second Temple period can help regarding the understanding of the size and location of the halachic Temple Mount and in particular, defining the stade mentioned by Josephus in connection with the perimeter of the outer court will enable us to identify the location of the halachic Temple Mount.

1. *The Stade of Josephus*

Different sources provide different lengths for the stade, ranging from 177.25 to 192.25 meters.[11] We shall make use of what turns out to be the average between these figures, i.e. 186 meters. This decision, however, is not simply an average between minimum and maximum figures. Thus, the length of the Greek stade is based on that of the Greek foot, which equals 0.31 meters[12] and because a Greek stade

---

[9] See D. Sperber, 'Measures and Weights in Judaism,' *Ha-Encyclopaedia ha-Ivrit*, 22 (1970), cols. 236–238.

[10] A major proponent of this view is A.Z. Kaufman. See, for example, A.Z. Kaufman, 'The Shape of the Ancient Temple Mount (Har Habayit),' *Judea and Samaria Research Studies: Proceedings of the Sixth Annual Meeting 1996*, Tel-Aviv 1997, pp. 111–123 (Hebrew).

[11] The stade is a unit of distance taken from the Greek stadium, which was used for track and field competitions. The stade was not uniform; different stadiums in Greece, for example, used different distances: in Olympia it was 192.25 meters; in Epidaurus, 181.30 meters; in Delphi, 177.55 meters; in Athens, 184.96 meters. See *Pauly Realencyclopaedie der Classischen Altertumswissenschaft*, Stuttgart 1929 vol. IIIA2, cols, 1930–1974.

[12] S. Hornblower and A. Spawforth, *The Oxford Classical Dictionary*, Oxford and New York 1996, pp. 942–943, s.v. measures. There were minor variations here as

is equal to 600 feet, the length of a stade may be calculated as follows: 600 × 0.31 = 186 meters.[13] The length of a *Byzantine* foot is recorded on an inscription found in the vicinity of the aqueduct near Bethlehem. This Byzantine period inscription provides the length of the foot used in Palestine three centuries after the time of Josephus and this works out to be .3089 meters long, i.e., within 1.1 mm of 0.31 meters mentioned above as the length of the Greek foot. The extremely minimal discrepancy may be due to an error by the artisan who engraved the inscription,[14] and it should be kept in mind that in antiquity there was no official, standard unit of length (the equivalent of the standard meter in Paris today, for instance). Each measuring device used by an artisan had its own degree of accuracy, resulting in the occasional discrepancy. In this particular case, the length of the Byzantine foot is 0.3089 meters; hence, the length of a Byzantine period stade works out to be 600 × 0.3089 = 185.34 meters, quite close to the figure of 186 meters cited above.

The figure of approximately 186 meters is further confirmed by the description of Josephus of the perimeter wall of Masada:

> The subsequent planning of the place [Masada] engaged the serious attention of King Herod. For first he enclosed the entire summit, a circuit measuring seven stades, with a wall of white stone, twelve cubits high and eight broad (*War* 7.286).[15]

Josephus specifies that the length of the wall is seven stades and it has been measured to be approximately 1300 meters.[16] Dividing 1300 meters by 7 stades results in 185.71 meters per stade, once again quite close to the figure of 186 cited above.

---

well. Thus, for example, the Olympic foot was 0.32 meters, the Pergamene one was 0.33 meters, the Attic was 0.2957 and the Aeginetan was 0.33.

[13] See n. 11.

[14] F.M. Abel, 'Inscription Grecque de L'Aqueduc de Jerusalem avec la Figure du Pied Byzantin,' *Revue Biblique*, 35 (1926), 284–288.

[15] Thackeray's translation, which we cite here, reads 'furlongs'. We have changed it to stades based on the Greek text and for consistency.

[16] See M. Avi-Yonah, 'The Excavations of Masada 1963/64: Preliminary Report,' *Israel Exploration Journal*, 15 (1965), 69 and n. 45. The circumference with all its windings is approximately 1,400 meters, while in a straight line it measures 1,300 meters which corresponds exactly to the seven stades mentioned by Josephus. Cf., however, E. Netzer, *Masada III: The Yigael Yadin Excavations 1963–1965—Final Reports: The Buildings, Stratigraphy and Architecture*, Jerusalem 1991, p. 605. Netzer estimates the circumference to be approximately 1,290 meters.

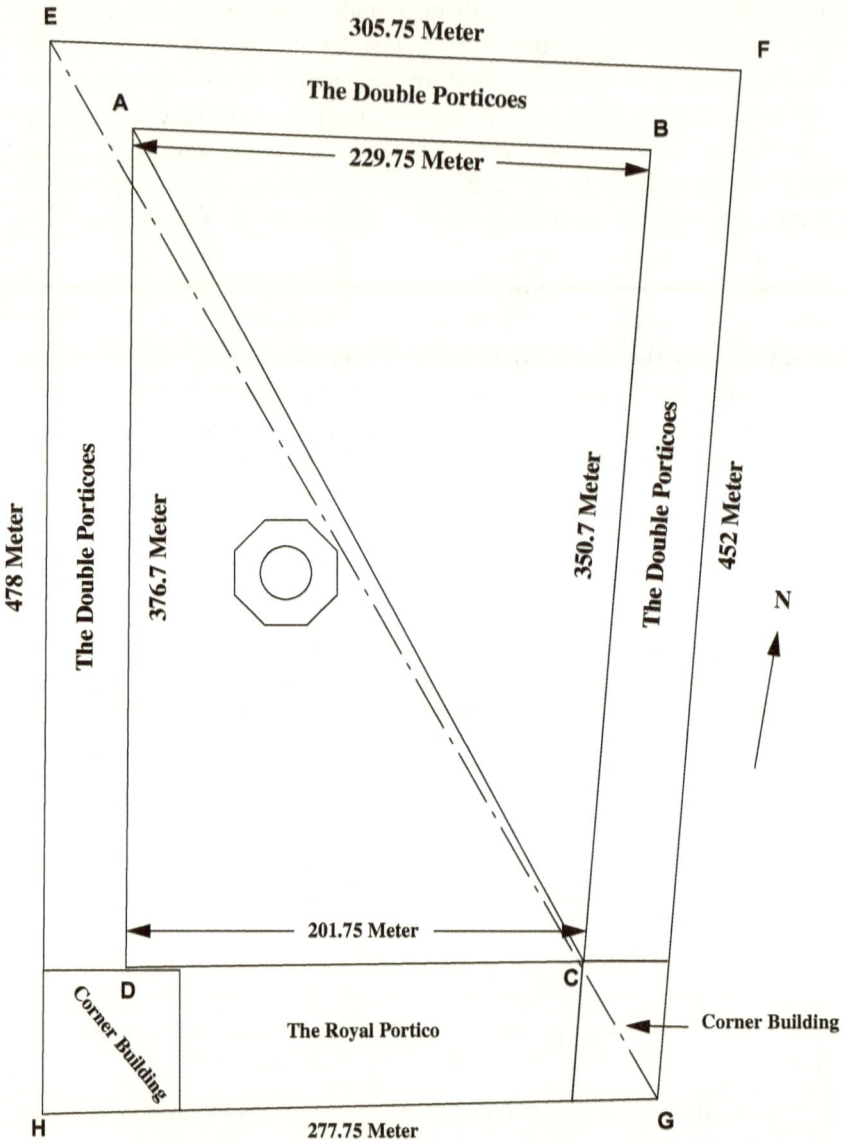

Fig. 1. The Outer Court Lay Out, Superimposed on the Herodian Temenos.

THE 'HALACHIC TEMPLE MOUNT' AND THE 'OUTER COURT' 213

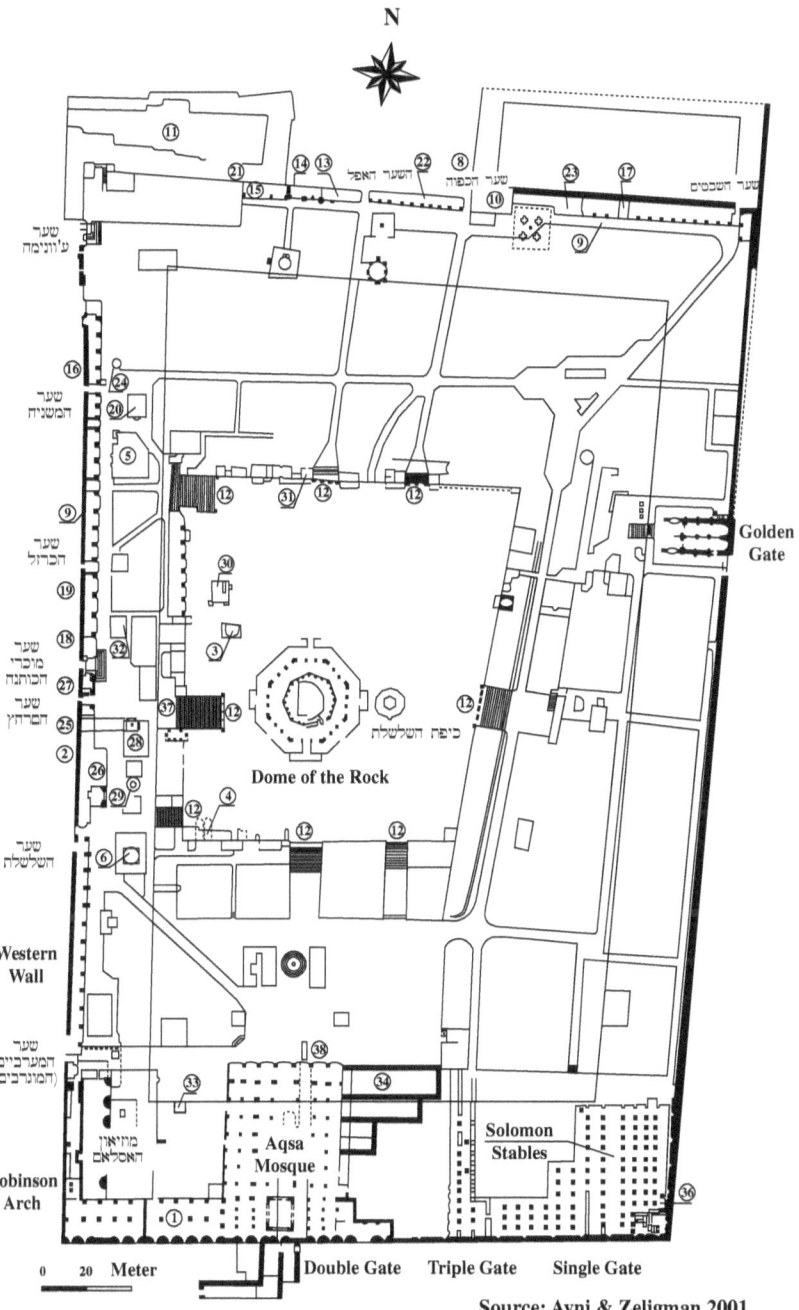

Map 1. The Inner Perimeter of the Herodian Porticoes Superimposed on the Temple Mount.

We have thus calculated the length of a stade based on two archaeological finds: the aqueduct inscription near Bethlehem and the perimeter wall of Masada and the two figures differ by only 0.2%. Hence, the average stade in the Herodian period was 185.53 meters. In other words, a stade was approximately 186 meters long.

2. *The Cubit in the Temple*

In most cases, the units of length used in the sources describing the Temple and the Temple Mount buildings are cubits (M Middot and Josephus).[17] There are various opinions as to the size of a cubit. This paper assumes that a cubit was 0.56 meters, as Aryeh Ben-David has shown and apparently this is true for both Josephus and Middot.[18]

TEMPLE MOUNT AND OUTER COURT

1. *The Herodian* Temenos *according to Josephus*

The *temenos* compound was redesigned and essentially rebuilt in the Herodian period. The main features of this compound were the fortified walls and a spacious area enclosed by these walls. This compound is described by Josephus as follows:

> Nor was the superstructure unworthy of such foundations. The porticoes, all in double rows, were supported by columns five and twenty cubits high—each a single block of the purest white marble—and ceiled with panels of cedar. The natural magnificence of these columns, their excellent polish and fine adjustment presented a striking spectacle, without any adventitious embellishment of painting or sculpture. The porticoes were thirty cubits broad, and the complete circuit of them, embracing the towers of Antonia, measured six furlongs. The open court was from end to end variegated with paving of all manner of stones (*War* 5. 190–192).

This Herodian *temenos* was, in fact, immense, and much larger, for instance, than those of the temple of Jupiter Heliopolitan at Baalbek

---

[17] There were different types of cubits. See, in general, E. Stern, 'Measures and Weights,' *Ecyclopaedia Biblica*, IV, cols. 848–852 (Hebrew).

[18] A. Ben-David, 'Ha-Midda ha-Yerushalmit,' *Israel Exploration Journal*, 19 (1969), 159–169; idem, 'The Hebrew Phoenician Cubit,' *Palestine Exploration Quarterly*, 110 (1978), 27–28. Ben-David presents archaeological evidence showing that in the late Second Temple period, the length of a cubit consisted of six handbreadths, which was 56 cm.

or the temples of Bel and Baalshamin at Palmyra.[19] Many Jews of Palestine and some Jews from the Diaspora came to the Temple during the pilgrimage festivals, and the expansion of the pre-Herodian *temenos* was undoubtedly intended to ensure sufficient physical space for the masses of celebrants.[20]

2. *Archaeological Evidence*

The Herodian compound has been measured a number of times and a number of maps have been prepared reflecting the measuring and measurements of the mount. After the Six-Day War, the IDF Engineering Corps also measured the Temple Mount and their measurements are probably the most accurate.[21] The sacred compound today extends over 13.5 hectares. The dimensions of the temenos according to the measurements of the IDF Engineering Corps are:

1. northern wall—305.75 meters
2. southern wall—277.75 meters
3. western wall—478 meters
4. eastern wall—452 meters

We can calculate the area of the *temenos*, indicated by the letters EFGH, by dividing the compound into two triangles (see fig. 1): the southwestern triangle (EHG) and the northeastern triangle (EFG). The calculation of the area of the triangles is facilitated by the fact that the southwestern angle of the temenos is 90 degrees, while the northeastern angle (EFG) is 92.5 degrees. A simple calculation of the triangles shows that the area of the sacred compound to be 13.5 hectares. Adding up the length of the walls of the *temenos* gives us 1513.5 meters (8.14 stades) as the perimeter of the sacred compound. This information is used below to calculate the size of the Herodian outer court.

---

[19] See Levine, *Jerusalem*, p. 232 and the literature cited there. Herod was following a Hellenistic plan popular at Rome which called for the construction of an artificial platform surrounded on three sides by porticoes and on the fourth by a basilica (royal portico or stoa).
[20] *Ibid.*, pp. 248–252.
[21] S. Goren, *Har ha-Bayit*, Jerusalem, 1992, pp. 178–184.

3. *Josephus on the Inner Perimeter of the Herodian Porticoes*

Josephus describes the Herodian porticoes surrounding the Outer Court as follows:

> The porticoes were thirty cubits broad, and the complete circuit of them (*ho de pas kuklos auton*), embracing the tower of Antonia, measured six stades. (*War* 5.192)

There are two possible ways of understanding this sentence. One is that it refers to the outer perimeter of the *temenos*, which is the same as the outer perimeter of the porticoes, including the walls of the tower of the Antonia. However, in such a case Josephus undoubtedly would have used the phrase *peribolos*, which he does not use here.[22]

The other option is that Josephus is referring to the inner perimeter of the porticoes; i.e., the six stades are the outer perimeter of the Outer Court (= the perimeter of the polygon ABCD in fig. 1.) and reflects how one would walk around the porticoes along the outer edge of the Outer Court.

Because of the problem with the first option, it would seem that the second one is to be preferred.[23] As we remember, six stades would be 1116 meters (6 × 186 = 1116) and we shall return to deal with this figure later.

Calculation of the Perimeter of the Outer Court: Archaeological Data and Josephus

Josephus describes the Outer Court in great detail (*War* 5.184–192; *Antiquities* 15.391–399, 410–416). His account of the high exterior walls and the gates in the western and southern walls enhances our knowledge about the compound, giving us a good picture of the structure of the Herodian *temenos*. Josephus sums up his impression of the compound and walls as follows:

> Both (porticoes) were (supported) by a great wall, and the wall itself was the greatest ever heard of by man. (*Antiquities* 15.396)

---

[22] See Rengstorf *Concordance*, III, p. 387, s.v. *peribolos*. This word, as we saw above, means the area surrounded and protected by a wall (i.e., the outer defensive wall). Josephus uses *kuklos*. See Rengstorf, *Concordance*, p. 142, s.v. *kuklos*. While *kuklos* can have some aspects of a wall, the wall element is far more prominent in *peribolos*.

[23] This is also the conclusion of Hollis, *Archaeology*, p. 34.

There were porticoes on the eastern, northern, and western sides; the Royal Portico was on the southern side. Even non-Jews—in fact, everyone except those women who were not yet ritually pure following menstruation—were permitted to enter the outer court. As Josephus writes:

> The Outer Court was open to all, foreigners included; women during their impurity were alone refused admission. (*Against Apion* 2.103)

The perimeter of the walls of the present Temple Mount is 1514 meters (8.14 stades, as stated above). This does not match the perimeter reported by Josephus (six stades- 1116 meters). Therefore, it would seem that the six stades should be attributed to the outer perimeter of the Outer Court. Below is a description of the areas surrounding the outer court.

In *War*, Josephus explains that double porticoes were built on the Herodian *temenos* adjacent to the walls. These porticoes were on the eastern, northern, and western sides, whereas the Royal Portico was on the south. Josephus describes the width of the double porticoes surrounding the Outer Court as follows:

> The porticoes, all in double *rows* . . . *were* thirty cubits broad. (*War* 5.190–192)

Josephus was being precise when he wrote 'porticoes' in the plural. He is referring to three porticoes forming the shape of a capital Greek letter *pi*, adjacent to the walls of the Temple Mount. The double porticoes are the three additional ones, also in the shape of a capital Greek *pi*, located within the first one, resulting in one portico inside another, or as the Babylonian Talmud says: 'Rehaba citing R. Judah stated: The Temple Mount had a double portico, one portico being within the other' (BT Sukkah 45a; BT Pesahim 13b, 52b; BT Berakhot 33b).

On the size of the porticoes Josephus writes:

> And he surrounded the Temple with very large porticoes, all of which he [Herod] made in proportion (to the Temple). (*Antiquities* 15.396)

The width of these porticoes, according to Josephus, was about 30 cubits, as we saw above in *War* 5.191. If a 'standard' portico was 30 cubits wide, then two rows mentioned in Josephus were 60 cubits wide.

On the southern side Herod built the Royal Portico:

> The fourth front of [the Herodian temenos] ... facing south ... had over it the Royal Portico, which had three aisles.... Now the columns (of the portico) stood in four rows, one opposite the other all along— the fourth row was attached to a wall built of stone ... they made three aisles among them, under the porticoes. Of these the two side ones corresponded and were made in the same way, each being thirty feet (*podes*) in width.... But the middle aisle was one and a half times as wide.... (*Antiquities* 15.411–415)

As can be seen, Josephus uses 'feet' to describe the width of the aisles of the Royal Portico. In an earlier study, it has been shown that the word 'foot' (*podes*) is probably a mistake and that the text instead should read 'cubit' (*pexus*).[24] Based on this, we have used cubits for our calculations below instead of feet.

Thus, if we add up the distances between the columns, we find that the Royal Portico was 105 cubits wide. This is calculated as follows: Two rows of standard-width porticoes, each 30 cubits wide, total 60 cubits. The middle portico was one and a half times as wide as a standard portico, i.e., 45 cubits (30 + 30 + 45 = 105).

The length of the royal portico (according to *Antiquities* 15.415) was one stade. However, Josephus describes the royal portico as extending along the entire length of the southern wall, from the western wall of the Temple temenos to its eastern wall. The length of the southern wall, as measured in modern times, as we saw above, is approximately 278 meters—obviously longer than the distance reported by Josephus. The difference between the two numbers is 92 meters (278−186 = 92). This difference is explained by the fact that while the inner length of the Royal Portico was one stade, in each of the two corners of the southern wall of the Herodian temenos, the eastern and western ones, there were square structures through which one could enter the Royal Portico, whether at ground level or to the upper stories through staircases in these structures.[25]

In determining the perimeter of the Outer Court, it is also necessary to determine and then to subtract the measurement of the thickness of the walls of the archaeological temenos. These walls, above the level of the Temple Mount, were approximately eight

---

[24] Y. Peleg and E. Baruch, 'The Measures of the Royal Stoa in the Temple Mount according to Josephus Flavius,' in A. Faust and E. Baruch (eds.), *New Studies on Jerusalem: Proceedings of the Seventh Conference, Ingeborg Rennert Center for Jerusalem Studies* (Ramat-Gan, 2001), 151–157.

[25] B. Mazar, *The Mountain of the Lord*, Garden City, New York 1975, p. 112.

cubits (4.5. meters) thick, as we know from electromagnetic measurements of the lower parts of the temenos walls that are visible today.[26] Subtracting the area covered by the four porticoes as well as the measurement of the thickness of the walls of the Royal Portico built on top of the retaining walls of the archaeological temenos (the Temple Mount) leaves us with the area defined by Josephus as the 'Outer Court.'

The Inner Perimeter of the Porticoes: Dimensions of the Herodian Temenos and Josephus

To calculate the inner perimeter of the porticoes, it is necessary to subtract the area of the porticoes and the walls surrounding the archaeological temenos, as we mentioned before. To do this it is first necessary to calculate the inner length of the porticoes on the eastern, western, and northern sides of the temenos. On these sides, an area of 68 cubits wide around the walls of the archaeological temenos should be subtracted from the outer length of the porticoes. This represents the width of the porticoes there, 60 cubits, and the thickness of the wall, 8 cubits. On the south, an area of 113 cubits wide must be subtracted, this representing the width of the Royal Portico, 108 cubits, and the thickness of the walls, 8 cubits. As we remember, the dimensions of the temenos are based on the measurements provided by the IDF Engineering Corps (see above).

This inner perimeter is represented by polygon ABCD (see fig. 1). The length of the northern side of the Outer Court (AB) is calculated by subtracting from the northern side of the temenos the width of the eastern and western porticoes (0.56 × 68 × 2 = 76 meters). Hence, the length of the northern side (AB) is 305.75–76 = 229.75 meters. The length of the southern side of the Outer Court is determined by subtracting from that side the width of the eastern and western porticoes (0.56 × 68 × 2 = 76 meters). Hence, the length of the southern side (CD) is 277.75–76 = 201.75 meters. The length of the western side of the Outer Court is established by subtracting the width of the northern and southern porticoes (0.56 × 68 = 38 meters; 0.56 × 113 = 63.3 meters). Hence, the length of the western

---

[26] A. Warszawski and A. Peretz, 'Building the Temple Mount: Organization and Execution,' *Cathedra*, 66 (1992), 10 (Hebrew).

side (AD) is 478–63.3–38 = 376.7 meters. The eastern side of the Outer Court is found by subtracting the width of the northern and southern porticoes (0.56 × 68 = 38 meters; 0.56 × 113 = 63.3 meters). Hence, the length of the eastern side (BC) is 452–63.3–38 = 350.7 meters. The total perimeter of the polygon ABCD is AB + BC + CD + DA = 1158.9 meters. This is almost exactly the same as the figure reached by Hollis, who unfortunately did not provide any clear indication as to how he arrived at it.[27]

The Perimeter of the Halachic Temple Mount according to Tractate Middot

The Tractate Middot describes the Temple Mount as an area covering 500 by 500 cubits, i.e., 250,000 square cubits, without stating its shape.[28] The perimeter of the Temple Mount is, therefore, 2000 cubits which is 1120 meters (0.56 × 2000 = 1120 meters).

Tentative Summary: Perimeter of the Outer Court or Temple Mount

We have so far calculated the perimeter of the Outer Court by three different methods:

1. Based on the archaeological data, i.e., the data relevant to the present temenos, based on measurements of the IDF Engineering Corps, minus the areas of the porticoes in the four corners of the temenos. Reference was also made to Josephan data. The perimeter, based on this method is equal to 1159 meters.
2. By determining the outer perimeter of the area of the Temple Mount according to Mishnah Middot. This produced a figure of 1120 meters.
3. By multiplying the figure of six stades mentioned by Josephus. This produces a result of 1116 meters.

The average of these three figures produces a result of 1132 meters with a maximum deviation from the average of 2.3%. The similar

---

[27] Hollis, *Archaeology*, p. 36. Hollis cites the figure of 3800 feet, which is or 1158.2 meters or 6.25 stades.

[28] As stated above, in ancient times, area was phrased as a square of the length. See Sperber, 'Measures and Weights in Judaism,' col. 37.

results produced would seem to indicate that our calculations and methodologies are correct.

Calculating the Area of the Temple Mount (Outer Court)

We will calculate the area of the outer court by dividing the polygon ABCD into two triangles: the southwestern one (ADC) and the northeastern one (ABC) (see fig. 1). It should be remembered that the figures we shall use are from the IDF Engineering Corps and Josephus.

In the southwestern triangle (ADC), the southern side (201.7 meters) lies at a right angle to the western side (376.7 meters). The southern side is therefore the height of the western triangle. Thus, the area of the triangle, by multiplying the base by the height and dividing the product by two is 376.7 × 201.7/2 = 37990.2 square meters. Regarding the area of the northeastern triangle (ABC), the base of the eastern triangle is the eastern side of the inner polygon (350.7 meters). The height of the triangle is equal to the northern side of the polygon, with a slight correction.[29] Hence, we can calculate the area of the eastern triangle by multiplying the base by the height and dividing by two: 228.8 × 350.7/2 = 40137.6 square meters.

The two areas of the triangles that make up the polygon ABCD yields 37990.2 + 40137.6 = 78127 square meters or 249,132 square cubits.[30] We remember that the area of the Temple Mount, according to the Mishnah, was 250,000 sq. cubits. This result differs only by 0.35% from the dimensions given in Mishnah Middot.

Summary

The Outer Court in the writings of Josephus and the Temple Mount as described by R. Eliezer b. Jacob in M Middot are the same, and the polygon ABCD gives us their size and shape. The measurements presented in these different, independent sources are amazingly similar,

---

[29] The height of the triangle is actually equal to the northern side of the polygon (229.7) × cos 2.5° = 228.8 m.
[30] To convert square meters into square cubits, we divide it by 0.56^2; i.e., 78127/(0.56 × 0.56) = 249,132 square cubits.

and both correspond to the perimeter of the present archaeological Temple Mount compound (the temenos) to an astonishing degree. Josephus is describing the Outer Court in the Herodian period and stating the perimeter in terms of the inner perimeter of the porticoes. R. Eliezer b. Jacob, in contrast, is discussing the area of the halachic Temple Mount, which is identical in area to the outer court as described by Josephus.

CONVERSION TO JUDAISM IN THE SECOND TEMPLE PERIOD: A FUNCTIONALIST APPROACH[1]

SETH SCHWARTZ

I would like in this paper to embed a history of conversion in an account of some issues in the social and political history of Jewish Palestine in the Second Temple period. Shaye Cohen has famously argued that religious conversion was introduced around the time of the Maccabean Revolt or shortly thereafter, that its introduction may be traced to the influence of Greek political thought, and that it reflects a change in mentalities generated by the Antiochan Persecution and the subsequent revolt, a shift from the conception of Judaism as an ethnicity to that of Judaism as a religion and/or a political affiliation.[2] I do not wish to reject Shaye Cohen's history of the conversion ritual, which I find convincing. Nor would I simply reject his account of the causes of and cultural changes involved in the introduction of conversion, though I would argue that his account is too simple, monocausal and starkly binary. Instead, I would like to emphasize continuities which Cohen elides, suggesting that the introduction of the ritual is just one episode in a long history, and one which marks a change primarily in—pardon the marxizing language—ideological superstructure, brought to bear on a systemic tension

---

[1] An earlier version of this paper was delivered at the 2001 meeting of the Association for Jewish Studies, at a session organized by Louis H. Feldman. It is offered as a modest tribute to Professor Feldman, my first Greek and Latin teacher and one of my earliest scholarly role models. I would like to thank S.D. Goldhill for his advice on the Athenian citizenship law of 451/0 B.C.E., and Sam Thrope for his indispensable research assistance.

[2] Or, more correctly, in the revised version of the article, an 'ethno-religion': S. Cohen, *The Beginnings of Jewishness*, Berkeley: University of California Press, 1999, 109–39. But the piece remains wedded conceptually to the binary opposition. Note for example the following, from p. 138: 'Thus even as they were becoming more "nationalistic" and "particularistic", the Judaeans/Jews were becoming more "universalistic" by extending citizenship to other peoples and allowing individuals to convert to Judaism...'.

Cohen distinguishes in this piece between conversion as a shift in political affiliation, in the case of the judaization of Idumaea and Galilee, and religious conversion as described in Judith and 2 Maccabees—a distinction which is once again heuristically useful but too sharp—see below.

present in ancient Jewish society for centuries before and after the Maccabean Revolt. To put it differently, I am suggesting that we may profit by shifting our attention from the ritual means by which foreigners entered into some relationship with the Jews to the nature, causes and contexts of such relationships.[3] In brief, I would like to argue[4] that conversion functioned to resolve the tension between the need for interethnic elite alliances—a need created by the political and economic fragmentation of the eastern Mediterranean world generated by geography and fostered by the Assyrian, Persian, and Hellenistic empires—and the increasingly socially important demand made by Jewish religious norms that the Jews keep separate from their neighbors.[5] When the fragmentation, and the interethnic friendships which were its corollary, were brought to an end by the centralizing tendencies of the Roman imperial state in the course of the first century C.E., conversion, now attested mainly in diaspora communities, changed functions.

Interethnic Friendship

From the beginning of the Iron Age until the early Roman Empire, most national/ethnic units in the eastern Mediterranean world were very small—a fact which may be regarded as more or less the state of nature in a part of the world split into narrow coastal plains, rocky and broken hill-country and desert, with a few fertile river valleys. Of course geography does not tell the whole story. The region was ruled for most of the first millennium B.C.E. by a series of empires which worked either by fostering and attempting to control local particularisms, in the case of the Achaemenids and their Macedonian heirs, or by rarely intervening in their regular functioning, under the Assyrians and Babylonians.

In this world, interethnic friendship, the best relatively recent account of which is Gabriel Herman's (of whose book, especially pp.

---

[3] Cf. G. Herman, *Ritualised Friendship and the Greek City*, Cambridge: Cambridge University Press, 1987, 32–3, on relationships of 'amity', relying on Pitt-Rivers.

[4] Expanding some observations Morton Smith made in passing in his discussion of conversion in *Palestinian Parties and Politics that Shaped the Old Testament*, New York: Columbia University Press, 1971, 163; 178–82.

[5] On the fragmentation of the Mediterranean world, see in detail P. Horden and N. Purcell, *The Corrupting Sea: A Study of Mediterranean History*, Oxford: Blackwell, 2000, 9–25. Indeed, this is one of the themes of the book.

73–115, the following paragraphs offer a partial summary), gradually became an important social institution, and one which crossed political, cultural and even religious boundaries.[6] Ultimately, such friendships were generated by the inherent fragility of an eastern Mediterranean economy based, except perhaps in Egypt, on subsistence dry-farming. In such an economy, there was an inevitable tendency for the most productive land to become concentrated in the hands of the few, while the many small-holders gradually descended into relationships of clientele, tenancy and even bondage with their wealthier neighbors, as they sought to protect themselves against the effects of frequent crop-failure, invasion, and so on. But the wealthy themselves, though they occasionally disposed of large quantities of surplus, were vulnerable to the same disasters, and so they sought protection by befriending their counterparts in neighboring districts. Such friendships involved exchanges of gifts and pursuit of commercial partnerships, including marriage.[7] They provided a way for local elites to protect their wealth, and acquire more wealth, in a way which could benefit the inhabitants of their home districts—for example by giving them access to supplies of grain in years of crop failure—and so enhance the elites' prestige and authority there.[8] Friendships also provided them with places of refuge, and with access to more manpower than they could raise from among their local dependents.[9]

All of these functions can be illustrated from Jewish history in the Second Temple period, primarily from the history of the Hasmonean and Herodian dynasties—for which we have the richest information. In addition, the marriages which were a frequent by-product of the friendships are attested in the book of Nehemiah (13:19–31; cf. Ez 9–10) and in some of Josephus's stories of the high priests of the

---

[6] *Ritualised Friendship*.

[7] On the association of interethnic friendship and marriage, see Herman, *Ritualised Friendship*, 36.

[8] On the frequency of crop failure in the central Mediterranean, and the coping strategies of farmers there, including establishment of relationships of social dependency and friendship, see P. Garnsey, *Famine and Food Supply in the Graeco-Roman World: Responses to Risk and Crisis*, Cambridge: Cambridge University Press, 1988, 8–16; 55–68.

[9] The classic case of the last is the Persian pretender Cyrus the Younger's Ten Thousand, raised in 401 B.C.E. from among his Greek *xenoi*—see Herman, *Ritualised Friendship*, 98–101.

fourth and third centuries B.C.E.[10] For an example of the functioning of friendship, in the form of gift exchange, we have the episode in which Hyrcanus II's receipt of horses from his friend Malikos king of the Nabataeans served Herod as the pretext for executing the aged priest.[11] The high priests of Jerusalem were normally enriched by their ancestral friendships with leading families of Ammon and Samaria, but sometimes the latter turned the tables on them, as the Ammonite/Jewish Tobiad family did in the opening scene of the partly fictional Tobiad Romance, in Josephus, Ant 12.160–236, when Joseph son of Tobias outbid his high priestly kinsman for the lucrative tax-farming contract for Palestine (more on this below). When Jason the Oniad was expelled from Jerusalem, he fled across the Jordan to his friends there, though they later turned against him, and several Hasmoneans were able to draw on the resources of Nabataean and Ituraean friends (and kinfolk) when they went campaigning.[12]

Now it bears emphasizing that contrary to what the authors of Ezra-Nehemiah among many other ancient Jewish writers tell us and to what many nowadays are more or less automatically inclined to believe, such friendships, though they certainly involved some interchange of cultural, not just material, goods, and depended on and probably functioned to produce a kind of compartmentalized 'international' elite culture, were not in fact primarily engines of 'assimilation' or acculturation. Rather they were mechanisms for assuring the viability of small-scale local ethnic cultures and political entities which might otherwise have been defenseless against imperial intervention, war, or economic catastrophe.

Separation

It was into this social and economic system that a set of Jewish authorities promoting a religious ideal of extreme separatism intruded,

---

[10] Ant 11.302–47, with discussion of S. Cohen, 'Alexander the Great and Jaddus the High Priest According to Josephus', *AJS Review* 7–8 (1982–3) 41–68; AJ 12.160.

[11] Ant 15.174–6; and see B. Shaw, 'Tyrants, Bandits and Kings: Personal Power in Josephus', *JJS* 44 (1993) 176–204, especially 192.

[12] 2 Macc 4.26, with comments of Abel ad loc., and 5.6–10; on the Nabataean and Ituraean friends of the Hasmoneans see discussion in S. Schwartz, 'Herod, Friend of the Jews', in J. Schwartz, Z. Amar and I. Ziffer, eds., *Jerusalem and Eretz Israel: Arie Kindler Volume*, Tel Aviv: Bar-Ilan University and Eretz Israel Museum, 2000, 70–1; Shaw, 'Tyrants', 193–4.

either at the times of Ezra and Nehemiah in the fifth century B.C.E. if we follow the biblical account, or shortly thereafter, if we are more skeptical. Particularists were of course not unknown in the ancient eastern Mediterranean. Many early biblical texts certainly manifest a tendency to ethnic particularism;[13] furthermore, in 451/0, almost contemporaneously with the administration of Ezra, Pericles is said to have introduced a law at Athens restricting citizenship to the children of two citizens—a measure meant, among other things, to make life difficult for traditional aristocratic families—with their long histories of intermarriage—in that democratic city.[14] (These developments were concurrent with Athens' consolidation of its maritime empire. This is no coincidence, since the empire was among other things a system of trade and of wealth distribution conducted by the state, not by aristocratic families).[15] What distinguished the new Jewish restrictions from either earlier Israelite or Athenian particularism— though it clearly bears a family resemblance to them—is their conception in terms of sanctity, and their *apparent* inescapability. Furthermore, unlike the Athenian case, in which tribute received from subject cities compensated for, in fact greatly exceeded, the wealth formerly brought in by personal alliances (considerable though that sometimes was),[16] Ezra and Nehemiah are not said to have introduced any similar compensatory policies. They introduced only internal redistributive ones (Neh 5:1–19) and furthermore believed that God would reward the Jews with prosperity if they divorced their foreign spouses (Ez 9:12). In theory, if Ezra and Nehemiah's rules were effective, Judaea was, all things being equal, a poorer place after their administrations than before.

But was legally enforced separatism effective? I would argue that it was at least partly so, though some Judaean elites worked out ways of evading it, in some circumstances. As an example of the legislation's

---

[13] Well discussed by Cohen, *The Beginnings of Jewishness*, 241–62.

[14] See Aristotle, Constitution of the Athenians 26.3; for parallels, see commentary of J.E. Sandys, *Aristotle's Constitution of the Athenians*, London – New York: MacMillan, 1893, 107; F. Miltner, 'Perikles', *RE* 19.1, 760.

[15] At the same time, as Cynthia Patterson stressed, Athenians now feared 'that their traditional self-identity as Athenians was being lost or sacrificed with the growth of Athens into a cosmopolitan urban center and ruler of a maritime empire' (*Pericles' Citizenship Law of 451/0 B.C.*, Salem: Ayer Press, 1981, 132–3). On the law as anti-aristocratic, see, e.g., S.C. Humphreys, 'The Nothoi of Kynosarges', *JHS* 94 (1974) 93–4.

[16] See Herman, *Ritualised Friendship*, 82–8.

effectiveness, though also of its evadability, I mention a story Josephus tells in Ant 11, in which a Zadokite priest, apparently in the middle of the fourth century B.C.E., marries the daughter of Sanballat, the Achaemenid governor of Samaritis and probably himself a Samaritan rather than a Persian, and is expelled from Jerusalem as a result. Now caution is in order: this story is clearly part of a propaganda war between Judaeans and Samaritans, because the expelled priestly miscreant, together with several of his equally sinful Judaean associates, go on to form the foundation of the Samaritan priesthood.[17] Nevertheless, it remains remotely possible that the story has some factual basis and so informs us that there were Judaean elites who even in the fourth and third centuries strove to maintain their traditional alliances, perhaps having found ways to defend them in terms of Jewish law, despite the opposition of other Judaeans.

The continuation of one such alliance, though, is in fact relatively reliably attested, and this information may help us understand how the religious difficulties raised after Nehemiah by interethnic alliances could be resolved. I refer to the traditional alliance between the Zadokite high priests and the Tobiads of trans-Jordan. This relationship is attested for the fifth century, when according to Nehemiah Tobiah the Ammonite maintained an office in the Jerusalem temple; and for the third century, when, according to Josephus the Zadokites and Tobiads were still intermarrying.[18] Some segments of the Tobiad family later allied themselves with Judah Maccabee, according to 2 Maccabees, and the fact that Simon the Hasmonean gave his son, probably born in the 160s, the name Hyrcanus, a name almost unknown outside the Tobiad family, may suggest the establishment of a friendship between the families, not necessarily excluding marriage.[19]

---

[17] See Cohen, 'Alexander the Great', and S. Schwartz, 'John Hyrcanus I's Destruction of the Gerizim Temple and Judaean-Samaritan Relations', *JH* 7 (1993) 9–25.

[18] For a powerful, illuminating, but not wholly convincing argument that this episode belongs where Josephus placed it, in the second century, see D. Schwartz, 'Josephus' Tobiads: Back to the Second Century?', in M. Goodman, ed., *Jews in a Graeco-Roman World*, Oxford: Clarendon Press, 1998, 47–61; for an account that attempts to integrate archaeological and some literary sources (though not the 'Tobiad romance'), see C.C. Ji, 'A New Look at the Tobiads in 'Iraq al-Amir', *LA* 48 (1998) 417–40.

[19] See S. Schwartz, 'A Note on the Social Type and Political Ideology of the Hasmonean Family', *JBL* 112 (1993) 305–9.

It will be recalled that the presumable ancestor of the dynasty is not only persistently described in the book of Nehemiah as an Ammonite, but was also the mortal enemy of Nehemiah. Nevertheless, there were peculiarities in the family history which may have eased their gradual judaization. The fact that 'the sons of Tobiah' appear in a list of returned Judahite exiles (Ez 2:59–60), though admittedly as a clan whose Israelite ancestry could not be established, probably indicates that someone had claimed a Jewish origin for the family (and perhaps also that the editor of the book of Ezra disagreed)—in a way reminiscent of Nikolaos of Damascus' claim much later that Herod was not of Idumaean origin, as everyone thought, but was impeccably descended from the Judahite *benei ha-golah* (Ant 14.9).[20] Likewise, the very name Tobiah probably tells us something about the family's Judaean connections, and/or their partial accommodation to Judaean religious norms, at just the time when Nehemiah rejected them as Ammonites. But even in the middle of the third century, a generation before the dramatic date of Josephus's Tobiad Romance, one member of the family, the Toubias of the Zenon papyri, demonstrated a shockingly casual religious laxity in beginning a letter to his friend the Ptolemaic courtier Zenon by thanking the gods—an action whose significance should not be hastily dismissed.[21] How are we to explain all this? First, the Tobiad family may have been large and ramified, with some branches more and some branches less assimilated to Judaism—though it may be instructive that the Jewish branch of the family which serves as the subject of Josephus's tale is still described as violating Jewish law persistently and unself consciously.[22] Still, it may be that whatever partial religious accommodations they were willing to make, and whatever obfuscations of their ethnic background, were enough to convince at least some elements in the Jerusalemite priesthood that they were fit to marry.

---

[20] On the nature and composition of the biblical list of returned exiles, see J. Blenkinsopp, *Ezra-Nehemiah*, Philadelphia: Westminster Press, 1988, 41–7, 83–4.

[21] CPJ 1.4. For some discussion (accompanying the argument that the Tobiads were devotees of Aphrodite [!]), see Ji, 'A New Look', 435–6; and further, C. Orrieux, 'Les papyrus de Zénon et la préhistoire du mouvement maccabéen', in A. Caquot, et al., eds., *Hellenica et Judaica: Hommage à Valentin Nikiprowetzky Z'L*, Louvain: Peeters, 1986, 329–33.

[22] See in general D. Gera, *Judaea and Mediterraean Politics, 219–161 B.C.E.*, Leiden: Brill, 1998, 36–58.

I would suggest then that in the period after Nehemiah, the practice of elite interethnic friendship and marriage could be partly preserved by the non-Judaean partner's assertion of (no doubt often fictive) claims of ethnic kinship with the Jews, and partial accommodation to their religious norms. It does not follow that the entire system of interethnic alliances as practiced before Nehemiah was preserved in this way. Thus, though Samarians could, in their dealings with Judaeans, emphasize their shared Israelite heritage, this was apparently not enough to convince all upper class Judaeans to marry them, as we have seen, though it may have worked for some. And it may have been very difficult indeed for Judaeans to maintain alliances with those who were in a weaker position to claim ethnic/religious kinship with the Jews than the Tobiads or the Samarians were. Still, claims of ethnic kinship are indeed likely to have been the main mechanism which in the fourth and third centuries allowed small numbers of upper class Jews to retain friendships with, and marry, their neighbors. As an extreme case, we may remember here the alleged correspondence between the Spartan king Areus and the Judaean high priest Onias, in which the king announced the discovery of his descent from Abraham, or so the Jews later claimed.[23] Claims of kinship in general played a very important role in Hellenistic diplomacy—a fact which may have made the fabrication of such claims natural for ambitious Judaean aristocrats and their non-Judaean friends.[24] Still, we must suppose that such claims were not always effective; there is no evidence of intermarriage between the Zadokite, or for that matter, the Hasmonean, family and the Spartan royal family—though even later there was probably more to the friend-

---

[23] 1 Macc 12:1–23; Ant 12.115–7; 13:165–70. 2 Macc 5.9 also knows about the *syngeneia* (kinship) of Judaeans and Spartans. The most detailed recent discussion of this episode is E. Gruen, *Heritage and Hellenism: The Reinvention of Jewish Tradition*, Berkeley: University of California Press, 1998, 253–68—Gruen is skeptical not only about the original correspondence between Areus and Onias, but also about that between Jonathan and the Spartans in the 150s, on the grounds of its political inutility. This is a weak argument in any case, but in addition neglects the fact that the later correspondance was primarily an exchange of pleasantries, a token of friendship, not meant to secure tangible political advantage. For a less skeptical view, see P. Cartledge and A. Spawforth, *Hellenistic and Roman Sparta: A Tale of Two Cities*, London: Routledge, 1989, 36–7; see also J. Sievers, 'Josephus, First Maccabees, the Three Haireseis—and Cicero', *JSJ* 32 (2001) 241–51.

[24] See the evidence assembled in O. Curty, *Les parentés légendaires entre cités grecques: catalogue raisonné des inscriptions contenant le terme syngeneia et analyse critique*, Geneva: Droz, 1995.

ship of Herod and C. Julius Eurykles, the Spartan adventurer-king, than meets the eye (Ant 16.300–10).[25] In sum, it is quite likely that the religious particularism introduced by Ezra and Nehemiah had some effect on people's behavior, and on social, political and economic life in Judaea. Indeed, it is probably in this light that we should understand the argument the author of 1 Maccabees attributed to the Jewish reformists (1.11): 'Let us a make a covenant with the nations roundabout, since from the time that we separated from them, many evil things have befallen us'.

The case of Onias and Areus also reminds us, though, that in the Hellenistic and early Roman periods, the eastern Mediterranean world was changing, for Jews and others, in the direction of greater integration, and so, people began to look beyond the neighboring districts for friends.[26] A Judaean high priest of the third or second century B.C.E. might have been interested in cultivating a friendship with a king of distant Sparta because the Judaeans' Ptolemaic overlords and allies, Sparta and Rome were increasingly thinking of themselves as components of a single political network, in opposition to the Seleucids and *their* clients and allies.[27] This integrative tendency was still embryonic in the third century, but became more significant as Roman influence, and then power, in the eastern Mediterranean grew. And as it did, aristocrats, even in a small and marginal district like Judaea, grew ever more interested in looking farther afield for their alliances and friendships than the traditional Ammanitis and Samaria. And just as integrative pressures were growing, so too was the importance of separatism, in the wake of the Maccabean revolt.

---

[25] See Cartledge and Spawforth, *Hellenistic and Roman Sparta*, 100–1, for the suggestion that the friendship of Herod and Eurykles (a local agitator who had risen to kingship in the triumviral period through friendship with senatorial grandees—exactly like Herod) was of long standing, and connected to the traditional *syngeneia* of the Jews and Spartans.

[26] For a full account see E. Gruen, *The Hellenistic World and the Coming of Rome*, Berkeley: University of California Press, 1984.

[27] Though there is no need to follow Gruen in seeking a specific political or diplomatic goal in the friendship between Judaeans and Spartans.

Conversion

I would not wish to speculate about why conversion replaced earlier models, including fictive kinship, at the moment that it did—again, I do not reject Cohen's explanation, though as I've already remarked, I suspect matters were more complicated. Among other things, conversion may not in fact have been very different from fictive kinship, conceptually speaking—a slight, but fateful, rearrangement.[28] And this fact may actually complicate discussion of the motivation for the change. Rather, I would like to concentrate on its effects, which are well attested.

In fact, the earliest historical conversions to Judaism, those of the Idumaeans towards the end of the reign of Hyrcanus I (as the event must now be dated), and of the Ituraeans soon after, may well have drawn as much on the old fictive kinship+partial religious accommodation model as on any new conversion model (Ant 13.254–7; 318). Several scholars have supposed that the Hasmoneans drew primarily on traditions of family relations between the nations (the Ituraeans could have claimed descent from Yetur, son of Ishmael, son of Abraham: Gen 25:15) as embodied in the shared practice of male circumcision. This would explain why the option of conversion was not offered to the 'Greeks' of Palestine, if they did not in fact normally convert after conquest. It may also help explain in Jewish legal terms the likelihood that the accommodation of the conquered peoples to Judaism was gradual, not immediate, and perhaps never complete.[29]

There were other similarities with the older model, too. Though the Hasmonean conversions differed from earlier cases of gradual judaization by being in some measure forced, and by apparently

---

[28] On the importance of kinship in the Hasmonean conversions, see M. Smith, in *CHJ* 3.198–213; this factor is neglected by Cohen in *Beginnings of Jewishness*, 109–40.

[29] For more detailed discussion, see, in addition to Cohen, my *Imperialism and Jewish Society*, 36–42; 51–2. For a different, but I would argue complementary, approach to the Hasmonean conversions, see S. Weitzman, 'Forced Circumcision and the Shifting Role of Gentiles in Hasmonean Ideology', *HTR* 92 (1999) 37–59, who argues that they were generated by the Hasmoneans' need to adapt their traditional hostility to gentiles, and the associated view that only pious Jews should live in the borders of the Holy Land (as suggested by the story that Mattathias had forcibly circumcised [Jewish] babies in Judaea—1 Macc 2:46), to a situation in which they depended on gentiles, both friendly or manipulable neighbors and foreign mercenaries, for their political survival.

(though we actually cannot be entirely certain about this) involving not individual families but entire nations, the fact remains that the main role the conquered nations play in Josephus's account before the Great Revolt is that their leading families formed 'friendships' with the Hasmoneans.[30] Since the leading Idumaeans and Ituraeans already enjoyed friendships with other important neighbors, like the Nabataeans or the Ituraean rulers of principalities outside Hasmonean territory, and because they themselves had some control over their compatriots, the Hasmoneans are plausibly said to have acknowledged their political utility by yielding to their overtures. Thus, Alexander Yannai befriended Antipas grandfather of Herod, who himself had friends in Nabataea and in the coastal cities of Palestine;[31] the same king is also said in a problematically late source to have used the services of a Galilean grandee in a campaign against the Nabataeans.[32] The civil war between Yannai's sons, one of whom was connected by marriage to the rulers of an Ituraean principality in the Beqaa Valley (Ant 14.126), increased the importance of friendships, but also tended to restrict them sharply to the immediate region, on the one hand—since the combatants needed local manpower above all—and the Roman senate, on the other.[33] But only the former could actually generate marriages at this point: what Roman senator would have considered marriage into a Jewish aristocratic family advantageous? So in this period we hear little about marriage alliances between Jews and people outside the immediate eastern Mediterranean neighborhood.

The period beginning with Herod's reign and ending in 66 was last great era of interethnic friendship, and marriage, for the Jews. Herod himself seems to have avoided marrying the daughters of other near eastern vassal kings. Though most of his marriages can be seen as components of an elite friendship,[34] Herod's chief concern

---

[30] Cf. Weitzman, 'Forced Circumcision', 56–8; Schwartz, 'Herod, Friend of the Jews'; Shaw, 'Tyrants, Bandits, and Kings'.

[31] Ant 14.10: '... they say that he (Antipas) made friendship with the Arabs who lived adjacent to him, and with Gazaeans and Ascalonites, having won them over with abundant and large gifts.'

[32] Georgius Syncellus, *Ekloge Chronographias* (ed. Dindorf), I 558–9, with discussion in Schwartz, 'Georgius Syncellus' Account of Ancient Jewish History', *Proceedings of the Tenth World Congress of Jewish Studies*, B.II (Jerusalem, 1990), 1–8, especially 4.

[33] These issues are discussed in detail in my 'Herod, Friend of the Jews'.

[34] Notwithstanding Josephus's assertion that the tension between Herod's daughter-in-law, the Cappadocian princess Glaphyra, and the other inmates of the royal

was to maintain his friendships with Roman senators, still off-limits for marriages, and with prominent Jews. This latter concern is what his choice of wives apparently reflects. But Herod also saw to it that his relatives and some of his children married into the families of other local dynasts, and that if the spouses were male, they submitted to circumcision, which probably implies conversion to Judaism. This practice was continued by his descendants. So, Herod's sister attempted to marry the Nabataean Syllaeus, who, however, rejected conversion;[35] his son Alexander married the daughter of Archelaus, king of Cappadocia (Ant 16.11), and other descendants married into the Jewish but socially climbing family of Philo of Alexandria, that of Azizus king of Emesa in northern Syria, and of Polemo, king of Cilicia (Ant 19.277; 20.137–47). A marriage into the quasi-Seleucid family of Antiochus IV of Commagene failed because the prince in question refused to be circumcised (Ant 20.139), while a daughter of Agrippa I married, for the first but not the last time in the history of the Herodian family, into a prominent Roman family. But the Roman in question, Antonius Felix, was of servile origin and, Josephus implies, did not submit to circumcision (Ant 20.143). Nevertheless, their son, who died in the eruption of Vesuvius, was named Agrippa, testifying to the persistence of family ties despite the dissolution of their attachment to Jewish norms.[36]

I would claim, then, that one of the effects of the introduction of conversion, if not its intention, was to broaden the potential objects of interethnic friendship, in a world in which elite friendships were customarily conducted at longer distance, and with nations ethnically and culturally more remote from the Jews, than had been customary, or practical, in the fifth and fourth centuries B.C.E. Of course, it did not always work because the foreigner in question did

---

gynaikeion was caused by Herod's invariable practice of selecting wives for their beauty, not their families (*di' eumorphian ouk apo genous*—JW 1.477), This claim is absent in Ant 16.193, where Glaphyra is presented merely as relatively more noble than the other royal women, which is undeniably true. For exhaustive discussion, see N. Kokkinos, *The Herodian Dynasty: Origins, Role in Society and Eclipse*, Sheffield: Sheffield Academic Press, 1998, 206–45; somewhat too schematically: P. Richardson, *Herod: King of the Jews and Friend of the Romans*, Columbia: University of South Carolina Press, 1996, 43–4. Josephus's claim may conceivably be true of some of Herod's more obscure wives.

[35] Herod asked Syllaeus 'to be enrolled in the customs of the Jews', Ant 16.225.

[36] For extensive discussion of the marriages of the Herodians, see Kokkinos, *The Herodian Dynasty*, 246–340; S. Schwartz, *Josephus and Judaean Politics*, Leiden: Brill, 1990, 110–69.

not always agree to be circumcised or live as a Jew, and the descendants of Alexander son of Herod are said by Josephus to have gradually allowed their ties to Judaism to lapse (Ant 18.139–40).

Religious Conversion?

Of course, once introduced, conversion could in principle serve religious, not merely socio-economic needs.[37] Indeed, the tale of Ruth the Moabite shows that even before the introduction of conversion, the religious accommodation perhaps customarily associated with elite interethnic marriages could assume special importance, at least in the fantasies of the pious. In the two earliest accounts of conversion *stricto sensu*, though, marriage is not a factor at all: both fictional converts, Achior the Ammonite in the book of Judith (14:10), and Antiochus IV in 2 Maccabees (9:12–7), are motivated by their experience of the power of the God of Israel (the story of Achior, like the book in which it is embedded, has paradoxical elements which will not detain us here), and later converts discussed by Josephus, especially the royal family of Adiabene (Ant 20.17–96), are likewise said to have been motivated primarily by piety.[38] In considering the latter, we should not overlook the peculiar religious history of the Tigris and Euphrates Valleys in the Roman imperial period (explored not long ago by Garth Fowden),[39] home of the first Christian kingdom, Adiabene's neighbor Edessa, and subsequently of several types of schismatic Christianity, and of Manichaeism. It would not be absurd to speculate that the Adiabenians' Judaism, like their neighbors' later embrace of minority religions of the neighboring empires, was somehow related to their location in the imperial border zone, and that it gave them a foothold in both empires (it's short term effect was to produce a political shift toward Rome and away from Parthia. This topic demands separate treatment). Nevertheless, they are not said to have married into any great Judaean families (notwithstanding the apparently erroneous contention which has entered the

---

[37] Cf. Cohen, *Beginnings of Jewishness*, 129–35.
[38] On which see now D. Schwartz, 'God, Gentiles, and Jewish Law: On Acts 15 and Josephus's Adiabene Narrative', in H. Cancik, H. Lichtenberger, P. Schäfer, eds., *Geschichte-Tradition-Reflexion: Festschrift für Martin Hengel zum 70. Geburtstag* I, Tübingen: Mohr (Siebeck), 1996, 263–82.
[39] *Empire to Commonwealth: Consequences of Monotheism in Late Antiquity*, Princeton: Princeton University Press, 1993.

scholarly tradition that they were related to the Herodians), and there seems little reason to doubt that in their dealings with Judaeans, which included several famous acts of *euergesia* (Ant 20.49–53; 101), they emphasized not their family connections but their Jewish piety. Josephus wrote that their pious generosity was still remembered among the Jews, and the occasional mentions of the family in rabbinic literature show that memory of them lasted far beyond Josephus's lifetime.[40] Their case demonstrates, in other words, the generative force of ideological superstructure—once conversion was reconceived as a religious ritual, it could attract the religious, or at least force the canny to represent themselves as such.

Let me briefly summarize. Before the High Roman Empire, political and economic conditions had generated an enduring tendency among wealthy landowners in the eastern Mediterranean to cultivate friendships, including marriage, with their counterparts in neighboring districts. Such friendships helped insure the viability of what were otherwise small and fragile polities, and are well attested among Jews, among others. But the requirement that the Jews keep separate from their neighbors, imposed sometime in the Persian period, interfered with the regular functioning of the system of interethnic friendships. In some cases they were now impossible, but in a few, the restrictions could be evaded by claims of fictive kinship and by partial religious accommodation. Conversion was introduced at a time when the political, social and economic tendency in the eastern Mediterranean was toward greater regional integration. So it functioned to enable for the Jewish elites geographically more widespread and scattered friendships than would have been possible if such friendships had continued to rely on fictive kinship alone. But the introduction of conversion also made it possible to become Jewish without any connection to marriage, as apparently in the case of the Adiabenian royal family, and of some others mentioned by Josephus.

---

[40] For a convenient collection of material, see *JE* sub v. 'Helena'.

JEWS AND GENTILES FROM JUDAS MACCABAEUS TO JOHN HYRCANUS ACCORDING TO CONTEMPORARY JEWISH SOURCES

Israel Shatzman

The revolt of Mattathias and his sons and the military successes of Judas Maccabaeus generated a significantly important change in the conditions of the Jews of Eretz Israel and in their relations with Gentiles, both those who bordered upon Judaea and those who lived at some distance but had Jewish settlements within their territories, notably in Transjordan. This change evolved and stemmed from the new political conditions of the Jews of Judaea. Now, for the first time after the downfal of the old kingdom of Judaea, the Jews and their leaders, freed to some extent from foreign rule, be it the Persian, Ptolemaic or Seleucid empire, were called to determine the kind of relations and attitude they should adopt vis-à-vis Gentiles. As a result of the military success the political rule of Jews over Gentiles could be envisaged as a realistic possibility, and a Jewish policy, with regard to potential Gentile subjects as well as neighbouring Gentile tribes, cities and other political entities, had to be defined. Naturally the neighbouring peoples had a cause to be concerned by the rise of the military power of Judas Maccabaeus. They might choose to render active support to the Seleucid government to quell the Jewish revolt, to remain neutral, watching for opportunities that could be exploited for political and other advantages, or even to cooperate with the Jews in order to attain political independence, admittedly a theoretical rather than realistic possibility.

This state of things prevailed after the death of Judas Maccabaeus. As long as Jonathan, Judas' successor as leader of the Hasmonaean forces, was considered a rebel by the Seleucid authorities, there was no reason for him to deviate from the policy of his dead brother, even though no immediate decisions had to be taken because Jonathan's power and sphere of influence were very limited for a number of years. When Jonathan was appointed, by Alexander Balas, High-Priest, governor and military commander of Judaea, he was invested with legally based position, ceasing to be considered a rebel by the

Seleucid authorities; paradoxically from then on he had to apply cautious policy with regard to the neighbouring peoples in order to maintain his position and good relations with the Seleucid king. Not only had he to take into account interests of foreign policy, but the integration into the established external political institutions obliged him to neglect or to limit the application of purely Jewish norms and Biblical commandments. Simon basically followed suit, and so did John Hyrcanus for not a few years after his accession. However, with the increase of the power of the Jewish state and the decline of the Seleucid kingdom, Hyrcanus became independent and felt free to determine his policy towards the Gentile peoples, both those who came under his rule and those with whom he stood in confrontation.

What was the policy of the Hasmonaean rulers towards the neighbouring peoples and what actions were required to implement this policy? What considerations shaped the Hasmonaean foreign policy? What changes took place in the Hasmonaean foreign policy in the period from Judas to John Hyrcanus? How Jewish society viewed and reacted to the Hasmonaean policy towards the neighbouring Gentiles? What problems arose due to the changing relations with the Gentiles? How was enisaged and depicted the Gentile attitude towards Jews in Jewish writings? Direct and indirect answers to these and akin questions may be found, sometimes in detail and sometimes in part or indirectly, in contemporary Jewish writings. In the following I intend to present the evidence relating to these questions as well as to show that the works discussed reflect not only the attitude of their authors towards Gentiles but also express, explicitly and implicitly, a certain view of and position in regard to the Hasmonaeans.

I Maccabees

Many, perhaps most scholars are of the opinion that I Maccabees was written during the reign of John Hyrcanus; for reasons explained elsewhere I find this dating of the work convincing.[1] The author

---

[1] See, e.g., A. Momigliano, *Primee linee di storia della tradizione Maccabaica* (Roma 1931), 34–6; M. Smith, 'Rome and the Maccabean Conversions—Notes on *I Macc.* 8', in E. Bammel, C.K. Barrett and W.D. Davies (eds.), *Donum Gentilicium: New Testament Studies in Honour of David Daube* (Oxford 1978), 1–7; K.D. Schunk, *1 Makkabäerbuch* (Gütersloh 1980), p. 292; B. Bar-Kochva, *Judas Maccabaeus. The Jewish Struggle against the Seleucids* (Cambridge 1989), 152–68; S. Schwartz, 'Israel and the

takes a pro-Hasmonaean view, and since this is patently clear, and generally agreed upon, there is no need to demonstrate it here. It stands to reason that what he writes on Jewish relations with and attitude towards 'the nations' (τὰ ἔθνη), that is, Gentile peoples, was acceptable to the Hasmonaean rulers; it is doubtful, though, that his work was written and regarded as an official Hasmonaean history, for several details and episodes depicted by the author cannot have been to the liking of the Hasmonaeans. Notwithstanding this minor qualification, I Maccabees provides the best surviving evidence on the relations between Jews and Gentiles from a Hasmonaean point of view.[2]

Right in the first chapter, the author presents his negative view of the Jews who sought to remove the barriers that distinguished between Jews and Gentiles: 'In those days there came forth out of Israel lawless men (*paranomoi*), and persuaded many, saying: 'Let us go and make a covenant with the nations that are round about us; for since we separated ourselves from them many evils have come upon us' (1:11). It should be noticed that the background for these words is the attempt of some Jews to obliterate their religious self-identity. The author's wrath is directed against the Hellenisers, who aimed at forgoing their Jewishness (1:13–14). It is not social contacts that come under attack, and certainly one cannot find here any evidence of or allusion to previous fundamental hostile relations (but see below). However, Antiochus IV's persecution of the Jewish religion and his attempt to enforce a foreign, Gentile cult brought about

---

Nations Roundabout: I Maccabees and the Hasmonaean Expansion', *JJS* 42 (1991), 33–38. See also my forthcoming book, *The Hasmonaeans in Graeco-Roman Historians and Jewish Sources*, III.i. A dating in the early years of Alexander Jannaeus (J.A. Goldstein, *I Maccabees* [Garden City, New York 1976], pp. 62–4) or in the early decades of the first century B.C.E. (E. Schürer, *The History of the Jewish People in the Age of Jesus*, revised and edited by G. Vermes, F. Millar and M. Goodman, I–III [Edinburgh 1973–87], I, 181) seems to me untenable.

[2] On the author of I Maccabees as an official Hasmonaean historian see already A. Geiger, *Urschrift und Übersetzungen der Bibel* (Breslau 1857), 206. In his comment on the defeat of Joseph and Azaria, the commanders who went to battle against direct orders by Judas Maccabaeus, the author expresses his basic view of the Hasmonaeans: 'But they [i.e. Joseph and Azaria] were not of the seed of those men, by whose hand deliverance was given unto Israel' (5.61–62). Here and in the following I use, with a few changes, W.O.E. Oesterley's translation of I Maccabees in R.H. Charles, *The Apocrypha and Pseudepigraphica of the Old Testament in English*, Oxford 1913). Goldstein (n. 1, *passim*, esp. 62–89) goes into extremes in his assumption that whatever the author wrote was aimed at throwing positive light on the Hasmonaeans.

a complete change in Jewish-Gentile relations. The struggle for adherence to and preservation of the Torah, that is, the Law, was at the same time a war for physical survival against the Gentiles, as witnessed by what Mattathias' followers said when informed of the death of those Jews who had refused to fight on the Sabbath: 'If we all do as our brethren have done, and do not fight against the Gentiles (τὰ ἔθνη) for our lives and our ordinances, they will soon destroy us from off the earth' (2:40). Judas is ascribed with the following speech, delivered before the battle against Apollonius: 'They come unto us in fulness of insolence and lawlesssness, to destroy us and our wives and our children, and to spoil us' (3:20–21). From then on 'the nations' are perceived and presented as a collective entity that poses a menace for the physical and religious existence of the Jewish people. The war is waged not only against the Seleucid government but also against the neighbouring peoples, who are considered as willing partners, committed to the persecution of the Jewish religion.

At first sight, this might seem as a completely new situation, a direct consequence of the nefarious deeds of Antiochus IV. However, the starting point of the work is relevant for the understanding of the author's view of the relations between the Jews and 'the nations'. According to the historical perception of the author, the remote political background which had made possible these inimical relationships to arise had been the conquest by Alexander of the East; Antiochus IV, a 'wicked shoot' (ῥίζα ἁμαρτωλός) (1:10), the Jewish Hellenizers and the Gentiles, each and every one of them, were responsible for the outburst of the hostilities. Indeed, Antiochus' persecution and the Hasmonaean uprising started off the formation of conscious, aggressive Jewish identity, characterized by segregation and strict demarcation of the lines between Jews and Gentiles.[3]

The author's view that the 'nations roundabout Judaea', motivated, as they were, by sheer hatred to the Jews, their religious practices and ways of life, supported the persecution of Antiochus IV is presented openly and clearly in his description of their reaction to the consecration of the new altar and the renewal of the daily sacrifices at the Temple by Judas:

---

[3] These topics cannot be discussed here. See E. Schwarz, *Identität durch Abgrenzung: Abgrenzungprozesse in Israel im 2. vorchristlichen Jahrhundert.* Frankfurt 1982; S.J.D. Cohen, 'Religion, Ethnicity, and "Hellenism" in the Emergence of Jewish Identity in Maccabean Palestine', in P. Bilde, T. Engberg-Pedersen, L. Hannestad and J. Zahle (eds.), *Religion and Religious Practice in the Seleucid Empire* (Aahrus 1990), 204–223.

And it came to pass, when the Gentiles round about (τὰ ἔθνη κυκλόθεν) heard that the altar had been built and the sanctuary dedicated, as aforetime, that they were exceeding wroth. And they determined to destroy those of the race of Jacob that were in the midst of them, and they began to slay and to destroy among the people (5:1–2).

The hostile nations were the Idumaeans, the Sons of Baean, the Ammonites, various peoples living in Galaaditis and Galilee, as well as Acre, Tyre and Sidon (5:3–9). All these nations sought to destroy Israel; hence ensued Judas' campaigns, which necessarily took on the form of a merciless war. Thus the campaign against the Sons of Baean is described as follows: 'And he [i.e. Judas] remembered the malice of the Sons of Baean, who were unto the people a snare and stumbling-block, lying in wait for them in the ways. And they were shut up by him in the towers; and he encamped against them, and utterly destroyed them, and burned with fire the towers of the place, and all that were therein' (5:4–5). In his expedition in Transjordan Judas was told by the Nabataeans he met there that the Jews of Galaaditis were about to be attacked by their enemies, who intended to destroy them all (5:25–27). Judas then attacked the city of Bosora: 'and he took the city, and slew all the males with the edge of the sword, and took all the spoils, and burned it (i.e. the city) with fire' (5:28). After routing the forces of Timotheus, a Seleucid commander with some authority in Transjordan, Judas besieged a town whose name has not been preserved clearly in the extant manuscripts:[4] 'And he turned aside to... and fought against it, and took it, and slew all the males thereof, and took the spoils thereof, and burned it with fire'.[5] After suffering another defeat, near the city of Raphon, the forces of Timotheus sought to find shelter in the temple at Karnaim, probably of the Syrian goddess Atargatis.[6] The victorious Jews pursued them: 'And they took the city, and burned the temple with fire, together with all that were therein. And Karnaim was overthrown' (5:44). The city of Ephron succumbed to the same fate for

---

[4] *I Macc.* 5:35. Cf. Joseph. *AJ* 12:340. See F.-M. Abel, *Les Livres des Maccabées* (Paris 1949), 98–9; Goldstein (above n. 1), 302.

[5] See Bar-Kochva (n. 1), 353–357. A Seleucid *strategos* by that name is mentioned in II Maccabees (12:2). For the less likely possibility that two persons by that name were involved in the campaigns of Judas, a Seleucid commander and a local chieftain, *phularches* (*II Macc.* 8:32), see Goldstein (n. 1), 296–7.

[6] On the cult of this Syrian deity see P. Bilde, 'Atargatis/Dea Syria: Hellenization of her Cult in the Hellenistic-Roman Period', in P. Bilde *et alii* (n. 3), 159–187.

not letting Judas' army pass through it: 'and they fought against the city all that day and all that night; and the city was delivered into his hands; and he destroyed all the males with the edge of the sword, and rased the city, and took the spoils thereof, and passed through the city over them that were slain' (5:50–51). These measures that characterized the wars of Judas were also applied in the campaign against the Idumaeans, notably Hebron: 'And Judas and his brethren went forth, and fought against the Sons of Esau in the land toward the south; and they smote Hebron and the villages thereof, and pulled down the strongholds thereof, and burned the towers thereof round about' (5:65). From Hebron Judas turned westward: 'And Judas turned to Azotus, to the land of the Philistines (εἰς "Αζωτον γῆν ἀλλοφύλων), and pulled down their altars, and burned the carved images of their gods, and took the spoils of their cities' (5:68).

Several comments regarding these descriptions are apposite. First, the author puts the responsibility for the outbreak of the hostilities on the nations roundabout Judaea: they took the initiative in conspiring against and attacking the Jews; they aimed at a total destruction of the Jews. Second, the war conducted by the Hasmonaeans was, therefore, a defensive war, Judas committing the very deeds the enemies intended to accomplish. Third, in a short while the war took on another aspect: it was directed against the gods of the Gentiles, as Judas demolished and set in fire temples and places of cult of the enemies. In doing so, Judas reacted to the relgious persecution which Antiochus IV had ordered and in which implementation the 'nations roundabout' participated.[7] Fourth, in certain cases Judas was willing to cooperate or to come to terms with Gentiles: not only with a remote state like Rome (8:1–32) or with the more close by Nabataeans (5:25), but even with the Seleucid commander Nicanor (7:26–30). The last case shows that the Gentiles were responsible for the continuation of the hostilites, for Nicanor plotted to seize Judas by a trap and threatened to burn down the Temple.

A different Hasmonaean policy towards the neighbouring nations is noticeable under the leadership of Jonathan. The author of I Maccabees reports only one case of a destruction during the years when Jonathan was a rebellious leader, but depicts it as a blood revenge. I refer to the killing of the Hasmonaean John by the Sons of Iamri

---

[7] Cf. S. Schwartz (above n. 1), 21–29.

near Medaba; a short while later Jonathan and his followers killed in an ambush a great company of the tribe, and the author concludes this account with the comment: 'And (thus) they avenged fully the blood of their brother' (9:36–42). This kind of killing, belonging in the sphere of personal, tribal relations, has nothing to do with religious or national-cultural wars, which are the subject under discussion. The only relevant case reported concerns the battle of Azotus, which Jonathan fought against Apollonius, the Seleucid commander who went over to Demetrius II. The defeated forces of Apollonius tried to find shelter in the temple of Dagon at Azotus: 'And the horsemen were scattered in the plain; and they fled to Azotus, and entered into Beth-dagon, their idol's temple, to save themselves. And Jonathan burned Azotus, and the cities round about it, and took their spoils; and the temple of Dagon, and them that fled into it, he burned with fire' (10:83–84; cf. 11:4). This exceptional case, the only one reported during the 18 years of Jonathan's leadership, is presented as a reaction to the provocation of Apollonius (10:70–74), not as an implenetation of a general policy. It is true that Jonathan's troops set Antioch in fire, but that had nothing to do with the Jewish-Gentile conflict, for there they were fighting in behalf of Demetrius II (*I Macc.* 10:44–48).

As well Simon's actions, even while his brother was still alive, betray the emergence of a new policy. The two brothers transferred their allegiance from Demetrius II to Antiochus VI, who appointed Simon *strategos* of the coast 'from the Ladder of Tyre to the border of Egypt' (10:59). During his siege of Beth-Zur, Simon concluded an agreement with the besieged, according to which they were allowed to leave unharmed, and the city was preserved and occupied by a Hasmonaean garrison (11:64–65). Suspecting that the people of Joppa intended to hand over it over to Demetrius II, Simon conquered the town and garrisoned it, but did no harm to the inhabitants (12:33–34). It was only after Tryphon captured Jonathan that Simon expelled the local population, who could not be trusted, and strengthened his hold of Joppa (13:11). During the siege of Gazara, Simon's forces breached the city wall, burst inside and could treat the local population as was quite normal at this stage of a siege.[8] Simon,

---

[8] Several examples may illustrate the way victorious generals treated the population of conquered cities in the Hellenistic period. When Alexander the Great took Thebes in 335 he killed a great number of the men, sold into slavery the surviving

however, yielded to the entreaties of the local population and was content with a mild treatment; he only: 'drove them out of the city, and cleansed the houses wherein the idols were ... And he put all uncleanness out of it' (13:43–48). He applied the same policy in the siege of the Acra, whose defendants were forced to capitulate: 'he cast them out from thence; and he cleansed the Acra from pollutions' (13:49–50). Simon's policy was then to expel the Gentile population, not to destroy it, and to purify and resettle the conquered cities. In fact, only on one occasion does the author of I Maccabees report of physical annihilation of Gentiles during Simon's reign: his son John Hyrcanus burned down the field-towers in which the survivors of Cendebaeus' army sought to find refuge (*I Macc.* 16:10).

Alongside the change in policy and actions taken by Jonathan and Simon towards the neighbouring nations, as compared with those of their brother Judas, the description of the tense relations between the Jews and 'the nations' is almost entirely modified and the mutual enmity is played down or seldom referred to. There is not even one single passage, sentence or phrase in the entire part devoted to Jonathan (9:23–12:39) that mentions any enmity or hostile intentions, on either side, on account of the bloody confrontations which had erupted in the days of Mattathias and Judas as a result of the persecution of Antiochus IV. According to the narrative of I Maccabees, the motives and aims of the wars of this period were purely political: Jonathan took active part in the struggle for personal power in which were involved in succession, on the Seleucid side, Demetrius I, Alexander Balas, Demetrius II, Tryphon and Antiochus VI, as well as Ptolemy VI. During these years Jonathan was able to cooperate with almost every one of the contestants for long or short periods, shifting his support from one to another according to the circum-

---

population, including women and children, and demolished the city (Diod.Sic.17:9–14; Arrianus, *Anab.* 1:7–9). For the atrocities perpetrated by the tyrant Agathocles after the conquest of Syracuse and Segesta see Diod.Sic.17:7–9; 20:71. When Agathocles conquered Utica in 307 he slaughtered the population (Diod.Sic.20:54–55). Dion, in Macedonia, was destroyed and burnt down by the Aetolian commander Scopas in 219 (Polyb.4:62). In the same war Philippus V burned down Metropolis and destroyed Othoria, whose defendants had managed to escape (Polyb.4:64); the same fate befell Oineadae (Polyb.4:65). For the killing of the population of Sardis, setting of fire and looting, by Antiochus III, in 214, see Polyb.7:18. For the execution or sale into slavery of prisoners of war and civil population in conquered cities see the discussion and lists in W.K. Pritchett, *The Greek State at War*, 5 (Berkeley and Los Angeles 1991), 205–242.

stances. So did the other players in this game of power, motivated as they were by political, not religious considerations. Ptolemy Philometer VI, for example, did nothing to help the people of Azotus who complained about the destruction of the temple of Dagon by Jonathan (11:4–6). It is noteworthy that enmity and fear of the Hasmonaean leader were expressed by Jews, the Hellenizers and, apparently, other internal opponents.[9] The only time when the basic enmity cropped up, according to the author, occurred after Tryphon deceitfully captured Jonathan: 'And all the Gentiles that were round about them sought to destroy them utterly, for they said: They have not a man (that is) leader and (who will) help (them); now therefore let us fight against them, and take away their memorial from among men' (12:53).

As well in the account of Simon's reign the author rarely mentions enmity between Jews and Gentiles. The first time he refers to it is in the context of Tryphon's attack on Judaea, directly following the above quoted passage (13:1–6); that is, it belongs to the same affair. The hostile relations are referred to only once more, namely in the account of the formal decision passed by the people to legitimize Simon position as High-Priest and leader (14:27–49). As is explained in the decision itself, it was taken because Simon and his brothers have succeeded in defending the Temple and the Law and in stultifying the intention of the enemies to destroy the country (14:29–31). In other words, the reference is to past events, not to a recent outbreak of hostilities. Furthermore, the conquest of the Acra and its consequences are described in the following vein: 'And in his days things prospered in his hands so that the nations were taken away of their (the Jews') country; and they also that were in the city of David, they that were in Jerusalem, who had made themselves a citadel, out of which they issued, and polluted all things round about the sanctuary, and did great hurt unto its purity (these he did expel); and he made Jews to dwell therein, and fortified it for the safety of

---

[9] *I Macc* 9:23, 25, 29, 58, 61, 69, 73; 10:14, 61, 64; 11:21, 25. These passages show that the majority of the population of Judaea supported Alcimus after the battle of Elasa and that the author of the I Maccabees regarded the Jewish 'leaders of the country' evil persons. However, after the repeal of the persecution not every one who did not support Judas was perforce a Hellenizer. It is precisely in these passages that the pro-Hasmonaean bias of the author is revealed. For the opponents to the Hasmonaeans see J. Sievers, *The Hasmonaeans and their Supporters: From Mattathias to the Death of John Hyrcanus I* (Atlanta 1990), Chap. 3, esp. 100–103.

the country and of the city; and he made high the walls of Jerusalem. And king Demetrius confirmed him in the High-Priesthood in consequence of these things, and made him one of his friends, and honoured him with great honour' (14:36–9). In this account the Gentiles are not perceived collectively; rather, the author draws a distinction between those who constituted a menace and caused harm to the people and the Temple, and others with whom it was possible to cooperate. Obviously, far from being pleased with the conquest of the Acra, Demetrius II decided to bestow titles on and cooperated with Simon because he needed his support in his war against Antiochus VI and Tryphon. Like Jonathan before him, Simon was willing to render help to the Seleucid king because there was a political gain to make by taking such a step. These relations of *do ut des* presumably reduced to some extent the hostilities between the Jews and the 'nations round about' Judaea. Yet, it would seem that the intentions attributed to the Gentiles, after the capture of Jonathan, indicate that, from the author's point of view, the basic hostility, which had broken out at the time of the persecution and the Hasmonaean rise, and the potential of conflict persisted, at least latently.

The author's view of the relations with the Gentiles may furthered be explored by an examination of the loaded phrase 'the nations roundabout us' (τὰ ἔθνη κυκλόθεν), which is employed for the second time in 5:1–2 (above, p. 237). He uses it to refer to the Jewish-Gentile antagonism on four more occasions. In the letter the Jews of Galaaditis sent to Judas Maccabaeus to rescue them from 'the nations roundabout us', it clearly means a specific localized situation (5:10). This is also the meaning of the phrase in the report pf Judas' spies concerning the army of Timotheus (5:38). To learn from the context of the third case, the reported talk of Josephus and Azariah who initiated an attack on Jamnia (5:56–8), the phrase refers to people living close to Judaea. Apparently this is also the meaning of the phrase in the last case, when it is employed to describe the bewilderment and apprehensions of Israel after the capture by Tryphon of Jonathan, 'who feared that all the nations roundabout them sought to exterminate (ἐκτρῖψαι) them' (12:53), that is, the surrounding nations would join Tryphon in his imminent attack on Judaea. The phrase 'the nations roundabout' is a precise rendering of the Hebrew term הגויים סביב (מ), or העמים סביב, which occurs in various books of the Bible almost always to denote the religious differences and enmity prevailing in the relationships between the people of Israel and other peoples and nations living in Eretz Israel and the adjacent regions.[10] Several books of the Bible have also the phrase 'their enemies roundabout' (אויביהם מסביב). No doubt the author of I Maccabees adopted the Biblical phrase in his depiction of the contemporary conflict between Israel and the Gentiles since he envisaged it as a continuation of the old conflict.

The question arises, therefore, whether the Gentile-Jewish hostility and destructive confrontation concern, in the author's view, all Gentiles or only those living in Eretz Israel and the surrounding regions. The first possibility seems, at first sight, to have support in the address of Simon to the people in anticipation for the invasion of Tryphon. After mentioning the wars of the Hasmonaeans in defence of the Law, the sanctuary and Israel, in which all his brothers had died, he continues: 'I shall take revenge for my nation (ἔθνος), for the sanctuary and for wives and children, since all the nations (πάντα τὰ ἔθνη) have assembled out of hatred to exterminate us' (13:6). However, the special circumstances at the time have to be taken into consideration: the capture of Jonathan and the killing of his bodyguard, one thousand men. Naturally the Jews of Judaea were dismayed and feared that Tryphon would invade Judaea in order to impose again the Seleucid rule and would be supported by the Gentile population of Eretz Israel and the surrounding regions; the latter had been subdued by Jonathan, acting as he did in behalf of Alexander Balas and Antiochus VI. Even the inhabitants of Antioch had suffered terribly when Jonathan's troops had come to rescue Demetrius II.[11]

---

[10] *Deut* 6:14; *Judg* 2:12; *I kings* 5:11 (non-inimical context); *Jer* 25:9; *Ezek* 36:4, 7; *Joel* 4:11, 12; *Zecc* 12:2, 6; 14:14. Note that גויים (*goyim*) and עמים (*'amim*) are often used as synonyms, e.g., *Gen.* 25:23; *II Sam.* 22:44; *Jes.* 2:2–3; 25:7; 49:22; *Jer* 10:2–3; *Zecc* 12:3. The term *'amim* is translated in the LXX sometimes as ἔθνη (*Deut* 6:14; *Jes* 2:3; 25:7; *Jer.* 10:3) and sometime as λαοί (*Judg* 2:12; *Zecc* 12:25). The term *goyim* is probably always translated as ἔθνη (*I Kings* 5:11; *Jes* 2:2; 25:7; 49:22; *Jer* 10:2; 25:9; *Ezek* 36:4, 7; *Joel* 4:11–12; *Zecc* 12:3). The only exception I know of is the use of λαοί in *Zecc* 14:14. If such inconsistency for *'amim* characterizes the Greek translation of I Maccabees, there is no way to know the distribution of the term τὰ ἔθνη in this work between *'amim* and *goyim* in the original Hebrew version.

[11] For the operations of Jonathan, and of Simon, and the grievances of the cities and the countryside population see *I Macc* 10:75–6; 12:33–4 (Joppa); 11:4–5 (Azotus); 11:47–51 (Antioch); 11:59–60 (Simon appointed *strategos* of the coastal plain); 11:61–2 (Gaza besieged, its suburbs burnt and looted, and forced to hand over hostages); 11:66–7 (Beth-Zur besieged and taken). The campaigns of Jonathan extended as far as Damascus and Hamath (11:60, 62; 12:25–32). *Pace* Goldstein (n. 1), 440, the

Hence, both in 12:53 and 13:6 the phrase 'all the nations' refers not to all peoples living on earth but rather to those involved in the wars of the Hasmonaean brothers. Of the four other cases when the phrase is employed, two clearly denote a specific group of people, namely those who enlisted in the army of Timotheus (15:38, 43). In the third case we are told that Judas and his brothers won great respect from all Israel and 'all the nations who heard of their name' (5:63). Thus 'all' is qualified here, and in any case the context does not necessarily imply inimical attitudes.[12] The phrase seems to mean a universal Jewish-Gentile hostile confrontation only once: Judas trusts that God will help his army destroy the camp of Gorgias at Ammaus so that 'all the nations will know that there is one who redeems and saves Israel' (4:11). Yet, the real message of Judas' words is that victory over Gorgias' army will deter those nations that contemplate to attack Israel. In other words, 'all the nations' is directed at nations who attack or might attack, of their own accord, Judaea and the Jews. Thus, from the point of view of the author, the Jewish-Gentile antagonism does exist, but the eruption of violent hostilities depends, to a large measure, on specific circumstances and may be restrained and avoided. His description of the vicissitude in the the Hasmonaean foreign policy lends support to such a view.

The change in the Hasmonaean policy towards the Gentiles and the apparent disappearance of open hostilities took place during the struggle between Alexander Balas and Demetrius I for the Seleucid throne. As the two contenders sought support from every quarter, they granted honours and rights to the Hasmonaean leader.[13] Jonathan decided to support Alexander Balas and persisted in his loylaty to him. At first he was appointed High-Priest and 'friend of the king' (*filos basileos*) and later on *strategos* and *meridarches* of Judaea; in addition he was raised to the rank of 'first friend'.[14] This new position

---

absence of the definite article in *I Macc* 11:60, in contrast to 7:8, suggests that Jonathan crossed the river (Jordan), and not transversed the Trans-Euphrates province.

[12] Cf. *I Kings* 5:11. In *I Macc.* 1:42 the phrase has nothing to do with Jewish-Gentile relationships.

[13] *I Macc.* 10:1–50. For an excellent account see the posthumous study of M. Stern, *Hasmonaean Judaea in the Hellenistic World: Chapters in Political History* (Jerusalem 1995), 27–35 (Hebrew).

[14] *I Macc.* 10:65. On the titles and ranks in the administration of the Hellenistic kingdoms see E. Bickermann, *Institutions des Séleucids* (Paris 1938), 40–50; C. Chrimes Atkinson, 'Some observations on Ptolemaic Ranks and Titles', *Aegyptus* 32 (1952),

of Jonathan provides the explanation for the change in the Hasmonaean policy, which is understandbly reflected in the narration of the author of I Maccabees. As M. Stern writes, 'the head of the Hasmonaean house became a well known figure throughout the kingdom, and the wish to play a role in the Seleucid politics was from then on a hallmark of the foreign policy of Jonathan to his last day'.[15] As a high-ranking Seleucid official, and not only High-Priest, he could not allow himself to carry out a systematic policy of destruction of Gentile cities and temples. Due to his attempt to participate as an equal partner in the political game, he had to deviate from the policy pursued by his brother Judas towards Gentiles. The same consideration holds good for Simon. When he and his brother transferred their allegiance from Demetrius II to Antiochus VI, the latter appointed Simon *strategos* of the Palestinian coast 'from the Ladder of Tyre to the border of Egypt' (*I Macc.* 11:59).

It looks pretty clear that the author of I Maccabees reports with approval and takes positive view both of the policy of destruction pursued by Judas Maccabaeus and of the policy maintained by Jonathan and Simon. According to his description, the latter refrained from general physical annihilation of the population of those cities and places which they were able to conquer or annex to Judaea, although they did abolish all signs of pagan worship. Usually they expelled the Gentile population from the sites under their rule, and in one case even this normative measure was not carried out, that is, in Joppa. When Simon took control of that city he let the pagan local population remain there (12:33–4), quite obviously because he was an official of the Seleucid king Antiochus VI, who had appointed him *strategos* of that region (above). This and the other cases indicate that, in contrast to Judas who arguably treated the enemies according to the Deuteronomic rules that ordained the 'ban' (*herem*), that is, the annihilation of the Canaanites,[16] Jonathan and Simon reckoned that they had to modify the policy of their dead brother

---

204–14; C. Habicht, 'Die herrechende Gesellschaft in den hellenistichen Monarchien', *Vierteljahrschrift für Social-und Wirtschaftsgeschichte* 45 (1958), 1–16.

[15] Stern (n. 13), 36 (my translation).

[16] See *Deut* 7:1–2; 20:16–7. Examples: *Deut.* 2:31–4; 3:3–4 (Sihon, Og and their cities); *Josh* 6:21–4; 8:24–8 (Jericho and 'Ai). On the *strata* of the Deuteronomic rules of war, notably the ban (*herem*) see A. Rofé, *Deuteronomy: Issues and Interpretation* (London and New York 2002), 149–67, with the literature there cited (= *Journal for the Study of the Old Testament* 32 [1985], pp. 23–44).

in order to promote and maintain their international political position.

The decision of Jonathan and Simon not to exterminate the Gentile population of the cities conquered could be justified, for example on the ground that those Gentiles were not one of the seven peoples that Israel was ordained to destroy upon the conquest of the Promised Land.[17] Furthermore, in his study of the laws regulating the relations of the Israelites to the Canaanites, M. Weinfeld has elucidated that the Covenant code of Exodus orders to *expel* the pre-Israelite inhabitants of the Land of Israel, and that the priestly code in Numbers commands to *dispossess (horish)* them, which can mean either expulsion or extermination. One could therefore find Biblical support for the deviation from the Deuteronomic laws concerning the ban of the Canaanites. There is much to say for the view of M. Weinfeld, who refers explicitly to the policy of Simon and implicitly to that of John Hyrcanus, that 'in their [i.e. of the Hasmonaeans] time the [Deuteronomic] law was taken out of its context, in order to be adjusted to reality to which it did not apply'.[18] But this need not imply that the descriptions of Judas Maccabaeus' campaigns that are modelled on the Deuteronomic law of *herem* are false. Rather, the author succeeds in this way to represent a change of policy, which makes sense in view of the different religious and political conditions under which Judas, on the one hand, and Jonathan and Simon, on the other hand, had to conduct their campaigns.[19]

Since the author of I Maccabees ended his history with the succession of John Hyrcanus to the position of his father Simon, there is no way to know how he would have depicted the captue of Medaba and Samoga in Transjordan, the forced Judaization of the Idumaeans, the conquest of Shechem, the destruction of the Samaritan temple and town on Mount Gerizim, and the demolition of Samaria, which

---

[17] Cf. Schwartz (above n. 1), 32 n. 59

[18] See M. Weinfeld, 'The Ban on the Canaanites in the Biblical Codes and its Historical Development', in A. Lemaire and B. Otzen (eds.), *History and Traditions of Early Israel* (Leiden 1993), 142–60, cited at 155 n. 37.

[19] *Contra* S. Schwartz (n. 1), 30–32, who highlights the apparent contradiction between accounts that seem to be influenced by Deuteronomic concepts and accounts that betray the influence of Priestly terminology: the purification of the Temple and the conquest of Gazara and the Acra. However, the modern distinction between Deuteronomic and Priestly sources in the Bible cannot serve as a criterion to distinguish between false and real elements in the narrative of I Maccabees, although the author surely exaggerated in glorifying the bloody victories of Judas, as did many ancient historians on other occasions.

are all reported by Josephus.[20] New, instructive evidence relating to some of these conquests and destructive actions of John Hyrcanus have been provided by archaeological finds in recent years. They have shown that he launched upon these campaigns not earlier than the year 112 B.C.E.[21] If the author of I Maccabees wrote his work in the early years of Hyrcanus' reign, as I think he did, he could not have possibly reacted to this change in the Hasmonaean foreign policy. Since, however, he described, generally speaking, in positive manner both the deeds of Judas and those of Jonathan and Simon, it stands to reason that he will have also presented a sympathetic account of John Hyrcanus' policy. What led Hyrcanus to adopt this policy is a question I'll try answer in my conclusion.

II MACCABEES

The extant II Maccabees is an abridgement of Jason of Cyrene's lost work that comprised five books. Unlike I Maccabees, which covers the history of the Hasmonaeans to the death of Simon in 135 B.C.E., II Maccabees ends its story with the victory of Judas Maccabaeus over Nicanor in 161 B.C.E. The date of Jason, who is mentioned only once in this work (2:23), and is not otherwise known, and of the composition of the abridgement is disputed. I adhere to the view that Jason of Cyrene probably wrote his history in the first Hasmonaean generation; the abridgement seems to have been composed during the reign of John Hyrcanus' rule, some time after 124 B.C.E.[22] But even if a later date were to be accepted for Jason's work and its abridgement, say the first third of the first century

---

[20] Joseph. *BJ* 1:63–6; *AJ* 13:254–8, 275–280.
[21] See R. Barkay, 'The Marisa Hoard of Seleucid Tetradrachmas Minted in Ascalon', *Israel Numismatic Journal* 12 (1992/3), 21–6; D. Barag, 'New Evidence on the Foreign Policy of John Hyrcanus', *ibid.*, 1–12. For details see below.
[22] See, e.g., B. Niese, 'Kritik der beiden Makkabäerbücher nebst Beiträgen zur Geschichte der makkabäischen Erhebung', *Hermes* 35 (1900), 277–93; Abel (n. 4), XLII–XLIII; J.-G. Bunge, *Untersuchungen zum zweiten Makkabäerbuch* (Diss. Bonn 1971), 195–202; A. Momigliano, 'The Second Book of Maccabees', *Classical Philology* 70 (1975), 81–8; R. Doran, *Temple Propaganda: The Purpose and Character of 2 Maccabees* (Washington 1981), 111–3. For a concise account with an extensive bibliography see Goodman, in Schürer (n. 1), III.1, 531–7. For the view that the abridgement was written in the year 143/142 see D.R. Schwartz, *The Second Book of Maccabees* (Jerusalem 2004), 16–19 (Hebrew).

B.C.E.,[23] this would not distract the least from the importance and relevance of the testimony of II Maccabees for our purpose. It is well to bear in mind that one focus of the book is upon the achievements of Judas: the author extols his devotion to the Lord and his exploits in defending Jews loyal to the Law. It is evident that the author, be it Jason or the epitomator, aimed at presenting a glorified account of this hero.

Of the beginning of the Maccabaean revolt, the author writes:

> Now as soon as Maccabaeus had got his company together, the Gentiles (τὰ ἔθνη) found him irresistible, for the Lord's anger was now turned into mercy. He would surprise and burn both towns and villages, gaining possession of strategic positions, and routing large numbers of the enemy.[24]

The author depicts here Judas as the agent who carries out God's mission; the destruction of the enemies and their towns and villages is perceived as heavenly retribution, which they fully deserve because of their wickedness. Thus, after defeating Timotheus and Bacchides and killing more than twenty thousand men of their troops, the Jews celebrated their victory and 'burned Callisthenes and some others, who had set fire to the sacred gates, and who had fled into a small house for refuge; thus these men did receive a reward worthy of their impiety (δυσσέβεια)'.[25] Later on Judas defeated again Timotheus, who fled to the fortress of Gazara. Judas' men stormed the wall and 'set fire to the the towers, kindling fires and burning the blasphemers alive' (10:36). One gets the impression that the burning of towers, fortresses, houses and the defeated themselves was the normal way Judas dealt with the enemies following his victories.

In a certain respect the account of Judas' war against the Idumaeans is particularly instructive (10:15-23). The Idumaeans kept harassing the Jews and gave shelter to those who fled from Jerusalem after its recovery by Judas; obviously the reference is to Hellenized Jews.

---

[23] The thesis of J.A. Goldstein, *II Maccabees: A New Translation with Introduction and Commentary*, (Garden City, N.Y. 1983), 16-19, 71-83 and *passim*, that the work was written by 86 B.C.E. to counter the pro-Hasmonaean propaganda of I Maccabees and is pervaded by an extremely anti-Hasmonaean bias seems to me to go beyond the evidence. I deal with this question in my forthcoming book (n. 1), III.i.

[24] *II Macc.* 8:5-6. Here and in the following I use, with a few changes, J. Moffatt's translation of II Maccabees in R.H. Charles, *The Apocrypha and Pseudepigrapha of the Old Testament in English*, Oxford 1913.

[25] *II Macc.* 8:33. For the difficulty concerning the reading of this verse see Abel (n. 4), 395; Goldstein (n. 23), 340-41.

Judas then attacked the Idumaeans, allegedly killing twenty thousand men. About nine thousand men fled to two towers. In Judas' absence, some of Simon's men, who were investing the towers, succumbed to bribery and let some of the besieged escape. Judas arrived and 'accused them of selling their brethren for money, by setting their enemies free to fight against them' (10:21). He executed these men as traitors, stormed the towers and destroyed twenty thousand men (the author apparently has forgotten that only nine thousand men had taken refuge in these two towers). The message the author conveys to his readers is clear: Judas waged a total war against those who attacked the Jews, especially those who collaborated with the Hellenized Jews of Jerusalem. There was no room for compromise, and Judas exhibited devotion to his mission by destroying all these enemies, as well as some of his own men, namely the corrupt ones who compromised with the enemy.

The same message is implied in the account of Judas' war against the people of Joppa, who killed the Jewish inhabitants of their city (12:3–7). Judas made a night attack on the harbour, set fire to the wharves, burned the ships and destroyed those who took refuge there. Unable to break into the city itself he left, but intended to return and 'to extripate the entire community of Joppa (τὸ σύμπαν τῶν Ἰοππιτῶν ἐκριζῶσαι πολίτευμα) (12:7). Judas also raided the harbour of Jamnia and burned it, forestalling the intention of the town-people to destroy the Jews who lived there. In the wars in Transjordan, he attacked the strongly fortified city of Caspin, which was inhabited by a mixed population, blasphemous Gentiles (12:13–16). Judas' men captured the city and massacred an enormous number of people, 'so much so that the adjoining lake, which was two stades broad, looked as though it were filled with the deluge of blood'. Judas then confronted again Timotheus and destroyed about thirty thousand men of his host (12:23: διέφθειρέ τε εἰς μυριάδας τρεῖς ἀνδρῶν). He proceeded to attack Carnaim and its temple, namely of the Syrian goddess Atargatis, where he slaughtered twenty-five thousand people (12:26: κατέσφαξε μυριάδας σωμάτων δύο καὶ πεντακισχιλίους). The difference in the verbs and nouns used here by the author (ἄνδρες—σώματα, διέφθειρε—κατέσφαξε) is telling: those killed in the battle were troops, whereas those killed in Carnaim were women and children who had been sent, by Timotheus, before the battle to find refuge in a city supposed to be impregnable (12:21). Once again the message is clear: Judas was relentless in the pursuit of the enemy, killing everyone he captured and sparing neither women nor children. This kind of slaughter also befell the city of Ephron, where twenty-five thousand people were destroyed (12:27-8). Of course the reported numbers of the enemies killed are inflated and imaginary, but they are noteworthy as reflecting one line of thinking of the author: the more Gentiles Judas destroyed, the better he served the cause of Israel. Still, one city, Scythopolis, proved an exception, for the local Jews testified to the goodwill and humane attitude of their neighbours (12:29-31).

Finally, it is instructive to note the way Judas treated the body of Nicanor (15:30-35). The 'accursed', 'impious' (μιαρός, δυσσεβής) Nicanor had sinned in stretching out his right hand towards the temple and swearing to level it to the ground, to demolish the altar and to build a temple to Dionysus if Judas was not delivered to him (14:33). Therefore Judas cut his head, arm and tongue and brought them to Jerusalem; he cast out the tongue to be eaten by birds of prey but hung the arm at a site facing the temple and the head close to the citadel: 'a clear and conspicuous sign (ἐπίδηλον ... καὶ φανερὸν ... σημεῖον) to all of the Lord's help'. The defeat of Nicanor, the treatment of his body and the public decision (κοινὸν ψήφισμα) taken to commemorate that day of victory conclude the work: since from that time 'the city was held by the Hebrews'.[26] Thus this was the final lesson the author wished to import to his readers: a total war of extermination should be waged against Gentiles who constituted a menace to the people of Israel and to the worship of God, and the fate of Nicanor was meant to serve as a warning to hostile Gentiles.

The First and Second Books of Maccabees differ between themselves in various and not a few respects including content, details, use of documents, chronological framework and beliefs. They also

---

[26] *II Macc.* 15:37: Τῶν οὖν κατὰ Νικάνορα χωρησάντων οὕτως, καὶ ἀπ' ἐκείνων τῶν καιρῶν κρατηθείσης τῆς πόλεως ὑπὸ τῶν 'Εβραίων, καὶ αὐτὸς αὐτόθι τὸν λόγον καταπαύσω. See on this Goldstein (n. 23), 501-2. That the Jews cut Nicanor's right arm and head and brought them to a site facing Jerusalem is the version of I Maccabees (7:47), which does not mention the other details concerning the treatment of Nicanor's body in Jerusalem. For the view that the version of I Maccabees is to be preferred because that of II Maccabees implies the defiling of the Temple precinct by contact with a dead Gentile, contrary to the prevailing Halakhic regulation, see Bar-Kochva (n. 1), 371. His interpretaion is disputed by R. Wilk, 'The Abuse of Nicanor's Corpse', *Sidra* 8 (1992), 53-7 (Hebrew), who discusses in detail the Talmudic sources which deal with the treatment of Nicanor's body, but concludes, for other reasons, that the vesrsion of I Maccabees is more reliable.

differ in that I Maccabees, written originally in Hebrew, shows marked influence of Biblical historical writing, whereas II Maccabees is a Greek composition in form, syntax and style.[27] It is abundant in dramatic scenes, emotive descriptions of gruesome cruelty and exemplary courageous behaviour and edifying speeches, in short elements of historical writing that characterized the trendy works of historians like Duris of Samos and Phylarchus.[28] The question arises whether these two Jewish works, the one a basically Biblical kind of history and the other a typically Hellenistic history differ in their presentation of the encounter between the Jews under the leadership of the Hasmonaeans and the τά ἔθνη roundabout. Needless to say, a comparison of these two works is limited to the period of Judas, for II Maccabees ends with the victory over Nicanor.[29]

I Maccabees recognizes the existence of a fundamental difference between the Jews and the Gentiles of Eretz Israel and the adjacent regions, which is the source of potential inimical relations that may burst into active hostility. Once this happens, it is imperative to fight uncompromisingly against the Gentiles. For the author of this work, this is what occurred under the rule of Antiochus IV; the wars of Mattathias and Judas against the Gentiles were an opportune occasion to implement the Deuteronomic laws, and hence were modelled on the wars of Joshua against the Canaanite peoples.[30] The

---

[27] On the style and motifs of I Maccabees see Abel (n. 4), XXIII–XXIV; Goldstein (n. 1), 10,12–4. On II Maccabees see Doran (n. 22), 24–46 (including a refutation of alleged cases of Semiticism); J. Geiger, 'The History of Judas Maccabaeus: One Aspect of Hellenistic History', *Zion* 49 (1983/4), 1–8 (Hebrew); Bar-Kochva (n. 1), 171–82.

[28] For three instances see *II Macc.* 6:10; 7:1–38; 14:41–6. On II Maccabees as belonging to the genre of rhetorical or pathetic history see Niese (n. 22), 300–301; E. Bickermann, *Der Gott der Makkabäer* (Berlin 1937), 147; C. Habicht, *2 Makkabäerbuch* (Gütersloh 1976), 189; A. Momigliano, 'Greek Historiography', *History and Theory* 17 (1978), 8; Doran, (n. 22), 84–97; Geiger, (n. 27); Bar-Kochva (n. 1), 173–7.

[29] Whether Jason of Cyrene ended his story with the victory over Nicanor (thus Habicht [n. 28], 173–4) or after the death of Judas Maccabaeus (thus Goldstein [n. 1], 27, 33, 80) is a matter of speculation. One cannot rule out the possibility that he went on to describe the history of Jonathan and Simon.

[30] The hostility of I Maccabees to Gentiles have been emphasized by S. Schwartz, (n. 1). Cf. Bickerman (n. 28), 27–32. E. Gruen, *Heritage and Hellenism: The Reinvention of Jewish Tradition* (Berkeley and Los Angeles 1998), 4–6, argues that the wars were conducted against the surrounding Gentiles, not against Greek or Hellenized cities. However, Judas sent his brother Simon to save the Galilaean Jews from the attacks initiated by Sidon, Tyre and Ptolemaïs, certainly Hellenized cities (*I Macc.* 6:14–5, 21–3), and Judas himself conducted war against Azotus (5:68), probably a Hellenized city to some extent. True, other wars were conducted against the local, surrounding population, but the difficulty is that, in absence of evidence, the extent of the Hellenization of many cities, like those of Transjordan, is unknown.

attitude of II Maccabees to the Gentiles is more articulated. For the author of this work, the wars of Judas against the Gentiles were justified because these Gentiles were blasphemous and had attacked Jews. Yet cases of friendly relations between Jews and Gentiles as well as humane behaviour of Gentiles are noticed, notably the indignation of many foreigners over the murder of Onias III (4:35–6), the sympathy of the Tyrians for the Jewish envoys who brought complaints against Menelaus and were unjustly executed (4:49), the attempt of Ptolemy Macron, a high-ranking Seleucid official, to rectify the injustice done to the Jews (10:12), and the good relations between the people of Scythopolis and the local Jews (12:30). These instances have been construed by scholars to claim that the author of II Maccabees is not hostile to non-Jews as such.[31] One needs to be more precise.

The author of II Maccabees is indignant and uncompromising in showing hostiltity at the attempt to Hellenize the Jewish people, whether by Jews or foreigners does not make any difference. The sharp contrast he draws is between Judaism and Hellenism (4:10–15), between Judaism and barbarians (2:21), which is an ironical inversion of the distinction Greeks used to make between themselves and barbarians, i.e. all the other peoples.[32] The essence of the persecution is the abolition of the Law and of all the traditional religious practices and manners of life of the Jews, on the one hand, and the forcible, atrocious imposition of Greek cults, sacrificial practices and social behaviour (6:1–10). It is instructive that the author equates ἀλλοφυλισμός with Ἑλληνισμός.[33] The term ἀλλόφυλοι is used only twice, both times in a context that connects it to the pollution of the Temple, that is, its Hellenization; in other words, the 'foreign-

---

[31] See, e.g., Momigliano (n. 22), 86; Goldstein (n. 1), 34; *idem* (n. 23), 444; Doran (n. 22), 110–11.
[32] Cf. Goldstein (n. 23), 192, 230.
[33] *II Macc.* 4:13: ἀκμή τις Ἑλληνισμοῦ καὶ πρόβασις ἀλλφυλισμοῦ. Note the context: on his appointment as High-Priest Jason πρὸς τὸν Ἑλληνικὸν χαρακτῆρα τοὺς ὁμοφύλους μετέστησε (4:10); and then the Jewish priests: τὰς δὲ Ἑλληνικὰς δόξας καλλίστας ἡγούμενοι (4:15). Similarly in 6:24 αλλοφυλισμός surely means all Gentiles, Greeks inclusive. That the object of the king's orders was to achieve a change over to Greek customs (τὰ Ἑλληνικά) is explicitly told on two occasions (6:9; 11:24). Hence, it is wrong to argue, as does S. Zeitlin, 'The Names Hebrew, Jew and Israel', *Jewish Quarterly Review* 43 (1952/3), 365–79, at 372–3, that αλλοφυλισμος refers to Gentiles who were not Hellenes. See also J. Lieu, 'Not Hellenes but Philistines? The Maccabees and Josephus Defining the "Other"', *Journal of Jewish Studies* 53 (2002), 246–63, at 250.

ers' are Hellenizers.³⁴ It is also worth to note that the citizens of Ptolemaïs, a Hellenized city, furiously objected to the agreement Lysias made to restore the religious liberty to the Jews.³⁵ This perception and representation of the persecution and of the Hasmonaean revolt has a bearing on the author's use of the term τὰ ἔθνη, only fourteen times, compared with forty-six times in I Maccabees. In one case it refers to a pro-Jewish attitude (4:35–6), and in some cases the context shows that the reference is to Hellenizers.³⁶ On two or three occasions the use of the term has nothing to do with the contemporary conflict.³⁷ In the other instances, 'the nations' are some specific, local Gentiles (12:13) or part of the Seleucid army (8:9, 16; 14:15; 15:8). One case is particularly instructive (6:13–5): according to the author, impious people (δυσσεβοῦντας) are punished immediately by God if they are Jews; if they are of the 'other nations' (τῶν ἄλλων ἐθνῶν), God punishes them when their sins reach completeness (πρὸς ἐκπλήρωσιν τῶν ἁμαρτιῶν). This use of the term reveals a somewhat different attitude than that expressed by the author of I Maccabees in his employment of the phrase 'the nations roundabout'.

Despite the differences it appears that, given the foregoing analysis, I Maccabees and II Maccabees have also much in common from the viewpoint taken here. Although the authors differed in their stance on the nature of the relations between Jews and Gentiles and in their interpretation of the purpose of the wars—particularly those of Judas Maccabaeus—they justified the wars and the punishment of the enemies of Israel. Both works extol Judas, the Hasmonaean hero, for his devotion to save Jews and to destroy Gentiles. The

---

³⁴ *II Macc.* 10:2, 5. I follow F. Millar, 'The Background to the Maccabean Revolution: Reflections on Martin Hengel's "Judaism and Hellenism"', *Journal of Jewish Studies* 29 (1978), 1–21, esp. 17–20, in holding that the cult introduced by Antiochus IV was Greek, not syncretic; *contra* Bickermann (n. 28), 90–116; M. Hengel, *Judaism and Hellenism. Studies in their Encounter in Palestine during the Early Hellenistic Period* (Eng. trans.) (Tübingen 1974), 292–303. See also Collins, in J.J. Collins and G.E. Sterling, *Hellenism in the Land of Israel* (Notre Dame, Indiana 2001), 51–2.

³⁵ *II Macc.* 13:23–5. The author's version is that Lysias actually offered sacrifice and respected the Temple, which of course had to be first restored as the Jewish Temple. In contrast, in *I Macc.* 5:1 it is the 'nations roundabout', not a Hellenized city, who are enraged. For the anti-Jewish enmity of the people of Ptolemaïs see also *II Macc.* 6:8, with the reading Πτολεμαέων ὑποτιθεμένων. See on this Bickermann (n. 28), 121–2 with n. 6; Abel (n. 4), 362–4; Goldstein (n. 23), 276–8.

³⁶ *II Macc.* 6:4; 10:4; 14:14; perhaps also 8:5.

³⁷ *II Macc.* 1:27 (Nehemia's prayer—twice). This in fact also holds true for 11:3.

authors clearly approved of the zeal of Judas to carry out his mission, and they even seem to have indulged in detailing the extermination of the enemies, both the traditionally hostile peoples like the Edomites and the Hellenized inhabitants of coastal cities like Joppa, Jamnia and Azotus. The authors readily reported the annihilation of the armies of the enemies, the capture and destruction of cities of the Gentiles and the killing of their civilian population. By these deeds Judas, as well as Jonathan according to I Maccabees, served well the Lord and the people of Israel.

The Book of Jubilees

Unlike I Maccabees and II Maccabees that narrate contemporary or recent events, Jubilees pretends to deal with the remote past, but is not a historical work. It recounts the story of the Bible from the Creation to the establishment of Passover, that is, Genesis and the first twelve chapters of Exodus. Within this framework, an angelic revelation allegedly presented to Moses on Mount Sinai, the author inserts many changes in and additions to the Biblical narrative, presumably some traditional and some of his own invention. No doubt the stories of the Patriarchs were rewritten by the author to display a model of behaviour that should be followed, and it may be assumed that the additions and the modifications reflect conemporary or recent conditions and issues. The composition of the work cannot be dated precisely; internal evidence and historical considerations may point to a date after the fall of Judas Maccabaeus, probably under Jonathan, although this is disputed.[38] According to one view, references to the

---

[38] For a concise exposition, with extensive bibliography, of the content, date of composition and views of modern scholars see Vermes, in Schürer (n. 1), III,1, 308–18. Add O.S. Wintermute, in J.H. Charlesworth (ed.), *The Old Testament Pseudepigrapha*, 2 (Garden City, N.Y. 1985), 35–50. On the date of the work see in particular the detailed discussion of J.C. VanderKam, *Textual and Historical Studies in the Book of Jubilees* (Misoula 1977), 214–85. For arguments to date the work ca. 168 B.C.E. see G.W.E. Nickelsburg, *Jewish Literature between the Bible and the Mishnah* (Philadelphia 1981), 77–9; J.A. Goldstein, *Semites, Iranians, Greeks and Romans: Studies in their Interactions* (Atlanta, GA 1990), 161–79. Their arguments do not seem to me to carry conviction. *Pace* Nickelsburg, the danger of Hellenization and of Jewish-Gentile contacts did continue even after the termination of the persecution in 164 B.C.E.; one has only to take into account the fortifications constructed and the garrisons placed in Judaea by Bacchides (*I Macc.* 9:50–53). For the view that the work is a purely literary composition, lacking allusions to any specific events, see R. Doran, 'The Non-Dating of Jubilees: Jub 34–38,23; 23:14–32 in Narrative

Idumaeans indicate that it was written at the time of John Hyrcanus, who conquered Idumaea,[39] but it is possible that the allusions to his exploits were included in a later redaction of the original work.[40] Be that as it may, and although the Hasmonaeans are not mentioned, the work clearly sheds light on thorny religious-political problems that have been troubling the Jewish society of Judaea since the days of Antiochus IV. As such, it provides instructive evidence, even if the author represents views of a minor sectarian group.[41]

Several major topics that concern the relations between Jews and Gentiles are prominent in Jubilees and hence are relevant for the present discussion. I'll single out the following:

1. Circumsion. This sign of the Covenant of the Lord that differentiated Israel from the Gentiles, especially the Greeks, was neglected by the Hellenizing Jews and became a major issue during the persecution of Antiochus IV.[42] In Jubilees the subject is brought up by the Angel of Presence, who alerts Moses to the future neglect of

---

Context', *Journal of Jewish Studies* 20 (1989), 1–11. His arguments are not entirely convincing; the composition surely post-dated I Enoch.

[39] See R.H. Charles, *The Book of Jubilees* (London 1902), LVIII–LXVI; D. Mendels, *The Land of Israel as a Political Concept in Hasmonaean Literature* (Tübingen 1987), 68–81.

[40] On several stages of redaction see G.L. Davenport, *The Eschatology of the Book of Jubilees* (Leiden 1971), 10–18, 32–46; M. Delcor, in *Cambridge History of Judaism*, 2 (1989), 436. For the view that chapters 37–38 do not reflect historical events, that is, neither a reflection of Judas' wars against the Idumaeans (Vanderkam's interpretation) nor of the conquest of Idumaea by John Hyrcanus (Mendel's view), see C. Werman, *The Attitude Towards Gentiles in the Book of Jubilees and Qumran Literature Compared with Early Tanaaic Halakha and Contemporary Pseudepigrapha* (Diss. Jerusalem 1995, Hebrew), 17–22. She argues that the author created a tradition, or used current traditions, in order to depict the relations between Jacob and Esau as he saw them: an eternal enmity. The first part of the argument is not persuasive, for since the author lived in the second century B.C.E., which is accepted by Werman (34–5), the contemporary violent conflict with the Idumaeans—be it in the time of Judas or of John Hyrcanys makes no difference—could surely serve as a proof of the eternal enmity and as a motivation to highlight it.

[41] For a brief summary of opinions on the sectarian identification of the author (Pharisee, Essene, Hasidaean) see Vermes, in Schürer (n. 1), III.1, 313–317. For the view that Jubilees, particularly 23:16–20, describes the origin of the Essenes see M. Kister, 'Concerning the History of the Essenes—A Study of the *Animal Apocalypse*, the *Book of Jubilees* and the *Damascus Covenant*', *Tarbiz* 66 (1986/7), 1–18 (Hebrew).

[42] *I Macc.* 1:15,48,60–61; *II Macc.* 6:10. On Jubilees as a sectarian reaction to the cultural models of Hellenism see the interesting study of F. Schmidt, 'Jewish Representations of the Inhabited Earth during the Hellenistic Period', in A. Kasher, U. Rappaport and G. Fuks (eds.), *Greece and Rome in Eretz Israel* (Jerusalem 1990), 119–40, esp. 132–4 ('The Book of Jubilees holds the hellenized Jews responsible for the disorder of the period, but first addresses its criticism at the Syrians, the descendants of Canaan, and the Seleucids, sons of Japhat', p. 133).

circumcision by the sons of Israel: 'And now I announce unto thee that the children of Israel will not keep true to this ordinance, and they will not circumcise their sons according to all this law; for in the flesh of their circumcision they will omit this circumcision of their sons, and all of them, sons of Beliar, will leave their sons uncircumcised as they were born'.[43] It has been argued that this evidence merely reflects Halakhic disputes concerning circumcision and nakedness, which may have been part of the causes for the emergence of the Essenes in the early Hasmonaean period. But those who separated themselves because of such Halakhic disputes were certainly extremely critical of the behaviour of the Hellenized Jews in these respects, and hence the attempt to deny any connection between the stance of the author on these topics and the Hellenization movement is not cogent.[44] At any rate, it is clear that for the author circumcision distinguished fundamentally Jews from Gentiles.

2. Marriage. Rebecca's severe warning to Jacob not to marry a Canaanite woman reveals the author's stance regarding this subject (25.1). The story of the massacre of the Shechemites by Simon and Levi is retold at length, clearly with one purpose: to admonish against inter-marriage (30:1-17). The marrying of a Gentile wife by an Israelite man and of an Israelite woman by a Gentile is entirely prohibited: 'And if there is any man who wishes in Israel to give his daughter or his sister to any man who is of the seed of the Gentiles he shall surely die, and they shall stone him with stones; for he hath wrought shame in Israel; and they shall burn the woman with fire, because she has dishonoured the the name of the house of her father, and she shall be rooted out of Israel ... And do though, Moses, command the children of Israel and exhort them not to give their daughters to the Gentiles, and not to take for their sons any of the daughters of the Gentiles, for this is abominable before the Lord'.[45]

---

[43] *Jub.* 15:33. See also 15:23-26, 34. Here and in the following I use R.H. Charles' translation of Jubilees in his *The Apocrypha and Pseudepigrapha of the Old Testament in English*, Oxford 1913.

[44] For the view that the issues of nakedness (3:31; 7:20) and circumcision were raised by the author merely as part of an internal Jewish Halachic dispute see Kister (n. 41), 6-7 n. 26, followed by Werman (n. 40), 30-31. Kister and Werman emphasize the fact that the persecution of Antiochus IV is not mentioned in Jubilees, but one may regard what the author says on the abandonment of circumcision as an illusion to those Jews who obeyed the orders of the Seleucid king.

[45] *Jub.* 30:7, 11. Still, marriage with circumcised Gentiles is perhaps implied to be possible: 'We will not give our daughter to a man who is uncircumcised' (30:12).

3. *Segregation.* Eating or any social association with the Gentiles are forbidden. Thus Abraham tells Jacob: 'And do though, my son Jacob, remember my words, and observe the commandments of Abraham, thy father: separate thyself from the nations, and eat not with them: and do not according to their works, and become not their associate; for their works are unclean, and all their ways are a pollution and abomination and uncleanness' (22:16).

4. *Enmity and the future fate of the Gentiles.* The author posits the existence of fundamental enmity between the Israelites and the adjacent Gentile peoples. The enmity against the Philistines is expressed in the curse of Isaac (24:28–33). The Philistines will be completely destroyed and uprooted: 'And no remnant shall be left to them, nor one that shall be saved on the day of the wrath of the judgement; for the destruction and rooting out and expulsion from the earth is the whole seed of the Philistines (reserved), and there shall no longer be left for these Caphtorim a name or a seed on the earth' (30). Likewise it is hostility that comes to the fore in the war Jacob wages against the seven kings of the Amorites: they are killed, and although peace is made, it is to endure only with the subjugation of these peoples (34:1–9). The war fought by Jacob and his sons against Esau and his sons involves Gentiles all around Israel to the south, east, north and west: Edomites, Horites, Moabites, Ammonites, Aramaeans (or Edomites) and Philistines. They are all defeated, and peace is made with the Edomites who are put to servitude.[46] Earlier the author has expressed a more radical view about the future fate of Canaan: 'Be thou ware, my son Jacob, of taking a wife from any seed of the daughters of Canaan; for all his seed is to be rooted out of the earth. For, owing to the trangression of Ham, Canaan erred, and all his seed shall be destroyed from off the earth and all the residue thereof, and none springing from him shall be saved on the

---

On Jewish attitudes towards inter-marriage, including its ban in Jubilees, see e.g., S.J.D. Cohen, 'From the Bible to the Talmud: The Prohibition of Intermarriage', *Hebrew Annual Review* 7 (1983), 23–39; C. Werman, 'Jubilees 30: Building a Paradigm for the Ban on Intermarriage', *Harvard Theological Review* 90 (1997), 3–36; C. Hayes, 'Intermarriage and Impurity in Ancient Jewish Sources', *Harvard Theological Review* 92 (1999), 3–36.

[46] *Jub* 38:2–14. As 'Aram' often stands for Syria in the Greek translation of the Bible, its mention here might be a reference to the Seleucid empire. See Bickermann (n. 14), 4–5. According to Werman (n. 40), 176 n. 37, 'Aram' (ארם) is a mistake for 'Edom' (אדם) which was the original reading. For the peoples who came to support Esau and his sons see also 37:6–10. The 'Kittim' mentioned there most probably refer to Greek soldiers. On the fate of Canaan see below.

day of judgement' (22:20–21). Indeed it is not only Canaan who is doomed, but all the heathen: 'And as for all the worshippers of idols and the profane, there shall be no hope for them in the land of the living, for they descend into Sheol' (22:22). Perhaps this radical position is to be associated with the next issue.

5. The Land of Canaan. Jubilees treats to a great length the subject of the ownership of, or the right to rule, the Land of Canaan, that is, Eretz Israel. This is brought up in the author's attack against Canaan, the son of Ham:

> And Canaan saw the land of Lebanon to the the river of Egypt, that it was very good, and he went not into the land of his inheritance to the west (that is to) the sea, and he dwelt in the land of Lebanon, eastward and westward from the border of Jordan and from the border of the sea. And Ham, his father, and Cush and Mizraim, his brothers, said unto him ... Dwell not in the dwelling of Shem; for to Shem and to his sons did it come by their lot. Cursed art thou ... But he did not hearken unto them, and dwelt in the land of Lebanon from Hamath to the entering of Egypt, he and his sons until this day. And for this reason that land is called the land of Canaan.[47]

The usurpation of the land by Canaan is contrasted with the behaviour of Madai, son of Japhet. He too did not like the land assigned him by lot, but managed to acquire the land of Media by a peaceful agreement (*Jub.* 10:35). Who were the peoples considered by the author as 'Canaan' at the time of his writing is not too difficult to infer: those who lived in 'the land of Lebanon to the river of Egypt'; 'eastward and westward, from the border of Jordan and from the border of the sea'; 'from Hamath to the entering of Egypt'. The author thus had in mind the coastal, Phoenician cities from Sidon or Tyre in the north to Raphia or Rhinocorura in the south; the population living in the inland regions on to the Jordan, from the Baq'a of Lebanon to the south of Idumaea; and possibly the inhabitants of Transjordan from Batanaea to, say, Edom.

It should be borne in mind that in asserting that the land of Canaan was Shem's lot, the author of Jubilees squarely deviates from the Biblical account (*Gen.* 10:15–20), according to which that land was indeed Canaan's possession. Hence, there can be no doubt about the issue adressed by the author, viz. the right to rule the Land of Israel. If then this polemical writing stemmed from a particular polit-

---

[47] *Jub.* 10:29, 31, 33. For the full version see *Jub.* 8:10–10:35 (Cf. *Gen.* 10:1–11:19).

ical situation, which is most likely, one may regard it as part of a dispute concerning the right of the Hasmonaeans to carry out an expansionist policy that aims at taking control of the Land of Israel.

According to one suggestion, the polemic may be understood as an answer to an accusation raised by Gentiles against the legitimacy of the Hasmonaean conquests. Manetho's and, possibly, Lysimachus' slanderous versions of the Exodus story could have been exploited for this purpose.[48] This line of inquiry has been astutely pursued by H. Lewy: as Jubilees provides the earliest testimony for the conroversy about the ownership of Canaan, and as it was written, in Lewy's view, in the last decades of the Hasmonaean period, its rewritten version of the stories of Genesis was intended to give religious justification for the Hasmonaean conquest against accusations made by Gentiles and based on legal arguments.

Lewy takes as the starting point for this interpretation a story told by Procopius, in which the accusation of illegal conquest by Joshua indeed manifestly appears (*Vandal.* 2.10:13–20). He points out that in that story, which may be associated with a Talmudic tradition that testifies to a dispute over the ownership of the Land of Canaan, the accusation is made by Phoenician refugees. Another clue for the identification of the original accusers is the fact that the Land of Canaan is rendered several times Phoenicia in the Septuagint and several other sources. Added to this is the supplanting of the name 'Canaanites' by 'Phoenicians' in Greek writers. All these pieces of evidence, Lewy argues, indicate that under the impact of the warlike, expansionist policy of the Hasmonaeans Hellenized Phoenicians denounced the Jews for their illegal conquests.[49]

---

[48] On Manetho and Lysimachus (introduction, text, English translation and commentary) see M. Stern, *Greek and Latin Authors on Jews and Judaism*, 1 (Jerusalem 1974), 62–86, 382–8. On Lysimachus see B. Bar-Kochva, 'Lysimachus of Alexandria and the Hostile Traditions concerning the Exodus', *Tarbiz* 69 (2000), 471–506 (Hebrew), but, *pace* Bar-Kochva, I still think that the time of Lysimachus cannot be determined with certainty.

[49] See H. Lewy, 'Ein Rechsstreit um Boden Palästinas im Altertum', *Monatschrift für Geschichte und Wissenschaft des Judentums* 77 (1933), 84–99, 172–80, esp. 90–96. For valuable comments on the stance of the author of Jubilees regarding the reconquest of the Land of Israel see Mendels (n. 39), 64–81. However, his basis for dating the work, namely that John Hyrcanus had completed his conquests by the year 125, has been proven wrong, for we now know that John Hyrcanus' expansionist wars began not earlier than 113; see Barag n. 21; I. Shatzman, 'The Integration of Judaea into the Roman Empire', *Scripta Classica Israelica* 18 (1999), pp. 49–84, at 67–9). Hence, inferences and arguments related to the 120's can hardly be sustained.

Ingenious as it is, Lewy's interpretation of the polemic of Jubilees with regard to the ownership of the Land of Canaan is open to several objections. First, if the illegal ownership of Judaea formed a major theme in the writings of anti-Jewish Hellenistic authors, it is surprising that it is not explicitly attested in the surviving fragments and testimonis of those authors. Even Lysimachus, who vehemently attacks and vituperates the Jews, does not bring up the question of illegal ownership, referring only to the invasion of the country and laying emphasis on horrible sacrilegious behaviour. Besides, he was not a Hellenized Phoenician but, to judge from the focus of his work on Egyptian history, a Greek author from Ptolemaic Egypt. Second, without the later sources, which post-date the Bar-Kochva revolt, it is hardly possible to detect an anti-Jewish denunciation behind the polemic of Jubilees; moreover, the accusation in those sources could have stemmed from a situation that emerged in the post-Second Temple period. Indeed, and this is the third objection, no linking texts are available to bridge the enormous chronological gap between Jubilees and the late sources adduced by Lewy. Fourth, Josephus could have hardly ignored the issue of Jewish illegal conquest and ownership of Judaea—if that had been a charge brought up by anti-Jewish authors. As it is, he does not deal with it, neither in the Jewish Antiquities nor in the Against Apion, works where one should expect him to do so. Finally, written originally in Hebrew, the work would have been ineffective as an answer to accusations made in Greek. Although one cannot be sure that the Greek translation was first made as late as its first appearance in Christian literature, not earlier than the third century C.E., this is enough to indicate that the author did not address a Greek audience.

It is therefore better to seek another explanation, and there is one at hand, namely to associate the polemic with an internal Jewish issue. The invective may well be construed as an exhortation to take control of Eretz Israel, unjustly usurped by 'Canaan', that is, the nations roundabout Judaea. It stands to reason that the military confrontations with the neighbouring nations, which burst out in the wake of the persecution of Antiochus IV and which play a major role in I Maccabees and II Maccabees, forced the Jews of Judaea to take a position about the objects of those engagements. Opinions varied, as may be inferred from various indications in our sources, and it is plausible to regard the polemic as part of a Jewish debate on the merits, dangers and religious justification of the expansionist

Hasmonaean wars. In sum, the author adresses his words to a stirred up Jewish audience, one that is trying to shape its future.⁵⁰

Jubilees is clearly not a historical work and the author is not interested in presenting an accurate, detailed account of the military exploits and political achievements of the Hasmonaeans. The issue he addresses in these chapters is the confrontation between the Jews of Judaea and their neighbours, Greeks and non-Greeks alike. The basic attitude revealed is that of hatred towards and fear from the Gentiles surrounding the people of Israel. They pose a menace that can be eliminated only with their destruction or subjugation by war. The author of Jubilees thus exhibits a more extreme attitude towards the nations roundabout Israel than that of the authors of I Maccabees and II Maccabees. Harsh treatment of those nations would be the kind of action endorsed and exhorted by the author and his milieu. In view of the considerable number of fragments of the original Hebrew work that were found in several caves at Qumran, the author probably belonged to the Qumran sect or to a proto-circle of it.⁵¹ At any rate, it is likely that the author of such a work will have welcomed the aggressive policy pursued by the Hasmonaeans against the Gentile peoples adjacent to Judaea, particularly the destructive actions of Judas Maccabaeus or of John Hyrcanus. The restraints adopted by Jonathan and Simon could hardly be to his liking, and it is more than doubtful that he will have endorsed the Judaization policy of John Hyrcanus.

---

⁵⁰ Cf. P.S. Alexander, 'Retelling the Old Testament', in D.A. Carson and H.G. Williamson (eds.), *It Was Written: Scripture Citing Scripture* (Cambridge 1988), 99–121, who writes: 'The powerful anti-Canaanite thrust of this section, coupled with the assertion of the rights of Shem descendants to the "land of Canaan", should surely be seen as propaganda for the territorial expansion of the Hasmonaean state' (102–3). I find it unlikely that the polemic of the author against Canaan is a purely theological discussion; *contra* M. Kister, *Journal of Jewish Studies* 44 (1993), 288 n. 40; Werman (n. 40), 101–2 n. 107. But Werman (n. 40), 333–8, is right to emphasize that the author envisages complete destruction of the nations living in the Land of Israel and the eventual rule of the Sons of Jacob over the entire world.

⁵¹ See, e.g., Nicklesburg (n. 38), 73–80; Wintermute (n. 38), 44; Delcor (n. 40), 435; G. Boccaccini, *Beyond the Essene Hypothesis* (Grand Rapids, Michigan 1998), 86–7.

Conclusion

Jubilees's attitude towards the Gentiles appears as well in The Testaments of the Twelve Patriarchs, a composite work that originated in the second century B.C.E.[52] The author/s of these works approved of or even encouraged the conducting of wars in order to annihilate the Gentiles, to demolish their tempels and to destroy their cities. In the Testament of Levi the killing of the Shechemites is depicted as part of a divine plan to destroy the Canaanites and to grant the country to Israel.[53] Admonition against marriage with Gentile, Canaanite women is emphasized in the Testament of Judah.[54] It is also worth to bear in mind that according to the Book of Esther, the Jews mercilessly killed their enemies: five hundred men in Shushan and seventy-five thousand people throughout the kingdom (9:5–6, 15). It emerges that the annihilation of enemies who posed a menace to the existence of the Jews was considered as natural. But of course there is a difference: Jubilees and the Testaments of the Twelve Patriarchs endorse and call for the destruction of the Gentiles on religious grounds; in Esther it is a reaction to a specific attempt to massacre the Jews. What is the significance of these views and attitudes with regard to the Hasmonaean policy towards Gentiles?

According to I Maccabees and II Maccabees, as has been shown, Judas Maccabaeus annihilated the Gentile enemies, destroyed their cities and demolished their cult sites, a policy he carried out whenever he had the opportunity to do so. One may argue that in all or most such cases he responded to actions or threats made by the Gentiles and did not act on his own initiative. But then it may be counter-argued that the implementation of a policy depends, more often than not, on particular circumstances. Moreover, and in any case, it is noteworthy that Judas' actions accord well with the views enunciated and the lines of action exhorted by the authors of Jubilees and the Testaments of the Twelve Patriarchs. The manner Jonathan and Simon conducted their campaigns and foreign relations, how-

---

[52] On the nature of this work and its affinities with Qumran and other Jewish writings see, e.g., O. Eissfeld, *The Old Testament: An Introduction* (Eng. trans.) (New York-Evanstone 1965), 630–36; G. Vermes and M. Goodman, in Schürer (n. 1), III.2, 767–80, Delcor (n. 40), 438–43); Boccaccini (n. 51), 86–7.

[53] Testament of Levi 7:1. See also 2:2; 5:3–4; 6:2–6; Testament of Simon 6:3–5; Testament of Judah 3:1–8; 4:1–2; 5:5; 6:3–5; 7:3.

[54] Testament of Judah 11:1; 16:4; 17:1.

ever, is conspicuously not congruous with such views and attitudes. Certainly the political circumstances were different, and perhaps Jonathan and Simon found a way to justify on religious, not political, grounds their not following the deeds of their dead brother. Whether the new policy reflects a real and comprehensive change in their attititudes towards the 'nations roundabout' rather than the need to yield to practical political considerations may be doubted. Yet there were Jews—few, many or a substantial part of the population—who held to the view that it was religiously ordained to pursue the war against the Gentiles, who should be eliminated from the Land of Israel. These Jews will have criticized the political conduct of Jonathan and Simon as a wrong policy, a religiously criminal failure to carry out the divine commands concerning the Gentiles. Hence one may suggest that John Hyrcanus renewed the aggressive policy against the Gentiles adjacent to Judaea, being mindful of and sensitive to the criticism that had been directed against his father and uncle.

Before suggesting another explanation, it will be useful to present in brief various finds which have been unearthed in archaeological excavations in several sites during the last two decades or so, and which show that Josephus erred in reporting that John Hyrcanus launched upon aggressive campaigns against neighbouring Gentile cities and peoples soon after the death of Antiochus Sidetes VII in 129 B.C.E.[55] To judge by the excavations of and coins found in Tel Beer-Sheva, the Hellenistic temple there was demolished and the site abandoned some time after 112/11.[56] Archaeological evidence indicates that the local temple of Lachish suffered destruction, probably during the Hasmonaean conquest of Idumaea.[57] The latest Seleucid coin found in a hoard in Marisa (of the mint of Ascalon) is of the year 113/2 and no later Seleucid coins were found in the entire area of the city; 68 coins of John Hyrcanus were discovered in the

---

[55] Joseph. *BC* 1:62–3; *AJ* 13:254–8. For a good survey and discussion of the finds see G. Finkielsztein, 'More Evidence on John Hyrcanus I's Conquests: Lead Weights and Rhodian Amphora Stamps', *Bulletin of the Anglo-Israel Archaeological Society* 16 (1998), 33–63.

[56] I. Shatzman, *The Armies of the Hasmonaeans and Herod* (Tübingen 1991), 55–6; A. Kushnir and H. Gitler, 'Numismatic Evidence from Tel Beer-Sheva and the Beginning of the Nabatean Coinage', *Israel Numismatic Journal* 12 (1992–3), 13–20, esp. 16–8.

[57] Finkielsztein (n. 55), 48, 55 n. 6; no details are given.

site. The latest funerary inscription known dates from the year 112/1. Two Rhodian amphora stamps are dated with certainty after 108/7. A Lead weight inscription attests to the existenc of an *agoranomos* (Agathocles) of the city in the year 108/7. Some evidence points to the existence of Jewish ritual baths (*miqwa'ot*). The excavations in the site of the lower city indicate that the buildings were not set in fire or demolished deliberately but collapsed sometime after they had been abandoned.[58] The latest coins, except those of the Hasmonaeans, uncovered on Mount Gerizim are dated to 112/1 or 111/10; 52 coins are of John Hyrcanus and 480 of Alexander Jannaeus, but only about a half of the 13000 coins found in the site have been identified. Clear signs of burning and destruction are in evidence in all the areas excavated in the site, except the one where the Hasmonaean coins were discovered.[59] The latest amphora stamp found in Samaria is dated about 110 and the latest coin known with certainty from the site is of the year 112/1. The excavations of the site have supplied considerable evidence for the siege and destruction of the city.[60] The latest datable amphora stamp from Tel Istabah (Scythopolis) is from about 108 and the latest Seleucid coins are of Antiochus VIII and Antiochus IX; traces of a general fire were unearthed in the site.[61]

---

[58] For a comprehensive account see Finkielsztein (n. 55), 33–42, 47–8, and for the hoard Barkay (n. 21). A. Kloner reported in several of his publications of the destruction of Marisa as a result of its conquest by John Hyrcanus; see, e.g., 'The Economy of Hellenistic Maresha', in Z.H. Archibald, J. Davies, V. Gabrielson and G.J. Oliver (eds.), *Hellenistic Economies* (London and New York 2001), 103–31, at 111. In my visit to the site, guided by A. Kloner, I was not able to notice signs of burning or destruction, and therefore raised the possibility that the population of Marisa continued to live there for some time after the Hasmonaean conquest (n. 56, 97). For the view that there was no burning or demolition of the inhabited area see Finkielsztein (n. 55), 47, who confirmed it to me by personal communication. At my request Prof. Kloner looked again at the matter and wrote to me that 'there are no indications of burning, but of abandonment', and I wish to thank him for this information.

[59] For the latest report see Y. Magen, 'Mt. Gerizim—A Temple City', *Qadmoniot* 120 (2000), 74–118, esp. 114–5, 118 (Hebrew). For a previous report see Y. Magen, 'Mount Gerizim and the Samaritans', in F. Manns and E. Elliata (eds.), *Early Christianity in Context: Monuments and Documents* (Jerusalem 1993), pp. 91–148, esp. 103–4, 119–20, 142–3, but the number of the coins found has tremendously increased.

[60] Shatzman (n. 56), 61 with n. 97; Finkielsztein (n. 55), 40–41.

[61] R. Bar-Nathan and G. Mazor, 'Beth-Shean in the Hellenistic period', *Qadmoniot* 107–108 (1994), 87–91 (Hebrew); Finkielsztein (n. 55), 40–42.

This archaeological evidence makes clear that John Hyrcanus started his campaigns shortly after the year 113 B.C.E.; Josephus' wrong chronology of those campaigns may have stemmed from his being confused by his sources, notably Nicolaus of Damascus. On the other hand, not only does the archaeological evidence corroborate the conquest of Marisa, Shechem, Mount Gerizim, Samaria and Scythopolis, but also provides additional information, that is, concerning places not reported by Josephus to have been conquered: Beer-Sheva and Lachish.[62] The precise chronological sequence of the campaigns cannot as yet be determined with certainty,[63] and it may be added that the conquest of Adora, Medaba and Samoga is known only thanks to Josephus, but there is no reason to doubt the reliability of his report. It is more important to observe that Josephus seems to provide a clue for the understanding of the circumstances and considerations that led John Hyrcanus to launch upon aggressive campaigns shortly after the year 113. He narrates that Hyrcanus revolted from the Macedonians after the death of Antiochus Sidetes; that his country flourished during the reigns of Alexander Zebina and especially during the reign of the brothers/cousins Antiochus VIII and Antiochus IX; and that Hyrcanus amassed enormous sums of money, taking advantage of the wars between the contenders for the Seleucid throne (*AJ* 13:272–4). The war between Antiochus VIII and Antiochus IX had started *ca.* 115 and went on for many years, exhausting both of the two antagonists (*AJ* 13.327). These pieces of information suggest that about 113–112 John Hyrcanus, who had probably utilized the peaceful years to build up his military resources, came to the conclusion that the time was opportune to take advantage of the general decline in the Seleucid power, and particularly of the Seleucid sibling war. Before launching upon his massive military campaign, he apparently sent envoys to Rome and got a *senatum consultum*, which supported Hyrcanus' territorial claims against Antiochus son of Antiochus, that is, Antiochus IX Cyzicenus.[64]

---

[62] See above n. 20. For the conquest of Scythopolis see also Syncellus I, 559 (Dindorf) and cf. *Megilat Ta'anit* 10 with the scholium thereto.

[63] For suggestions see Barag (n. 21), 8–11; Finkielsztein (n. 55), 56–60.

[64] Joseph. *AJ* 14:247–55. On the struggle between the Seleucid contenders see F. Millar, in Schürer (n. 1), I, 132–3, 208–9. On the *s.c.*, its date and relation to the campaigns of John Hyrcanus see also Shatzman (n. 49), 66–9. It is well to bear in mind that Hyrcanus started recruiting foreign mercenaries some time after his settlement with Antiochus VII (*BJ* 1:61; *AJ* 13:249).

It is then very likely that John Hyrcanus renewed, in certain respects, the policy of Judas Maccabaeus by the time he realized the political conditions had changed. In other words, the decline of the Seleucid rule and the increase of his own resources and power made it possible for him to ignore the political considerations that had induced Jonathan and Simon to accept restraints in the conduct of their campaigns and foreign affairs. Such an explanation need not exclude the possibility that consideration for internal criticism of the foreign policy of his father and uncle contributed to his decision to launch upon expansionist wars. But John Hyrcanus did not simply renew Judas' policy. To judge both by the archaeological evidence and by the information of Josephus, Gentile temples, as well as the Samaritan temple on Mount Gerizim, were indeed demolished, and several cities of the Gentiles did suffer destruction. But there were cities that were spared. Moreover, in Idumaea Hyrcanus hit upon an entirely new means to solve the problem of the encounter with the Gentiles, that is, their Judaization. He could not possibly allow the Idumaeans to stay in Idumaea as Gentiles. On the other hand, their expulsion would have ruined a large region, and was probably considered dangerous both on political and military grounds. Their Judaization, even under duress, was to solve the problem.[65]

The conquests of John Hyrcanus should not be regarded merely as exploitation of opportune circumstances. In a certain, important respect they enunciated a basic Hasmonaean, and Jewish, attitude towards Gentiles living in the Land of Israel; that is, John Hyrcanus sought to implement the aspiration that had emerged in the time of Judas to rule Eretz Israel. According to the author of I Maccabees (15:33), even Simon, who was constrained to apply moderation in his relations with the Gentiles, asserted in his answer to Antiochus VII: 'We have neither taken other men's land, nor have we possession of that which appertaineth to others, but of the inheritance of our fathers; howbeit, it was had in possession of our enemies wrongfully for a certain time'.[66]

---

[65] On the novelty of Judaization cf. S.I.D. Cohen, *The Beginnings of Jewishness* (Berkeley and Los Angeles 1999), 118. Cohen goes on (119–25) to suggest various considerations and possible Biblical models that could have induced and may have been utilized by John Hyrcanus to introduce this new policy.

[66] It is a real pleasure to contribute this article to a volume in honour of Prof. Louis H. Feldman, whose *Jew and Gentile in the Ancient World*, as well as his numerous other publications, have taught us all so much about the relations between Jews and the 'others' in the Graeco-Roman world.

THE ANCIENT LISTS OF CONTENTS OF JOSEPHUS' *ANTIQUITIES*

Joseph Sievers

In almost the entire Greek and Latin manuscript tradition, each book of Josephus' *Antiquities* is preceded by a somewhat schematic list of its contents.[1] Although printed in most editions and in some translations (LCL, Reinach, Nodet), these lists have received scarce attention from scholars. Since Louis Feldman's contributions to the study of Josephus have spanned the entire range of the works of Josephus, especially the *Antiquities*, a systematic study of these lists may be a small but fitting tribute to his endeavors and achievements.

Ancient Summaries, Chapter Headings, and Lists of Contents

> Die Geschichte des Kapitels (*caput*, κεφάλαιον) ist noch nicht geschrieben und auch ich gedenke nicht sie hier zu geben: es würde ein ganzes Buch daraus.[2]

The ancient reader, not unlike the postmodern individual suffering from information overload, was apt to seek information about the contents of a book before reading through it, or to have it summarized at some point. Ancient authors and 'editors' sought to fill this need in various ways. Historians such as Polybius and orators like Isocrates provided summaries often called κεφάλαια (LSJ: 'summing

---

[1] I would like to thank the staff of the Bodleian Library and of the Biblioteca Apostolica Vaticana for granting me access to some of the manuscripts discussed here. Thanks are due also to the library of the Deutsches Archäologisches Institut (Rome), the Pontificia Università S. Croce, and the Pontifical Biblical Institute for providing me with material otherwise not easily available. I am grateful to Prof. Martin Goodman, Oxford, and to Prof. Guglielmo Cavallo, Rome, for helpful suggestions. My colleague Prof. Frederick Brenk, S.J., graciously undertook to carefully read a semi-final version of this paper. Any remaining errors are of course my own responsibility.

[2] 'The history of the chapter (...) has not yet been written, nor do I intend to present it here: it would take an entire book.' Hermann Mutschmann, 'Inhaltsangabe und Kapitelüberschrift im antiken Buch,' *Hermes* 46 (1911): 93–107, here 95.

up').[3] Chariton's *Callirhoe*, a popular novel composed c. 25 B.C.E.–50 C.E., contains summaries of the previous books in 5.1.1–2 and 8.1.1. G.P. Goold, its most recent editor, comments on the first of these summaries: 'This recapitulation, modeled on the summaries introducing Books 2, 3, 4, 5, and 7 of Xenophon's *Anabasis*, has suggested that *Callirhoe* was conceived as a publication in two rolls, Book 5 beginning the second' (LCL [1995] p. 231). In this comment we run up against the question of authorship because Carleton S. Brownson in his edition of the *Anabasis* expresses an *opinio communis* when he states that 'All these summaries must have been the work of a late editor' (LCL rev. ed. 1998, 146). It seems to be unclear whether such an editor was active before the composition of the *Callirhoe* or later.

Such summaries need to be distinguished from the lists of contents found at the beginning of each book of Josephus' *Antiquities* and of other historical writings. A first question is one of terminology. If we search Niese's text of Josephus' *Antiquities*, we look in vain for a noun defining these lists. The Latin mss. edited by Blatt use a formula that includes the words *expliciunt capitula* (roughly 'here end the chapter headings') at the end of the list of contents of Books 3, 4, and 5.[4] The Codex Vaticanus Graecus 147 (14th century), which contains most of *Ant.* 3–15, in its present form opens with a Greek table of contents entitled Πίναξ, listing the folio number on which each book begins. The lists in which we are interested here, however, are incorporated in the text and identifiable primarily through the initial letter written in larger uncial script.[5] In the Budé edition of Diodorus Siculus, instead, the list of contents at the beginning of each book is sometimes entitled Πίναξ (so Books 14 and 19). In the case of Josephus' *Antiquities*, Niese in his editions uses the designation '*Argumenta*,' Schreckenberg calls the same '*Hypotheseis*.'[6] Thackeray

---

[3] Polybius 1.13.8; 1.65.5; 3.5.9. Cf. Paul Pédech, *La méthode historique de Polybe* (Paris: Belles Lettres, 1964), 47. Isocrates provides summaries '... breaking up the discourse, as it were, into what we call general heads' (τὰ καλούμενα κεφάλαια) Speech 15.68 (*Antidosis*; Norlin, LCL).

[4] Franz Blatt, *The Latin Josephus*. Part I. *Introduction and Text: The Antiquities, Books I–V* (Aarhus: Universitetsforlaget, 1958).

[5] In the Oxford Codex Bodleiensis Misc. Graecus 186 (*O* in Niese) the lists of contents of *Ant.* 1–10 are set off from the text through indentation and in particular through red initial letters.

[6] Heinz Schreckenberg, *Die Flavius-Josephus-Tradition in Antike und Mittelalter* (Leiden: Brill, 1972) 180–81.

treats the same texts in an appendix entitled 'An Ancient Table of Contents' but on the same page he speaks of 'summaries of contents.'[7] Nodet and other French authors refer simply to 'sommaires.' Hence it seems important to first clarify the terminology and its meaning across different languages.

A 'Table of Contents' is generally placed at the beginning or end of an entire volume, not split into different parts for each 'book.' It also normally includes reference to folio, page, or section of a volume. Reynolds and Wilson correctly identify the table of contents as one of the advantages of the codex over the book roll.[8] But here we are not dealing with tables of contents in the strict sense. *Hypothesis* is a term used for the front matter added to Greek drama, including an outline of the plot as well as other information.[9] It is occasionally used with reference to rhetorical works[10] but is hardly if ever applied to the works of historians. The French 'sommaire' is a very general and vague term that does not highlight the specificity of the lists of contents prefixed to individual books of Josephus' *Antiquities* and to other works. The terms 'capitulum/a' ('chapter[s]') and Πίναξ ('table of contents,' but also 'writing tablet' [with catalogue entry]) are attested in pre-modern usage but are ambiguous. Thus the most unambiguous term may be *argumentum*. It and its plural *argumenta* are not ancient designations, but they are in current use by palaeographers and codicologists and have been used by classical philologists.[11]

---

[7] *Josephus*. Vol. 4 *Jewish Antiquities I–IV* (trans. H.St.J. Thackeray; LCL; Cambridge, Mass.: Harvard University Press, 1930), 636.

[8] Leighton D. Reynolds and N.G. Wilson, *Scribes and Scholars: a Guide to the Transmission of Greek and Latin Literature* (2nd ed.; Oxford: Clarendon Press, 1974), 31.

[9] The use of such a system ultimately goes back to Aristophanes of Byzantium (c. 257–180 B.C.). These summaries found only limited application in non-dramatic texts. See Bernhard Zimmermann, 'Hypothesis,' *DNP* 5 (1998), 819–20.

[10] For twelve speeches of Isocrates we have *hypotheseis* of varying length, attributed to an anonymous grammarian. They mention the occasion and context of the speech in addition to offering a brief summary. Their form is quite different from the *argumenta* for the *Antiquities* or other works. *The Kellis Isocrates Codex (P.Kell. III Gr. 95)* (ed. K.A. Worp and A. Rijksbaron; Dakhleh Oasis Project: Monograph 5; Oxford: Oxbow, 1997), a recently found mid-fourth century wooden codex, contains three speeches by or attributed to Isocrates. Two are preceded by a brief *hypothesis* (*Ad Demonicum* lines a–d [p. 59] and *Ad Nicoclem* lines a–d [p. 91]). These *hypotheseis* are much shorter than the ones attributed to the anonymous grammarian and have been added to the ms. by a second scribe (*ibid.*, p. 24). Clearly they were not part of the text by Isocrates.

[11] See Denis Muzerelle, *Vocabulaire codicologique: Répertoire méthodique des termes français relatifs aux manuscrits* (Rubricae 1; Paris: CEMI, 1985), #433.06 (with figure 159). 'Argument' is here defined as 'Analyse du contenu d'un texte ou d'une de ses

The closest descriptive English equivalent seems to be 'list of contents.' The English term 'argument' includes as one of its meanings 'an abstract or summary esp. of a literary work'[12] and may serve as a suitable equivalent of the Latin but in order to avoid any ambiguity, here the Latin term will be used.

The question of when, how, by whom, and for what specific purpose these *argumenta* were composed has rarely been addressed, and scholars treating this topic do not always seem to be aware of earlier discussions.[13] No exhaustive treatment of the subject will be attempted here, but some data that are rarely considered together will be surveyed in a way that may prove helpful for further studies.

The earliest manuscript that includes the end of one book and the *argumenta* and the beginning of the following one seems to be Codex Vaticanus Graecus 1288, dated to the second half of the fifth or the early sixth century.[14] It contains the end of Book 79 and the

---

parties, placée en tête de ce texte ou de cette partie.' 'Sommaire' is given as an equivalent not only of 'Argument' but also of 'Table,' (here meaning table of contents) (#433.07). An Italian definition of 'Argomento,' based on Muzerelle's, is provided by Marilena Maniaci, *Terminologia del libro manoscritto* (Addenda 3; Rome: Istituto Centrale per la patologia del libro, 1996), p. 218 (with figure 173). There does not seem to be a comparable English handbook. The closest equivalent appears to be Michelle P. Brown, *Understanding Illuminated Manuscripts: A Guide to Technical Terms* (London: The British Library – The Paul Getty Museum, 1994). As its title states it concentrates on manuscript illumination and does not have an entry for '*argumentum*' or related terms.

[12] *Merriam-Webster's Collegiate Dictionary* (10th ed.; Springfield, Mass.: Merriam-Webster, 1994).

[13] Jean Irigoin ('Titres, sous-titres et sommaires dans les œuvres des historiens grecs du Ier siècle avant J.-C. au Ve siècle après J.-C.,' in *Titres et articulations du texte dans les œuvres antiques. Actes du colloque international de Chantilly 13–15 décembre 1994* [ed. J.-C. Fredouille et al.; Collection des Études Augustiniennes Série Antiquité 152; Paris: Institut d' Études Augustiniennes/Turnhout: Brepols, 1997], 127–34) makes no reference to Etienne Nodet's discussion of the topic in 'Jésus et Jean Baptiste selon Josèphe,' *RB* 92 (1985): 497–524 or to Nodet's edition and discussion of the texts in *Flavius Josèphe, Les Antiquités Juives* (Paris: Cerf), vol. 1 (1990, ³2000), X–XII; vol 2 (1995), V–VI. Nor does Nodet refer to Irigoin in his more recent treatments of the topic: *Baptême et resurrection: Le témoignage de Josèphe* (Paris: Cerf, 1999), 127–32; *Flavius Josèphe, Les Antiquités Juives* (vol. 3; Paris: Cerf, 2001), V–VII. Neither Nodet nor Irigoin seem to be aware of Hermann Mutschmann, 'Inhaltsangabe und Kapitelüberschrift im antiken Buch,' *Hermes* 46 (1911): 93–107 or of Richard Laqueur's article 'Ephoros,' (*Hermes* 46 [1911]: 161–206, in which he discusses Josephus (167–175) and the question of *argumenta* (178–188). I have not seen B.-J. Schröder, *Titel und Text: Zur Entwicklung lateinischer Gedichtüberschriften. Mit Untersuchungen zu lateinischen Buchtiteln, Inhaltsverzeichnissen und anderen Gliederungsmitteln* (Berlin-New York: De Gruyter, 1999).

[14] Available in facsimile *Cassii Dionis Cocceiani Historiarum romanarum lib. LXXIX–LXXX*

beginning of Book 80 of Cassius Dio's *Roman History*, composed in the early part of the third century. The *argumenta* of Book 80 consist of several short numbered phrases, generally beginning with περί ('About...') or ὡς ('How...'). A concluding sentence indicates the number of years covered in this book. It is followed by a list of the consuls for those years. The same scheme is followed in later mss. for earlier books of Dio's *History*. They generally also include an opening sentence τάδε ἔνεστιν ἐν τῷ ('the following are the contents of...' plus book number, author, and title). The *argumenta* in Josephus' *Antiquities* have an identical structure and similar wording (obviously without lists of consuls).

A similar procedure is followed in the *Ecclesiastical History* of Eusebius of Caesarea (c. 260–340 C.E.). Here Eduard Schwartz has adduced important reasons to show that the *argumenta* go back to the author himself.[15] Similarly, Marrou has shown that the *argumenta* of Augustine's *City of God* on the whole were authored by Augustine himself.[16] Thus the question arises whether also other, and earlier, authors provided their works with lists of contents. This question is generally answered in the affirmative for the *Natural History* by Pliny the Elder (d. 79 C.E.), in which the entire first book consists of a list of contents for the remaining Books 2–37. At the end of his introductory letter Pliny claims 'quid singulis contineretur libris huic epistulae subiunxi' ('I have appended to this letter a table of contents of the several books').[17] He also admits that he has adopted this system from the book by [Valerius] Soranus (d. shortly after 82 B.C.E.) entitled ἐποπτίδες ('Women admitted to the highest grade of the mysteries'[?]). Pliny was followed by Aulus Gellius in his *Attic Nights*, who after his preface provides a list of contents, book by book.[18]

---

quae supersunt. (preface by P. Franchi de' Cavalieri; Leipzig: Harrassowitz, 1908). See Irigoin, 'Titres, sous-titres et sommaires' (note 13 above), 131.

[15] Eusebius *Werke* 2. Bd. *Die Kirchengeschichte* ed. Eduard Schwartz (GCS Eusebius 2.3; Leipzig: Hinrichs, 1909), CLI–CLIII. Giorgio Pasquali (*Göttingische Gelehrte Anzeigen* 1909, p. 285) has shown the same for Eusebius' *Life of Constantine*.

[16] H.-I. Marrou, 'La division en chapitres des livres de *La Cité de Dieu*,' *Mélanges J. De Ghellinck*, (Gembloux: Duculot, 1951), 239.

[17] *Preface* 33 (Rackham, LCL).

[18] On Pliny and Gellius see Peter L. Schmidt, 'Paratextuelle Elemente in lateinischer Fachprosa,' in *Titres et articulations du texte dans les œuvres antiques. Actes du colloque international de Chantilly 13–15 décembre 1994* [ed. J.-C. Fredouille et al.; Collection des Études Augustiniennes Série Antiquité 152; Paris: Institut d' Études Augustiniennes/Turnhout: Brepols, 1997], 223–32, esp. 225–30.

Among earlier writings, the manuscript tradition includes *argumenta* at the beginning of several extant books of the *Library of History* of Diodorus Siculus (written c. 60–30 B.C.E.).[19] Irigoin assumes but does not argue that these *argumenta* go back to Diodorus himself.[20] In the same context he also states, apparently without foundation, that Dionysius of Halicarnassus in his *Roman Antiquities*, which began to appear in 7 B.C.E., used the same technique. Dionysius does refer to a resumptive summary (ἀνακεφαλαίωσις) at the end of his first book (1.90), but this is not given in the form of *argumenta* and follows rather than precedes the material summarized. No *argumenta* are provided for the other extant books.

Of interest for the use of *argumenta* are also the column headings found in a few papyri. They were added by a different hand than that of the scribe of the regular text and fairly fully preserved in the Didymus papyrus, dated to the early second century C.E. by its first editors.[21] Similarly, though badly damaged, such column headings are visible on P.Herc. 558.[22]

Laqueur has studied the column headings of the Didymus papyrus and found that they do not correspond well to the layout of the particular manuscripts they are part of. Therefore, argues Laqueur,

---

[19] On this see the Richard Laqueur's posthumous study, based in part on his *Habilitationsschrift* completed in 1907, *Diodors Geschichtswerk: die Überlieferung von Buch I–V* (ed. Kai Brodersen; Frankfurt am Main: P. Lang, 1992), 24–25. Laqueur considers the *argumenta* of Books 1, 4, and 11 late additions, or rather substitutions, for lost ones. He emphatically attributes the other *argumenta* to Diodorus himself (*ibid.* 73). Elsewhere he argues that Diodorus does not mention his name in the proem to his work, because he includes it in the *argumenta* (R. Laqueur, 'Ephoros,' *Hermes* 46 [1911]: 195).

[20] 'Titres, sous-titres et sommaires' (note 13 above), 130.

[21] *Didymi de Demosthene commenta* ed. H. Diels and W. Schubart (Leipzig: Teubner, 1904), IV.

Column headings: 'paginae sive columnae voluminis titulis illius alterius, ut videtur, scribae manu superscriptae sunt.' No specific dating for the column headings is provided.

[22] See Tiziano Dorandi, 'La rassegna dei filosofi di Filodemo,' *Rendiconti dell'Accademia di Archeologia, Lettere e Belle Arti di Napoli* 55 (1980): 31–49; cf. Mario Capasso, *Manuale di papirologia ercolanese* (Galatina, Lecce: Congedo, 1991), 165. Wilhelm Crönert, the first editor ('Herkulanensische Bruchstücke einer Geschichte des Sokrates und seiner Schule,' *Rheinisches Museum für Philologie* Neue Folge 57 [1902]: 285–300), noticed the remains of what he called 'Kapitelüberschriften' (chapter headings). He also noted that they were added later, by a different hand (291 n. 1). Though according to Crönert these are the earliest 'chapter headings' in any manuscript, he refers to an even earlier usage in inscriptions and cites as examples *Die Inschriften von Magnesia am Maeander* (ed. O. Kern; Berlin: Speman, 1900) #98 and #100 of the 2nd cent. B.C.E.).

they existed before and independent of the preserved manuscript copy. Laqueur distinguishes four types of column headings:

1. Introduced by τίς (Col. 2, 7, 8, 11, 14)
2. Introduced by ὅτι (Col. 2, 9, 10, 13)
3. περὶ with genitive (Col. 4, 8, 11 [bis], 12, 14)
4. Nominative (Col. 6, 10)

He further argues that they follow the same pattern as the *argumenta*, first visible for us in the *Library of History* of Diodorus.[23]

Nothing like *argumenta* is preserved in historians earlier than Diodorus. However, there are some intriguing indications in the work of Polybius. In the fragmentary proem at the beginning of the second decade of his work (11.1a.1), he states that some people might ask themselves why he has not included προγραφαί, as earlier authors did, but has used προεκθέσεις instead. Both these terms can roughly mean 'preface,' but evidently for Polybius they are not synonymous. In his work, προεκθέσεις are defined as summaries concerning single Olympiads. They are included in the text as integral part of the work (11.1a.4). As for προγραφαί, they have a less secure status. In Walbank's translation 'they are held in little account and get destroyed.'[24] As a matter of fact, nothing of what Polybius called προγραφαί is preserved for his work. Already Laqueur took this precarious position of the προγραφαί to mean that they were not part of the text itself but prefixed to it in some way. He explicitly identified them with the *argumenta* of later works: 'die προγραφαί sind nichts anderes als unsere argumenta.'[25] Walbank thinks that these lists of contents by Polybius

---

[23] R[ichard] Laqueur, 'Die litterarische Stellung des Anonymus Argentinensis,' *Hermes* 43 (1908): 220–28, here 221–22.
[24] ὀλιγορούμενον καὶ φθειρόμενον τὸ τῶν προγραφῶν γένος (11.1a.3) transl. F.W. Walbank, *A Historical Commentary on Polybius* (3 vols.; Oxford: Clarendon, 1957–79), 2:267. This translation follows the acute observations by Richard Laqueur ('Ephoros,' *Hermes* 46 [1911]: 178–88) who discusses the distinction between προγραφαί and προεκθέσεις in Polybius. Paton's translation of the same passage 'prologues (προγραφαί) were now neglected and had degenerated in style' (LCL) goes in an entirely different direction, followed by Pédech (*La méthode historique de Polybe*, 509–10 n. 78), who comments on this phrase 'Les mots... ne signifient pas que les προγραφαί sont endommagées par des accidents matériels ou négligées par les copistes, mais que c'était, á l'époque de Polybe, un genre dédaigné et corrompu (par l'abus de la rhétorique).' However, degeneration 'in style' is nowhere specified in the Greek text. Also, it would be odd for Polybius to notify the reader that he had been using a literary genre that was disdained and corrupted.
[25] 'Ephoros,' *Hermes* 46 (1911): 181.

were 'either attached to the outside of the scroll' (citing Jerome, *Commentary on Ezechiel,* Preface to Book 5 [CCSL 75.185] in support) 'or preceding the text, but inside.'[26] Mutschmann considered three possibilities, namely, that the *argumenta* were originally written on the inside or on the outside of the book roll, or on a separate label attached to it.[27] A systematic study of literary papyri may yet enlighten us further on the question of how and where *argumenta* were first used.

As a result of this preliminary survey of primarily historical works it is clear that the use of *argumenta* has to be distinguished from the tables of contents of codices. *Argumenta* at the beginning of each book predate the codex form and are most suited to the book roll. While some *argumenta* were supplied late and are unevenly represented in the manuscript tradition (as for example for Josephus' *War*), others unquestionably go back to the author's time, if not to the author himself.

The arguments against the authenticity of the extant *argumenta* are generally based on the following points: (a) greater variation in the manuscript tradition when compared to the main text of the work; (b) sloppiness, uneven coverage, incompleteness, and downright errors in the lists of contents.

These issues are similar for most extant *argumenta*. If we take into consideration the position of the *argumenta* as front matter on book rolls, clearly distinguished from the main text, and more liable to loss or mutilation, point (a) loses its probative force. Point (b) is weakened if we take into account that *argumenta* may have been considered an optional aid to the reader, and were perhaps added not by the author himself but by one or more assistants.[28]

The *Argumenta* in Josephus' *Antiquities*

From all of the above one may deduce that it is a priori possible that the *argumenta* go back to the original 'edition' of the *Antiquities*. In this case, however, external factors can only suggest the *possibility*

---

[26] *A Historical Commentary on Polybius*, 2:266. Laqueur, to whom he attributes the latter view, does not seem to discuss the precise position of the προγραφαί.

[27] 'Inhaltsangabe und Kapitelüberschrift,' 100.

[28] Mutschmann ('Inhaltsangabe und Kapitelüberschrift,' 99) suggests that such a technical task may have been entrusted to a 'Corrector.'

of the provenance of the *argumenta*. Close study of the lists of contents themselves may provide some more specific indications. Such a study has so far been done only by Nodet, for *Ant.* 1–7 and 18.[29] Other authors have provided only brief but sometimes helpful hints.

Alfred von Gutschmid proposed that the 'Summarien' (= *argumenta*), if not composed by Josephus himself, were produced by a 'servus litteratus,' by order of Josephus.[30] Thackeray expressed a similar view: '[T]hough it is improbable that these ... chapter headings are the production of his [Josephus'] pen, they may well not be far removed from him in date. They are ostensibly written by a Jew (...), and the phraseology occasionally suggests the hand of one of the author's assistants.'[31] Laqueur in his detailed study of paratextual elements in ancient historians argued that Josephus, just as Diodorus, wrote προγραφαί (= *argumenta*). He noted that the author's name is regularly mentioned in these *argumenta* and that this would explain the absence of the name in the proem to the *Antiquities*.[32] Schreckenberg in a brief discussion proposes, against von Gutschmid, that the *argumenta* may have been produced by an ancient book dealer.[33] His strongest point against Josephan authorship are the inconsistencies between the text of the *Antiquities* and the *argumenta*. Nodet, instead, uses the same observations to argue for the opposite conclusion: the *argumenta* were written by Josephus, as an outline prepared *before* the composition of the *Antiquities*. This would

---

[29] 'Jésus et Jean Baptiste selon Josèphe,' *RB* 92 (1985): 497–524; *Baptême et Résurrection*. Paris: Cerf, 1999, 127–32.

[30] In Julius Euting, *Nabatäische Inschriften aus Arabien* (Berlin: Reimer, 1885), 87. The only specific evidence cited in support, namely the correct chronology of Herod's reign in the *argumenta*, is weak. However, undoubtedly von Gutschmid knew the subject matter of ancient summaries of contents because in the same year he completed his critical edition of the *Prologi* of Pompeius Trogus (*M. Iuniani Iustini Epitoma Historiarum Philippicarum Pompei Trogi* ed. Franciscus Ruehl. Accedunt *Prologi in Pompeium Trogum* ab Alfredo de Gutschmid recensiti. Leipzig: Teubner, 1907, lii–lxii, 251–64). These *Prologi* are very terse and somewhat similar in form to *argumenta*. They are quite different from the more extensive Epitome. On Gutschmid see also Niese's dedication page in his *Flavii Iosephi Opera* (vol. 1; Berlin: Weidmann, 1887), III: '... si quis postea ex hac editione utilitatem aliquam perceperit, Gutschmidi is memor esto.'

[31] *Josephus*. Vol. 4 *Jewish Antiquities I–IV* (trans. H.St.J. Thackeray; LCL; Cambridge, Mass.: Harvard University Press, 1930), 637. This evaluation is of course based upon a controversial idea particularly dear to Thackeray: the role of assistants in the composition of Josephus' works.

[32] 'Ephoros,' *Hermes* 46 (1911): 195. In the *War*, which lacks ancient *argumenta*, Josephus introduces himself by name in the proem (1.3).

[33] Schreckenberg, *Flavius-Josephus-Tradition*, 181.

explain why some of the topics mentioned in the *argumenta* are developed at great length while others are touched upon only briefly and yet other topics are introduced in the *Antiquities* without any counterpart in the *argumenta* or in a different sequence.[34]

In his recent study on the subject, Jean Irigoin discusses examples of *argumenta* or similar elements in writings from early imperial Rome. Without ever referring to any of the scholars mentioned in the preceding paragraph, he argues that Josephus in the *Antiquities* simply conformed to the well-established pattern of historical writing.[35] In this context, implicitly contradicting Nodet, he denies that *argumenta* represent outlines or 'scaffolding' used by the author for the composition of his work.[36] Thus the question of the origin and purpose of the *argumenta* of Josephus is again wide open. The only way to make progress seems to be a close analysis of the *argumenta* themselves. Here it is obviously impossible to provide a line-by-line commentary. Only certain examples, spread over different books, will be taken into consideration.

Book 1[37]

Niese's text contains the heading Τά δε ἔνεστιν ἐν τῇ πρώτῃ τῶν Ἰωσήπου ἱστοριῶν τῆς Ἰουδαϊκῆς ἀρχαιολογίας ('These are the contents of the first [book] of Josephus' account of the Jewish/Judean Antiquities'), apparently based on mss. S and L. As noted above, this is a fairly standard form of heading for *argumenta*, found also in manuscripts of Dio and other authors. Niese's heading follows exactly that in the edition by Haverkamp (1726). It is repeated in the same way in Nodet (1990), whereas Oberthür (1782) and Dindorf (1845) give a different heading. In the Loeb Classical Library edition, such

---

[34] *Baptême et resurrection: Le témoignage de Josèphe* (Paris: Cerf, 1999), 127–32.

[35] 'Ce souci de respecter les règles non écrites d'un genre littéraire, l'histoire, est confirmé par la présence de sommaires de chaque livre dans des manuscrits grecs et dans la traduction latine de Josèphe.... Josèphe montre que, grâce à son long séjour à Rome, il a appris à se conformer à tous les principes du genre historique' ('Titres, sous-titres et sommaires' [note 13 above], 131).

[36] 'Titres, sous-titres et sommaires,' 130.

[37] The numbering system for the *argumenta* adopted here for easy reference is that of LCL, which for Books 1–10 is based on Niese, who follows a substantial part of the manuscript tradition. For Books 11–20, LCL continues to number each item, while Niese, in accordance with the weaker ms. evidence, discontinues numeration. Nodet has created his own, more detailed, numeration.

a heading is always omitted except for Books 15–17. The numbered *argumenta* are preceded by a reference to the proem. It is introduced in almost exactly the same words as that of Diodorus.[38]

#i: The first topic is the creation of the world. It is described in language that is uncommon in Josephus. The word σύστασις ('beginning,' 'basis') is a Josephan hapax legomenon in *Ant.* 15.194 but is found here in reference to the beginning of the world.

#iii: Nodet in his notes on the *argumenta* correctly indicates many omissions and several transpositions and inconsistencies. In this last category, by way of example, one may draw attention to the statement that Noah settled in the Plain of Shinar (*Ant.* 1 #iii; Nodet: s4), whereas according to *Ant.* 1.109–110 (based on Gen 11:2) his descendants did so, after Noah's death (Gen 9:29; *Ant.* 1.104).[39] Josephus' poor recall of the details of Scripture may possibly be claimed to account for this inconsistency.

#vii: A little further on, however, we read 'How Abraham, our ancestor, having left the land of the Chaldeans, occupied what was then called Canaan but now Judea' (τὴν τότε μὲν Χαναναίαν νῦν δὲ Ἰουδαίαν λεγομένην, Nodet: s8). At first sight, this note offers valuable information for dating the *argumentum* because officially the country was no longer called Judea after 132 C.E.[40] The expression quoted in Greek, however, agrees verbatim with a quote from Book 4 of the *Histories* of Nicolaus of Damascus as given in *Ant.* 1.160 and could have been copied for the *argumentum* at any time. It is hardly likely that Josephus in his outline would have cared to remind himself who Abraham was and how the name of his country changed. Similarly, it seems unlikely that for an outline he would copy out

---

[38] Diodorus, Book 1: Προοίμιον τῆς ὅλης πραγματείας. Josephus, *Ant.* 1: Προοίμιον περὶ τῆς ὅλης πραγματείας ('Proem concerning the whole treatise'). As noted above, the *argumentum* of Book 1 of Diodorus in its present form is a late addition.

[39] Flavius Josèphe, *Les Antiquités Juives*. Vol. 1: *Livres I à III*. Text, translation, and notes by Étienne Nodet et al. (Paris: Cerf, ³2000), 1–1*; cf. X–XII.

[40] During the Bar Kochba revolt, 'Israel' was the name used by the revolutionaries. See David Goodblatt, 'From Judeans to Israel: Names of Jewish States in Antiquity,' *JSJ* 29 (1998): 1–36, esp. 28–36. After the Bar Kochba revolt it became the province of Syria Palaestina. The new name was not applied entirely consistently. See E. Mary Smallwood, *The Jews under Roman Rule from Pompey to Diocletian* (SJLA 20; Leiden: Brill, 1976; corrected repr. 1981), 463–64, 529, 552; Fergus Millar, *The Roman Near East 31 B.C.–A.D. 337* (Cambridge, Mass.: Harvard University Press, 1993) 107–8. In the Mishnah, there are references to Judea, as distinct from Galilee (*m. Šeb.* 9:2; *Pes* 4:5). When, however, the entire country is meant, the expression ארץ ישׂראל ('Land of Israel') is used (*m. Demai* 6:11; *m. Šeb.* 6:1; *m. Miqw.* 8:1).

this information from Nicolaus. Thus, against Nodet, the author of (this section of) the *argumentum* is almost certainly someone other than Josephus.

One more general observation may point to the method of working of the author of the *argumenta*. Quite often, there is a close verbal parallel with a text in the body of the *Antiquities*, frequently the opening sentence of the material summarized (so at *Ant*. 1 #vi; #viii; #ix, and passim). For other peculiarities of the *argumenta* of Books 1–7 one may consult the detailed and helpful notes in Nodet's edition.[41]

Book 12

#ii: Ptolemy II Philadelphus is correctly identified as a son of Ptolemy I Soter, whereas in *Ant*. 12.11 he is simply his successor. This summary statement covers Josephus' entire paraphrase of the *Letter of Aristeas* (*Ant*. 12.11–118).

#iii reads 'How the kings of Asia honored the Judean *ethnos*, and made [the Judeans] citizens in the cities founded by them.' Strictly speaking, this is a summary of just one paragraph, *Ant*. 12.119, with strong verbal parallels.[42] The continuation of such favors by Roman authorities, even by Vespasian and Titus (12.120–128) is absent from the *argumentum*, as is Antiochus III's conquest of Palestine and the documents quoted in this connection (12.129–153).[43]

#iv covers the entire Tobiad romance (12.154–236) in one nominal phrase. The lemma ἐπανόρθωσις ('rectification') appears only twice in the body of the works of Josephus (*Ant*. 11.157; 16.263).

---

[41] See in particular his discussion (*Antiquités Juives. Livres I–III*, 2 n. 89) of the concluding formula for the *argumentum* of *Ant*. 1 attested only in ms. O: 'The book covers a period of 3008 years according to Josephus, of 1872 according to the Hebrews, of 3459 according to Eusebius.' Nodet's harmonization of data here seems somewhat fanciful, but his thesis that the reference to Eusebius is a gloss and cannot be taken as a terminus post quem for the *argumenta* as a whole is basically sound. See also his *Baptême et résurrection*, 127.

[42] In *Ant*. 12.119, the recipients of the honors are consistently the Ἰουδαῖοι, without the awkward implicit change from ἔθνος (singular) to individual citizens (plural). It seems easier to explain the *argumentum* as an infelicitous rendering of 12.119 than the other way around.

[43] One may of course consider under this heading the privileges granted by Antiochus III to Jerusalem and to certain Judeans (*Ant*. 12.138–153); but these regard tax exemptions, temple worship, and observance of Jewish law even outside Judea. The subject of citizenship is never addressed.

#v limits itself to refer to the brief letter of the Spartan king Areus to the Jerusalem high priest Onias (*Ant.* 12.225b–228a), which is inserted within the story of the Tobiads.

#vi Στάσις τῶν δυνατῶν Ἰουδαίων πρὸς ἀλλήλους καὶ ὡς ἐπεκαλέσαντο Ἀντίοχον τὸν Ἐπιφανῆ ('The civil strife of the powerful among the Judeans against each other and how they called upon Antiochus Epiphanes for assistance'). Here the *argumentum* clearly reflects the language—and the situation—of *War* 1.31–32a rather than *Ant.* 12.237–245. The narrative of the *War* begins at 1.31 with the following words: Στάσεως τοῖς δυνατοῖς Ἰουδαίων ἐμπεσούσης καθ' ὃν καιρὸν Ἀντίοχος ὁ κληθεὶς [ἐπικληθεὶς B Herwerden] Ἐπιφανὴς διεφέρετο.... Neither στάσις nor δυνατοί are found in the partial parallel in the *Antiquities*. Furthermore, in *Ant.* 12.240 Menelaus and the Tobiads go to Antiochus to request permission to abandon their ancestral laws, whereas in *War* 1.32a the Tobiads flee to Antiochus and ask for his military intervention, because they have been ousted from Jerusalem. Here the author of (this part of) the *argumentum* clearly follows the *War* against the *Antiquities*.

#vii Whereas the language for Antiochus' capture of Jerusalem is fairly standard and close to *Ant.* 12.246, the expression τὸν ναὸν ἐσύλησε ('he plundered the temple') exactly replicates *War* 1.32. In *Ant.* 12.357 a similar expression is contained in Antiochus' deathbed confession about the plundering of the Jerusalem temple, while *Ant.* 12.247, which should be summarized here, reads χρήματα πολλὰ συλήσας ('having plundered much money'), without any reference to the temple. *Ant.* 12.249–250 gives a confused report that Antiochus despoiled the temple during his second 'visit' to Jerusalem. Neither 1 Maccabees nor the *War*, nor the *argumentum* of the *Antiquities* know of such a second visit.[44]

#viii 'How, when Antiochus did not permit the Judeans to use their ancestral laws (τοῖς πατρίοις νόμοις χρῆσθαι), only Mattathias the son of Asamonaios (μόνος ὁ Ἀσαμωναίου παῖς Ματταθίας) despised the king and defeated the generals of Antiochus (τοὺς Ἀντιόχου στρατηγοὺς ἐνίκησεν).' The first part of this statement uses language

---

[44] Cf. Emil Schürer, *The History of the Jewish People in the Age of Jesus Christ (175 B.C.–A.D. 135)* (rev. ed. by G. Vermes, F. Millar et al.; Edinburgh: Clark, 1973–87), 1:152–53 n. 37. Even those scholars who argue for two visits of Antiochus to Jerusalem (169 and 168 B.C.E.) would place the despoiling of the temple during the first visit. See Christian Habicht, *2. Makkabäerbuch* (*JSHRZ* 1.3; Gütersloh: Mohn, 1976), 224 n. 5,1 a.

that is common in the *Antiquities*. The second part, however, is again much closer to the *War*. Mattathias is called the son of Asamonaios only here and in *War* 1.36, whereas *Ant.* 12.265, which supposedly is summarized here, has Mattathias the son of Joannes the son of Symeon the son of Asamonaios.[45] *War* 1.37 uses almost identical language for his victory over the Seleucids (νικᾷ τε τοὺς Ἀντιόχου στρατηγούς), which has no basis or parallel in 1 Maccabees or in the narrative of the *Antiquities*.

#ix The death of Mattathias, at a ripe old age, is described in conventional terms frequently used in the *Antiquities* but not in the corresponding narrative, and never in the *War* (cf. *Ant.* 5.232, 254, 271, 274; 8.1, 211; 11.158; 18.194; 20.240). The passing of the command to his sons (παραδόντος δὲ τὴν τῶν πραγμάτων προστασίαν τοῖς παισίν) uses the same language as *Ant.* 12.285, where however the command is inherited specifically by Judas (διεδέξατο δὲ τὴν προστασίαν τῶν πραγμάτων ὁ παῖς αὐτοῦ Ἰούδας).

#x 'How his son Judas after fighting the generals of Antiochus brought the Judeans back to their ancestral constitution (εἰς τὴν πάτριον ... πολιτείαν) and was appointed high priest by the people.' Language about the Judeans' ancestral constitution is entirely absent from the *War*, but frequent in the *Antiquities* (4.191; 13.2, 245; cf. 12.240, 280). The rededication of the temple and the restoration of Torah observance, however, are nowhere described in these terms. Judas did not become high priest but is given that title here as in *Ant.* 12.414, 419, 434, never in the *War*. The entire statement is so general that it can cover almost the entire career of Judas. Marcus notes that this section is misplaced, with some of it belonging after #xii, while the reference to the high priesthood would belong after #xx.[46] It may, however, be regarded as a resumption of the summary statement in *Ant.* 12.286.

The remaining sections (##xi–xxii) summarize events for the rest of Book 12. The organizing principle, however, is not the even coverage of events, but every section has as its subject another person or persons,[47] usually a king or military leader, regardless of the

---

[45] In Hebrew and Aramaic the term 'son' can of course mean more generally '(male) descendant' (cf. Josh 22:27; 1 Kgs 10:30).

[46] *Josephus*. Vol. 7 *Jewish Antiquities, Books XII–XIV* (trans. R. Marcus; LCL; Cambridge, Mass.: Harvard University Press, 1943), 707 n. a.

[47] A similar tendency may be observed in Book 1 ##x–xix, Book 8, and especially Book 13.

length of the narrative. Judas is the subject only of sections #x, #xiii (expeditions to Ammon and Gilead) and #xxii (his death). His other activities are listed in sections where his opponents are the subject. The first expedition of Lysias (#xv) is curiously out of place. It is listed approximately in accordance with the relative chronology of 2 Maccabees, not that of the *Antiquities* or its source, 1 Maccabees.[48] The failure of Bacchides' mission (#xix ἄπρακτος ἀνέστρεψε) is described in terms used in Josephus only at *Ant.* 15.349.

Book 13

The *argumentum* for Book 13 is more detailed than those for earlier books. Its language, contrary to some of the central sections of Book 12, shows no particular affinity with the *War*. As noted above, in almost every section a different leader, often a Seleucid king, is the subject. This scheme leaves large gaps in the summary. One very significant gap appears between #xix (defeat of Antiochus Cyzicenus *Ant.* 13.276–277 || *War* 1.65) and #xx (reign of Aristobulus I *Ant.* 13.301–319 || *War* 1.70–84). Here the story of the famous banquet given by Hyrcanus, and his alleged shift from Pharisees to Sadducees, recounted at length in *Ant.* 13.288–298, is entirely absent. Less conspicuous, but perhaps also significant, is the omission of any reference to the first presentation of Pharisees, Sadducees, and Essenes in the *Antiquities* (*Ant.* 13.171–173).[49] Both these passages, as I have tried to show elsewhere, are later additions to the text of Josephus.[50] Their absence from the *argumentum* should be noted, even though it is insufficient evidence to support Nodet's contention that the *argumenta* were written before the composition of the *Antiquities*. A further indication may be seen in *Ant.* 13 #i, where Jonathan is explicitly introduced as Judas' brother. This information seems to be provided for the benefit of the reader and not part of an outline for the author's own use.[51]

---

[48] See my *Synopsis of the Greek Sources for the Hasmonean Period: 1–2 Maccabees and Josephus, War 1 and Antiquities 12–14* (SubBi 20; Rome: Editrice Pontificio Istituto Biblico, 2001), XI.
[49] Cf. Nodet, *Flavius Josèphe. Les Antiquités Juives* Vol. 1, p. XI n. 1.
[50] 'Josephus, First Maccabees, Sparta, the Three *Haireseis*—and Cicero,' *JSJ* 32 (2001), 241–51.
[51] Cf. *Ant.* 5 #iv.

Book 14

If the *argumentum* for Book 13 is more detailed than those of earlier books, the one for Book 14 is even more prolix, with thirty-seven relatively long sections. Nonetheless, different parts of the book are very unevenly covered. Sections ##i–xx cover only *Ant.* 14.4–97. In the later sections, long narrative portions are not summarized (#xxxvi inadequately covers *Ant.* 14.394–467) and the many documents (*Ant.* 14.145–155, 185–267, 306–323) receive only one brief non-inclusive reference (#xxvii). One might argue that these changes of style point towards different authors. However, even in other books we encounter sometimes long (e.g., *Ant.* 3 #ix), sometimes extremely short (*Ant.* 1 #xvi) phrases and smaller or larger numbers of sections. As Laqueur has shown in a different context, the genre *argumentum* allowed for different forms (four according to him) within the same composition.[52]

#i The Hasmonean fortress in Jerusalem, later renamed Antonia, is here called *Baris*, whereas the passage being summarized here (*Ant.* 14.5) speaks of the *Akropolis*. The parallel in *War* 1.121 has Antonia. The nearest use of the term *Baris* is found slightly earlier in the *War* (1.118), where the name is explained in the context of the reign of Queen Alexandra. In the *Antiquities*, the identification of *Baris* and *Akropolis* occurs solely at 15.403. The verb ἰδιωτεύειν ('to live as a private citizen') is used here for Hyrcanus instead of the noun in *Ant.* 14.7. The verb is used only five times in Josephus, three times in *Ant.* 15–16.

#iv summarizes a short passage about the intervention of Scaurus, sent by Pompey to Syria. While *Ant.* 14.29 and *War* 1.127 are closely parallel, only in the *War* and in the *argumentum* is Pompey called Μάγνος ('the Great').

#ix The language here is a mixture of expressions from *War* 1.135–137 and *Ant.* 14.50–52: δικαιολογέομαι ('to plead one's cause' *Ant.*), ἠνάγκασε . . . γράψαι ('forced him . . . to write' *War*), τῇ αὑτοῦ χειρί ('in his own hand' cf. *Ant.*).

#xii '. . . how the partisans of Hyrcanus admitted him [Pompey] into the Upper City, while those of Aristobulus fled to the Temple' (Marcus, LCL). Here the wording is largely taken from *War* 1.140–143, which is different from the parallel in *Ant.* 14.57–58. The Upper

---

[52] See n. 23 above.

City is not specified in either passage, but topographically this specification is plausible.

#xiii Pompey's capture of the Lower City in addition to the temple is explicitly mentioned only here.

#xv The phrase τὴν Ἰουδαίαν ποιήσας φόροις ὑποτελῆ ('making Judea subject to tribute') reflects in part *War* 1.154 with its reference to the countryside as well as to Jerusalem, where the *Antiquities* speak only of Jerusalem. The rest of the expression, however, is found almost verbatim in *Ant.* 14.74 (καὶ τὰ μὲν Ἱεροσόλυμα ὑποτελῆ φόρου Ῥωμαίοις ἐποίησεν).[53] Ὑρκανὸν ἀποδείξας ἐθνάρχην ('appointing Hyrcanus ethnarch') has no equivalent in the two narratives of Josephus. In documents reported in Josephus, Hyrcanus II bears the title of ethnarch only from the time of Caesar on.[54] Some scholars, however, argue that Pompey indeed gave him that title, that Gabinius deprived him of it (cf. *War* 1.169), and that Caesar merely reinstated him as ethnarch.[55] In the passage being summarized here, *Ant.* 14.73 mentions only Hyrcanus' reinstatement as high priest. In the parallel passage in *War* 1.153, however, the participial construction is precisely that of the *argumentum* (ἀποδείξας Ὑρκανὸν ἀρχιερέα). The rest of this section of the *argumentum* closely parallels *Ant.* 14.79 and *War* 1.157, leaving out the reorganization of Palestine by Pompey (*Ant.* 14.74b–76) as well as Josephus' considerations concerning the misfortune of Jerusalem (*Ant.* 14.77–78).

#xxii The destination of Pompey's flight is here given as Epirus (a name absent from Josephus' works), in northwestern Greece, while *Ant.* 14.123 and its parallel in *War* 1.183 have Pompey fleeing across the Ionian See, without specifying the destination. As a matter of fact, he sailed to Dyrrhachium, slightly to the north of Epirus.

---

[53] Daniel R. Schwartz ('Josephus on Hyrcanus II,' in *Josephus and the History of the Greco-Roman Period: Essays in Memory of Morton Smith* [ed. F. Parente and J. Sievers; Leiden: Brill, 1994], 218) suggests that *Ant.* 14.74–76 closely follows the account of Nicolaus of Damascus.

[54] The references to Hyrcanus as ethnarch in *Ant.* 14.148, 151 are a separate problem. At least in the present arrangement of the text, the documents in *Ant.* 14.145–155 are assigned to Caesar's time, while in reality they may refer to Hyrcanus I, over half a century earlier.

[55] M. Stern, *Hasmonean Judaea in the Hellenistic World: Chapters in Political History* (Hebr.), (ed. D.R. Schwartz; Jerusalem: Yad Izhak Ben-Zvi, 1995), 213; Miriam Pucci Ben Zeev, *Jewish Rights in the Roman World* (TSAJ 74; Tübingen: Mohr, 1998), 49.

#xxiv A prominent role is assigned to Hyrcanus II, in line with *Ant.* 14.127, 131–132 but unlike in the *War*.

#xxv Permission to rebuild Jerusalem's city walls is given to Hyrcanus (as in *Ant.* 14.144), whereas in *War* 1.199 that permission is given to Antipater.

#xxxvii refers to the execution of Antigonus, the last Hasmonean king, briefly mentioned at *Ant.* 14.490. The majority of mss. attributes the death to Sossius and Herod (ὑπὸ Σοσσίου καὶ Ἡρώδου Ἀντίγονος διεφθάρη). One Greek ms. (L) and the Latin translation show an awareness of the problem: In reality Antigonus was executed by Mark Antony, after he had been defeated by Herod and Sossius, and had surrendered himself to Sossius.

Book 15

#i repeats the reference to the execution of Antigonus, as it is repeated and expanded at *Ant.* 15.9, quoting Strabo. This repetition as well as the reference to the capture of Jerusalem described in the previous book suggests that the *argumentum* here is based on the full text of the *Antiquities*.

#ii Ὃν τρόπον Ὑρκανὸς ὁ πρῶτος βασιλεὺς Ἰουδαίων καὶ ἀρχιερεὺς ἀφεθεὶς ὑπὸ τοῦ τῶν Πάρθων βασιλέως Ἀρσάκου πρὸς Ἡρώδην ὑπέστρεψεν ('In what way Hyrcanus the first king of the Judeans and high priest returned to Herod after being released by the Parthian king Arsaces'). Marcus and Wikgren note that 'There is a confusion here of Hyrcanus (II) with his grandfather, John Hyrcanus, and of the earlier king Arsaces with Phraates of our present text.'[56] A better explanation of this obviously erroneous statement seems to be available. If we look at the passage being summarized we find fairly similar wording in *Ant.* 15.11–12. There, however, Ὑρκανὸν τὸν πρῶτον ἀρχιερέα γενόμενον, εἶτα βασιλέα clearly has a different meaning, correctly translated by Marcus (LCL) 'Hyrcanus, who had first been made high priest and then king.' Thus adverbial πρῶτον has mistakenly been rendered as an adjective by the author of the *argumentum*.[57]

---

[56] *Josephus*. Vol. 8 *Jewish Antiquities, Books XV–XVII* (trans. R. Marcus and A. Wikgren; LCL; Cambridge, Mass.: Harvard University Press, 1963), 539 n. b.

[57] The Latin version, however, avoids this mistake: 'Quo pacto Hyrcanus, antea Judaeorum rex et pontifex, a Parthorum rege Arsace dimissus ad Herodem rediit.'

Book 18

Nodet in his detailed study of the *argumentum* for Book 18 proposes that it was drawn up by Josephus in preparation for writing the *Antiquities*, and was partly based on the *War*. While none of the transpositions he indicates bring the *argumentum* closer to the sequence of events in the *War*, his observations regarding the inadequacies of the *argumentum* to summarize *Ant.* 18 are correct.[58]

#vi This section of the *argumentum* deals with the Samaritans scattering bones in the Temple at Passover. It asserts that 'they defiled the people for seven days,' a statement without basis in the extant narrative. Niese in his *editio minor* as well as Feldman (LCL), suppose a lacuna in the report about this incident (*Ant.* 18.30). Here as in other instances, as noted by Schreckenberg, the *argumenta* may be of assistance in textual questions.[59]

Conclusions: Date and Provenance of the *Argumenta*

As early as Polybius, historians and other authors were concerned with providing their readers with a systematic overview of their work. Although this practice was certainly not generalized, traces of it can be found as early as the first century B.C.E. in a papyrus from Herculaneum. In the first and second centuries C.E., encyclopaedic works such as Pliny's *Natural History* and the *Attic Nights* by Aulus Gellius provide a list of contents after the preface and before the body of the work. For works of some historians (Diodorus, Josephus, Cassius Dio, Eusebius), we have more or less detailed lists of contents (*argumenta*) at the beginning of each book. Their textual transmission is much more unstable than that of the body of the work. Nevertheless, there are good indications for considering these elements part of the original 'published' version.

---

[58] As Nodet correctly notes ('Jésus et Jean-Baptiste selon Josèphe,' 503–4), the intervention of the high priest Joazar in the *argumentum* follows and cuts short the rebellion initiated by Judas the Galilean against the census (*Ant.* 18 #iii). In *Ant.* 18.3–4, instead, the high priest's intervention is mentioned before the incitement to a tax rebellion by Judas the Gaulanite. In the *War* (1.118), neither the high priest nor the outcome of Judas' revolt is specified.

[59] Schreckenberg (*Flavius-Josephus-Tradition*, 181) cites *Ant.* 13.268, 301, 370 as examples.

The *argumenta* for Josephus' *Antiquities* show a wide variation in the amount of detail provided. The main criterion for their composition was clearly not to cover the *Antiquities* in a uniform manner. Sometimes a long—or brief—section of a book is summarized under one heading, because it is based on a particular source.[60] At other times the same type of material is lumped together under one heading, even though dispersed in the narrative. Elsewhere, one section is devoted to each king or military leader discussed, regardless of the length of the narrative.

We are dealing with a large amount of data that often seem to lead to conflicting conclusions. Since the textual basis for the *argumenta* is relatively uncertain, all conclusions based on individual data have to remain tentative. Some elements, however, become reasonably clear.

1. The author of the *argumenta* is 'ostensibly' Jewish, as Thackeray remarked. Abraham is called 'our' forefather (*Ant.* 1 #vii; cf. *Ant.* 1.158); 'our' people served the Moabites (*Ant.* 5 #v); Demetrius presented gifts to 'our' people (*Ant.* 13 #iv).
2. Christians took great interest in the *Antiquities* and were early on, from the third century at the latest, involved in their textual transmission.[61] The fact that the *argumenta* show no Christian influence suggests an early date.[62]

---

[60] See the *Letter of Aristeas* (*Ant.* 12 #2, covering 12.11–118), the Tobiad romance (*Ant.* 12 #iv for 12.154–236), relations with Sparta (*Ant.* 12 #v for 12.225–228), Asineus and Anileus (*Ant.* 18 #xx for 18.310–379), the story of Queen Helena and her family (*Ant.* 20 #viii for 20.17–96). Josephus' list of high priests (*Ant.* 20.224–251) and many other clearly identifiable blocks of material, some derived from special sources, are omitted from the *argumenta*.

[61] Christian interpolations in the texts of Josephus are first attested in Origen (d. 253 C.E.), but may predate his time. See Heinz Schreckenberg, 'Josephus in Early Christian Literature and Medieval Christian Art,' in Heinz Schreckenberg and Kurt Schubert, *Jewish Historiography and Iconography in Early and Medieval Christianity* (CRINT 3.2; Assen: Van Gorcum, 1992), 57–63; Fausto Parente, 'Sulla doppia trasmissione, filologica ed ecclesiastica, del testo di Flavio Giuseppe: Un contributo alla storia della ricezione della sua opera nel mondo cristiano,' *Rivista di Storia e Letteratura Religiosa* 36 (2000), 3–51, esp. 12, 15, 49.

[62] On the reference to Eusebius at the end of the *argumentum* of Book 1 see n. 41 above. A reference to 'de baptista Iohanne' is extant only in Latin (*Ant.* 18 #xiii) and is relegated to the critical apparatus by Niese and Feldman (LCL) as a gloss. If anything, it shows that Christian interpolations were possible but that the author of the *argumenta* was clearly not guided by Christian interests, since neither the *Testimonium Flavianum* (*Ant.* 18.63–64) nor Jesus, nor the death of James (*Ant.* 20.199–203) are mentioned anywhere in the *argumenta*.

3. A terminus ante quem for the *argumenta* of the *Antiquities* is their Latin translation commissioned by Cassiodorus (c. 490–c. 583 C.E.), for the Latin *argumenta*, attested in relatively early manuscripts, agree on the whole with the Greek ones.
4. Nodet's suggestion that the *argumenta* constituted Josephus' outline before he wrote the *Antiquities* seems to be a brilliant solution to the striking inconsistencies between *argumenta* and text of the work. In support of his hypothesis one may adduce that they are at times closer to the content *and wording* of the *War* than of the *Antiquities*, and sometimes mix elements from both works.
5. Yet, there are other indicators that suggest that, as in the case of other ancient authors, the *argumenta* were provided for the benefit of the reader and are not fortuitous remains of the author's outline. (see *Ant.* 1 #vii; 13 #i).
6. In some instances, the *argumenta* reflect use of a text of the *Antiquities* similar to the one known to us (see especially *Ant.* 14 #xxxvii and 15# 1; 15 #2). It does not appear feasible to assign just these sections to a later redactor.
7. Thus, the author of the *argumenta* seems to have known different (but not all) sources and stages of composition of the *Antiquities*, had a fair acquaintance with Jerusalem topography (*Ant.* 14 ##i, xii), and had a less than perfect knowledge of the geography of Greece and/or Roman history (*Ant.* 14 #xxii). Whether he knew the *Histories* of Nicolaus of Damascus (a principal source for both the *War* and the *Antiquities*) seems an intriguing but hard-to-verify possibility.
8. If it is hard to see the *argumenta* as Josephus' own composition, Gutschmid's suggestion of a 'servus litteratus' (or Thackeray's 'assistant') does not seem as farfetched as it had appeared to me when I began my research for this paper.[63]
9. In any case, the *argumenta* deserve to be included in any edition or translation of the *Antiquities*. They need to be studied for the questions they raise concerning the development, edition(s), and transmission of the text. And they need to be seen in the context of similar phenomena in other works of Hellenistic and Roman historiography.

---

[63] On the process of composition in ancient authors see now Tiziano Dorandi, *Le stylet et la tablette: Dans le secret des auteurs antiques* (Paris: Belles Lettres, 2000). On the use of assistants see pp. 29–38, 64, 117, and passim.

If these tentative and very open-ended conclusions go in some measure beyond the work of Louis Feldman,[64] they could not have been reached without much that I have learned from him.

---

[64] He does not include the *argumenta* in *Flavius Josephus*. Transl. and commentary ed. Steve Mason. Vol. 3 *Judean Antiquities 1–4. Translation and Commentary* by Louis H. Feldman (Leiden: Brill, 2000).

INDEX OF SOURCES

Hebrew Bible

Genesis
10:1–11:19	262
10:15–20	262
11:2	281
15	35
17	30, 35, 37
17:14	39
19	37
19:3	37
25:15	232
25:23	247
29:33	149
33:16	154

Exodus
19:15	38
28:9 [+LXX]	151
28:17–20 [+£]	151
39:10–13 [+£]	151

Leviticus
21:18	155
26:15	39
26:42	37

Numbers
27	33
36	33

Deuteronomy
2:31–4	249
3:3–4	249
6:14 [+LXX]	247
7:1–2	249
31:16	39
20:16–7	249

Joshua
6:21–4	249
8:24–8	249
22:27	284

Judges
2:12 [+LXX]	247
13:5	153
14:19	163

1 Samuel
1:11 [+ LXX, £, *4Qsam^a*]	153
1:22 [+ *4Qsam^a*]	153
1:24	161
2:25	143
6:7–14	150
7:11 [+LXX, £]	150
8:12 [+LXX, £]	148
9:13 [+LXX, £]	150
10:3 [+ LXX, £, *4Qsam^a*]	161
10:4 [+ LXX, £]	168
10:27[a] [+*4Qsam^a*]	153–4
12:25	157
14:8–10 [+LXX]	143
14:45 [+LXX]	143
16.2 [+£]	150
17:43 [+LXX, £]	147, 163
19:18 [+LXX [B, V], £]	150
19:22 [+LXX, £]	147
20:30 [+ LXX, £, *4Qsam^a*]	147, 163
21:3 [+LXX, £, *4QSam^b*]	152
22:6 [+ LXX, £]	163
23:25 [+LXX, £]	149
25:2 [+LXX, £]	149
25:3 [+ LXX, £, *4Qsam^a*]	161
25:18	161
26:11 [+ LXX, £]	161, 163
28:1 [+*4Qsam^a*]	154, 162
28:19 [+£]	147
29:1 [+ LXX, £]	162
29:1 (LXX [B])	154
31:13 [+ LXX, £]	162
31:2 [+LXX, £]	147

2 Samuel
2:21 [+ LXX, £]	163
3:26 [+LXX, £]	150
3:3 [+ LXX, £, *4Qsam^a*, p. 156]	155
4:4 f. [+£]	147
5	147
5:4–5 [+£]	147
5:6 [+ LXX, £, *4Qsam^a*]	155
5:8	155
6:7 [+ LXX, £, *4Qsam^a*]	156
6:13 [+ LXX, £]	162

7:8.12.14	165	*Zechariah*		
8:9–10 [+LXX, £]	148	12:2	247	
9.6 f. [+£]	147	12:3 [+LXX]	247	
10:6 [+ LXX, £, 4Qsam^a^]	162	12:6	247	
11:6 [+4Qsam^a^]	154	12:25 (LXX)	247	
16:1	161	14:14 [+LXX]	247	
16:21–2	144			
17:1	144	*Psalms*		
17:27 [+LXX, £]	149	7	67	
19:11 [+LXX]	143	7:3	43, 45, 47	
21:16 [+LXX]	144	7:12	45, 49–50	
22:44	247	115:16	18	
24:15 [+LXX]	144			
24:17 [+ LXX, £, 4Qsam^a^]	156–8	*Esther*		
24:20 [+ LXX, 4Qsam^a^]	158	9:5–6	266	
		9:15	266	
1 Kings				
1:6 f. [+ LXX, £]	148	*Daniel*		
1:8 [+LXX]	145	9:24	126	
2:10	147			
5:11 [+LXX]	247	*Ezra*		
5:11	248	2:59–60	229	
10:30	284	6.1–2	181	
19:14–8	165	7	182	
		7.27	182	
Isaiah		9–10	225	
2:2 (LXX)	247	9:12	227	
2:2–3	247			
2:3 (LXX)	247	*Nehemiah*		
25:7 [+LXX]	247	5:1–19	227	
49:22 [+LXX]	247	13:19–31	225	
Jeremiah		*1 Chronicles*		
10:2 (LXX)	247	2:42–9	161	
10:2–3	247	3:1	156	
10:3 (LXX)	247	11:5	155	
25:9 [+LXX]	247	13:10	156	
33:25	39	15:22	156	
		15:26	162	
Ezekiel		18	148	
4:12	11	18:9	148	
4:13	11	19:6	162	
9	55	21	158	
36:4 [+LXX]	247	21:16	157	
		21:17	157	
Joel		21:20	158	
4:11	247	29:2 [+LXX, £]	150	
4:11–2 (LXX)	247			

Apocryphal/Deuterocanonical Books

Judith
14:10	235

1 Maccabees
1:10	240
1:11	231, 239
1:13–4	239
1:15	259
1:42	248
1:48	259
1:60–1	259
2:40	240
2:46	232
3:20–1	240
3:32	170
3:33	170
3:38	171
4:11	248
4:14–5	172
4:17	171
4:55–63	171
4:55–6	171
5:1–2	241, 246
5:3–9	241
5:4–5	241
5:10	246
5:25–7	241
5:25	242
5:28	241
5:35	241
5:38	246
5:44	241
5:50–1	242
5:56–8	248
5.61–2	239
5:63	248
5:65	242
5:68	242, 255
6:14–5	255
6:21–3	255
7:8	248
7:26–30	242
7:27–30	171
7:47	254
8:1–32	242
8:17	203
9:23	245
9:23–12:39	244
9:25	245
9:29	245
9:36–42	243
9:50–3	258
9:58	245
9:61	245
9:69	245
9:73	245
10:1–50	248
10:14	245
10:44–8	243
10:59	243
10:61	245
10:64	245
10:65	248
10:70–4	243
10:75–6	247
10:83–4	243
11:4	243
11:4–5	247
11:4–6	245
11:21	245
11:25	245
11:47–51	247
11:59	249
11:59–60	247
11:60	247–8
11:61–2	247
11:62	247
11:64–5	243
11:66–7	247
12:1–23	230
12:25–32	247
12:33–4	243, 247, 249
12:53	245–6, 248
13:1–6	245
13:6	247–8
13:11	243
13:43–8	244
13:49–50	244
14:27–49	245
14:29–31	245
14:36–9	246
15:33	270
15:38	248
15:43	248
16:10	244

2 Maccabees
1:27	257
2:21	256
2:23	251
4:10	256
4:10–15	256
4:11	203
4:13	256

4:15	256	10:15–23	252
4:26	226	10:21	253
4:32–34	173	10:36	252
4:35–6	256–7	11	172, 182
4:45–9	173	11:1	170–1
4:49	256	11:3	257
5:1	257	11:12	171
5:6–10	226	11:16–38	171
5:9	230	11:23–26	172
5:15	174	11:24	256
5:27	9	12:2	241
6:1–10	256	12:2	169, 173
6:4	257	12:3–7	253
6:8	257	12:7	253
6:9	256	12:13	257
6:10	255, 259	12:13–6	253
6:13–5	257	12:21	253
7:1–38	255	12:23	253
8:5	257	12:26	253
8:5–6	252	12:27–8	254
8:9	257	12:29–31	254
8:16	257	12:30	256
8:32	241	13:2	171, 173
8:33	252	13:3–8	171
9	182	13:23–5	257
9:12–7	235	14:14	257
10:2	257	14:15	257
10:4	257	14:33	254
10:5	257	14:41–6	255
10:11	171	15:8	257
10:12	256	15:30–5	254
10:12–3	169, 173	15:37	154

Old Testament Pseudepigrapha

Book of Jubilees		30:7	260
3:31	260	30:12	260
7:20	260	34:1–9	261
8:10–10:35	262	37:6–10	261
10:29	262	38:2–14	261
10:31	262		
10:33	262	*Letter of Aristeas*	
10:35	262	30	165
15:23–6	260		
15:33	260	*Testament of Judah*	
15:34	260	3:1–8	266
22:16	261	4:1–2	266
22:20–1	262	5:5	266
22:22	262	6:3–5	266
24:28–33	261	7:3	266
25:1	260	11:1	266
30	261	16:4	266
30:1–17	260	17:1	266

INDEX OF SOURCES

Testament of Levi		*Testament of Simon*	
2:2	266	6:3–5	266
5:3–4	266		
6:2–6	266		

Dead Sea Scrolls

1 QSam (1 Q7)		1Sam 21:3	152
1Sam 18:17–18	151	1Sam 23:9–17	152
2Sam 20:6–10	151		
2Sam 21:16–18	151	*4QSam^c*	
		1Sam 25:30–1	152
4QSam^b		2Sam 14:7–13	152
1Sam 16:1–11	152	2Sam 15:1–15	152
1Sam 19:10–17	152		
1Sam 20:26–42	152	*Covenant of Damascus*	
1Sam 21:1–9	152	12.12	37

New Testament

Matthew		5.36	94
3:4	9	7.58–60	97
24.19–21	99	11.29–30	95
		12.1–4	94
Luke		12.2	97
1:15	153	12.21–3	94
7:15	203	12.23	94
7:33	9, 12	15:5	7
		22:3	203
Acts of the Apostles		24:5	7
2.27–38	95	24:14	7
5:17	7	26:5	7, 203

Patristic Sources

Basil		Eusebius	
Epistle		*Ecclesiastical History*	
258.4	74	2	92
		2.5.6	92, 101
Clement		2.5.7	92, 101
Stromata		2.6.1	93
1.21.101.2–5	115, 120	2.6.3	101
1.21.101.5–102.1	110	2.6.8	93, 101
1.21.126.3	126	2.7.1	93
1.21.136.3	126	2.10.1	93
1.21.139.3	126	2.10.1	101
1.21.140.7	125	2.10.2	94
		2.10.10	94
Cohortatio ad Gentiles		2.12.2	95
9	119	2.19.1	95

2.23.1	95 [ff], 101	George Synkellos	
2.23.19	101	I, 559 (Dindorf)	269
2.23.20	95		
2.23.21	95–6	*Ekloge Chronographias*	
2.26.1–2	96	1.558–9	233
2.26.2	96		
3	92	Jerome	
3.5.2	97, 101	*Commentary on Ezechiel*	
3.5.3	97, 101	Preface to Chapter 5	
3.5.4	93	[CCSL 75.185]	278
3.5.4	98		
3.5.5–6	98	Origen	
3.5.6	93	*Contra Celsum*	
3.5.7	93	4.11	119
3.5.7	99, 101		
3.7.1	99, 101	Photius	
3.7.6	99	*Bibliotheca*	
3.7.7	100	33	105
3.7.8	100–1		
3.7.8–9	100	Tatian	
6.13.7	197	*Oratio ad Graecos*	
8.13.2	145	38	115, 120
9.6.3	145		
		Tertullian	
Praeparatio evangelica		*Apologeticus*	
9.42.2–3	199	19.3	119
10.10.15	112		

Greek, Latin and Persian Authors

Apuleius		67.14.2	85
The Golden Ass		68.1.2	82, 85
11.24.6	66	79	274
		80	275
Aristotle			
Athenaion Politeia		Diodorus Siculus	
26.3	227	1	281
		17:7–9	244
Arrianus		17:9–14	244
Anabasis		20:54–5	244
1:7–9	244	20:71	244
		34–35:1, 5	172
Chariton			
Callirhoe		Diogenes Laertius	
5.1.1–2	272	2.41	106
8.1.1	272		
		Dionysius of Halicarnassus	
Cassius Dio		*Roman Antiquities*	
2.9.44	60	1.90	276
3.11.44	60		
66.7.2	87, 89	Gellius	
67.14.1	82	X, 15, 16	60

INDEX OF SOURCES

Herodotus
Histories
I.132   74

Historia Augusta [Loeb]
I, Avidius Cassius, vii,
  244–247   60
II, 141   54
III, viii, 462–463   60
Commodus, 9.6   65
Life of Heliogabalus,
  3, 4–5; 7, 1 and 5–6   62

Nicolaus of Damascus
Histories
4   281

Plato
Politicus
276 b   194

Symposium
188 b–c   194

Pliny
Natural History
2–37   275
XXCIII, 10–11   51–2

Plutarch
Life of Lucullus
24   74

Polybius
The Histories
1.13.8   272
1.65.5   272
3.5.9   272
4:62   244
4:64   244
4:65   244
7:18   244
11.1a.1   277
11.1a.3   277
11.1a.4   277

Procopius
Vandal.
2.10:13–20   263

Servius
On *Aeneid* IV.323   184
On *Aeneid* VI.861   184

Strabo
Geography
15.3.13–14   73
15.3.14   74

Suetonius
Lives of the Caesars
I, The Deified Julius,
  lxxix, 102–103   60
I, The Deified Julius,
  lxxix, 104–105   60
II, xviii, 148–149   59
II, 185, Nero, 56   55
II, Domitian, 12.2   82, 86, 89
III, xxiv, 330–331   59
III, xxv   59
III, lxx, 392–393   55–6
V, x, vol. II, 20–21   59
VI, vii, 98–99   59
VII, vi, 236–237   59
VIII, vi, 294–297   59

Thucydides
V   181

Xenophon
Anabasis
2–5   272
7   272

Cyropaedia
8.7.3   74
8.3.24   74

Yasna
62.5–6   73

JEWISH HELLENISTIC SOURCES

Josephus
Antiquities
1   280–1, 290
1.i   281
1.iii   281
1.vi   282
1.vii   281, 290–1
1.viii   282
1.ix   282
1.x–xix   284

INDEX OF SOURCES

1.xvi	286	6.295	149
1–7	279, 282	6.296	161
1–10	280	6.313 f.	161
1.5	141	6.325	154, 162
1.5	202	6.336	147
1.6	205	6.377	163
1.12–3	141	7.9	147
1.104	281	7.15	163
1.109–10	281	7.21	156
1:129	163	7.34	150
1.158	290	7.61	155
1.160	281	7.81	156
1.212	193	7.83	156
1.227	193	7.85	162
1.304	149	7.103	205
1.309	193	7.107	147, 193
1.333	196	7.108	147
1.336	154	7.121	162
2.341	193	7.131	155
3–5 [Latin mss., Blatt]	272	7.213–216	144
3–15	272	7.217–221	144
3.165	151	7.230	149
3.168	151	7.259	143
3.182	193	7.299	144
3.284	193	7.324–9	144
3.321 [MSP]	192	7.327	157–8
4–11	166	7.328	157
4.72	153	7.330	158
4.118	192	7.346	144
4.191	284	7.377	150
4.303	205	7.389	147
5–7	141	8	284
5.v	290	8.1	284
5.iv	285	8.42	192
5.232	284	8.105 f.	154
5.254	284	8.144	202
5.271	284	8.211	284
5.274	284	8.346 f.	154, 162
5.278	153	9.208	141
5.344	153	10.173	193
5.347	153	10.210	141
6.28	150	10.218	141
6.40	148	11–20	280
6.48	150	11.79	192
6.55	161	11.157	282
6.68–9	153–4	11.158	284
6.110	143	11.302–47	226
6.128	143	11.304–5	104
6.157	150	11.313–47	104
6.222	147	12	282, 284–5
6.237	163	12.2	290
6.243	145, 152	12.ii	282
6.251	163	12.iii	282
6.280	149	12.iv	282, 290

12.v	283, 290	13.254-8	251, 267		
12.vi	283	13.268	289		
12.vii	283	13:272-4	269		
12.viii	283	13.275-80	251		
12.ix	284	13.276-7	285		
12.x	285	13.289	6		
12.xi-xxii	284	13.293	6		
12.xii	284	13.301	289		
12.xiii	285	13.301-19	285		
12.xx	284	13.318	232		
12.xxii	285	13.327	269		
12.xv	285	13.370	289		
12.4	192	14 [Budé]	272		
12.11	282	14	180, 182-3,		
12.11-118	282		185, 286		
12.115-7	230	14.i	286, 291		
12.119	282	14.xx	286		
12.120-8	282	14.iv	286		
12.122	186	14.ix	286		
12.129-53	183, 282	14.xii	286, 291		
12.154-236	282, 290	14.xiii	287		
12.160	226	14.xv	287		
12.160-236	226	14.xxii	287, 291		
12.225-8	290	14.xxiv	288		
12.225b-228a	283	14.xxv	288		
12.229	193	14.xxvii	286		
12.237-45	283	14.xxxvi	286		
12.240	283-4	14.xxxvii	288, 291		
12.246	283	14.4-97	286		
12.247	283	14.5	286		
12.248	172	14.7	286		
12.249-50	283	14.9	229		
12.265	284	14.10	233		
12.280	284	14.29	286		
12.285	284	14.50-2	286		
12.286	284	14.57-8	286		
12:340	241	14.73	287		
12.357	283	14.74	287		
12.414	284	14.74-6	287		
12.419	284	14.74b-76	287		
12.434	284	14.77-8	287		
13	284-6	14.79	287		
13.i	285, 291	14.86	186		
13.iv	290	14.123	287		
13.xix	285	14.126	233		
13.xx	285	14.127	288		
13.2	284	14.131-2	288		
13.165-70	230	14.144	288		
13.171, 293	6	14.145-55	286-7		
13.171-3	285	14.148	287		
13.196	193	14.149	180		
13.245	284	14.151	287		
13.249	269	14.185-267	177, 286		
13.254-7	232	14.186	181		

INDEX OF SOURCES

14.247–55	269	19.278–90	183
14.306–323	286	20.viii	290
14.394–467	286	20.17–96	235, 290
14.490	288	20.49–53	236
15	288	20.97	94
15.i	288, 291	20.97–98	94
15.ii	288, 291	20.101	95, 236
15–16	286	20.112	95
15–17	281	20.137–47	234
15.9	288	20.139	234
15.11–2	288	20.143	234
15.174–6	226	20.180–1	95
15.194	281	20.197ff	95
15.349	285	20.197–203	95
15.373	6	20.199–203	290
15.391–9	216	20.224–251	107, 290
15.396	216–7	20.240	284
15.400	208	20.263	192
15.403	286	20.263–5	105
15.410–416	216		
15.411–5	218	*Bellum Judaicum*	
15.415	218	1	192
15.417	183	1.3	203
16	182–3, 185	1.16	205
16:11	234	1.17	204–5
16.160–78	177	1.31	283
16.161	177	1.31–32a	283
16.175	186	1.32	283
16.183	196	1.32a	283
16.186	204	1.36	284
16.187	203	1.37	284
16.193	234	1:61	269
16.225	234	1:62–3	267
16.263	282	1.63–6	251
16.300–310	231	1.65	285
17.41	203	1.70–84	285
18	279, 289	1.108–9	203
18.iii	289	1.118	286, 289
18.vi	289	1.121	286
18.xiii	290	1.127	286
18.xx	290	1.135–7	286
18.3–4	289	1.140–3	286
18.17	8	1.153	287
18.30	289	1.154	287
18.63–4	290	1.157	287
18.139-40	235	1.169	287
18.194	284	1.183	287
18.257–60	92	1.199	288
18.317–379	290	1.477	234
18.319	192	1.596	98
19 [Budé]	272	2.119	6, 8
19	107	2.129	7
19.34–51	94	2.134	10
19.277	234	2.137	6

2.143	9	6.423–8	98
2.147–149	10–1	6.435	98
2.150	7	7.110	186
2.162	203	7.218	84
2.166	8	7.255	8–9
2.169–170	93	7.264	193
2.175–177	93	7.286	211
2.227	95	7.318–19	101
2.239	101	7.327	101
2.254–6	95		
2.261–3	95	*Contra Apionem*	
2.306	96	1.2	196
2.307	96	1.6–28	195
2.390	101	1.7.13.57	192
2.465	96	1.9	201
3.293	101	1.10–1	201
3.352	203	1.11	201
3.404	101	1.12	201
3.484	101	1.55.73.213.288	192
3.494	101	1.20	201
4.104	101	1.21	201
4.196	208	1.29	201
4.323	101	1.29–43	195
4.362	101	1.36	201, 203
4.366	101	1.38	201
4.370	101	1.38–40	200
4.402–405	8	1.42	201
4.573	101	I 46	192
4.622	101	1.46	194
5.39	101	1.47–56	195
5.60	101	1.50	205
5.184–192	216	1.58–9	195
5.190–2	214, 217	1.59	195
5.191	217	1.54	141, 202–4
5.192	208–9, 216	1.58	192
5.193	208	1.69–218	195
5.194	183	1.69–160	195, 199
5:324	151	1.72	196
5.343	101	1.73	202
5.367–8	101	1.78	123
5.378	101	1.85–103	116
5.412–3	101	1.86–7	123
5.424–5	99	1.88	116
5.512–9	99	1.94	117
5.566	99	1.103	117
5.559	101	1.116	202
6.110	101	1.160	201
6.127	101	1.161	196, 199
6.193–213	99	1.161–217/18	195–6
6.250–1	101	1.162	192
6.288–304	100	1.162	194
6.38–40	101	1.198	194
6.411	101	1.198	192
6.420	99	1.209	192

1.210	192, 194	1.309	193–194
1.211	192, 194	1.320	201
1.213-4	196	2.16	116
1.215	196, 199, 201–2	2.17	123
		2.46	197
1.215-8	196, 199	2.103	217
1.216	196, 199, 200–2, 204	2.146	193
		2.156	116
1.216-7	202	2.196	193
1.216-8	200	2.208	193
1.217	196, 199–201, 204	2.281	193
		2.291	193–4
1.217-8	200		
1.218	195–202, 204–6	*Life*	
		1–6	203
1.218b	201	9	203
1.219	195	11	9
1.220-2	200	14	9
1.221	200	40	192
1.230-232	117	191	203
1.231	116	336	192
1.237	123	417	142
1.257	193		
1.260	194	Philo	
1.260	193	*Hypothetica*	
1.269	194	11.1–2	6
1.269	193	11.14–17	10
1.287	205		
1.289	193	*De somniis*	
1.306	193	2:34	149

RABBINIC LITERATURE

Mishna		*Bava Qama*	
		1:2	37
Berakhot		1:3	32
3:3	32		
		Sanhedrin	
Demai		7:6	50–2
6:11	281	10:1	39
Shevi'it		*Avot*	
6:1	281	2:2	135
9:2	281	3:11	40
Pesachim		*Tamid*	
4:5	281	1:1	11
Nedarim		*Middot*	
3:11	30	2:1	207, 209
		2:5	209

INDEX OF SOURCES

Mikva'ot
8:1   281

Tosefta

Berakhot
3.7   37
3.9   35

Sota
10:1   46

Sanhedrin
11:4   37
12:9   39

Menahot
13:22   135

Palestinian Talmud

Berakhot
1 3d   35
3 6b   33
4.2 7d   175
9 [end] 14d   40

Peah
16b   40
17a   35

Pesahim
1.1, 27a   138

Megillah
74d   35

Hagigah
76d   35

Nedarim
3.14 38b   30

Sanhedrin
27c   40

Babylonian Talmud

Berakhot
6b–7b   46–7
7a   43
16b   37
33b   217
48b   29, 34
49a   30–1, 34

Shabbat
33a   35, 39
55a   67
132a   30
133a   30
137b   39

Pesahim
13b   217
17a   58
52b   217
69b   30

Yoma
85b   40

Sukkah
45a   207

Megila
18b   62

Yevamot
5b   30
46b   38

Ketubot
72a   131

Gittin
23b   32, 37
60b   35

Qiddushin
41b   32

Sanhedrin
38b   40
60b–61a   76
65a–b   43
99a   40
113b   46

Shavuot
13a   40

Avoda Zara
2a–4b   49
3b   49
4a–b   43
4b   46–7

Hullin
10b   131

INDEX OF SOURCES

Keritot
3b 76
7a 40

Midrash

Exodus Rabah
5:14 58
23:3 58

Eichah Rabah
3:3 58

Mekhilta
Bahodesh
2 38
3 38
7 37

Pesikta DeRaba
39b 58

Sifra
Behuqotai 8, 112c 37

Shoher Tov
To Isaiah 49:3
  58

Tanhuma
To Exodus 5:1–2
  [printed ed.] 58
To Exodus 5:1–2
  [Buber 19] 58
Re'eh [Buber 60] 58

Megilat Ta'anit
10 269

Medieval and Later Sources

R. Asher Ben Yehiel (Rosh)
Piskei HaRosh
Pesahim, 1:3 131

Codex Vaticanus Graecus
147 272
1288 274

R. David Ibn Zimra (Radbaz)
Teshuvot Radbaz HaHadashot
§ 51 132–4

R. Eliezer Ben R. Joel Halevi
Sefer Ra'avyah
§428 (Aptowitzer 2:60) 136–7

Magen Avraham
On Orech Hayim 187.3 34

Maharam Halawah
On bPes 4b 136–7

R. Manoah of Narbonne
Sefer Hamenuhah
On Hilkhot Hamez and
  Mezuzah, 2:17 130, 135

Meiri
On Berakhot 48b 34
On Pesahim 4a 129

R. Moshe ben Nahman (Ramban)
Hiddushei Ha-Ramban
On bHul 10b 131, 137

R. Moshe Isserlish (Ramah)
Commentary on Shulchan Aruch
Orah Hayim 187.3 34

R. Nissim of Gerona (Ran)
Commentary on Rav Alfasi (Rif)
Pesahim §689 133, 135, 138–9

Hiddushei Haran
On bPes 4b 131, 133

Otzar HaGeonim
p. 49–50, no. 123 34

Otzar Piskei Hageonim
199 [?] 129, 135, 138

Penei Moshe
On yPes 1.1, 27b

Qorban Netanel
Commentary on Piskei HaRosh
Pesahim 1:6 134

Rashi
Commentary on the Talmud
On Berakhot 20b 33
On Pesahim 64b 75

R. Saadyah Gaon [?]
Sidur Rinat Yisrael [Sefarad, Edot Hamizrah]
116 36

Siddur Tefilat Rahel
316 38, 41

Sheyarei Qorban
On yPes 27b 129, 133

R. Shlomo ibn Aderet (Rashba)
Hiddushei HaRashba
On bHul10b 131, 135, 139

Torat HaBayit
Hilkhot Shehitah, Sha'ar 1, 7b 131

Tosafot
On Berakhot 20b 34
On Arakhin 3a 34

Tosafot HaRosh
On Berakhot 20b 34

Tuv Yerushalayim
On yPes 1.1, 27b 134, 140

R. Yehiel Michel Epstein
Aruch Hashulhan
Orah Hayyim 437:7 129

Rav Yom Tov ben Avraham (Ritba)
Hiddushei HaRitba
On bKet 72a 131

INDEX OF SCHOLARS CITED

Abegg (Jr.), Martin, 151
Abel, Felix-Marie, 211, 241, 251–2, 255, 257
Aburabia, Amram, 36
Adler, William, 109–110, 112–4, 118, 125
Albeck, Hanokh, 44
Alexander, Loveday, 57
Alexander, Philip S., 57, 265
Alföldi, Andreas, 58, 66
Alon, Gedaliah, 17
Aptowitzer, Victor, 136–7
Asaf, Simha, 36
Assmann, Jan, 117
Atkinson, C. Chrimes, 248
Attridge, Harold William, 196–7
Avi-Yonah, Michael, 211

Baer, Yitzhak, 25
Barag, Dan, 251, 263, 269
Barkay, Rachel, 251, 268
Bar-Kochva, Bezalel, 196, 238, 241, 254–5, 263–4, 268
Bar-Nathan, Rachel, 268
Barnes, Timothy, 109, 116
Barrera, Julio Trebolle, 166
Barthélemy, Dominique, 146, 164
Baruch, Eyal, 218
Baumgarten, Albert, 1–2, 6, 11–13, 203
Bausani, Alessandro, 68
Beard, Mary, 52, 56, 62
Beck, Roger, 65, 69
Becker, Yaakov, 16, 20
Ben Zeev, Miriam Pucci, 116, 178–180, 183, 185–188, 287
Ben-David, Aryeh, 214
Ben-Yehudah, Nachman, 17
Bergmeier, Roland, 1–2
Bickerman, Elias, 8, 170, 182, 255
Birnbaum, Philip, 33
Black, Matthew, 197
Blatt, Franz, 272
Blenkinsopp, Joseph, 229
Blum, Léon, 196, 201
Boccaccini, Gabriele, 265–6
Boring, M. Eugene, 124

Boyce, Mary, 68–9, 71–5
Boyd, James W., 71
Briant, Pierre, 181
Bringmann, Klaus, 173
Brock, Sebastian, 166
Brodersen, Kai, 276
Broshi, Magen, 96
Brown, Michelle P., 274
Bunge, Jochen-Gabriel, 251

Calabi, Francesca, 196, 201
Calmeyer, Peter, 70, 73
Capasso, Mario, 276
Cartledge, Paul, 230–1
Ceriani, Antonio, 146
Charles, Robert Henry (R.H.), 239, 252, 259–260
Choksy, Jamsheed K., 72
Christ, Wilhelm, 115, 121–2
Clark, Peter, 69
Clauss, Manfred, 65
Clermont-Ganneau, Charles, 183
Cohen, Naomi G., 62, 206
Cohen, Shaye J.D., 1–2, 29, 106, 223, 226–8, 232, 235, 240, 261, 270
Collins, J.J. (John Joseph), 104, 116, 257
Conzelmann, Hans, 124
Coser, Lewis, 5
Cotton, Hannah M., 203
Cribiore, Raffaella, 105
Crönert, Wilhelm, 276
Cumont, Franz, 64–5
Curty, Olivier, 230

Davenport, Gene L., 259
Davies, John, 180
Dawson, L., 3
De Jong, Albert, 74
De Lagarde, Paul, 146
Delcor, Mathias, 259, 265–6
Denis, Albert-Marie, 196–8
Desideri, Paolo, 180
Diels, H., 276
Dindorf, Wilhelm, 111
Doran, Robert, 251, 255–6, 258
Dorandi, Tiziano, 276, 291

INDEX OF SCHOLARS CITED 309

Dorival, Gilles, 165
Douglas, Mary, 1, 5
Drijvers, Hendrick Jan Willem (H.J.W.), 66
Droge, Arthur J., 125, 196
Du Person, Anquetil, 75
Duchesne-Guellemin, Jacques, 65
Dumont, Louis., 5, 11
Dvornik, Francis, 57

Eilers, Claude, 177, 179–180, 187–8
Eissfeldt, Otto, 266
Elbogen, Ismar, 36
Eliav, Yaron Zvi, 207
Elman, Yaakov, 43, 45
Elsas, Christoph, 76
Epstein, Jacob Nahum, 127
Eshel, Esther, 10
Euting, Julius, 279

Farrar, Frederic William, 112
Fears, Julius Rufus, 52, 60–1
Feldman, Louis, 81, 270, 289–290, 292
Ferguson, John, 48, 62–3, 123, 151–2, 198, 201, 205
Field, Frederick, 146
Finkelstein, Louis, 32, 26
Finkielsztein, Gerald, 267–9
Finley, Moses I., 180
Fishwick, Duncan, 58
Flint, Peter, 151
Fowler, W. Warde, 57
Frankel-Goldschmidt, Hava, 42
Freese, John Henry, 106
Friedman, Shama Yehuda, 133
Früchtel, Ludwig, 115, 120
Fuks, Alexander, 89

Garnsey, Peter, 225
Geiger, Abraham, 239, 255
Geiger, Joseph, 255
Gellner, Ernest, 3
Gelzer, Heinrich, 125
Gera, Dov, 170–2, 229
Gershevitz, Ilya, 64
Gifford, Edwin Hamilton, 112
Gilat, Yitzhak Dov, 133
Gitler, Haim, 267
Glare, P.G.W., 84
Goldstein, Jonathan A., 239, 241, 247, 252, 254–8
Goldstein, Moshe, 131
Goodblatt, David, 281

Goodman, Martin, 53, 82, 84, 89, 103, 121, 124, 197, 199, 187, 239, 251, 266
Goodspeed, Edgar Johnson (E.J.), 203
Gordon, Richard Landsey (R.L.), 64
Gordon, Richard, 51, 56
Goren, Shlomo, 215
Grätz, Heinrich, 126
Greenfield, Jonas C., 203
Grenet, Frantz, 69, 73–4
Griffin, Miriam, 82, 87
Grossman, Avraham, 34, 42, 127
Gruber, Meyer, 57
Gruen, Erich, 116, 230–1, 255
Gruenwald, Itamar, 3–4
Gutschmid, Alfred von, 115, 121–2, 124, 279

Habermann, Avraham Meir, 36
Habicht, Christian, 172, 249, 255, 283
Hadas-Lebel, Mirielle, 17
Halivni, David, 138
Halsberghe, Gaston H., 62
Hanson, J., 197
Hardwick, Michael E., 91
Harl, Marguerite, 165
Harrington, Hannah, 12
Haverkamp, Siwart, 280
Helm, Rudolf, 108–9, 111
Hengel, Martin, 104, 169–170, 257
Herbert, Edward D., 152
Herman, Gabriel, 224–5, 227
Herr, Moshe David, 104–5
Herwerden, B., 283
Hill, Christopher, 3–4
Hinnells, John R., 64–5, 75
Hohl, Ernest, 60
Holladay, Carl R., 103, 108–111, 196–7, 201
Hollis, Frederick James (F.J.), 209, 216, 220
Holmes, Robert, 146
Honigman, Sylvie, 178, 185
Horden, Peregrine, 224
Hornblower, Simon, 210
Horowitz, Wayne, 171
Houghton, Arthur, 171
Humphreys, Sarah C., 227
Hyman, Aharon, 63

Ilan, Yaacov David, 131, 133, 137
Irigoin, Jean, 274–6, 280

Jackson, A.V. Williams, 73
Jacoby, Felix, 103, 106, 108–112, 115, 197
James, Montague R., 151
Ji, Chang-ho C., 228–9
Jones, Arnold Hugh Martin (A.H.M.), 83
Jones, William Henry Samuel (W.H.S.), 110

Kampen, John, 169
Karst, Joseph, 108
Kasher, Aryeh, 198, 201
Katz, Jacob, 3
Kaufman, Asher Zelig, 210
Kern, Otto, 276
Kister, Menahem, 259–260, 265
Klausner, Joseph, 15–27
Klawans, Jonathan, 7
Kloner, Amos, 268
Kohut, Alexander, 76
Kokkinos, Nikos, 106, 234
Kosovsky, Moshe, 128, 133, 135
Kotwal, Firoze M., 71, 73
Krauss, Samuel, 53
Kushnir, Alla, 267

Lamb, George, 105
Landau, Tamar, 177
Laqueur, Richard, 179, 276–9, 286
Lavagne, Henri, 65
Lawlor, Hugh Jackson, 92
Le Rider, Georges, 171
Levine, Lee I., 207–9, 215
Levi-Strauss, Claude, 186
Lévy, Isidore, 198
Levy, Jacob, 76
Lewin, Benjamin Menashe, 30, 34
Lewis, Charleton T., 83
Lewy, Hans, 198, 263–4
Lichtenstein, Eliyahu, 131
Lieberman, Saul, 30–31, 33, 35, 46, 127, 131, 135, 138
Liebeschuetz, John H.W.G., 48, 52
Lieu, Judith, 256
Lloyd-Jones, Hugh, 197
Lommel, A. Herman, 64

MacMullen, Ramsay, 64
Magen, Yitzhak, 268
Magie, David, 54, 60
Magness, Jodi, 11
Malandra, William M., 73
Maniaci, Marilena, 274

Marchesi, J.M., 68
Marcos, Natalia Fernández, 146
Marcus, Ralph, 284, 286, 288
Marincola, John, 180, 183
Marrou, Henri, 105, 275
Martin, Luther H., 65
Mason, Steve N., 1, 13, 91, 177, 184, 203, 292
Mattingly, Harold, 81–7
Mazar, Benjamin, 218
Mazor, Gabi, 268
Meherjirana, Erachji, 71
Mendels, Doron, 19, 259, 263
Merkelbach, Reinhold, 65
Meshorer, Ya'akov, 82
Metzger, Bruce, 145
Mez, Adam, 146
Milikowsky, Chaim, 105
Millar, Fergus, 54, 84, 103, 121, 124, 239, 257, 269, 281, 283
Miltner, F., 227
Moehring, Horst, 179, 182
Moffatt, James, 252
Momigliano, Arnaldo, 181, 238
Mommsen, Christian, 58
Moscowitz, Leib, 138
Mosshammer, Alden Adams (A.A.), 108–110, 113–4, 118
Munnich, Olivier, 165
Mutschmann, Hermann, 271, 274, 278
Muzerelle, Denis, 273

Netzer, Ehud, 211
Neubauer, Adolf, 62
Neusner, Jacob, 69
Nickelsburg, George William Elmer (G.W.E.), 258
Niebhur, Helmut Richard, 3
Niese, Benedictus, 251, 255, 272, 280, 289–290
Nigosian, S.A., 69
Nodet, Étienne, 141–2, 167, 271, 273–4, 279–282, 285, 289
Norena, C.F., 84
North, Christopher Richard, 56

Oberthür, Franz, 280
Oesterley, William Oscar Emil (W.O.E.), 239
Orrieux, Claude, 229
Oulton, John, 92

Parente, Fausto, 287, 290
Parsons, James, 146

INDEX OF SCHOLARS CITED

Parsons, Peter, 197
Pasquali, Giorgio, 275
Paton, William Roger, 277
Patterson, Cynthia, 227
Pédech, Paul, 272, 277
Peleg, Yehoshua, 218
Pelletier, Andre, 205
Peretz, Avraham, 219
Pietrzykowski, Michael, 62–3
Pines, Shlomo, 76
Price, Simon R.F., 53, 58
Pritchett, William K., 244
Puech, Aime, 198
Purcell, Nicholas, 224

Radin, Max, 205
Rajak, Tessa, 106–8, 113, 115–6, 124, 205
Rappaport, Uriel, 173–5
Raspe, Lucia, 116
Ratner, Ber, 136
Ratzhabi, Yehuda, 36
Reinach, Theodore, 198
Rengstorf, Karl Heinrich (K.H.), 208, 216
Reynolds, Leigton D., 273
Richardson, Peter, 234
Rijksbaron, Albert, 273
Ritmeyer, Kathleen, 209
Ritmeyer, Leen, 209
Robert, L., 58
Rofé, Alexander, 249
Rokéah, David, 205–6
Rolfe, John C., 55–6, 60, 86
Rosenthal, Eliezer, 127
Rubin, Nisan, 40
Runia, David T., 200
Ryberg, Inez Scott, 55–7
Ryland, J.E., 120

Safrai, Shmuel, 37, 40
Saiz, José Ramón Busto, 146
Sanders, Ed Parish (E.P.), 6
Sandys, John Edwin, 227
Schäfer, Peter, 81, 89, 116
Schafler, Samuel, 17, 23
Schiffman, Lawrence, 4
Schmidt, Francis, 259
Schmidt, Peter L., 275
Schreckenberg, Heinz, 91, 99, 272, 279, 289–290
Schröder, Bianca-Jeanette, 274
Schubart, Wilhelm, 201, 276
Schubert, Kurz, 91

Schunk, K.D., 238
Schürer, Emil, 103–4, 121, 124, 197, 200, 239, 251, 258–9, 266, 269, 283
Schwartz, Daniel, 196, 228, 235, 287
Schwartz, Eduard, 275
Schwartz, Seth, 105, 115, 125, 204, 226, 228, 232–4, 238, 242, 250–1, 255
Schwarz, Eberhard, 240
Scullard, Howard Hayes, 46
Shaked, Shaul, 76
Shapira, Anita, 17
Shatzman, Israel, 263, 267–9
Shaw, Brent, 226, 233
Short, Charles, 83
Shotter, Davis Colin Arthur (D.C.A.), 81, 83
Showalter, Daniel N., 52
Sievers, Joseph, 230, 245, 287
Sirinelli, Jean, 115
Sivan, Emmanuel, 5
Smallwood, E. Mary, 281
Smith, Morton, 224, 232, 238
Spawforth, Antony, 210, 230–1
Sperber, Daniel, 210, 220
Stählin, Otto, 115, 120
Stein, Stephen, 12
Sterling, Gregory E., 104–5, 186, 257
Stern, E., 214
Stern, Menahem, 82, 89, 104, 116, 119, 121, 124, 170, 248–9, 263, 287
Stern, Sacha, 54
Strauss, Claude-Levy, 5
Strugnell, John, 2
Sussmann, Yaacov, 137–8
Sydenham, Edward, 81–7

Tabory, Joseph, 29
Tal, Shlomo, 33, 36
Talmon, Shemaryahu, 6
Taylor, Joan, 9
Tcherikover, Victor, 89, 169
Teixidor, Javier, 63
Thackeray, Henry St. John, 146, 159–160, 195–6, 201, 205, 208, 272–3, 279, 290
Thomas, Rosalind, 184–6
Toren, Hayim, 16, 20
Touati, Charles, 25
Tov, Emanuel, 146, 159
Tuffin, Paul, 109–110, 112–4, 118
Turcan, Robert, 48, 62, 65

Ulansey, David, 64
Ulrich, Eugene, 151–3, 160–2, 164

VanderKam, James C., 258
Vanggaard, Jens H., 60–1
Vardapet, Eghishe, 68
Vermes, Geza, 121, 239, 258–9, 266, 283

Wacholder, Ben Zion, 104, 110–1, 124, 197–9, 201
Waddell, W.G. (William Gillen), 117
Walbank, Frank William (F.W.), 277
Walter, Nikolaus, 121–2, 196–198
Wardman, Alan, 48, 54–5
Warszawski, Avraham, 219
Weber, Max, 3
Wehrli, Fritz, 197
Weinfeld, Moshe, 250
Weiss, Avraham, 43
Weitzman, Steven, 232–3
Werman, Cana, 259–261, 265

Whitaker, Molly, 115, 120
Wikgren, Allen, 288
Wilk, Roman, 254
Williamson, Callie, 186–7
Wilson, Bryan, 3, 5–6
Wilson, Nigel G., 273
Wilson, W., 120 [?]
Winterbottom, Michael, 86
Wintermute, O.S., 258, 265
Wittfogel, Karl A., 66
Worp, Klaas Anthony (K.A.), 273

Yaavetz, Zvi, 60
Yarsheter, Ehsan, 79
Youtie, Herbert C., 203

Zaehner, Robert Charles, 68–9
Zeitlin, Solomon, 256
Zerubavel, Yael, 17
Ziegler, Ignaz, 53
Zimmermann, Bernhard, 273
Zinner, Gavriel, 129

www.ingramcontent.com/pod-product-compliance
Lightning Source LLC
Chambersburg PA
CBHW021354290426
44108CB00010B/239